Irish Human Rights Law Review
2010

Irish Human Rights Law Review 2010

Editor
Donncha O'Connell

CLARUS PRESS

Published by
Clarus Press Ltd,
Griffith Campus,
South Circular Road,
Dublin 8.

Typeset by
Eimer Neville,
Compuscript Ltd,
Shannon Industrial Estate,
Shannon, Co. Clare

Printed by
ColourBooks Ltd,
105 Baldoyle Industrial Estate ,
Baldoyle,
Dublin 13

ISBN

978-1-905536-08-5

Citation

This work may be cited as [2010] 1 IHRLR

About the Editor

Donncha O'Connell is currently a Visiting Senior Fellow at the Centre for the Study of Human Rights, LSE. He is on sabbatical from the School of Law, NUI Galway where he teaches Constitutional Law, European Human Rights, Processes of Law Reform and Equality Law: Principles & Thematic Application. He was Dean of Law at NUI Galway from 2005-2008. Donncha is the Senior Irish member of FRALEX, the legal expert group that advises the EU Agency for Fundamental Rights based in Vienna and was, from 2002-2006, the Irish member of the EU Network of Independent Experts on Fundamental Rights. From 1999-2002 he was the first full-time Director of the Irish Council for Civil Liberties, a NGO founded in 1976 by Kader Asmal and Mary Robinson. He is currently a member of the Board of Directors of the London-based NGO, INTERIGHTS — The International Centre for the Legal Protection of Human Rights, and has, in the past, been a board member of the Free Legal Advice Centres (FLAC) Ltd and Amnesty International Ireland. He is also on the Advisory Board of the Public Interest Law Alliance (PILA), a project of FLAC, and is chairperson of the Programme Forum of FOMACS, a collaborative public media project based in DIT. Donncha co-edited (with Mike Milotte) five monographs in the Irish Academic Press series, *Justice in Controversy*, and writes and speaks extensively on public law and human rights issues. He is also a member of the Board of Directors of Druid Theatre Company.

About the Assistant Editor

Siobhán Cummiskey is the Managing Solicitor of the Irish Traveller Movement Independent Law Centre. She is a course contributor to the Certificate in Human Rights Law at the Law Society of Ireland and lectures in Constitutional Law at Independent Colleges. Siobhan has worked with the European Human Rights Advocacy Centre in London, Vigil India Movement in Bangalore, the Legal Aid Department of Malawi, the Irish Human Rights Commission and the International Human Rights Network.

Acknowledgements

This inaugural edition of the *Irish Human Rights Law Review* has had a gestation period akin to a marathon but we will sprint to the second and subsequent editions on an annual basis. That is a promise! I would like to thank each of the sixteen contributors, not just for the quality of their contributions but for their forbearance with the protracted editorial process leading to this publication. I would also like to thank the Assistant Editor, Siobhan Cummiskey, for her very valuable work on the manuscript as it progressed. David McCartney of Clarus Press remained steadfast in his commitment to this publication when others would have given up and his constant good humour and common sense was and is greatly appreciated.

The final stage of the editing process took place while I was a Visiting Senior Fellow at the Centre for the Study of Human Rights, LSE. My colleagues there — Zoe Gillard, Sara Ulfsparre, Christine Chinkin, Conor Gearty, Carol Prendergast, Kirsteen Shields, Kai Moller, Margot Salomon, Alasdair Cochrane, Claire Moon and my fellow Irish temporary exile, Caroline Fennell — provided an atmosphere that was friendly and conducive to seeing this project through to completion. I will remember this time in the heart of London, a city of infinite distraction, with great fondness and am grateful to my own university, NUI Galway, for the generous period of sabbatical leave that enabled me to avail of the fellowship at LSE.

Donncha O'Connell,
Centre for the Study of Human Rights,
London School of Economics & Political Science.

March 2010

Contents

Inaugural Editorial

We sometimes struggle to find anniversaries of significant events on which to hang other less significant events as if the suggested symmetry, which is usually coincidental, entailed some kind of poetic beauty. In that spirit of coincidental symmetry it is (merely) appropriate to launch a new scholarly review dedicated to human rights in 2010, the sixtieth anniversary of the signing in Rome of the European Convention on Human Rights (ECHR) following the establishment of the Council of Europe.

Despite some serious tension between the Irish and British delegations in the negotiations that led to the creation of the Council of Europe in 1949 arising from the so-called "sore thumb policy" then pursued by the Irish — whereby every opportunity was used to raise the issue of Irish partition as a human rights violation — there was significant agreement between the Irish and British on the contents of the ECHR. De Valera was, notably, effective in this process pointing up a quaint historical irony given that his then prominent foe, Churchill, provided inspiration for the Convention in earlier speeches calling for a pan-European codification of the common law by means of a convention or charter protecting civil and political rights as a democratic bulwark against totalitarianism.

Ironies persist. Now the Conservative Party in the United Kingdom — one of the parties of Churchill — is committed to repealing the UK Human Rights Act of 1998, the Act that incorporates the ECHR into UK law, and replacing it with a "British" Bill of Rights. This proposal is controversial, even within the Conservative Party, and it ignores the very "Britishness" of the ECHR with its focus on a dated but valuable set of civil and political rights. Those who are accused of favouring "rights inflation' or of being "rights supremacists" complain about the ECHR for precisely this reason, that it doesn't go far enough. Sixty years on, the European Convention on Human Rights seems somewhat unloved.

And, yet, its achievements are remarkable. The Convention and the European Court of Human Rights are heralded as the outstanding success story of regional rights protection. Competition for this accolade is, admittedly, not keen. The European Court of Human Rights, although hybrid in character by comparison to other so-called constitutional courts, has earned the healthy respect of national apex courts (in Europe and beyond) on a broad range of human rights issues. The Court has, occasionally, shown a tendency to be inconsistent and unattractively pragmatic but what collegiate court has not exhibited such fallibility consistent with the human fallibility of its individual parts?

The ECHR has been of critical importance in both parts of the island of Ireland since the 1950s. This was recognised in the Belfast / Good Friday Agreement of 1998 where the Convention was viewed, for better or worse, as providing a "neutral" benchmark of minimal rights protection for the island as a whole. It was in the context of the Agreement that the legislation to give further effect to the ECHR in Irish law was proposed. While the ECHR Act 2003 has, predictably, been undramatic in its impact to date, it has normalised recourse to the Convention in domestic legal practice, something which was happening anyway prior to incorporation, and may yet add some value in areas of law where domestic standards fall short of Convention standards.

The debate on indirect incorporation of the ECHR revealed a strange defensiveness on the part of certain commentators about the relative merits of the Irish Constitution of 1937, but it also revealed a somewhat misplaced enthusiasm on the part of rights advocates about the added-value, in terms of substantive rights protection, to be gained under the Convention. Colm O Cinneide characterises this tension as one between "particularism" and "cosmopolitanism".

But perhaps the debate was merely a shadow of the real debate in Irish constitutional jurisprudence which is — since cases like *Sinnott* and *TD* that hinged on the distinction between commutative and distributive justice — about where to draw the line in applying the separation of powers doctrine and how far the judicial branch should go in deferring to the Legislature and Executive, especially on matters of socio-economic justice.

This tension was sharply revealed (ironically, on an issue of commutative justice) in the recent Supreme Court (3:2) decision in *Meadows v Minister for Justice, Equality & Law Reform* [2010] IESC. The majority in this case has dented the established Irish application of "Wednesbury reasonableness" (Hibernicised as "O'Keeffe reasonableness") as the appropriate standard of scrutiny in judicial review of administrative actions. The apparent judicial embrace of the alternative standard of "anxious consideration" or "anxious scrutiny" was not driven by zealous devotion to the ECHR or international human rights standards generally but the jurisprudence on which it drew was influenced by the Convention, as was acknowledged by Mr Justice Fennelly.

In his trenchant dissent in *Meadows,* Mr Justice Hardiman gave vent to a deeply-felt scepticism about anxious consideration in withering terms:

> "The phrase is used in different senses, which any outside observer of judicial developments must find thoroughly confusing. But such observers are mostly lawyers, academic or otherwise, and are almost invariably *partis pris,* whose strong taste for novelty, and specifically for the extension of the domain of the law, leads them to pass lightly over the absence of rigour or even of specific meaning, in the phrase as now used. They do this, seduced by the intoxicating prospect it has come to represent of a dramatic judicial incursion into the political and administrative field."

Without entering into an involved discourse on the points at issue in *Meadows* (a topic that will be considered in the next issue of this Review), the passage of Hardiman, J, just quoted, serves to illustrate a problem of general but fundamental concern raised by rights sceptics in respect of rights enthusiasts. The suggestion seems to be that those who favour more recourse to international human rights instruments favour more recourse to the courts as an effective way of advancing human rights. There is some truth in this rather reductive assertion but it does insufficient justice to the idealism of those who view the rule of law differently than those who, by virtue of their positions, ordain the prevailing judicial orthodoxy. The difference is, essentially, between those who see separation of powers as a means to achieving the rule of law and those who see the separation of powers as an end in itself.

Undoubtedly, some see human rights as a source of proxy public morality or "new civic religion", a code of conduct for a post-modern age. According to this view, instead of just raising awkward questions human rights provide a comprehensive set of answers. Human rights, like religion, are about certainty and not doubt.

This can, of course, limit our imagination causing us to see human rights-based solutions solely or mainly as judicialised solutions. Thus, the necessarily political dimension of the struggle for rights — and it usually is a struggle — is problematised to the point where political processes are by-passed in favour of transcendent judicial intervention. In this crudely cast dilemma, when politics is the problem the courts become the solution. Social movements and the mobilisation of people in the name of ideals seem like a relic of the past although, in less prosperous times like now, this may change.

The foregoing is, admittedly, a caricature of the rights enthusiast but one which is deployed to great effect by those who, depending on the occasion and the audience, embellish or mask their real objection to certain human rights. A more balanced and humorous representation is to be found in Conor Gearty's book of unusual brevity but rich insight, *Can Human Rights Survive?* (Cambridge University Press, 2006), in which he states:

> "Human rights people are stuck, required without the support of many symbols to practise their beliefs in exactly those places — developed modern societies — where belief in anything is hard enough and belief in something moral apparently rooted in nature hardest of all. They are the disciples of an idea rather than a sacred text or even a holy (much less a divine) person, and the closest they get to congregational worship is the occasional drinks party after a human rights lecture. (They are usually too polite for the solidarity that comes from public protest)."

The human rights community must address these issues of substance and presentation even if they feel that criticisms levelled by their detractors are unfair. Too much time is spent on winning arguments about textual formulae that may or may not affect actual outcomes for actual human beings. Having one's sense of virtue crystallised in a text — whether international or domestic — is not its own reward.

Perhaps it is more useful to see human rights instruments — whether constitutional or otherwise — as the beginning rather than the end of dialogue. Thus, in his book, *The Negotiable Constitution: On the Limitation of Rights* (Cambridge University Press, 2009), Gregoire Webber argues that constitutional rights are "under-determinate" and suggests that: "…citizens frame and adopt constitutional rights in a manner that leaves the resolution of rights disputes to a *later day*." The unfinished business of the Constitution is progressed, *inter alia*, by the Legislature.

In the Irish context this raises a very real practical problem which partially explains the enthusiasm of some for recourse to judicial and quasi-judicial solutions. That is the problem of a weak Legislature controlled in most vital respects by the Executive with no serious capacity to hold the Executive to account. This has recently been decried by the Ombudsman, Emily O'Reilly, for transforming the constitutional ideal of some balance as between branches of government into a fiction. Undue judicial deference to the political branches of Government will inevitably entail a disproportionate deference to the Executive.

The apparent disdain for politics on the part of some rights enthusiasts offends judges and others who are alive to the dangers of judicial trespass on the political domain. But it may well indicate an astute appreciation on the part of such enthusiasts of the dysfunction at the heart of the Irish polity. This dysfunction may, of course, be an intended consequence of the 1937 Constitution. More benignly, it may be something that remains uncorrected by operation of the constitutional mandate. Why, then, are more people not protesting about this instead of studying legal texts and briefing solicitors? What is missing in our political life animated by a public morality that one would expect to draw on an ethic of civic republicanism?

In his book, *Ship of Fools* (Faber & Faber, 2009), Fintan O'Toole writes about this in the most forceful terms:

> "The Irish had been taught for generations to identify morality with religion, and a very narrow kind of religion at that. Morality was about what happened in bedrooms, not in boardrooms. It was about the body, not the body politic. Masturbation was a much more serious sin than tax evasion. In a mindset where homosexuality was much worse than cooking the books, it was okay to be bent as long as you were straight. This nineteenth-century ethic was not pushed aside by the creation of a coherent and deeply rooted civic, democratic and social morality. It mostly collapsed under its own weight of hypocrisy. The familiar code of values, the language in which right and wrong could be discussed, lost its meaning before Irish society had fully learned to speak any other tongue."

What O'Toole identifies so eloquently cannot be solved by a lazy liberalism that replaces the discarded moral framework once provided by religion with a comprehensive manifesto for goodness and happy outcomes passed off as "human rights". At a more conscious, strategic level we must not rely on the external imposition of 'progressive' solutions for want of the energy required to convince fellow citizens of the objective merit of such solutions. This view of human rights as a holistic catalogue of trendy and progressive answers to troubling questions is utterly devoid of meaning and purpose.

The *Irish Human Rights Law Review*, which will be published on an annual basis, will challenge this view of human rights devoid of real meaning by focusing mainly but not exclusively on human rights values distilled in human rights law. It is not because law is seen as the be-all and end-all of human rights protection and promotion that this focus will be adopted but because this area of law now requires a more rigorous treatment as a mainstream area of growing relevance to domestic legal practice.

In a common law jurisdiction domestic legal practice is never hermetically sealed from "external" or "foreign" influence but the influence of international human rights law could be greater. The recent restatement of dualism in classical and unreconstructed terms by Chief Justice Murray in the case of *McD v L & Another* [2009] IESC 81, the case involving a dispute between a lesbian couple and their gay male sperm donor, was unsurprising. But dualism is no more than an enabling mechanism in the Constitution that invites Parliament to achieve a greater integration of municipal and international law by means of legislative or constitutional incorporation.

This understanding of dualism is consistent with a fair appreciation of the aptitude of the Constitution's primary framer, De Valera, in the international domain. He was an avowed nationalist and a capable internationalist. When judges restate their understanding of the relevant provision of De Valera's constitution — Article 29.6, which requires some act of legislative incorporation before an international instrument can be enforced by a court — they are not objecting to international law *per se* but, rather, describing the absence of a necessary political act required in a dualist system. The real issue is, therefore, political. Unless and until the Oireachtas gives further effect to international human rights instruments in domestic law they will remain of no more than persuasive authority before the Irish courts. In the case of the ECHR this "problem" may well be solved by EU accession to the Convention but that will only add to the confusion with other, arguably more important, international instruments.

A necessary part of the effort to "patriate" international human rights obligations, or at least to create a more active "dialogue" between international and municipal systems, is a vibrant, critical discourse on the domestic legal and political significance of those instruments of human rights protection to which the State is a party. In this annual Review we will endeavour to provide a space in which these issues can be discussed in a rigorous and scholarly manner. This inaugural edition contains articles and case notes on a diverse range of topics including: the right to a fair trial, the work of the Irish Human Rights Commission, privacy, equality, immigration, children's rights, housing rights, jurisdictional issues pertaining to the European Court of Justice and European Court of Human Rights, freedom of expression and recognition of same-sex marriage. In subsequent editions we will revisit some of these topics and deal with other issues of academic and practical concern.

Donncha O'Connell,
Editor.

Part I

Feature Articles

The Dreyfus Case a Century on — Ten Lessons for Ireland & Australia*

The Hon Justice Michael Kirby AC CMG**

The *Dreyfus* Affair

It may seem strange for an Australian judge to cross half the world to come to Dublin to talk about the *Dreyfus* affair. Yet, as I shall show, it is a tale worth retelling because it has modern resonance. The case has lessons both for Ireland and Australia. Indeed, as I hope to demonstrate, it is remarkably up-to-date in the instruction it gives to present day citizens and particularly to lawyers.

It is exactly a century since Alfred Dreyfus, the French soldier who was Jewish, was finally cleared of the offence of high treason. At the time, with Gallic hubris, he was described as the most famous man in the world since the death of Napoleon.[1]

Yet today, in both of our countries, the events involving Dreyfus, the story of the trials he underwent on the charge of providing military secrets to Imperial Germany, is largely forgotten. My purpose is to retrieve memories of what happened. In his *Philosophy of History*, Hegel remarked that people and governments have never learned anything from history. I am not sure that this is true of the Irish people. But I am here to ensure that we rekindle the memories.

In its time, Dreyfus's ordeal became an illustration of how human institutions can go wrong. Lawyers know that human justice can fail. Pride and patriotism can swamp concern for the individual. All too easily, this can happen when that individual is a member of a minority subjected to irrational hatred — as Dreyfus, the Jew, was and as others in the century that followed have often been.

The *Dreyfus* case was a warning of the Holocaust, of the show trials of Hitler, Stalin and Pol Pot, and of the occasional failings of elected democracies that marked the twentieth century. The warning was not sufficiently recognised a century ago. We should reflect on its lessons today so that we do not repeat its mistakes.

It is in the detail that the real wrongs of the *Dreyfus* affair are to be found. The greatest wrong was not the mistaken conviction of Dreyfus for treason. No human

* Law Society of Ireland Annual Human Rights Lecture, 29 June 2006. An earlier version of this lecture was delivered in Melbourne, Australia, on 26 March 2006.

** Retired Justice of the High Court of Australia. The author acknowledges the assistance of Mr Adam Sharpe, legal research officer of the High Court of Australia, with Irish materials.

[1] M Burns, *France and the Dreyfus Affairs* (Bedford/St Martin's, 1999), vii.

effort is wholly immune from error.[2] What was important was how the conviction came about in the first place; how it was reconfirmed in the face of mounting evidence; and how, ultimately, institutions of government and other powerful forces elevated the insistence on Dreyfus's guilt above the demonstration of his innocence. Maintaining his guilt became a badge of honour for elements in the Army, the Church, the government and the population at large. Even today in France, streets and statues to honour Dreyfus are desecrated. In France, anti-Semitic murders still happen.[3] In Australia, violence occurs against ethnic and religious minorities that shocks citizens who are convinced that the multicultural ideal will spare the country from the worst of such prejudice. Although sectarian violence has greatly receded in Ireland, it still exacts a price, as was seen in a recent murder in Ballymena.

So come back a hundred years to when the *Dreyfus* affair was on the lips of most informed people.[4] How did this happen? Why should we give any thought a century later to events that occurred so long ago in a world so different?

Sources of Anti-Semitism

To find the answers to these questions it is necessary to dig deep into an unattractive but common human tendency. A root cause of the *Dreyfus* affair was anti-Semitism. The fear and hatred of Jews in France arose because of several factors: their minority numbers; their exclusive, counter-majoritarian, habits; their close involvement in money lending and finance; their often unusual clothing; their distinctive culinary habits; and their disproportionate educational and professional success. Above all, there was the supposed "blood guilt" of Jews for the death of Jesus Christ. The foundation for this blood guilt was a passage in St Matthew's Gospel, when Pontius Pilate, the Roman Governor of Judea, offered to release Jesus but the Jewish people of Jerusalem chose Barrabas for release and said to Pilate, of Jesus, "His blood be on us, and on our children".[5] Those nine words occasioned a terrible hatred.

Until recent times at church services at Easter, the hatred was reinforced by prayers for the conversion of "the perfidious Jews"; by deep feelings of animosity towards the Jews amongst many Christians and others; and by governmental, political and religious attitudes that fuelled anti-Semitism throughout Europe and beyond.

---

[2] EC Hughes, *Men and Their Work* (1958) cited in O Quick, "Outing Medical Error" (2005) 14 *Medical Law Review* 22 at 23.

[3] S Rotella, "Racism a Factor in Murder of Jew Says Magistrate", *Sydney Morning Herald*, 22 February 2006, p 13 (concerning the death in France in on 13 February 2006 of Ilan Halimi).

[4] See e.g. *Sydney Morning Herald*, 11 September 1899; *The WestAustralian*, 12 September 1899 cited in HL Rubinstein, "'A Disgrace to Christendom': Australian Reactions to the Dreyfus Affair" in (1994) 12 *Journal of Australian Jewish Historical Society* 467 at 467–468.

[5] St Matthew's Gospel, Ch 27, v 25. See also C Thornton-Smith, "Reactions of the Australian Catholic Press to the Dreyfus Case" (1997) 14 *Journal of Australian Jewish Historical Society* 57 at 64. *cf* JT Gross, *Fear-Anti-Semitism in Poland after Auschwitz* (Princeton, 2006), 134 ff, 257.

Revolutionary and Military Causes

It was a mark of the acceptance of notions of universalism and rationality after the French Revolution that they eventually gave rise to an edict of liberation for the Jews of France. Although prejudice endured, it waned in nineteenth century France. Gradually, notions of secularism, which reserved religion to a private zone, began to prevail. This was a feature of France in the *Belle Époque* that reassured Dreyfus, when accused, that he would be protected by the French legal system against any lingering hostility against Jews. After all, decades earlier, Christian symbols had been removed from French courthouses. The French *Declaration on the Rights of Man and of the Citizen* drew no distinctions on the grounds of race or religion. At first, Dreyfus's confidence was to prove misplaced.

The seeds of the affair were planted by the military humiliation of France in the Franco-Prussian War of 1870. The defeat of the army, still proud of the Napoleonic conquest of Europe, was a great blow to French honour and pride. The catastrophe was commonly attributed to the work of German spies. Only spying, it was believed, could explain the collapse of an army and nation so historical, glorious and unique. Paranoia over superior German spying capacity was never far from the surface in the last years of the nineteenth century. Financial collapse, economic depression and the political instability of the Third Republic turned conservative politicians and newspapers into messengers of fear and suspicion of the supposed enemies of the nation in their midst. The loss of Alsace and Lorraine made many of those who elected to live in France suspect in the eyes of fellow citizens. The popular Parisian newspapers pandered to these fears. This was especially so if those who remained were German-speaking, with German-sounding names or foreign appearance. It was particularly so if they were of the Jewish minority.

Discovery of the Bordereau

Into this mixture of fear, paranoia and suspicion intruded a remarkable event.[6] A document was discovered, apparently by a French concierge working in the Germany embassy in Paris. It was handed to French security which then worked in a section of the General Staff of the Army. Torn into six pieces, this memorandum (or *bordereau*) was a communication in French, apparently addressed to a German contact, about military secrets, including details about a new and secret French field gun. The document was signed with the initial "D". It suggested that a senior military official of France was providing secrets to the German military attaché in Paris.

The *bordereau* led immediately to a search for the culprit. That search led the senior members of the French Army to suspect Alfred Dreyfus. He was descended from a wealthy Jewish family from Alsace. He had made the French Army his career. He was a non-observant Jew who enjoyed an income many times greater than his military salary. He had been a top student. At the age of thirty, his outstanding service led him to be assigned to work in the Ministry of War in Paris, with the rank

---

[6] MP Johnson, *The Dreyfus Affair: Honour and Politics in the Belle Epoque* (1999).

of captain. For a soldier, he lived an unusually quiet family life. His misfortune was that the leaders of the French General Staff were openly anti-Semitic. They were determined, without delay, to rid the army of the alleged author of the inculpating document.

The *bordereau* was discovered in September 1894. By late October 1894, the conservative and right-wing Christian newspaper, *La Libre Parole*, was fed the news that the suspect in the spying was a Jewish officer. On a pretext, Dreyfus had been asked by a superior to write a letter based on the wording of the *bordereau*. Because of perceived similarities between the handwriting in the two documents, he was arrested and imprisoned. The Dreyfus affair had begun.

Conviction and Exile

In December 1894, Dreyfus stood trial before a court martial. He had an excellent lawyer who was convinced of the innocence of his client and demanded an open trial. However, the military judges insisted on a trial held behind closed doors. They said that this was essential to safeguard national security. Handwriting experts called by the army attested to the similarity of the writing in the *bordereau* and the sample of Dreyfus's writing. However, two superior experts called for the defence pointed to many dissimilarities in the writing. Dreyfus' lawyer was sure that his client would be free at the end of the trial.

As is now known, contrary to the basic rules of procedural fairness and also the French law governing courts martial, an officer of the War Ministry provided a secret dossier to the members of the court martial whilst they were deliberating. The dossier contained a letter from an Italian military attaché inculpating Dreyfus. Neither Dreyfus nor his lawyer was given access to this secret evidence. Nor did they know of its provision to the tribunal. The course adopted was later justified in the name of national security.[7] Vehemently professing his innocence, Dreyfus was unanimously convicted of treason. He was condemned to military degradation and perpetual deportation.

In an electric scene in the courtyard of the *École Militaire* in the centre of Paris, Dreyfus had his military insignia torn from his uniform and his sword broken in his presence. A famous cartoon of the time showed him bowed and downcast. But photography had arrived by 1894. A photograph showed him unbowed and erect. He declared in a voice that those nearby could hear: "I forbid you to do this to me". Because the square was so large, Dreyfus was led around its perimeter to be humiliated in front of the assembled army officers and antagonistic citizens. Yet he was far from humbled. Repeatedly he declared "Innocent! Innocent! Vive la France!". It was an unsettling response and it led several who witnessed it to quit the assembly in a state of disquiet.

However, the vast majority of witnesses were relieved by the quick resolution of the disgraceful episode. Dreyfus's protestations at the *École Militaire* were drowned out

---

[7] HT Tamplin (ed) "The Dreyfus Case" (1898) 15 *The Cape Law Journal* 23.

by cries "Death to the Jew!". In the legislature, politicians of all persuasions welcomed the outcome of the court martial and the eradication of a blemish on the honour of the French Army. Uncovering the treacherous spy so swiftly was a cause for congratulations to the government and the army. Even the radical politician, Georges Clemençeau, who was later to become a supporter of Dreyfus, asked Parliament why an ordinary soldier would be condemned to death for treason but a captain spared of his life? Politicians of the right, the left and of the centre, jumped on the bandwagon of excoriation. Dreyfus was sentenced to exile to Devil's Island off the coast of French Guinea, as soon as his petition for leave to appeal was rejected. On that island, he spent his time in solitary confinement in a malarious environment. But his spirit was not broken; nor that of his wife and brother.

A saga of iniquity began that represents the essence of the *Dreyfus* affair. The army had wanted no publicity and a quick conclusion to the matter. No motive had been shown why a wealthy captain, with a promising career and quiet domestic life, would have acted as claimed. The motive hinted at was Dreyfus's origin in Alsace, his knowledge of the German language and his Jewishness. Religious newspapers like *La Libre Parole* and *La Croix* supported the conviction whenever it was questioned. As the growing evidence of wrongdoing mounted, these forces in government, in the army and the Church railed against the questioners. For them, patriotism demanded unquestioning loyalty to the institutions of the state. Yet the questioners would not let up.

A Second Letter is Discovered

The case against Dreyfus began to collapse in March 1896 when a further letter was intercepted in the German embassy. This could not have been written by Dreyfus. He was safely locked away on Devil's Island. Because a new government had taken office in Paris, the *Dreyfus* file was reopened. Against his earlier belief, a military official, Georges Picquart, became convinced of the innocence of Dreyfus and of the guilt of another Army officer, Major Ferdinand Walsin-Esterhazy. Esterhazy, a big spending soldier, originally from Hungary, with a weakness for women and gambling, was identified by his stockbroker, de Castro, who saw a photographic reproduction of the incriminating *bordereau* in a newspaper and he recognised the writing. The facsimile had been published to confirm Dreyfus's guilt and to still the doubts. Instead, it shifted a spotlight to Esterhazy.

Esterhazy demanded a court martial to clear his name. In the heated atmosphere of the times, the army pulled out all the stops to reaffirm the guilt of Dreyfus and to clear Esterhazy. False rumours had been circulated that, before departing France, Dreyfus had confessed his guilt to military colleagues. In the face of his astonishing performance at the *École Militaire*, this story proved unconvincing. A leak from military headquarters to a sympathetic newspaper contained a mention, for the first time, of the existence of the incriminating secret file that had been provided to the court martial in 1894. This unintended slip propelled the Dreyfus family to petition the Chamber of Deputies for a review of the proceedings. The army transferred Picquart to a dangerous post in Tunisia, presumably in the hope that he would die or disappear there. Picquart did not oblige. Another conservative newspaper, unsympathetic to Dreyfus, *Le Matin,* boastingly published the *bordereau* as evidence of Dreyfus's guilt and de Castro saw it. However, an even bigger mistake was made.

It involved the interference by military operatives in the evidence that had been used to convict Dreyfus.

Forged messages were inserted in the evidence in the military file, naming Dreyfus as the spy. Eventually these forgeries were revealed as such. One of them, prepared by a master forger, came undone when examination under magnification showed a discrepancy between the size and colour of the lines in the paper at different parts of the reconstructed page. The identification of Dreyfus's name appeared on paper that had obviously been skilfully inserted into the original that had contained no such identification. It was like a modern case of reconstruction by photocopying. It showed the extent to which elements in the army would go to keep the *Dreyfus* case closed.

Émile Zola's Accusation

Esterhazy was acquitted by his court martial. Lucie Dreyfus's petition was rejected by the French legislature. At the end of 1897, the French Prime Minister declared to the National Assembly "[t]here is no Dreyfus affair whatsoever". Yet a group of civil libertarians and intellectuals had taken up the Dreyfus cause.[8] Their intervention was to prove decisive.

Émile Zola published the first of a series of public letters urging his fellow citizens to interest themselves in the wrongful conviction of Dreyfus. International handwriting experts denounced the opinions that had declared that Dreyfus was the author of the *bordereau*. Zola stepped up his public campaign. On 13 January 1898, in Clemençeau's newspaper *L'Aurore*, Zola wrote a letter to the President of the French Republic. It appeared under a full-page headline, composed by Clemençeau, "*J'accuse* ...!". French authors of great distinction, such as Marcel Proust and Anatole France, joined the campaign. But anti-Semitic hoodlums took to the streets to defend France against "Masons, Protestants and Jews".

By February 1898, the French League for Human and Civic Rights was founded to provide a focus for the voices asserting that the Dreyfus conviction was a miscarriage of justice. Contemporaneous with these developments was a heightened official resolve to affirm Dreyfus's conviction and to keep his file closed and out of public scrutiny. This resolve was at first vindicated by the outcome of Zola's public letter. Instead of the reopening the *Dreyfus* case, it resulted in a long prosecution of Zola for criminal libel. He was convicted and, after an appeal, retried and reconvicted. He fled to Switzerland and then to England where he awaited the outcome of the campaign. He was denounced personally and, not content with this, his critics also traduced his father.

Yet by August 1898 more senior army officers were beginning to share some of the doubts about the forged materials inserted into the army files. They secured the dismissal of Esterhazy from the army. When this occurred it was not for treason, but for "habitual misconduct". Yet even in the face of plain forgeries, the

[8] WE Dwight, "An Episode in the Affaire Dreyfus", 8 *Yale Law Journal* 272 at 272 (1898).

army at its highest level continued to cover up. Indeed, an inquiry was initiated against Picquart, on account of his work for a reopening of the *Dreyfus* case from within the army. Picquart was arrested and imprisoned. Still more violent anti-Semitic demonstrations broke out in Paris. Mobs in the streets asserted the guilt of Dreyfus and condemned the lack of patriotism of those who questioned that guilt. Evidence was not the concern of these people. Fear of German spies and of Jewish aliens was what drove them on. By December 1898, in response to the activities of the League for Human and Civil Rights, conservative forces founded the League of French Patriots. It was to survive the outcome of the *Dreyfus* case and to laud the "patriotic" officers who had forged documents in order to uphold the army's honour. Eventually, this body was to provide many of the personnel who initiated the anti-Semitic campaigns of Vichy France during the Second World War.

Second Trial and its Outcome

All of this notwithstanding, and despite the cover-up, by 1899 it had become impossible to keep the lid on the errors of the original *Dreyfus* trial. In June 1899 a Court of Appeal overturned the court martial verdict of 1894. Dreyfus was brought back to France for a new court martial. He was remanded in custody at Rennes. Foreign journalists noticed that, in the second court martial, conducted in a local high school, Christian symbols remained on the walls, as if to indicate that in military affairs, secularism would not intrude too far. In August 1899, a fanatic shot Dreyfus's lawyer in an attempt to kill him. The second trial opened a week later. Yet to the astonishment of foreign observers, Dreyfus was not acquitted. For the second time, this time by a majority verdict, he was found guilty of treason. The verdict was qualified by a rider of "extenuating circumstances". Dreyfus's imprisonment was reduced to ten years detention.[9]

The outcry against the second verdict was instantaneous and overwhelming. Within days the French Cabinet had recommended that Dreyfus should be pardoned by the President. Dreyfus only accepted the pardon on condition that he could continue to assert, and establish, his innocence. The French President agreed to this stipulation. The pardon issued. The Minister of War declared: "The incident is over".[10] Paris was preparing for the inauguration of the Universal Exhibition of 1900. The Chamber of Deputies passed an amnesty law. Many hoped that Alfred Dreyfus would quietly disappear into obscurity and old age. However, the turmoil was not so easily put to rest.

Vindication and Innocence

Several members of the Chamber of Deputies were gravely disquieted by the official conduct during the affair. This disquiet grew when the army itself, in October 1903, raised the possibility of a still further retrial of Dreyfus on charges of

---

[9] See Burns, above n 1, 176 describing the Rennes verdict and its immediate annulment.

[10] JD Bredin, *The Affair: The Case of Alfred Dreyfus* (1986); A David, *Famous Political Trials* (Learner, 1980) at 45.

treason. In March 1904, the Criminal Chamber of the Court of Cassation granted Dreyfus's request for a reinvestigation of his case. That investigation concluded with an outcome favourable to Dreyfus. The decision was referred to an extraordinary sitting of the Supreme Court of Appeal in November 2004. On 12 July 1906, after yet further inquiry, the Supreme Court of Appeal, with all three Chambers of France's highest court sitting jointly, annulled the Rennes verdict. It pronounced the acquittal and total rehabilitation of Dreyfus. It proclaimed his innocence. A week later, in the same courtyard of the *École Militaire* in Paris, Dreyfus was decorated a Knight of the Legion of Honour. When the crowd shouted "Long live Dreyfus!", he replied in the words he had used in that place twelve years earlier: "*Vive la France!*".[11] Picquart was there to witness the scene.

The Vichy Aftermath

A hundred years ago many observers declared that the ultimate outcome of the *Dreyfus* affair was a delayed vindication of French institutions and a reaffirmation of the civic equality of all citizens in the face of stigma and discrimination. Yet the case left a deep sense of disquiet among both supporters and opponents of Alfred Dreyfus. His supporters noted the long interval of denial, forgery and cover-up to which, even in a democratic country like France, great governmental institutions and high office-holders would stoop. His opponents continued to hate those who had supported Dreyfus. They considered that their damaging campaign had undermined French institutions and questioned the honour of the French army and the nobility of the nation: values that should be maintained at all costs — even, if necessary, at the sacrifice of a person like Dreyfus. Some of the anti-Dreyfusards would never believe his innocence. A number of them took their vengeance in the anti-Semitic laws of Vichy France. After 1942, that regime tightened the noose around the lives of the Jewish refugees in France and, ultimately, even French citizens of Jewish origin.

On the outer perimeter wall in one corner of the *École Militaire* in Paris, where the beginning and the end of the Dreyfus drama was played out, is a memorial. It records a group of French Jews who were ordered to assemble there, and were deported to the Nazi death camps with almost total loss of life and real loss of national honour. Anti-Semitism did not die out in France with the rehabilitation of Alfred Dreyfus. It lay in wait for further victims.

So what are the lessons for today that we should derive in Ireland and Australia, as we reflect on the story of Alfred Dreyfus in France a century ago? I do not presume to recount all of the lessons for Ireland. It would be inappropriate for me to do so. Yet there surely are lessons. Many would be the same as those that we can see in Australia where so many descendants from this nation have made their lives.

---

[11] AL Goodhart, "Three Famous Legal Hoaxes" (1968) 6 *Alberta Law Review* 1 at 9.

Ten Lessons for Today

Vigilance Against Miscarriages

The first lesson is that, whoever we are, but especially if we are judges and lawyers, we must be vigilant against miscarriages of justice.[12] It is easy for the mind, especially the lawyer's mind, to slip into formalism. Easy to forget the ultimate purpose of law and of its institutions. The fact that a trial has gone through all the correct procedures, and ostensibly conformed to legal forms, does not relieve us of the duty to consider any flaws that are alleged in the process, or the outcome, that amount to a miscarriage of justice.

Many serious injustices happen long before cases come before courts. If police investigation is defective or partisan, justice may never be rescued. If the prosecutor does not act fairly, the accusation may never be properly tested. If officials lie and falsely claim (as in the *Dreyfus* case) that an accused has confessed, great wrongs can follow.[13] This is why the High Court of Australia, in a series of decisions in the 1980s and 1990s, ultimately insisted on verification of confessions to officials. This insistence led Parliaments throughout Australia to provide for sound and video recording of them.[14] Vulnerable and inexperienced witnesses can sometimes undermine their own cases.[15] In such instances, it is not enough for a court to admit to lingering "anxiety".[16] Yet this was what the High Court did at the beginning and end of its reasons dismissing an appeal of Rupert Max Stuart, an Aboriginal accused of, and sentenced to death for, the murder of a young girl based on an uncorroborated and flawed confession.[17] In the end, it was a media campaign, the agitation of civil libertarians and the disquiet of some politicians and a Catholic priest, Father Dixon, that saved Max Stuart's life. It was not the Australian courts of justice.

There have been other recent instances of suggested miscarriages of justice in Australia where the courts have been divided. The *Lindy Chamberlain* case is an instance.[18] That case involved the trial and conviction of a young mother whose

---

[12] See AAS Zuckerman, "A Strategy for Reducing the Incidence of Miscarriage of Justice" (1993) 44 *Northern Ireland Legal Quarterly* 3.

[13] *The Queen v McKinney and Judge* (1991) 171 CLR 468. Also relevant was the decision upholding the right to legal representation of the indigent in serious criminal trials: *Dietrich v The Queen* (1992) 177 CLR 292; *cf* I Dennis, "Miscarriages of Justice and the Law of Confessions: Evidentiary Issues and Solutions" [1993] *Public Law* 291 at 291–301.

[14] See e.g. *Kelly v The Queen* (2004) 218 CLR 216 considering the *Criminal Law (Detention and Interrogation) Act* 1995 (Tas) s 8(1) and *Nicholls v The Queen* (2005) 219 CLR 196 and *Carr v Western Australia* (2007) 232 CLR 138 considering the *Criminal Code* (WA), s 570D(2).

[15] See e.g. *Tuckiar v The King* (1934) 52 CLR 335.

[16] *Stuart v The Queen* (1959) 101 CLR 1.

[17] *ibid*, at 3, 10 per Dixon CJ, McTiernan, Fullagar, Taylor and Windeyer JJ; *cf* MD Kirby, "The Stuart Case — Black and White Lessons for the Australian Judiciary" (2002) 23 *Adelaide Law Review* 195.

[18] *Chamberlain v The Queen [No 1]* (1983) 153 CLR 514; *Chamberlain v The Queen [No 2]* (1984) 153 CLR 521.

baby disappeared near Ayers' Rock in the centre of Australia. A wild dog (dingo) was first blamed for the death of the baby. The mother and her husband were members of a small minority religion. There was much media antagonism towards the mother. The mother was found guilty by a jury and convicted of murder of her baby. Once again, the eventual outcome of the saga was secured outside the courts. It followed a Royal Commission of Inquiry. Many more recent examples show an increased vigilance of Australian courts against the risks of miscarriage. This is usually a central issue in most criminal appeals.[19]

In *Mallard v The Queen*,[20] the importance to just outcomes of the fair conduct of a trial by the prosecution all criminal trials in Australia was given fresh emphasis by the High Court of Australia. In our criminal justice system, the prosecutor is not just another litigant, determined to win its case. Like the court itself, the prosecutor is subject to duties of fair conduct, which includes fairness to the accused. This is a universal feature of a fair criminal procedure.[21] Courts themselves are not exempt from it. The *Mallard* case had come to the High Court in 1997 and Mr Mallard had been refused leave to appeal.[22] I was a party to that refusal. It was only when further evidence was gathered and analysed by supporters, who believed in Mr Mallard's innocence, that the matter was returned to the courts on a petition of mercy. Only then was the evidence reopened, re-explored and found wanting. Even then, the petition was rejected in the intermediate court. But it was unanimously upheld by the High Court of Australia. Mr Mallard's decade in prison for murder was ended. Sadly there have been similar cases of miscarriage of justice in Ireland and Britain.[23] Many wrongful Irish convictions have taken more than a decade to be uncovered and corrected.[24]

The lesson of the *Dreyfus* case, and of countless cases since, is that decision-makers who have control over important decisions on behalf of society must always retain an open mind. They must never join a popular bandwagon. And society must maintain a questioning attitude towards officialdom. The persistent supporters of Dreyfus elevated a "duty to question" over the "duty to obey".[25] Some patriots and institutional conservatives at the time deeply resented this.[26] However, in the end, the questioners were proved right.

[19] *Weiss v The Queen* (2005) 224 CLR 300 where the relevant Australian cases concerning criminal appeals are collected.
[20] *Mallard v The Queen* (2006) 224 CLR 125.
[21] *Mallard v The Queen* (2006) 224 CLR 125 at 148 [57]ff.
[22] Noted *Mallard v The Queen* (1997) 191 CLR 646.
[23] Lord Steyn, "Human Rights: The Legacy of Mrs Roosevelt" [2002] *Public Law* 473 at 473–474.
[24] *Miscarriages of Justice: A Review of Justice in Error* (1999), describing Irish cases in England (pp 46–49); Northern Ireland (pp 298–300) and the Irish Republic (pp 304–308).
[25] Burns, above n 1, viii.
[26] *cf* B Dickson, "The Prevention of Terrorism Acts" in Clive Walker and Keir Sarmer (eds), *Justice in Error* (1993) 178.

Alert to Stigmatised Minorities

The second lesson of the *Dreyfus* case is that we should always be alert to the dangers of prejudice towards stigmatised minorities, especially people who are hated and feared because they are different.

There is no doubt that Dreyfus suffered — and was kept on Devil's Island long after his conviction could be seen by fair-minded observers as suspect. He was a Jew in a society with widespread and powerful, if usually latent, anti-Semitism. There are other such minorities, including in Australia. The Aboriginals, like Max Stuart. The communists, Arabs and Muslims. A minority I know well, a small proportion of the population like the Jews: the homosexual minority. Gays are still hated, feared and discriminated against, often, I am ashamed to say, at the behest of the same religious people who hated the Jews in France a century ago. Convicted prisoners, the mentally disabled and the unconventional are also easy targets. The rule of law and equality before the law forbid courts giving effect to such prejudices.

The lesson of the *Dreyfus* affair is that judges, prosecutors and advocates must be on their guard to ensure that prejudices do not affect official decision-making. From the start, the objective evidence against Dreyfus was extremely weak. There was no motive, no reliable confession, simply contested handwriting evidence and a spirited protestation of innocence. What filled the evidentiary deficit in the France of 1894 was anti-Semitism. In Ireland, as in Australia, we must make sure that we never make up an evidentiary deficit in a case with attitudes of fear or dislike against members of a minority. Attitudes of prejudice sometimes exist on the streets. They have no place in a court of law or other independent tribunal. These institutions do not answer to populism or prejudice. The commitment to equality before the law is tested by the way we treat vulnerable minorities. Members of the majority do not generally have to face this problem.[27]

Beware of Military Tribunals

Dreyfus was twice convicted by a military tribunal. The first conviction was reached on flimsy and unreliable evidence. The second conviction occurred in the face of demonstrable proof of innocence. Loyalty to the army swamped the evidence on both occasions. One member of the first court martial admitted that he had scarcely looked at the handwriting tendered to secure the conviction. For him, assertions by the most senior officials of the nation was enough to prove the accusation.

Loyalty, love of nation and belief in its institutions can be admirable virtues. In the modern world, patriotism has its place, at least in sporting contests. But there is a danger of tribunals deciding questions of liberty that operate outside the

---

[27] *Adelaide Company of Jehovah's Witnesses v The Commonwealth* (1943) 67 CLR 116 at 124 per Latham CJ.

independent courts.[28] This is why the independence of the courts, and the tenure of the judges, are so important for our freedoms.[29]

An examination of outcomes in the Australian Refugee Review Tribunal, after its members were not regularly (reappointed as they had previously been as a matter of course) shows a fall-off in decisions favourable to applicants for refugee status and a rise in decisions in favour of the Minister contesting the claim.[30] This is what can happen where decision-makers do not enjoy guaranteed tenure. It is true that such guarantees sometimes entail disadvantages. Occasionally, they can cloak individual inadequacies. However, over the centuries, judicial tenure has been a great protection for our liberties. It did not exist in the first or second tribunals that tried, and convicted, Dreyfus. Those military tribunals were not really independent. They displayed loyalty to the conception of the members of the nation and of their military superiors. An affirmation of civilian rule is crucial to the just trial of serious accusations. It is ironic today to read the American comments on the *Dreyfus* trials in the 1890s and their asserted superiority of American civil courts,[31] contrasting those comments with the more recent defence of United States military commissions at Guantánamo Bay.

In Australia, courts martial are an exception to the general principle of civilian courts for contested federal accusations.[32] In this, Australian law normally reflects a longstanding tradition of the common law restricting courts martial, essentially, to military accusations arising out of conduct on the battlefield.[33] However, a recent decision of the High Court of Australia has had the effect of expanding this exceptional military jurisdiction. It was my opinion, in that case, and still is, that we should not expand the jurisdiction and powers of military tribunals.[34] Doing so is contrary to our constitutional history and, in my view at least, to the Australian constitutional text.[35]

---

[28] B Dickson, "Law versus terrorism: Can law win?" [2005] *European Human Rights Law Review* 11.

[29] C Campbell, "'Wars on Terror' and Vicarious Hegemons: The UK, International Law and the Northern Ireland Conflict" (2005) *International and Comparative Law Quarterly* 321; C Walker, "The Commodity of Justice in States of Emergency" (1999) 50 *Northern Ireland Legal Quarterly* 164; *ASIC v Forge* (2006) 228 CLR 45 at 72 [54], 94 [124].

[30] Mary Crock, "Reviewing the Merits of Refugee Decisions: An Evaluation of the Refugee Review Tribunal" in Conference Proceedings, *Retreating from the Refugee Convention* (1997), Northern Territory University, Darwin.

[31] SD Thompson, "The Revision of the Dreyfus Case" (1899) 11 *Green Bag* 9 at 13: pointing to the need to "maintain the supremacy of the civil over the military power, and to purge themselves of the rank corruption and gross injustice which fester in the Dreyfus case".

[32] *Re Tracey; Ex parte Ryan* (1989) 166 CLR 518; *Re Nolan; Ex parte Young* (1991) 172 CLR 460 and *Re Tyler; Ex parte Foley* (1994) 181 CLR 18.

[33] Discussed in *Re Aird; Ex parte Alpert* (2004) 220 CLR 308 at 341 [103] citing *Re Tracey* (1989) 166 CLR 518 at 558 and *Burdett v Abbot* (1812) 4 Taunt 401 at 449–450 [128 ER 384 at 403].

[34] *Re Aird* (2004) 220 CLR 308. See also *White v Director of Military Prosecutions* (2007) 81 ALJR 1259. In *Lane v Morrison* (2009) 83 ALJR 993 the Military Court was declared unconstitutional.

[35] *cf* C Walker, "Army Special Powers on Parade" (1989) 40 *Northern Ireland Legal Quarterly* 1 at 31–33; J D Jackson, "The *Northern Ireland (Emergency Provisions) Act* 1987" (1988) 39 *Northern Ireland Legal Quarterly* 1 at 31–33.

Anyone in doubt about the defects that can intrude into military tribunals in fraught circumstances should consider the *Dreyfus* case, and especially Dreyfus's second trial at Rennes. These provide a reason for deep concern, mentioned by many observers, about the United States military commissions for trying prisoners kept for four years in the military base at Guantánamo Bay.[36] The subordination of military power to civilian power is one of the vital elements in a successful modern democracy. We must keep it unimpaired.[37]

Beware of Secret Trials

The *Dreyfus* case also teaches the great care that must be observed in deciding serious accusations behind closed doors. Hearing and deciding cases in secret, based on secret evidence, not made available to an accused or the public, was a serious flaw in Dreyfus's first trial. It was only repaired when, later, mistakenly hoping that it would condemn Dreyfus, a facsimile of the document on which he had been condemned, the *bordereau*, was published by a newspaper and helped to turn up the real culprit.

A general feature of our legal systems is a revulsion against secret trials.[38] Even where there is confidential information, courts must ordinarily be allowed to adopt expedients to keep the trial, and the evidence, as open as possible whilst treating sensitively material recognised as sensitive.[39] The light of public scrutiny must be shone on all serious trials. Otherwise, they may become a cosy self-fulfilling enterprise, denying fundamental rights to the accused.[40]

The fact that national security was repeatedly asserted as the reason for the secrecy of the *Dreyfus* trial demonstrates the need for appropriate caution and scepticism about the justification for such claims. Had it not been for the gradual emergence of the truth, the army and many other powerful interests in France would have closed the *Dreyfus* file. Most people would quickly have forgotten him. He would have rotted away on Devil's Island. Politicians of all persuasions, and the demonstrators on the streets, would have continued to denounce Dreyfus as a traitor. It was only a small band of supporters, and the gradual emergence of the truth, that saved this innocent man from such a fate. That was not the outcome of

[36] *cf Hamdi v Rumsfeld* (2004) 159 LEd 2d 578; 124 SCt; I Barker, "Human Rights in an Age of Counter-Terrorism" (2005) 26 *Australian Bar Review* 1 at 10.

[37] *cf* PA Thomas, "September 11th and Good Governance" (2002) 53 *Northern Ireland Legal Quarterly* 366 at 366–374; 380–390.

[38] See e.g. *Raybos Australia Pty Ltd v Jones* (1985) 2 NSWLR 47 at 50–58; *John Fairfax and Sons Ltd v Police Tribunal of New South Wales* (1986) 5 NSWLR 465; *In the Matter of an Application by the Chief Commissioner of Victoria Police* (2005) 79 ALJR 881 at 900 [114]; *cf Scott v Scott* [1913] AC 417 at 437–438.

[39] R Costigan, and PA Thomas, "Anonymous Witnesses" (2000) 51 *Northern Ireland Legal Quarterly* 326 at 335–357.

[40] M O'Neill, "EC Law and the regulation of British Anti-Terrorism Legislation: Does Gallager open the door to further EC challenges?" (1998) 1 *Contemporary Issues in Irish Law and Politics* 110 at 11–113.

the closed and secret trial which officialdom supported and defended. How many innocent people languish for lack of supporters and skilled advocates?

Protection for People of Conscience

The *Dreyfus* case also demonstrates the importance of protecting people of conscience. Protests might have been expected from Dreyfus's wife and brother: declaring his innocence and working for his vindication. Families are usually like this. They often cling to a belief in innocence in the face of overwhelming evidence to the contrary. The community tends to discount family claims, as the French community originally did in the case of the Dreyfus family's pleas.

What changed the outcome of the *Dreyfus* case was the adherence to the Dreyfus side of intellectuals and civil libertarians. In Australia and Ireland, there are people, some in the law, who do not much like intellectuals, criminologists and do-gooders. They are attacked as "egg-heads". In Australia, they often fall as the first victims to the tall poppy syndrome that has existed since the earliest convict days. Further, there are people who condemn civil libertarians and reject the legitimacy of their role. On some occasions, it is true, civil libertarians buck the system. They challenge authority with its important tasks to perform. Yet, it was the Dreyfus case that led to the establishment of the French League for Human and Civic Rights. Writers, philosophers, journalists and lawyers joined the League. It gave focus to the increasing disquiet about the Dreyfus conviction. It mobilised the belief that a serious wrong had occurred.

In Australia, Justice Lionel Murphy, a leading judge of my court, of Irish derivation, once explained that the world had been greatly improved by protestors objecting to injustice as they saw it. Sometimes they have brought the world around to their persuasion. Justice Murphy famously declared that Mr Percy Neal, an Aboriginal activist, was "entitled to be an agitator".[41] We must never forget that entitlement. We must defend it and uphold it.[42]

Eventually, some of the most important converts to the Dreyfus cause were officers of the French army. Commandant Georges Picquart became convinced that Dreyfus had been framed. Picquart paid for this belief, and the publication of his opinion, by being arrested, court martialled and imprisoned. Yet fortunately, he lived to see the vindication of his suspicions. He was present when Dreyfus was welcomed back to the *École Militaire* in 1906. But when he acted as he did, in defence of his conscience and his notions of the requirements of justice, Picquart could not have known the outcome. Some whistle-blowers are obsessive, misguided, intolerant people who will never accept even overwhelming evidence. But, as Picquart illustrates, some are important agents for truth. Where it is significant, and a person is suffering loss of liberty and of reputation, society must find ways to protect

---

[41] *Neal v The Queen* (1982) 149 CLR 305 at 316–317 per Murphy J.

[42] *cf* A Bunyan, "The War on Democracy and Freedom? — An Assessment of the War on Terrorism on Criminal Justice Civil Liberties" (2002) 12 *Irish Criminal Law Journal* 25.

conscientious officials and others who adhere to their understanding of the truth, even if sometimes they later prove wrong and misguided.

Picquart was not alone. A decade after Dreyfus's conviction and following his pardon, more senior army officers expressed doubts. True, the army leadership was complicit in the cover-up. Most of its leaders never accepted Dreyfus's innocence. But there were military people and officials of conscience and integrity who were eventually won round. Sadly, it took a long time.

Scrutiny of Authority

The *Dreyfus* affair is a story about spies. Acting on partial information, embracing a theory, defending national security and honour as they saw it, their "intelligence" and "proof" took France, a great democratic republic down the road where it seemed willing to sacrifice an individual to defend the supposed honour of the nation and its army.

The cover-up was remarkable. When a military officer prepared forged documents, and slipped them into the military file, he thought his ploy would never be discovered.[43] It would help prove what the forger "knew", in any case, was the truth. But the forgery was discovered. When its deception was revealed, the army officer involved committed suicide. Yet immediately, he was praised for his actions. They were called patriotic and well-meaning. A national collection was invited for the support of his widow.[44]

There are people who are so blinded by their concept of duty and patriotism, or misled by their participation in espionage, that they forget society's commitment to truth and justice. A civil society, respecting liberty, must always be defensive against such honour-blind people. It must beware of their cover-ups. It must retain a healthy scepticism about their accusations of anti-State activity. The terrible wrongs of the Gestapo in Germany, of the NKVD, Stalin's secret police, of Pol Pot's Khmer Rouge, and even of the House Un-American Activities Committee in the United States show what grave wrongs can be done in the name of patriotism and national security.[45]

Every society has a right and duty to protect its citizens against genuine threats to security. Yet, in the long run, the best guarantee against attacks on society is often a steady adherence to the institutions and ways of a temperate democracy. This steady adherence was demonstrated in Australia in 1951 by the decision of the High Court in the *Communist Party* case.[46] That decision invalidated a law designed to

---

[43] *cf* D Curtin, "Digital governance in the European Union anno 2002 - Freedom of information trumped by 'internal security'?" (2002) 12 *Irish Law Journal* 17.

[44] P Quillard, "The Henry Monument" cited in Burns, above n 1, 130.

[45] *cf* N Neligan, "Criminalising International Terrorism: The Criminal Justice (Terrorist Offences) Bill 2002" (2004) 9 *The Bar Review* 152; C Walker and Y Akdeniz, "Anti-terrorism laws and data retention: War is over?" (2003) 54 *Northern Ireland Legal Quarterly* 159 at 172–175.

[46] *Australian Communist Party v The Commonwealth* (1951) 83 CLR 1.

outlaw Australian communists. That case stands in marked contrast to the decision of the Supreme Court of the United States, at the same time, upholding the constitutional validity of a similar law to deprive communists in that country of their rights to assembly and to free speech, although these values are expressly guaranteed in the American Constitution.[47]

Maintenance of Secularism

Another lesson of the *Dreyfus* case is the importance of keeping religious beliefs separate from the institutions of the state and processes of the law. It is not a coincidence that, in December 1905, in the aftermath of the vindication by the Criminal Chamber of the Court of Cassation of Alfred Dreyfus's appeal, a law was enacted by the French legislature expressly establishing the separation of Church and State in France.[48]

France had been moving in the direction of secularism throughout the nineteenth century. However, the strong support for the forces lined up against Dreyfus by anti-Semitic elements in the Church, army and politics of France, led to a feeling of revulsion against these institutions when the injustice and cover-ups of the *Dreyfus* case were laid bare. Secularism was reinforced in France. It is still very strong.

A study of Australian Church journals in the years of the *Dreyfus* affair shows that they never reflected the antagonistic attitude to Dreyfus present in various Church-supported newspapers and other publications in France.[49] Instead, the Australian religious press noted the suggested double standards of the English media towards the French trials and the trials of the Irish and Boer accused in the British Empire. But the strong bias against secret military tribunals, that has long existed in English-speaking countries, was evident in Australia in reaction to the *Dreyfus* trials.

The institutions that grew up, supposedly to defend patriotism and the honour of the army and the nation in the *Dreyfus* case, were later to help spawn the extremist politicians and officials who led the anti-Semitism of the Vichy period of French history. It was not a noble time for adherents to the Christian religion or for the universal principles of that faith. It taught the need to keep the religious dimension private and for the state to protect, and defend *all* people in its jurisdiction and power, whatever their religion, ethnicity or other features of special difference.

If anything, the separation of religion and the state has become more important and urgent as the decades have passed. In the modern age, insistence upon legal enforcement of religious beliefs is again intruding into law and governance in many

---

[47] *Dennis v The United States* 341 US 494 (1951), Vinson CJ for the Court; Black and Douglas JJ dissenting.

[48] See C Thornton-Smith, above n 5, at 76ff for the concerns in the Australian Catholic community about the secular movement in France as it affected the Church.

[49] C Thornton-Smith, above n 5, 76ff.

countries.[50] Demands that religious law should predominate over the laws made by a civilian parliament need to be resisted where they adversely affect the basic civic rights of others. From contemporary experience, we know that religious majorities sometimes target vulnerable minorities. Those minorities may be Jews. But they may also be gays. Or members of the Baha'i faith. Or Muslims. Or Christians in some countries. In a modern, democratic and pluralistic state, the law should be there for everyone. People should not be punished for changing their religion or renouncing religion altogether. These are fundamental individual human rights.[51]

Respect for the right to religion and for the dignity of each religion does not extend to punishing people because they are of a different religion or because of characteristics attributed to that religion. In Australia, to a large extent, we have grown out of such sectarian attitudes. Such attitudes, between Catholics and Protestants and against Jews, were still present in my youth. The wrongs of the *Dreyfus* case demonstrated the perils of anti-Semitism. There are other like attitudes to members of other religions, ethnic and similar minorities.

Witnessing the ordeal of Alfred Dreyfus, Theodor Herzl, a founder of modern Zionism, reporting for the Viennese newspaper *Der Judenstaat*, came to the conviction that a separate national homeland for the Jews was essential. If Jews could not be protected in their liberties, even in comparatively liberal and secular France, Herzl believed they were in peril everywhere. The State of Israel was thus an indirect outcome of the affront to justice of the Dreyfus affair. In all societies, lawyers and other citizens must build a protection for religious and like minorities. However, there must equally be an insistence upon respect, under the law, for religious freedom. Religious freedom includes the right to change one's religion or to renounce religion altogether. The killing of apostates and of gays, women or other groups on supposed religious grounds has no place in the modern world. Respect for religious or cultural values must not involve the deprivation of the fundamental human rights of non-adherents or minority and dissenting adherents.[52]

Ambivalent Role of the Media

The media played an ambivalent role during the *Dreyfus* affair. On the one hand, in the earliest years, sections of the media inflamed the anti-Semitism so evident in the news reports and editorials of the Church-supporting newspapers such as *La*

---

[50] See e.g. RA Fenton, "Catholic Doctrine Versus Women's Rights: The New Italian Law on Assisted Reproduction" (2005) 14 *Medical Law Review* 73 at 75 concerning recent polarisation in the Italian Parliament over a law on assisted reproduction. There are many examples in many countries on many issues.

[51] See *Applicant NABD of 2002 v Minister for Immigration and Multicultural and Indigenous Affairs* (2005) 79 ALJR 742 at [55]-[145]; *cf* L Thio, "Apostacy and Religious Freedom – Constitutional Issues Arising from the Lina Joy Litigation" (2006) 2 *Malaysian Law Journal* 8.

[52] See e.g. the provision on this subject in the UNESCO *Universal Declaration on Cultural Diversity* of 2 November 2001 and the *Universal Declaration on Bioethics and Human Rights* of 19 October 2005 (art 12); *cf* R Inglehart and P Norris, "The True Clash of Civilisations", *Foreign Policy*, March/April 2003, 63.

Libre Parole and *La Croix*. These journals played their part in suppressing the early attempts to right the wrong of the Dreyfus convictions. They affirmed his guilt largely because of his Jewishness and because the institutions of the state were being accused.

On the other hand, the publication in *L'Aurore* of the famous letter by Émile Zola, "*J'accuse!*" was a turning point in the campaign for justice for Dreyfus. Liberal newspapers took up his cause. So did journalists from overseas.[53] The case became one of the earliest illustrations of global infotainment. Part of the media attention arose out of the genuine concern of a few journalists and editors, affronted by the apparent cover-up and injustice. Other journalists just liked a good story. Not a few, in Australia, England, and perhaps Ireland at the time, enjoyed pontificating about the superiority of British justice.

Ultimately, as Lord Russell of Killowen reported to Queen Victoria in 1899, the rehabilitation of Dreyfus was "brought about mainly by the efforts of Frenchmen". Dreyfus's trial had not occurred in the civil courts where his conviction would much earlier have been quashed.[54] Even Lord Russell felt obliged, somewhat condescendingly, to acknowledge that "with all his grossness and exaggeration, the name of Zola ought not to be omitted". Where the media failed was in identifying the systemic and deep-seated problems which the *Dreyfus* case illustrated. Amongst these, the issues of ultra-patriotism, the misuse of claims of national security and the ubiquity of anti-Semitism were inadequately addressed. They were soon to re-emerge with terrible consequences for Europe and the world.

Need for Institutional Changes

The need for institutional changes and improvements are illustrated by what happened to Alfred Dreyfus.[55] His case sounded a warning about anti-Semitism. Inadequately answered, this was to produce unparalleled suffering fifty years later, including in France.

Thinking on the *Dreyfus* case today, in Ireland and Australia, we can conclude that improvements in society's institutions are needed, including sometimes in the attitudes of officials who constitute those institutions.[56] Minimising the role of military tribunals; resisting secret trials; examining closely claims of national security; protecting stigmatised minorities: upholding secularism. All of these are necessities shown in stark relief by what happened to Alfred Dreyfus.

---

[53] See e.g. *The Times of London*, 23 December 1894 extracted in Burns, above n 1, 46–48.

[54] Lord Russell of Killowen to Queen Victoria, 16 January 1899 extracted from RB O'Brien, *The Life of Lord Russell of Killowen* (1901) in Burns, above n 1, 152.

[55] C Walker, "Terrorism and criminal justice: Past, present and future" [2004] *Criminal Law Review* 311; B Dickson, "The Prevention of Terrorism Act" in C Walker and Keir Starmer (eds), *Justice in Error* (1993) 178.

[56] *cf* C Campbell, "The Criminal Justice (Terrorism and Conspiracy) Act 1998" [1999] *Criminal Law Review* 941.

The awful happenings of the first half of the twentieth century, including the *Dreyfus* affair, led ultimately to the acceptance, after 1945, of notions of legally enforceable fundamental human rights. In Australia, we have accepted those notions as binding on the country, in the form of international treaty law. In some instances, we have also translated the notions into enforceable domestic law - such as the law on refugees, the law against racial discrimination, against sex discrimination and discrimination on the ground of sexuality, and on other topics. But we have still not taken the final institutional step of adopting, nationally, an enforceable Australian charter of fundamental rights.

Ireland was the first common law country after the United States to accept the concept of enforceable constitutional rights, subject to the remedies of constitutional review. Later, following this Irish example, Britain, Canada and New Zealand, in their different ways, have now done so, as have India, South Africa and the countries of the new Commonwealth of Nations. Such charters are no absolute guarantee against wrongdoing, cover-up and official mistakes. But they do afford an institutional protection for what are partly institutional problems. At the least, they shore up the values that set society's standards which need to be given weight when cases like *Dreyfus* come along.

Proffering Apologies for Wrongs

There is one final point. It is also illustrated by the *Dreyfus* affair.

In France, there was a persistent reluctance of the old anti-Dreyfusards to acknowledge the wrongs done to Alfred Dreyfus. They would blame everything and everyone except the elements that they adored - in the government, the army and the Church, which had assailed Dreyfus and played on anti-Semitic sentiments to keep him imprisoned.

By 1985, the French government, at its highest level, determined on a corrective. The socialist President, François Mitterand, commissioned a statue to honour Alfred Dreyfus. It was presented to the army for placement in the *École Militaire*. The army declined to accept it.[57] In 1988 it was placed in a corner of Tuileries Gardens in Paris. Soon after, it was daubed with painted swastikas. Anti-Semitic profanities were also marked on Dreyfus's tomb at the Montparnasse cemetery in Paris.

In 1994, during the centenary reflections on Dreyfus's arrest an official military history was published. Whilst literally accurate, it omitted many details and ignored the crimes committed by supposed "patriots" in the name of the honour of the French Army. The official account, written by Colonel Paul Gaujac, declared that "Dreyfus's innocence is the thesis generally accepted by historians".[58] That observation showed that some people will never admit error. For them, Dreyfus's guilt was still an open question — an equal hypothesis or an arguable thesis.

[57] Burns, above n 1, 189.

[58] P Gaujac, "A Theory of Innocence" quoted from *Le Monde*, 10 February 1994, extracted in Burns, above n 1, 189–190.

In 1998, President Jacques Chirac took a bold and healing step. He commemorated the centenary of Émile Zola's public letter "*J'accuse…!*". It had been written by Zola as a letter to the President of the French Republic. At last, a President of the Republic responded. He took the occasion to remind his fellow citizens of the "sinister forces, intolerance, injustice" that can "creep into the State's highest level". Half a century after Vichy, and a century after Dreyfus's ordeal, it was timely to make that acknowledgment frankly, openly and humbly. It was an acknowledgment of "what Émile Zola and Alfred Dreyfus are saying to us across the years".[59]

President Chirac emphasised the suffering of Alfred Dreyfus. He also pointed out that Dreyfus had known how to forgive. He declared that it is patriots of this kind, not shallow, prejudiced, discriminating, covering-up nationalists, who constitute "the conscience of humanity". It is they who teach their fellow citizens that love of country includes rejection of intolerance and hatred.[60] Blind patriotism and unquestioning belief in the nation, whatever its wrongs, is not the ethos of a modern, democratic civic society.

Neither in the Republic of Ireland nor in the Commonwealth of Australia have we condemned a fellow citizen for treason to an equivalent of Devil's Island or Guantánamo Bay.[61] Indeed, accusations of treason are rare in the modern history of either country since attaining full independence. But Australians have certainly made mistakes. Some we have repaired. Others we have failed to repair. We have shown discrimination against vulnerable minorities. Discrimination still exists. It exists not just in the streets. It exists in the law, in legal ways and in our hearts. We must all learn to recognise these mistakes. Like President Chirac, where wrongs are demonstrated, we must acknowledge them, express regret for them, learn from them and teach the next generation. That is the way to sustain the human journey towards greater human enlightenment.

The *Dreyfus* affair speaks powerfully to Jewish people everywhere, including in Ireland and Australia. This is especially so because of the genocide that quickly followed. But it also speaks clearly of wrongs done in Australia to Aboriginals, to Asian Australians, to Arab and Islamic Australians, to gays and other sexual minorities, to women, to the very old and young, to the mentally and physically disabled, to prisoners, refugees and to unconventional people. No doubt, in Ireland, it speaks clearly to people who have been wrongly branded under anti-terrorism laws; or wrongfully convicted of crimes in the general courts. We must not think that such wrongs are over or that full enlightenment has arrived. Dreyfus belongs to Jewish people. But he also belongs to all human beings. Down the years, and even down the centuries, his cry as he was sent to exile from the courtyard of the *École Militaire* in Paris will ring out as a warning against miscarriages of justice:

"Innocent! Innocent! Vive la France!"

---

[59] J Chirac, Letter of the President of the Republic on the Centenary of "J'accuse", January 1998, in Burns, above n 1, 199 at 192.

[60] *ibid*, 193.

[61] Although see *Victorian Council for Civil Liberties Inc v Minister for Immigration & Multicultural Affairs* (2001) 100 FCR 491; special leave refused in (2001) 205 CLR 694.

The Irish Human Rights Commission: The Early Years

Dr Alpha Connelly*

Introduction

On 25 July 2001, an unusual creature was born. It was a public body, brought into being by statute,[1] and called the Human Rights Commission. Born of political circumstances and in a time of cutbacks in the public sector, its survival, not merely its growth, was far from certain.

The impetus for the establishment of the Commission was the conclusion in 1998 of the Good Friday Agreement. The strength of the Agreement was that it was agreed not only by the British and Irish Governments but had been negotiated with the political parties in Northern Ireland and endorsed in referenda held both north and south of the border. In the negotiations preceding the Agreement, one of the concessions to nationalist demands was the creation of a human rights commission in Northern Ireland, and it was envisaged that a commission would also be established in the Republic. The possibility of the establishment of such a body in the South had been mooted by the Constitution Review Group a couple of years earlier, in 1996, when it reported to the Government on the areas where constitutional change may be desirable or necessary. Like many a good idea before, it would probably have been left to gather dust on a shelf but was taken down from the shelf, dusted off, and given life in response to political events, namely the efforts to bring about a lasting peace in Northern Ireland.

As might be expected, the Northern Commission was established first — in March 1999. The same political urgency not applying in the Republic, the southern Commission followed two years later, though it met in shadow form for a few months before its formal establishment.

The Commission was provided with a temporary office, and a temporary administrator was employed while it went about recruiting a chief executive. This took the best part of a year, and it took over another year to acquire and fit-out permanent premises and to recruit the necessary staff. The story is a familiar one by now. The Government decides to establish a public body, but the resources required are rarely provided for it to hit the ground running. Rather there is bureaucratic delay and legitimate demands for adequate resources, both human and financial, are resisted at official and occasionally at ministerial level.

---

* Chief Executive of the Irish Human Rights Commission 2002–2007. This paper has been written in a personal capacity, and any views expressed therein are those of the author only unless explicitly stated otherwise.

[1] The Human Rights Commission Acts 2000 and 2001.

Once a chief executive had been recruited, the necessary staff employed and permanent premises acquired and fitted out, major challenges still lay ahead. The Commission had to establish its credibility with a range of stakeholders, including Ministers, officials, politicians and non-governmental organisations, as a body which produced high quality research, heightened general awareness of the importance of respect for human rights, afforded sound advice to Government on the human rights dimensions of public policy and legislative proposals, and took legal action, as appropriate, to protect persons' rights. It had also to distance itself from its political birth, to operate in a professional manner, and be seen to speak, with an independent voice, on human rights matters.

In this article, I provide some basic information about the Commission and seek to give some idea of the challenges it faced in its crucial, early years. The article covers essentially the first five years of the Commission. Topics covered are the appointment procedure and membership of the Commission, its functions, its first Strategic Plan, key areas of work, casework and its participation in the Joint Committee with the Northern Ireland Human Rights Commission and in the International Co-ordinating Committee of national human rights institutions.

Appointment Procedure and Membership

On 20 December 1993, there was adopted within the context of the United Nations a set of principles relating to the status of national human rights institutions ("Paris Principles"). The Principles lay down global standards by which national institutions may be judged and place particular emphasis on independence and pluralism.

With regard to the composition of a national institution and the appointment of its members, the Principles provide that they:

> "...shall be established in accordance with a procedure which affords all necessary guarantees to ensure the pluralist representation of the social forces (of civilian society) involved in the promotion and protection of human rights, particularly by powers which will enable effective cooperation to be established with, or through the presence of, representatives of:
>
> (a) Non-governmental organizations responsible for human rights and efforts to combat racial discrimination, trade unions, concerned social and professional organizations, for example, associations of lawyers, doctors, journalists and eminent scientists;
> (b) Trends in philosophical or religious thought;
> (c) Universities and qualified experts;
> (d) Parliament;
> (e) Government departments (if these are included, their representatives should participate in the deliberations only in an advisory capacity)."[2]

[2] Para. 1 of the section "Composition and guarantees of independence and pluralism".

The Principles also provide that:

> "In order to ensure a stable mandate for the members of the national institution, without which there can be no real independence, their appointment shall be effected by an official act which shall establish the specific duration of the mandate. This mandate may be renewable, provided that the pluralism of the institution's membership is ensured."[3]

Some national human rights institutions are based closely on these principles. For example, the French National Consultative Commission on Human Rights includes among its large membership representatives of very many non-governmental organisations working in the human rights or humanitarian field, two members of Parliament, and several representatives of Ministers.[4]

The Government however chose a different method of appointing members of the Irish Commission. It chose not to follow the model whereby members are representatives of a specific sector of society. The legislation establishing the Commission states that its members shall broadly reflect the nature of Irish society.[5] It also provides that they shall be suitably qualified for appointment by reason of their "possessing such relevant experience, qualifications, training or expertise as, in the opinion of the Government, is or are appropriate, having regard, in particular, to the functions conferred on the Commission."[6] Moreover, a gender balance is ensured in that the legislation requires that not less than half of the members shall be men and that not less than half shall be women.[7] Members are appointed by Government.[8]

In order to aid it in the appointment of the first members of the Commission, the Government set up an independent selection body and expressions of interest were sought in appointment to membership of the Commission, apart from that of President. The selection body considered those who expressed an interest and drew

---

[3] Para. 3 of the same section.

[4] The composition of the French Commission was changed somewhat in 2007. Under Article 4 of Decree No. 2007-1137 of 26 July 2008, the Commission comprises the following members with the right to vote:

- 30 persons nominated by the principal non-governmental organisations working in the fields of human rights, international humanitarian law or humanitarian action and the principal trade unions;
- 30 persons with recognised competence in the field of human rights;
- One deputy and one senator;
- The "Médiateur de la Republique";
- One member of the Economic and Social Council.

Representatives of the Prime Minister and of interested Ministers may participate in the work of the Commission in a consultative capacity.

[5] Human Rights Commission Act, 2000, s 5(12).

[6] s 5(4).

[7] s 5(2) of the Human Rights Commission Act, 2000, as amended by the Human Rights Commission Act, 2001.

[8] s 5(3).

up an "A" and a "B" list of those it deemed most suitable for appointment. When the matter came before the Government for decision, the Government did not accept all those persons on the "A" list recommended for appointment and went outside it in some of its appointments. This resulted in considerable anger among non-governmental organisations, members of which had sat on the independent selection body, anger which the Government could not ignore. The outcome was that further legislation was passed, increasing the membership of the Commission from nine to fifteen and allowing onto the Commission most of the "A" list.

The members came from a variety of backgrounds. Lawyers, both academic and practising, were well represented, comprising just over half of the membership. Also included were a chartered accountant, a philosopher, a psychiatrist and a sociologist. One was a member of the Travelling Community. Many had a history of involvement with non-governmental organisations, and many possessed an in-depth knowledge and expertise in human rights.

The President of the Commission is directly appointed by the Government. The first President of the Commission, Mr Justice Donal Barrington, was a former judge of the Supreme Court but, unfortunately, had to resign due to ill health in the late summer of 2002. He was succeeded by Dr Maurice Manning, who has a background in academic life and in politics.

With such a rocky start, it was imperative that the members of the Commission negotiate their differences and pull together in the cause of the task assigned to them: the promotion and protection of human rights in Ireland.

Functions

The Paris Principles contain a long list of the responsibilities, or functions, which a national institution should possess. They also state that a national institution shall be given as broad a mandate as possible and that the mandate shall be clearly set forth in a constitutional or legislative text.[9]

The founding legislation of the Irish Commission confers on it a wide range of functions corresponding broadly to those listed in the Paris Principles.[10] They include the giving of advice to Ministers on legislative proposals, the making of recommendations to Government, participation in national and international fora for the protection of human rights and educational and promotional work.

The Commission also has a number of specifically legal functions. It may afford assistance to a person in legal proceedings involving an issue of human rights. It may take a case in its own name on behalf of a person or class of persons. It may also seek to participate, as appropriate, in proceedings before the High Court or the Supreme Court as *amicus curiae*.

[9] Paras. 2 and 3 of the section "Competence and responsibilities".
[10] See ss 8 to 11 of the Human Rights Commission Act 2000.

Furthermore, the Commission may, either of its own volition or at the request of an individual, conduct an enquiry "into any relevant matter" in furtherance of some of its other functions. This is a substantial power, backed up by criminal sanctions. For the purposes of an enquiry, the Commission may require the attendance of a person before it and the production to it of any information, document or thing relevant to the enquiry. Failure to comply with a requirement is enforceable by the Circuit Court and constitutes an offence for which a person shall be liable on summary conviction to a fine not exceeding £1,500 (€1,923) or imprisonment for a term not exceeding twelve months or both.

The political circumstances of the Commission's birth are directly reflected in one of the provisions relating to the functions of the Commission. The Good Friday Agreement envisages a joint committee of representatives of the two Human Rights Commissions, North and South, as a forum for consideration of human rights issues in the island of Ireland. The Agreement also specifically directs the joint committee to consider "among other matters, the possibility of establishing a charter, open to signature by all the democratic political parties, reflecting and endorsing agreed measures for the protection of the fundamental rights of everyone living in the island of Ireland." The Irish Commission is required by its founding legislation to take whatever action is necessary to establish and participate in the joint committee.

At the time of writing, the Commission had exercised all its functions bar two. It had not, of its own volition, held an enquiry. However, it regularly considered requests from persons for an enquiry, and had completed a report on its first enquiry — into a pensions matter.[11] It was also conducting a second enquiry — into the treatment of an alien who was denied leave to land in the State, though in possession of a valid visitor's visa.[12] The second function yet to be exercised by the Commission was the institution of legal proceedings for the purpose of obtaining relief in respect of any matter concerning the human rights of any person or class of persons. The Commission was actively trying to identify an appropriate case in order to trigger this function.

First Strategic Plan

The term "human rights" potentially covers a huge range of matters. Happily, the legislation governing the Commission confines it somewhat in that it limits the term for the purpose of the Commission's work to:

> "(a) the rights, liberties and freedoms conferred on, or guaranteed to, persons by the Constitution, and

---

[11] *The Self-Employed and the Old Age Contributory Pension Enquiry Report*, published in April 2007.

[12] A third enquiry was initiated in early 2007 into the treatment of persons with intellectual disabilities.

(b) the rights, liberties or freedoms conferred on, or guaranteed to, persons by any agreement, treaty or convention to which the State is a party."[13]

Even limited in this way to those human rights which are guaranteed by the Constitution and international agreements, the scope of the matters falling within the competence of the Commission remains vast. Wisely, therefore, in 2003, the Commission adapted a strategic plan for the period 2003 to 2006.[14] In the plan it identified those areas on which it would focus during this period and set forth the criteria for selecting these areas.

In considering those areas on which to focus, the Commission used a threefold classification of rights based on the traditional distinction between civil and political rights on the one hand and economic, social and cultural rights on the other. The third classification comprised matters which cannot easily be placed in one or the other of these categories but rather span both categories of rights.

Under the heading of civil and political rights, the Commission chose to concentrate on the administration of justice. In practice, it has adopted an expansive interpretation of this notion so as to include, for example, prisons rather than confining it to the operation of the courts.

The Commission did not adopt the same approach to economic, social and cultural rights. Instead of selecting one right in this category on which to concentrate, the Commission decided to undertake a major study of this category of rights in general, including in particular the issue of their enforceability, before turning to an examination of the enjoyment in Ireland of specific rights in this category. The reason for adopting this approach was that there appears to be little comprehension of this category of rights in Ireland. Whereas persons are generally familiar with civil and political rights, such as the right to freedom of expression or the right not to be unlawfully deprived of one's liberty, even if they do not conceptualise them as civil and political rights, there is a relatively low level of awareness of the human rights dimension of economic, social and cultural issues.

As to matters which span the two traditional categories of human rights, or as the Commission has called them, "cross-cutting issues", the Commission decided to focus on four. They were racism, persons with disabilities, gender, and equality and human difference.

Key Areas of Work

It is not possible to detail here all that the Commission has done in its key areas of work. Rather examples of its work in each of the key areas will be given in order to paint a general picture of what it did in its early years.

---

[13] Human Rights Commission Act 2000, s 2.

[14] *Promoting and Protecting Human Rights in Irish Society. A Plan for 2003–2006.* The Commission has since adopted a Second Strategic Plan for 2007–2011.

(i) Administration of Justice

Much of the Commission's work in the area of the administration of justice concerned legislative proposals referred to it by the Minister for Justice, Equality and Law Reform. Proposals referred to the Commission in this area were:

- the Criminal Law (Insanity) Bill 2002;
- the European Arrest Warrants Bill 2003;
- the General Scheme of a Garda Síochána Bill 2003;
- the General Scheme of a Criminal Justice Bill 2003;
- the Commissions of Investigation Bill 2003;
- the Transfer of the Execution of Sentences Bill 2003;
- the Criminal Justice Bill 2004;
- the General Scheme of the Criminal Justice (International Co-operation) Bill 2004;
- additional draft Heads of a Criminal Justice Bill 2004;
- further proposed amendments to the Criminal Justice Bill (Youth Justice);
- Coroners Bill 2006.

The impact of the Commission on these legislative proposals in terms of the amendment of the proposals in response to the Commission's views was mixed. Using this criterion, some of the more successful submissions of the Commission related to policing.

With regard to the General Scheme of a Garda Síochána Bill, the Commission had already published, in December 2002, a position paper entitled *A Proposal for a New Garda Complaints System*. In the position it took, the Commission was clearly influenced by the establishment of the office of Police Ombudsman in Northern Ireland and argued for the establishment of a comparable office in the Republic. In its views on the General Scheme of the Bill, the Commission reiterated its conviction that the most appropriate way of achieving an effective and independent investigation of complaints against members of the Garda Síochána was by establishing an office of Garda Ombudsman and urged the Minister to reconsider this issue. In its submission to the Minister, the Commission also expressed the view that policing is central to the protection of human rights in a democratic society, and that human rights should be at the core of policing philosophy and practice. When the Garda Síochána Bill was published, early in 2004, it was clear that amendments had been made to the proposals in the light of the Commission's views; and the Commission took the opportunity to issue further observations on the Bill. In its observations the Commission gave a detailed analysis of the extent to which its views had been taken on board in the drafting of the Bill and made a number of additional recommendations as to how the human rights aspects of the Bill might be strengthened.

Furthermore, while the Defence (Amendment) (No. 2) Bill 2006 was not formally referred to the Commission by the Minister for Defence, a staff delegation led by the chief executive met formally with officials of the Department of Defence involved in the drafting of the Bill. It was a most constructive meeting. The Bill updated aspects of military law, particularly in relation to courts martial and the ensuing Act contained several amendments which reflected the discussion at the meeting.[15]

Impact may also be assessed by reference to criteria other than the amendment of legislative proposals. All of the Commission's submissions are published and are available on its website www.ihrc.ie. In this way public awareness of the proposals and their human rights implications is heightened. Also, sections of society with a particular interest in certain proposals, such as politicians and non-governmental organisations, may be better informed about them as a result of the Commission's analysis and recommendations, and the Commission's views may feed through into the activities of these other persons and bodies.

Apart from its work on legislative proposals, the Commission also actively engaged with the Minister for Foreign Affairs on the issue of "extraordinary rendition", expressing its concern that US aircraft landing at Shannon airport might be transporting persons to secret locations in other countries for the purpose of interrogation in connection with suspected terrorism and subjected there to torture, other cruel, inhuman or degrading treatment, contrary to international human rights standards.

(ii) Economic, Social and Cultural Rights

In 2005, the Commission undertook a major research project on economic, social and cultural rights. The research dealt essentially with four matters:

- the nature of the rights;
- the status of the rights under international law;
- the various powers of redress and enforcement of the rights; and
- the current status of the rights in Ireland.

All the research, bar the second matter, was carried out in-house. Examination of the status of the rights under international law was outsourced and then integrated with the results of the rest of the research into a *Discussion Document.*

Towards the end of the year, the *Discussion Document* was launched at a major international conference on economic, social and cultural rights, hosted in Dublin by the Commission over two days. Speakers included distinguished academics and representatives of international organisations, such as the United Nations and the Council of Europe, working in the area as well as national experts.[16]

---

[15] The Chief Executive and staff also had most constructive meetings in 2006 with officials of the Department of Justice, Equality and Law Reform on the drafting by the Department of new Prison Rules and with officials of the Department of Foreign Affairs on the General Scheme of a Passports Bill. This Bill was formally referred to the Commission by the Minister for Foreign Affairs. Staff generally communicate with officials of the relevant Department when drafting the Commission's observations on legislative proposals.

[16] In 2006, the Commission initiated a consultation process by way of follow-up to the conference and publication of its *Discussion Document* with the intention of drawing up a report on economic, social and cultural rights.

In 2006, having undertaken a general study of economic, social and cultural rights, the Commission commenced its consideration of the enjoyment in Ireland of specific rights in this category. It chose to begin with the right to housing and to do so by way of a joint project with the Equality Authority.

In its early years, the Commission had no legislative proposals referred to it in this area. It was however approached by the Department of Health and Children, as part of a consultation process the Department was holding in relation to proposals to put the Health Information and Quality Authority on a statutory basis and to establish an Office of the Chief Inspector of Social Services within the Authority.

(iii) Racism

The Commission was also active in the area of racism, which it again broadly understood to include, for example, the human rights standards applicable to migrant workers and aspects of nationality and citizenship law.

In the latter part of 2003, the Commission undertook collaborative research with the National Consultative Council on Racism and Interculturalism ("NCCRI") on the international and EU standards of relevance to migrant workers and their families. On 5 April 2004, the results of this research were published under the title, *Safeguarding the Rights of Migrant Workers and Their Families. A Review of EU and International Standards: Implications for Policy in Ireland*. In their review, the two organisations emphasised the need for Ireland to manage labour migration so as to respect the rights of migrant workers and their families, while taking into account economic and employment initiatives. They further recommended the development of a coherent immigration policy in Ireland and that the State should become party to the International Convention on the Protection of the Rights of Migrant Workers and Members of their Families.[17]

The Commission's first engagement with an international treaty-monitoring process was in the area of racism. In 2004, it examined Ireland's First National Report under the Convention on the Elimination of All Forms of Racial Discrimination ("CERD") and prepared a submission to the UN CERD Committee based on its examination of this Report.

The matters on which the Commission focused were:

- the legal status of CERD in Irish law;
- the scale of the problem of racism in Ireland;
- awareness of racism in the context of the State's obligations under CERD to adopt effective educational programmes to combat racial discrimination and to promote friendship among racial groups;

---

[17] The Commission subsequently commented on the Immigration, Residence and Protection Bill 2008.

- the State's reservation in relation to freedom of expression and freedom of association[18];
- racist speech and freedom of expression;
- migrant workers;
- Travellers;
- asylum-seekers and refugees; and
- gender and racial discrimination.

It followed up its submission by sending a delegation to Geneva in March 2005 for the formal examination by the CERD Committee of Ireland's Report. The delegation was given the opportunity to address the Committee separately from the Government delegation in recognition of its independent status and was happy to avail of the opportunity, thereby becoming the first national human rights institution to address the Committee in its own right.[19]

The Commission's engagement with this process illustrates the way it approaches such activities in general. The Commission's operational values include a commitment to consultation and dialogue, to co-operation with other bodies active in the human rights field both at home and abroad, and to the avoidance of unnecessary duplication of work. It seeks to add value to work already being undertaken in the State to promote and protect human rights. It therefore liaised closely during the CERD process with other relevant public bodies and non-governmental organisations, both in drawing up its submission to the CERD Committee and during the formal examination by the Committee of Ireland's Report.

On 21 October 2003, the Commission published a paper entitled *Position of Non-National Parents and their Irish-Born Children*. This was prompted by a decision of the Supreme Court in which the Court held the non-national parents of children born in Ireland (the children thereby being entitled to Irish citizenship) had no automatic right to residency in the State. Some six months later it also decided to examine the proposed constitutional amendment which would prospectively remove the constitutional entitlement to Irish citizenship based on birth on the

[18] The reservation reads:

"Article 4 of the International Convention on the Elimination of All Forms of Racial Discrimination provides that the measures specifically described in sub-paragraphs (a), (b) and (c) shall be undertaken with due regard to the principles embodied in the Universal Declaration of Human Rights and the rights expressly set forth in Article 5 of the Convention. Ireland therefore considers that through such measures, the right to freedom of opinion and expression and the right to peaceful assembly and association may not be jeopardised. These rights are laid down in Articles 19 and 20 of the Universal Declaration of Human Rights; they were reaffirmed by the General Assembly of the United Nations when it adopted Articles 19 and 21 of the International Covenant on Civil and Political Rights and are referred to in Article 5(d)(viii) and (ix) of the present Convention."

[19] The Committee subsequently introduced a rapporteur system to follow-up on its observations on state reports. One of the Committee members, Morten Kjaerum, was appointed rapporteur, and the Commission met with Mr Kjaerum when he visited Ireland.

island of Ireland and leave this matter to be regulated by legislation. In doing so, the Commission saw its role not as an advocate for or against the proposed constitutional amendment, but as being to highlight relevant human rights issues, more especially those arising from the State's international human rights obligations.

The Commission also commented in 2004 on the draft Irish Nationality and Citizenship (Amendment) Bill, which had been referred to it by the Minister for Justice, Equality and Law Reform. It expressed the view that any proposed restriction of the right to citizenship should be considered in the wider context of serious shortcomings in immigration and asylum policy. It also recommended a more generous approach to the granting of rights of residence for humanitarian and employment purposes. It followed this up two years later with comments on the General Scheme of the Immigration, Residence and Protection Bill, also referred to it by the Minister for Justice, Equality and Law Reform.

(iv) Persons with Disabilities

The main contribution of the Commission during its early years to the promotion of the rights of persons with disabilities was in relation to legislative proposals and to the negotiations on an international convention on the rights of persons with disabilities.

On 11 September 2003, the Commission submitted to the Oireachtas Joint Committee on Education and Science written observations on the Education for Persons with Disabilities Bill 2003 (subsequently entitled the Education for Persons with Special Educational Needs Bill). It was concerned at the role given to school principals in the preparation of education plans. It was also critical of the minimal role assigned to parents and children in the preparation and review of education plans by Health Boards and by the National Council for Special Education. It favoured a presumption of mainstream education for children with disabilities. Where this would not be in the interests of a child, effective and adequate services should be provided.

Responding to legislative developments in this area, on 13 September 2003, the Commission co-hosted with the Law Society of Ireland and the National Disability Authority a conference on "Global Trends in Disability Law: Setting a Context for Irish Law Reform". Speakers at the conference included persons from the Office of the UN High Commissioner for Human Rights and from the Directorate General for Employment and Social Affairs of the European Commission.

In 2004, the Minister for Justice, Equality and Law Reform referred the Disability Bill to the Commission for its views. The Commission reviewed the provisions of the Bill in the light of relevant international human rights standards, and submitted its views to the Minister on 15 November 2004. It was critical of the Bill as being out of step with several basic international principles, such as the lack of effective mechanisms for the allocation of funding and the provision of services to secure progressive realisation of the economic and social rights of persons with disabilities and the lack of effective remedies in terms of the enforcement of orders for the provision of services. On 23 November 2004, representatives of the Commission appeared before the Oireachtas Joint Committee on Justice, Defence and Women's Rights in relation to the Bill.

The Commission was represented, from an early stage, in the international negotiations for a Convention on the Protection and Promotion of the Rights and Dignity of Persons with Disabilities. In 2002, the Commission was elected by the European Group of national human rights institutions to co-ordinate their contribution to the negotiations. The Commission was very active in this regard and its influence through the European Group was evident in the negotiations, particularly in relation to the provisions on the monitoring of State's obligations.[20]

(v) Gender

The Commission's second engagement with an international treaty-monitoring process related to the Convention on the Elimination of All Forms of Discrimination Against Women ("CEDAW"). As with CERD, the Commission examined the most recent report of the State under the Convention and submitted observations on it to the CEDAW Committee in January 2005. The observations concentrated on a select number of topics, namely:

- a review of the Irish Constitution from a gender perspective;
- a review of Ireland's methods of monitoring progress on the implementation of its obligations under the Convention;
- women and poverty;
- migrant women and women of racial and ethnic minorities; and
- older women.

In drawing up its observations, the Commission listened to what relevant non-governmental organisations were saying and liaised closely with those also actively engaged with the process.

It followed up its submission by sending a delegation to the formal examination by the CEDAW Committee of the State's report in July 2005 in New York. Immediately prior to the examination of the State's report, the delegation was accommodated in a slot normally devoted by the Committee to hearing representatives of non-governmental organisations and permitted to make an oral presentation to Committee members in its capacity as an independent national human rights institution. The delegation also approached and spoke to individual members of the Committee and suggested questions for them to put to the Government delegation. Its influence is clearly evident in the Concluding Comments of the Committee on its examination of Ireland's report.[21]

[20] A final text of the Convention was agreed by the UN General Assembly in December 2006. Ireland has signed the Convention and the Commission's focus has shifted to urging the Government to ratify it.

[21] At the time the Committee was considering what standing to afford national human rights institutions before it, and the delegation provided the Committee with a written submission arguing that national human rights institutions should be recognised as state bodies independent from Governments and be afforded the opportunity to be present and to address the Committee during its formal examination of the relevant state report.

During 2004, the Commission held three consultation meetings with key actors in the field of prostitution and, in light of the issues raised at the meetings, in 2005 it commissioned a major piece of interdisciplinary research into prostitution in Ireland.

(vi) Equality and Human Difference

The third time the Commission engaged with an international treaty-monitoring process was in relation to the Convention on the Rights of the Child ("CRC"). This time however it did so in a subsidiary and supplementary capacity to the Ombudsman for Children, given its policy of adding value rather than duplicating the work of other bodies. It met with two members of the CRC Committee who were visiting Ireland at the invitation of the Ombudsman and teased out with them those topics on which the Committee might particularly welcome comments from the Commission. It then drew up and made a short submission to the CRC Committee in May 2006, liaising very closely with the Office of the Ombudsman. The submission dealt with:

- children's rights in Irish law;
- children and the criminal justice system;
- children and poverty;
- family reunification;
- vulnerable groups of children, specifically Traveller children, children with disabilities, children from religious minorities or non-religious families, and trafficking in children.

The CRC Committee operates yet again differently to both the CERD and the CEDAW Committees. Prior to its formal examination of a State's report, it holds a pre-sessional hearing with representatives from relevant non-governmental organisations and national human rights institutions. The pre-sessional hearing was held in June 2006, and the Commission was represented at the hearing. It also attended the formal examination of Ireland's report in September 2006.

Much of the Commission's work in the area of equality and human difference has involved the outsourcing of research.

Early on, the Commission commissioned research on older people in long stay care. The results of the research were published in April 2003 as a consultation document which was widely circulated to relevant persons and bodies. The Commission was concerned that there is no legislation on the quality of care of older persons; that there is very little published up-to-date information on the quality of care in either public or private long stay care; that there are no clear rules about access to public long stay places; that the admission system lacks transparency; that there is a shortage of long stay care beds; and that the complaints and appeals procedures are inadequate. In the light of the results of this research, the Commission decided in 2005 to commission a further piece of research to assess the applicability of international human rights standards to the following specific areas:

- equality of treatment as between home, public and private care;
- the entitlement to care of older persons in such contexts;
- the adequacy of measures to ensure equality and equity in the availability of public provision places for older persons;

- the adequacy of legal protection for older vulnerable persons;
- the incidence of inhuman and degrading treatment in care;
- the right to an effective remedy; and
- the right to participate in decision-making.

In addition, the research was to examine relevant principles and practice in EU anti-discrimination law and the EU Charter on Fundamental Rights in relation to these areas.

Also in 2005, the Commission commissioned a major piece of research into the EU and international human rights standards applicable to opposite sex and same sex cohabiting couples. The research was timely. All the main political parties, as well as the Government, had come out in favour of recognising rights for same sex couples; and the Minister for Justice, Equality and Law Reform had established a Working Group to look at the matter. The research in the form of a report entitled *The Rights of De Facto Couples* was published on 12 May 2006, at a launch at which a copy of the report was formally presented to the Minister.

The Commission also participated in the Joint Equality and Human Rights Forum, which comprises a number of statutory equality and human rights bodies in Ireland and the United Kingdom and affords them the opportunity to meet in a formal structure to discuss matters of common interest. In June 2003, the Forum published the results of a joint research project undertaken by its members entitled *Re-thinking Identity: The Challenge of Diversity*. The research explored the multiple identities which people have. It dealt with disabled minority ethnic people , Black and minority ethnic women, lesbian, gay and bisexual people with disabilities, women with disabilities, young lesbian, gay and bisexual people, and young minority ethnic men.

Casework

While the key areas of work influence the exercise by the Commission of all its functions, other considerations also come into play in the exercise of its legal functions. For example, conditions are imposed by its founding legislation on the exercise of its enquiry function.

The main challenges facing the Commission in relation to casework were to clear a backlog of complaints, to introduce procedures for the efficient consideration of cases, to produce guidelines in respect of the exercise of its discretion and to publish booklets explaining to the public its legal functions and how they would be exercised.

Caseworkers were only recruited in 2003 and, by this time, a sizeable backlog of requests from persons that the Commission conduct an enquiry or afford them assistance had built up. That year criteria for the consideration of such requests were adopted, but a system of Committees established by the Commission to consider the requests did not prove efficient[22] and, in July 2004, the Commission

[22] The Commission established a Casework Committee from among its members to consider and decide upon requests and a Review Committee to consider further requests for review of negative decisions of the Casework Committee. From mid 2004, the Casework Committee ceased deciding upon requests and, following legal advice, the Review Committee was discontinued.

delegated its functions in relation to enquiry and assistance requests to the chief executive. This resulted in a substantial reduction of the backlog, with such requests requiring attention hovering around thirty at any one time; and, in December 2004, a casework database was introduced allowing for the better administration of casework communications.

At the time of writing, the Commission had received relatively few applications for assistance.[23] Most approaches from members of the public related to its enquiry functions, and the issues raised in the requests ranged across the whole field of human rights.

The Commission receives many queries from members of the public regarding human rights issues. The majority of queries fall outside the remit of the Commission and this will be explained to the persons concerned. The casework officers will also direct persons to where they may find appropriate assistance, for example, under the criminal and civil legal aid schemes, or to appropriate complaints mechanisms, for example, a regulatory professional body or the Ombudsman.

To assist the public, the Commission produced several leaflets during its early years detailing the criteria and procedures which it applies when considering enquiry and assistance requests, and later it published an information booklet on its legal functions.

Also, in April 2004, the Commission adopted guidelines in respect of its *amicus curiae* function. By the end of 2006, it had sought and been granted liberty to appear before the superior courts in three cases,[24] and has been asked by the judge in a High Court case whether it wished to make submissions in the case.[25]

A new dimension was added to the Commission's casework with the entry into effect on 31 December 2003 of the European Convention on Human Rights Act. The Act allows a party to a case to seek a declaration of incompatibility between a statutory provision or rule of law and the State's obligations under the provisions of the Convention.[26] Where such a declaration is sought, both the Commission and

[23] The Commission gave assistance in the form of legal advice to a naturalised Irish couple in respect of the denial of a visa to their minor child who wished to join them in Ireland, and assistance in the form of legal representation during *habeas corpus* proceedings to a person detained in a mental hospital.

[24] See *Dublin City Council v Jeanette Fennell*, Judgment of the Supreme Court, 12 May 2005; *Ann Lawrence and others v Ballina Town Council and others*, High Court Record No. 5813P/2003, 2005; *Edward Carmody v The Minister for Justice, Equality and Law Reform, Ireland and the Attorney General*, Supreme Court Appeal Record No. 082/2005.

[25] *Legal Aid Board v District Judge Patrick Brady, Health Service Executive and MG Notice Parties*, High Court Record No. 474JR/2005.

[26] s 5.

the Attorney General must be notified.[27] This allows the Commission to activate its *amicus curiae* function should it deem this to be appropriate. The Act also provides, in general, that public bodies should act in a way which is compatible with the State's obligations under the Convention[28] and that domestic law should be interpreted by the courts, in so far as is possible, to accord with the State's obligations under the provisions of the Convention.[29] Issues relating to the permeation into domestic law and practice of the Convention provisions are of interest to the Commission in terms of the exercise of its *amicus curiae* function.

Joint Committee

The Joint Committee of representatives of the two Human Rights Commissions envisaged by the Good Friday Agreement was set up shortly after the establishment of the Irish Commission in July 2001, and met formally for the first time in November 2001 (having previously met in shadow form in May 2001). The Committee decided that its membership would comprise all members of the two Commissions.

Early on the Committee set up a sub-committee to carry forward its consideration of the possibility of drawing up a charter of rights for the island of Ireland. The sub-committee prepared and circulated a pre-consultation paper on the charter and analysed the responses it received. The Committee also set up a sub-committee on racism. One of the first things this sub-committee did was to produce *A User's Guide to the International Convention on the Elimination of Racial Discrimination*. The Guide was published on 18 September 2003 on the occasion of a meeting of the Joint Committee in Belfast. Its purpose is to help non-governmental organisations, Black and ethnic minority groups, community organisations, pressure groups and others to use the mechanisms of CERD in the fight against racism in both parts of Ireland. A third sub-committee on emergency laws never really got off the ground and was discontinued. It was replaced by a sub-committee to identify research priorities and for general purposes.

In 2006, the sub-committees reviewed the work of the Joint Committee in their respective areas and started to draw up new work programmes, with a view to seeking dedicated funding from the Irish and British Governments to employ one or more persons to work on the programmes.[30]

International Co-ordinating Committee

The International Co-ordinating Committee oversees compliance by national human rights institutions with the Paris Principles and operates a system of

[27] s 6(1).
[28] s 3(1).
[29] s 2(1).
[30] A dedicated officer was appointed in 2008 to support the work of the Joint Committee. This officer is intended to act as a focal point for internal and external communications of the Joint Committee, as well as for joint policy and research work.

accreditation in this regard. The Commission is a fully accredited national human rights institution with "A" status, signifying compliance with the Paris Principles.

The International Committee also serves as a forum for the co-ordination of the activities of national human rights institutions globally and the discussion of matters of common interest. It holds an annual meeting in Geneva at which the Commission has been represented since its foundation.

The International Committee has four regional groups, including a European Group. The Commission is a member of the European Group and, in 2002, it co-hosted with the Northern Ireland Human Rights Commission, the biennial meeting of the European Group, as well as a Round Table of European national institutions, in Dublin and Belfast. At the biennial meeting of the Group in Berlin in 2004, the Commission was honoured to be elected as one of four members of the co-ordinating committee of the Group, and two years later it was elected to the chair of the Group.

Concluding Comments

Significant challenges faced the Commission in its early years. The recruitment of a chief executive and of an initial intake of staff and the acquisition and fit-out of permanent premises proved time-consuming, and it was only some two years after its establishment that the Commission was in anything like a position where it could exercise the range of its functions.

It managed to survive the damage cause to it at birth by a flawed appointment process. It exercised most of its functions. With the adoption of a Strategic Plan and the identification of key areas of work, its work became focused, and I think any reasonable observer would conclude that its output was impressive. All this was achieved through the expertise and commitment of Commissioners and the sterling work and high standards of a small team of staff.

There are of course areas in which the Commission might have done more or done better. It might have put more effort into increasing public awareness of its existence and functions, but with only one staff member working in this area and covering education as well, one has to be realistic as to what could be achieved. It might have more proactively sought to identify vulnerable groups whose voice is weak or unheard in public and political circles, but its outsourced research on older persons in long stay care has proven timely in this regard. Greater effort might have been made to persuade Ministers other than the Minister for Justice to refer legislative proposals in their areas to the Commission for its views on their implications for human rights in the State, but measures were taken in an attempt to redress this imbalance and both the Departments of Defence and of Foreign Affairs were receptive to approaches by the Commission. A more strategic approach might have been taken to the exercise of its legal functions, but it had started to address this question. More attention might have been given to cross-functional work in planning ahead, but its work, for example, on economic, social and cultural rights shows an awareness of this.

At the time the legislation for the establishment of the Commission was being drafted, the Taoiseach stated that it was his intention that the Commission be a model for others to follow, one that would set rather than follow standards of best international practice in this area. The Commission is on track to fulfil this ambition, but if the ambition is to be realised, good intentions must be backed up with required resources.

Even with additional resources, a focus needs to be maintained since the demands and expectations of such bodies as the Commission typically outstrip resources. And the development of its staff needs to be taken seriously since the Commission's credibility in the public sector and with its various stakeholders depends in large measure on the quality of its output, not merely the quantity. The Commission will always have its opponents: those who deride human rights; those who hold the view that the Irish courts adequately protect human rights and that there is no need for such a body as the Commission; those who pay lip service to human rights while showing little respect for them in practice. In the years ahead, the Commission will have to continue to confront obstacles placed in its path by its opponents. It has made a good start.

Aspirations Unfulfilled: The Equality Right in Irish Law

Colm O'Cinneide*

Introduction

Equality is a concept that is subject to multiple interpretations. It generates disputes both as to its meaning and the weight it should be given in legal and political debates. This paper aims to explore some of these controversies that surround the interpretation and application of what can be described as the "equality principle", and also examines how this equality principle is manifested in Irish law. Particular emphasis is placed upon the place of equality in the Irish constitutional order, given the symbolic and practical importance of constitutional values in shaping how the rest of the legal system functions. However, consideration is also given to how Irish anti-discrimination law attempts to give regulatory shape to the equality principle at the sub-constitutional level: this tends to be often more influential in terms of day-to-day impact that the equivalent constitutional jurisprudence. The potential impact of international human rights instruments, in particular the European Convention on Human Rights, is also examined, along with the possible implications of the requirement in the Belfast Agreement that Ireland provide an "equivalence" of rights protection as that applying in Northern Ireland. The conclusion is reached that a substantial gap exists between the place of equality as a fundamental value in the Irish Constitution, and how the equality principle is actually applied in the Irish legal system. This may require a re-assessment of what it means to "[cherish] all of the children of the nation equally", in the words of the 1916 Proclamation.

Equality: A Contested Concept

The right to "equality" is embedded in every major human rights instrument and constitutional system, in some form or other. It is recognised as a foundational right and primary value in modern democratic states. However, this "equality principle" has also proved to be slippery and elusive to define. There are multiple accounts in political philosophy of what normative meaning or meanings should be attached to the term "equality". In legal literature, there is a similar debate as to what a commitment to upholding equality entails in practice.[1] At the political level, arguments about the meaning and status of the principle of equality continue to generate considerable heat and light. Equality can mean wildly different and often conflicting things to different people, who might all assert passionately their commitment to "true equality".

---

* Reader in Law, UCL.

[1] See N Bamforth, "Conceptions of Anti-Discrimination Law" (2004) *Oxford Journal of Legal Studies* 713–715.

Aristotle's oft-quoted formulation of the equality principle as requiring like cases to be treated alike, and unlike cases to be treated unlike, just helps to illustrate the underlying problem.[2] As Weston and others have argued, equality is an "empty idea", in the absence of agreement as to what normative framework should determine when cases are alike and when they are different, and what forms of distinctions between individuals and groups are legitimate and which are not.[3] Several such possible frameworks exist, each of which often serve as the unarticulated foundation of many other political and legal theories.[4]

The umbrella term "formal equality" is often used to describe approaches that treat the equality principle as satisfied if rational justification exists for any distinctions that are made between persons in similar situations. However, defining what precisely constitutes a "rational" justification or a "similar" situation can be difficult. There is an absence of any real agreement in contemporary political and moral thought on what does or does not constitute a rational distinction, or as to when individuals should be treated as similarly situated.[5] Nevertheless, there is increasing agreement that certain types of distinction which relate to particular aspects of an individual's personality, such as race, gender or sexual orientation, should in general not be used to differentiate between persons. This has resulted in the development of an "anti-discrimination" approach to equality issues, which emphasises the illegitimacy of using characteristics such as race, ethnicity or gender, to distinguish between individuals in key areas of social activity. Both the basic "formal equality" approach and the by now relatively developed "anti-discrimination" framework can be classified as "process conceptions of equality", as they place their primary emphasis upon the method by which distinctions were made between individuals.[6]

Both of these approaches can be contrasted with "substantive" conceptions of equality", which place a greater emphasis upon the substantive *results* of social

[2] Aristotle, *The Politics* III.ix (Penguin, London, 1962), p 195–196.

[3] P Westen, "The Empty Idea of Equality" (1985) 95 *Harvard Law Review* 537. Commentators have questioned whether equality claims can ever serve as an adequate conceptual foundation for anti-discrimination law: for a discussion of this, see C O'Cinneide, "Fumbling Towards Coherence: The Slow Evolution of Equality and Anti-Discrimination Law in Britain" (2006) 57(1) *Northern Ireland Legal Quarterly* 57–101. See also O Doyle, "Direct Discrimination, Indirect Discrimination and Autonomy" (2007) 27(3) OJLS, 537–553.

[4] The following analysis of the different approaches to equality makes use of a form of categorisation that is well-established and often used in the academic literature. See S Fredman, *Discrimination Law* (OUP, Oxford, 2001), pp 21–22; S Fredman, *The Future of Equality in Britain* (EOC, Manchester, 2003); C McCrudden, "Theorising European Law" in C Costello and E Barry (eds.) *Equality in Diversity: The New Equality Directives* (Irish Centre for European Law, Dublin, 2003) 1; O Doyle, *Constitutional Equality Law* (Round Hall, Dublin, 2004) 14–21. As with all description of analytical frameworks, these categories can be reduced to over-simplified generalisations, and should be handled with due caution. Particular caution needs to be exercised about the tendency to classify any form of equality which one disagrees with as "formal equality".

[5] See Westen, at n 3 above.

[6] See Doyle, *Constitutional Equality Law*, 14.

practices and see the equality principle as requiring action to remove existing forms of disadvantage and social exclusion.[7] Particularly important are "group subordination" approaches, which aim to eliminate the disadvantages faced by the particular social groups that face serious and deeply entrenched forms of social exclusion.[8] Substantive equality analysis is linked (through an often uneasy relationship) to concepts of "equality of opportunity", which view the equality principle as satisfied by the creation of the necessary conditions to ensure a fair and equal starting point for all, while recognising that positive measures may be necessary to remove obstacles that obstruct this goal. "Minimalist" approaches to equality of opportunity emphasise the provision to all of at least a minimum level of access to certain core social goods, within the parameters of existing social structures. More "maximialist" approaches look for substantial shifts in existing social practices to ensure a much wider degree of access to these essential social goods.[9]

Often, elements of these different approaches, both process and substantive, are combined in legislation and case-law. Disagreements about the proper application of the equality principle are often actually disagreements about what approach or combination of approaches should be applied in a particular circumstance.[10] Differences of view also exist as to the extent to which legal regulation designed to further equality objectives should be used to alter existing social practices, interfere with market processes, and limit the freedom of action of individuals and corporations. In other words, how much "social engineering" should be conducted via equality and anti-discrimination law? How far should the impact of the equality principle, no matter how it is interpreted, extend?

This question links back to wider philosophical and political disputes about the relationship between equality, liberty, personal autonomy, and other moral values,

---

[7] See Doyle, *ibid*, p 18–20. See J Balkin and R Siegel, "The American Civil Rights Tradition: Anticlassification or Antisubordination?" (2004) 58 *U. Miami L. Rev.* 9. Sandra Fredman uses the term "substantive equality" to refer to what I have described as the "group disadvantage" approach. See S Fredman, *Discrimination Law* (OUP, Oxford, 2001), pp 21–22.

[8] See the seminal work of Owen Fiss on group disadvantage, in particular O Fiss, "Groups and the Equal Protection Clause" (1975) 5 *Philosophy and Public Affairs* 107.

[9] Equality of opportunity and group disadvantage approaches overlap to a considerable degree, in that both are concerned with securing equal opportunities for all social groups. However, proponents of group disadvantage approaches are often wary of a perceived tendency in equality of opportunity analysis to accept the existing contours of society as fixed and therefore to be mainly concerned with ameliorative reform than wholescale social transformation. As a result, theorists who adopt a group disadvantage approach are often more comfortable with "maximalist" conceptions of equality of opportunity approaches, and sometimes advocate the adoption of an "equality of outcomes" approach, on the basis that achieving equality of outcomes is the only way to ensure the existence of real equality of opportunity: see e.g A Phillips, "Defending Equality of Outcome" (2004) 12(1) *Journal of Political Philosophy* 1–19. However, it should also be noted that some "maximalist" accounts of equality of opportunity would reject a group-specific focus: see B Barry, *Culture and Equality: An Egalitarian Critique of Multiculturalism* (Polity, Oxford, 2001).

[10] See McCrudden, cited above at n 4.

as well as to the appropriate role of the state in modern mixed economies. A classic liberal approach might see the role of the equality principle in law as best confined to protecting individuals against unjustified and discriminatory harm inflicted by others, and reject any wider application of equality norms to justify major redistribution of resources, or the imposition of extra burdens upon individuals and corporate entities.[11] Other approaches are possible. In the Irish context, Doyle suggests that a distinction exists in the constitutional case-law between a reasonably generous application of the equality principle in the civil-political sphere, and a reluctance to apply the principle in a similar manner in the socio-economic sphere.[12] This distinction reflects what Doyle describes as a "liberal egalitarian" interpretation of the appropriate scope of the equality principle, which confines itself to protecting the individual against certain forms of prejudice, without being concerned with challenging the inherent inequalities of existing social structures.[13] More straightforwardly egalitarian approaches would be readier to apply the equality principle across a wider range of social activities. An example of a strong egalitarian approach would be that advocated by Baker, Lynch, Cantillon and Walsh, who argue for consideration to be given to the potential impact of the equality principle in the sphere of affective relationships, and for wholescale social transformation structured around a strong substantive equality approach.[14]

More questions arise as to when and if the equality principle should be given priority where it comes into conflict with other valued social goods, such as family values, social order and adherence to time-honoured modes of conduct and morality. For example, conflict has often arisen between the equality principle and certain social norms rooted in some religious beliefs: deciding which of these norms should be prioritised when they come into tension has been a constant source of controversy within Irish society.[15] The key question that arises when the equality principle (however interpreted) comes into conflict with other values is therefore often straightforward: how important is equality when it comes into tension with other social values?

Classical conservative critiques of the equality principle are essentially based on the argument that the values of social stability, respect for the organic development of society and deference to established moral reasoning should be prioritised over the application of the equality principle.[16] However, a preference for other social

---

[11] For a critique of "social engineering", see M Abram, "Affirmative Action: Fair Shakers and Social Engineers" (1986) *Harvard Law Review* 1312–26. For a discussion of liberal justifications for anti-discrimination law, see J Gardner, "Liberals and Unlawful Discrimination" (1989) 9 *Oxford Journal of Legal Studies* 1.

[12] Doyle, *Constitutional Equality Law*, 11–13.

[13] N Crowley, *An Ambition for Equality* (Irish Academic Press, Dublin, 2006), 14–18.

[14] See J Baker, K Lynch, S Cantillon and J Walsh, *Equality: From Theory to Action* (Palgrave-Macmillan, Basingstoke, 2004).

[15] It should be noted that the strong currents in support of the equality principle in mainstream religious thought should not be overlooked or downplayed: it will often be easy to apply equality and religious values in a complementary manner. See Doyle, *Constitutional Equality Law*, 5–8.

[16] Ireland's major contribution to classical conservative thought exemplifies this perfectly: see E Burke, *Reflections on the Revolution in France* (Pelican, London, 1969).

values to be given priority at times over the equality principle need not stem solely from the classic conservative perspective. Many liberal theorists give preference to individual autonomy over equality, while even communitarians may at times prioritise the maintenance of certain communal goods over the application of the equality principle.[17] Doyle suggests that in Irish constitutional case-law, the courts have tended to give preference to other constitutional values when they come into conflict with the equality principle, which has been "subordinated" in the overall value scheme of the *Bunreacht*.[18]

The argument is often made by Dworkin and others writing within the tradition of Rawlsian political philosophy that the entitlement of all individuals to equality of respect and concern should be recognised, in Dworkin's words, as the "sovereign virtue".[19] As discussed above, different accounts exist as to how this "virtue" should be defined and applied.[20] In general, however, adherents to this school of political philosophy suggest that "equality of respect" should be seen as *the* core guiding principle for a modern democracy, meaning that all individuals must be recognised by the state as equally entitled to participation and as possessing equal status before the law.

The extent to which this approach requires a departure from liberal individual approaches to equality is not always clear. "Equality of respect" as a term can cover a wide range of different and contrasting views about equality. Classical liberalism could sit comfortably with minimalist applications of this approach, which would resemble a "formal equality" approach. However, Rawls, Dworkin and others within this tradition tend to interpret "equality of respect" as requiring positive steps to guarantee some degree of *de facto* equality for all individuals within a society: they tend to adopt a more maximalist take on equality of opportunity and to favour something resembling substantive equality analysis. Indeed, "equality of respect" as a concept can be seen as an attempt to unify "substantive equality", "formal equality" and "anti-discrimination" approaches under the same roof. While the roots of this position lie in the conventional liberal emphasis upon individual autonomy and self-determination, proponents of strong "equality of respect" theories tend therefore to reject classical liberal doctrines of state non-intervention as insufficient to create the conditions that are required to generate meaningful equality of respect.

---

[17] For an interesting discussion of the relationship between liberal and communitarian views of equality, see W Lund, "Communitarian Politics and the Problem of Equality" (1983) 46 *Political Research Quarterly* 577–600.

[18] Doyle, *Constitutional Equality Law.*, 99–103.

[19] R Dworkin, *Sovereign Virtue: The Theory and Practice of Equality* (Harvard University Press, Cambridge, MA, 2000), especially chs 2 and 4.

[20] See the excellent and comprehensive discussion by R Arneson, "Equality of Opportunity", in Edward N Zalta (ed.) *The Stanford Encyclopedia of Philosophy*, Winter 2002 edition, available at http://plato.stanford.edu/entries/equal-opportunity/ (last accessed 15 May 2006). See also A Phillips, "Defending Equality of Outcome" (2004) 12(1) *Journal of Political Philosophy* 1–19.

"Identity" theorists such as Charles Taylor and Iris Marion Young argue along similar lines, except that equality of respect for different "identity" groups is emphasised.[21] Theorists from various critical perspectives, including feminism and critical race theory, also argue for a broad and wide-ranging application of the equality principle across the entire range of social, economic, familial, and political relationships.[22] This perspective is often combined with a critique of the classic liberal approach and even modern individualistic-orientated "equality of opportunity" theories. For many theorists adopting a critical stance, liberal individualist approaches, even those stemming from the Rawlsian camp, can "mask" and even reinforce existing inequalities, by largely limiting their focus to the individual and emphasising reform within existing social structures at the expense of addressing group or structural subordination.[23]

Other approaches adopt a much more sceptical stance towards equality and question the extent to which it should receive priority in the event of conflicts with other values. "Libertarian" schools of thought, best exemplified by the work of Robert Nozick, tend to regard the equality principle has having little or any normative force. For Nozick, the equality principle lacks the normative substance to justify government interference with individual autonomy.[24] As discussed above, the classic conservative perspective would place comparatively little value on equality, while some religious-centred viewpoints, elements of communitarian philosophy and certain strands of liberal political thought would prioritise other values. The place of equality in contemporary society remains uncertain and contested.

Equality in Irish Political Debate

Recent political debates in Ireland have highlighted the existence of this uncertainty that surrounds the interpretation, scope and priority to be given to the equality principle. The former Minister for Justice, Equality and Law Reform, Mr Michael McDowell TD, triggered an interesting controversy in June 2004 with his comments

---

[21] See C Taylor, "The Politics of Recognition", in A Gutmann (ed.), *Multiculturalism and "The Politics of Recognition"* (Princeton University Press, Princeton, NJ, 1992), 25–73; IM Young, *Justice and the Politics of Difference* (Princeton University Press, Princeton, NJ, 1990).

[22] See e.g. C MacKinnon, *Toward a Feminist Theory of the State* (1989); for an analysis of why feminist theory rejects conventional liberal assumptions about the appropriate scope of equality analysis, see F Olsen, "The Family and the Market: A Study of Ideology and Legal Reform" (1983) 96 *Harvard Law Review* 1497. See also A Phillips, *Which Equalities Matter?* (Polity, Cambridge, 1999).

[23] See J Baker, K Lynch, S Cantillon and J Walsh, *Equality: From Theory to Action* (Palgrave-Macmillan, Basingstoke, 2004); A Phillips, *Which Equalities Matter* (Polity, Cambridge, 1999); K Zappone, *Charting the Equality Agenda: A Coherent Framework for Equality Strategies in Ireland, North and South* (Equality Authority and Equality Commission for Northern Ireland, Dublin, 2001), available at http://www.equalityni.org/uploads/pdf/kzreport.pdf.

[24] R Nozick, *Anarchy, State and Utopia* (Basic Books, New York, 1974), especially Ch. 8. Libertarianism has rarely struck a chord in Irish political debates, but its influence in recent years has perhaps been more extensive than its current low profile in academic discussion would suggest.

that "a dynamic liberal economy like ours demands flexibility and inequality in some respects to function" and to provide "incentives".[25] This characteristic piece of McDowellian provocation produced some outraged responses from some of the then Minister's favourite targets, as well as a few more nuanced critiques.[26] However, McDowell's comments deserve close and serious consideration: they formed part of an overall critique of the perceived dangers of stretching human rights claims, and in particular equality claims, beyond a classic liberal approach of defending the individual against unjustified state intrusion. In McDowell's view, "[d]riven to a complete extreme, the current rights culture and equality notion would create a feudal society. A society so ordered, static, and where the Government tries to order everything by law, it would become as atrophied as a feudal society."[27]

Implicitly, the suggestion is being made here that the right to equality should best be conceptualised as an individual right to freedom from unfair discrimination, rather than as a much wider entitlement to some notion of substantive equality, equality of resources, or to equality of outcomes, which would carry with it a certain commitment to "social engineering". This classic liberalism contrasts greatly for example with the argument made by Baker, Lynch, Cantillon and Walsh that a genuine commitment to "equality" should entail a commitment to a wide and substantive equality of concern and respect, including recognition of the importance of equality of outcomes and of the need to transform existing social structures.[28] This difference of opinion reflects one of the major dividing lines in Irish political and legal debate at the moment. It is reflected in current political debates about the perceived neo-liberal orientation of Irish government policy since the mid 1990s. It also is a submerged theme in the ongoing debate about the enforceability of socio-economic rights in the Irish constitutional order triggered by the *Sinnott* case.[29]

Disputes about national and group identity and the appropriate scope of the equality principle also arise in debates about Ireland's increasingly ethnically and culturally mixed population. Media broadsides against "political correctness" and equality "bureaucrats" by commentators such as Kevin Myers can be seen as linked to a wider backlash in North America and Europe against attempts to give the equality principle a substantive application.[30] It also reflects distaste for "social engineering", as well as concern that priority will be given to group identity claims at the expense of "common values".

---

[25] See *The Irish Catholic*, 27 May 2004, in an interview with Herman Kelly.

[26] See Niall Crowley's measured comments in *The Irish Times*, 7th June 2004, "Equality is Central to Social Cohesion, The Economy and Greater Democracy".

[27] McDowell, *The Irish Catholic*, 27 May 2004.

[28] See J Baker, K Lynch, S Cantillon and J Walsh, *Equality: From Theory to Action* (Palgrave-Macmillan, Basingstoke, 2004).

[29] *Sinnott v Minister for Education* [2001] 2 IR 545. For a sample of the debate surrounding the issue of socio-economic rights, see G Hogan, "Directive Principles, Socioeconomic Rights and the Constitution" (2001) *Irish Jurist (n.s.)* 174; G Whyte, *Social Inclusion and the Legal System: Public Interest Law in Ireland* (IPA, Dublin, 2002) 9–57, 340–363; *Report o f the Constitution Review Group* (Stationery Office, Dublin, 1996), 235.

[30] See N Crowley, *An Ambition for Equality* (Irish Academic Press, Dublin, 2006), 182–185.

Such controversies about equality in Irish political and legal debate are not new. However, there has been a change in emphasis in recent years. Now, arguments about equality are about how far should the principle be applied, whether it should be given more of a substantive tinge, and whether it conflicts with newly cherished liberal values (which increasingly tend to be of the liberal-egalitarian, social liberal and neo-liberal varieties). In contrast, disputes about equality prior to the mid 1990s tended instead to concern its compatibility with deeply-embedded religious and social values. These "older" debates have not gone away. Abortion remains a lurking source of controversy and passionate disagreement, even if debates on this issue are often muted and cautious. Controversy also surrounds the cautious approach of the current government towards permitting the legal recognition of same-sex partnerships. However, demands rooted in substantive equality, "maximalist" equality of opportunity and critical perspectives for the transformation of existing social structures now rub up against neo-liberal and quasi-libertarian approaches as well as culturally conservative viewpoints. This has made current debates on equality in Ireland complex and multi-faceted a tendency accentuated by the fall-out of the recent economic crisis.[31] These debates about equality reflect its inherent ambiguity as a concept. They also reflect the uncertainty about the status and scope of the equality principle that has persisted in Irish law and politics since independence.

The Place of Equality in Irish Legal and Political Discourse

The concept of the equality of all citizens of Ireland was a central part of nationalist ideology in the run-up to independence.[32] It was linked to a rejection of ideologies of class associated with British rule and a concern with attempting to create a common citizenship with Protestant minorities. The rhetoric of equality featured prominently in the Proclamation of Independence in 1916, with its promise to "[guarantee] religious and civil liberty, equal rights and equal opportunities to all its citizens", and to "[cherish] all of the children of the nation equally. . ." It was also reflected in the mythology of the new state, with the intertwined relationship between nationalism and aspirations to equality of citizenship often presented as symbolically consummated by James Connolly leading the Citizens' Army into the Republican fold in 1916.[33]

This link between independence and a commitment to the equality principle was part of a wider conception of the establishment of the Republic as having introduced a new democratic and rights-based constitutional order. This new republican order was to be unencumbered by the denial of equality and subjection to state power associated with British rule. The classic expression of this concept can be found in the seminal

[31] Some leading proponents of the argument that priority should be given to the equality principle at the expense of traditional moral values in these debates of the 1980s have now become prominent sceptics about the desirability of any substantive turn in equality law and policy, which extends beyond the civil-political sphere: Minister McDowell would be an example. This again demonstrates the complexity of the issues that surround equality in the Irish context.

[32] See M Caulfield, *The Easter Rebellion*, (Gill and Macmillan, Dublin, 1995), p 97, for an account of the intertwined nationalist and socialist views of some participants in the Easter Rising.

[33] See K Allen, *The Politics of James Connolly* (Pluto, London, 1990).

judgment of Walsh J in *Byrne v Ireland*,[34] where the royal prerogative was held not to have survived the transition to the new constitutional order. Walsh J's decision can be seen as based partially upon a rejection of the implicit hierarchy of monarchy over the people at large inherent in the notion of the prerogative, as incompatible with a new constitutional system founded upon the sovereignty and equality of the Irish people.[35]

This concept of a rights-based democratic polity founded upon the principle of equality of citizenship is firmly rooted in the texts of the 1922 and 1937 Constitution. While the 1922 Constitution had no equality clause, its constant reiteration of the entitlement of "all citizens" of the Free State to basic civil and political rights, elementary education (Article 10) and participation in the democratic process reflected this emphasis on civil-political equality of citizenship.[36] De Valera went further, specifically inserting Article 40.1 into the 1937 Constitution to ensure that the text of the *Bunreacht* specifically recognised and protected equality as a fundamental right.[37]

However, the implementation in practice of this equality guarantee has tended to lack a degree of consistency, and its impact can best be described as muted. In both legislation and constitutional case-law, as well as in the formulation of public policy by the institutions of the state, the equality principle has suffered mixed fortunes. On the one hand, it has become part of the Irish constitutional background: it is one of the set of norms that are evoked in constitutional rights interpretation and find their way into political rhetoric as core values of the Republic.[38] Irish media and political

---

[34] [1972] IR 241. Note also the provisions of Article 50, whereby pre-Constitution laws are tested for "consistency" with this new constitutional order: see *State (Sheerin) v Kennedy* [1966] IR 379, 386; *Aughey v Attorney-General* [1989] ILRM 87, 90; *Murphy v Attorney-General* [1982] IR 241, 307, where Henchy J was of the view that an "inconsistent" pre-1937 piece of legislation had a "date of death" when the 1937 Constitution came into force.

[35] For a similar rejection of conceptions of "special status", see the Supreme Court in *Howard v Commissioners for Public Works* [1994] 1 IR 101, where the Court determined that there should be no presumption derived from the Constitution or from common law that a general statute did not apply to the State.

[36] Note too the provisions of Article 5 of the 1922 Constitution, now echoed in Article 40.2 of the 1937 Constitution (and significantly situated immediately after the equality clause in Article 40.1), that prohibits Irish citizens from being conferred with "titles of honour" without the prior approval of the Government.

[37] See the excellent analysis in Doyle, *Constitutional Equality Law*, 51–66.

[38] See e.g. the remarks made by President Mary McAleese at a conference, "The Long Revolution: The 1916 Rising in Context", at University College Cork, on Friday 27 January 2006, entitled "1916 - A View from 2006": "In the longer-term the apparent naïveté of the words of the Proclamation has filled out into a widely-shared political philosophy of equality and social inclusion in tune with the contemporary spirit of democracy, human rights, equality and anti-confessionalism... The kind of Ireland the heroes of the Rising aspired to was based on an inclusivity that, famously, would "cherish all the children of the nation equally – oblivious of the differences which have divided a minority from the majority in the past". That culture of inclusion is manifestly a strong contemporary impulse working its way today through relationships with the North, with unionists, with the newcomers to our shores, with our marginalized, and with our own increasing diversity." The text of the remarks is available at http://www.president.ie/index.php?section=5&speech=211&lang=eng (last accessed 15 May 2006).

discourse tends to assume that a rejection of hierarchy, combined with an egalitarian streak, is part and parcel of the Irish national character.[39] Equality concerns have featured prominently in the social partnership agreements, and before the Irish economy went into a downward spiral in 2008, various half-hearted policy initiatives were introduced to address questions of socio-economic deprivation.[40] A concern with formal equality is deeply embedded in the Irish legal system (see below).

However, the debit side of the balance-sheet shows a less rosy picture. The linking of nationalism with the equality principle has proved problematic. The commitment to cherish equally "all the children of the nation" has often taken the form of a focus upon securing equality rights for Irish citizens only.[41] Non-citizens falling outside of the warm embrace of the "nation" can be left in a terrain of considerably more limited constitutional and legal protection.[42] Even in its treatment of its citizens, the Irish Republic has not always given priority to the equality principle. The Free State made provision for reserved seats in the Seanad for Trinity College Dublin, which at the time served as a *de facto* set-aside of seats for the country's Protestant minority.[43] However, the perspectives of non-Catholic groups were rarely reflected in the legislation enacted by the Free State or subsequently by the Republic. WB Yeats's speech opposing legislative constraints on divorce in 1925 on the basis of the need for respect for minority views went unheeded[44]: in subsequent years, an equivalence was assumed to exist between what was deemed to be the appropriate legislative position and the views of the Catholic Church. The often implicit correspondence in nationalist ideology between the "nation", the "State" and the Catholic identity of the vast majority of the citizens of the Republic squeezed the room available for minority groups to assert themselves in the Irish public sphere, and often such groups were conceptualised as falling outside the definition of "Irishness".[45]

---

[39] See the following interesting comments of (the then Taoiseach) Bertie Ahern TD: "[T]he best qualities of the Irish are natural ability, tolerance, friendliness and sociability and an instinctive egalitarianism and solidarity ... our whole history over the past 2,000 years indicates that we are an adventurous and outward-looking people, seeking not to conquer, but to carry a message of hope and solidarity." See P Logue (ed.) *Being Irish: Personal Reflections on Irish Identity Today* (Oak Tree Press, Dublin, 2000), 1–3.

[40] See Government of Ireland (2002), *Building an Inclusive Society: Review of the National Anti-Poverty Strategy under the Programme for Prosperity and Fairness* (Department of Social, Community and Family Affairs, Dublin, 2002); The National Economic and Social Forum, *Partnership 2000: Development of the Equality Provisions*, Forum Opinion No. 1 (Stationery Office, Dublin, 1997); National Economic and Social Forum, *A Strategic Policy Framework for Equality Issues* (NESF Report No. 23, Dublin, March 2002).

[41] See e.g. the decision of *Lobe & Osayande v Minister for Justice, Equality and Law Reform* [2003] IESC 1 (23 January 2003), which confirmed that even non-citizens with a paternal link to children with a citizenship entitlement could be denied residence rights in the Republic.

[42] See J Casey, *Constitutional Law in Ireland* (3rd ed.) (Round Hall, Dublin, 2000), 71–73, 444–449. Casey downplays to an extent the limited nature of the rights afforded to non-citizens.

[43] See *The Seventh Progress Report: Parliament* of the All-Party Oireachtas Committee on the Constitution (Government Publications, Dublin, 2002), p 37.

[44] See 5 *Seanad Debs.*, cc. 435–443 (11 June 1925).

[45] See B Fanning, *Racism and Social Change in the Republic of Ireland* (Manchester University Press, Manchester, 2002), in particular his analysis of Irish anti-Semitism in the 1930s and 1940s, at pp 67–81.

Recent years have seen a substantial erosion of the close link between Catholic moral teaching and the institutions of the state. As with other European societies, the challenges posed to conventional social and legal practices by feminism, the gay rights movement and other forms of social activism have brought about profound changes. However, these changes, significant as they are, may gloss over persisting problems with the implementation of the Republic's commitment to securing equality for all. It could even be argued that the association of Irish identity with the values of republican egalitarianism and non-hierarchy has actually served to gloss over the extent of the issues surrounding inequalities and exclusion in Irish society.[46]

Irish Travellers remain a severely disadvantaged group, subject to structural discrimination, state neglect and active prejudice.[47] Homosexual couples are still placed in a subordinate position to heterosexual couples who choose to marry. Considerable levels of social exclusion persist.[48] Disabled persons often have difficulty accessing the essential services necessary to enable them to live independently and autonomously, free of dependence upon state or charitable paternalism.[49] Forms of intolerance and contempt that have been historically directed at the outsider within the Irish society, usually taking the form of the Traveller community, are now sometimes broadened in focus to encompass the new ethnic groups.[50]

Another set of issues arise as a consequence of the strong sense of fixed Irish cultural identity, celebrated endlessly in Guinness adverts and reinforced by the nationalist project of giving political expression to the "Irish people", conceived as a single

---

[46] Peader Kirby has critiqued what he has described as a "self-serving version of history" that denies historical and current patterns of exclusion in Irish society by instead celebrating uncritically its perceived integrity, unity and openness: see P Kirby, "Contested Pedigrees of the Celtic Tiger", in P Kirby, L Gibbons & M Cronin, *Reinventing Ireland: Culture, Society and the Global Economy* (Pluto, London, 2002), p 27.

[47] See Doyle, *Constitutional Equality Law*, 247–249; B Fanning, *Racism and Social Change in the Republic of Ireland* (Manchester: Manchester University Press, 2002); M MacGréil, *Prejudice in Ireland Revisited* (Survey and Research Unit, St. Patrick's College, Maynooth, Maynooth, 1996); G Whyte, *Social Inclusion and the Legal System: Public Interest Law in Ireland* (Institute of Public Administration, Dublin, 2002) 218–219; Irish Human Rights Commission, *Submission of the Irish Human Rights Commission to the UN Committee on the Elimination of Racial Discrimination* (IHRC, Dublin, 2005).

[48] See N Crowley, *An Ambition for Equality* (Irish Academic Press, Dublin, 2006), 6–8; P Kirby, *Celtic Tiger in Distress: Growth with Inequality in Ireland* (Palgrave, London, 2002).

[49] See the *Report of the Commission on the Status of People with Disabilities* (Stationery Office, Dublin, 1996). See also the still-relevant comments by Mervyn Taylor, TD, former Minister for Equality and Law Reform, on the occasion of the launch of the Report of the Commission on the Status of People with Disabilities, Cork, 18 November 1996: "People with disabilities are the neglected citizens of Ireland. They are angry – angry at a society that excludes them from almost every aspect of economic, social political and cultural life. They want equality, to move from a reliance on charity towards establishing basic rights…".

[50] See the various contributions in R Lentin and R McVeigh (ed.), *Racism and Anti-Racism in Ireland* (Beyond the Pale, Belfast, 2002).

entity. Other forms of cultural identity or affiliation tend to be classified as "alien" or "other", and as being essentially different to "Irishness".[51] This means that the influx of new groups becomes perceived as a problem, requiring careful management and control to minimise the perceived threat of harm to the established patterns of Irish society. As Gavan Titley has argued, Irish multicultural policy concentrates on managing cultural difference, seeing the influx of new groups as a fundamental shift from monocultural "old" Ireland to a new multicultural era of diverse, separate and potentially clashing forms of cultural identity. He suggests that "[t]his narrative of monochrome to technicolour implies that difference arrives with the newly immigrant Other, a fiction that not only airbrushes out the historical experiences of minority groups in Ireland, but implies that racism…is imported by the traveller rather than incubated in the social environment."[52] This can in turn result in an emphasis on managing and containing manifestations of racism among the "native" Irish populace, which tends to gloss over wider issues about the role of the state in acting or failing to act in this area.[53]

This strong sense of fixed and bounded Irish identity can also produce a closing of the ranks against attempts by "outsiders" to assume the mantle of "Irishness", exemplified in some of the rhetoric that surrounded the citizenship referendum in 2003.[54] The citizen/non-citizen distinction in Irish law has been widened in recent years, paralleling similar developments elsewhere. This tends to ensure that asylum-seekers and other non-nationals are often now left in a legal grey zone, with circumscribed rights and increasingly dependant upon the mercy and forbearance of the executive.[55]

---

[51] See the comments by Gavan Titley: "[i]n countless ways, the daily experience of social life and interaction produces negotiations and versions of what it is to be oneself, presumably including disparate and overlapping understandings of Irishness. Yet in general public discourse, a fixation with received and assumed notions of culture and multiculturalism has privileged concepts that involve exclusion as a condition of their discourse." See G Titley, "Everything Moves: Beyond Culture and Multiculturalism in Irish Public Discourse" (2004) 31 *The Irish Review* 11–27. See also L Gibbons, "Race against Time: Racial Discourse and Irish History" (1996).

[52] See also R Lentin, "Anti-Racist Responses to the Racialisation of Irishness: Disavowed Multiculturalism and its Discontents", in R Lentin & R McVeigh (ed.) *Racism and Anti-Racism in Ireland* (Beyond the Pale, Dublin, 2002), 226–238.

[53] For a comprehensive discussion and critique of this trend, see A Lentin, *Racism and Anti-Racism in Europe* (Pluto, London, 2004.)

[54] See C Costello, "Accidents of Place and Parentage: Birthright Citizenship and Border Crossings", in *The Citizenship Referendum: Implications for the Constitution and Human Rights* (Trinity College Dublin School of Law, Dublin, 2004), pp 25–28. See also B Ryan, "The Celtic Cubs: The Controversy over Birthright Citizenship in Ireland" (2004) 6(3) *European Journal of Migration and Law* 173–193. See also D O'Connell and C Smyth, "Citizenship and the Irish Constitution", in U Fraser and C Harvey (eds.), *Sanctuary in Ireland: Perspectives on Asylum Law and Policy* (Dublin, 2003).

[55] See the various contributors in U Fraser and C Harvey (eds.), *Sanctuary in Ireland: Perspectives on Asylum Law and Policy* (Dublin, 2003).

These inequalities lie at the heart of many of the political and media debates about equality, discussed above. Mainstream political debate in Ireland has often steered clear from direct clashes about equality, preferring to focus on other issues and indulge in casual affirmations about the egalitarian nature of Irish society. However, Ireland's "uniqueness" no longer sets us apart from global trends: like other European states, we must now squarely face the reality of embedded social and ethnic inequalities, whose persistence cannot be attributed just to our historic poverty and post-colonial status.[56] However, there are considerable divisions of opinion as to the extent and seriousness of the inequalities in Irish society, the scope of the state's obligations towards non-nationals or recently arrived ethnic groups, and the appropriateness of different forms of state intervention. Sceptics about the efficacy or appropriateness of state intervention, such as Michael McDowell, have tended to see the existence of these inequalities as inevitable and unavoidable in contemporary conditions of globalisation. Critics of the current trajectory of Irish law and policy take a different perspective.

Equality as a Constitutional Norm

Ultimately, political battles, social trends and economic processes will determine how these debates play out and whether these inequalities persist. Law cannot provide simple solutions. There are no legal mechanisms to magic these problems away, or to resolve the serious political disagreements that exist. Law, and even human rights frameworks, cannot wholly substitute for or replace social-political contests. However, the Irish Republic is a state founded upon a constitutional order that gives priority to individual rights within a democratic framework. Political debates about equality take place within this constitutional setting, the flawed but principled legacy of the idealist streak of the early days of independence. The structure of the state institutions established under the Constitution, its protection of certain basic rights, and the unenforceable Directive Principles set out in the text when taken together are supposed to "orient" political debate and the operation of the Irish legal system towards adherence to core constitutional values.[57] Disagreement can and will inevitably exist as to the best methods for upholding constitutional principles, and how they should be applied in particular circumstances. Nevertheless, the challenge for all constitutional actors is to work within this framework, and to give effect to (or at least not to deviate from) constitutional principles in law and policy.

Equality is one of these core constitutional values, enshrined in Article 40.1 and inherent in the underlying normative structure of the Constitution taken as a whole. As has been repeatedly stressed, equality is a contested principle. The Constitution does not necessarily commit constitutional actors to a particular approach to the equality principle, except perhaps to a basic requirement that legislation be rational as regards its application to different individuals and groups. However, strong

---

[56] F O'Toole, "A Less Important Ireland", 106 *Prospect*, January 2005.

[57] For a discussion of this concept of "orientation" and its role in how the UK Human Rights Act takes effect in the British legal system, see C O'Cinneide, "Democracy and Rights: New Directions in the Human Rights Era" (2004) 57 *Current Legal Problems* 175–211.

arguments can be made that the inherent logic of the Constitutional text, and its privileging of personal and democratic rights, mean that attempts to subordinate a particular social group, or to establish different classes of citizenship, or to withhold essential social goods from particular groups without real justification, would rub against the grain of Irish constitutional expectations. It would run counter to the idealistic roots of the Constitution, and to its commitment to human dignity. From this relatively uncontroversial deduction, it follows that some combination of the "formal equality", "anti-discrimination" and "substantive equality" approaches, perhaps best grouped together under the umbrella concept of "equality of respect" would constitute the "best fit" in interpreting the equality right set out in Article 40.1.[58]

As a consequence, constitutional actors, including the judiciary, the Oireachtas and other state institutions, should attempt at a minimum to respect the broad parameters of such an "equality of respect" approach, which should be seen as combining: i) a commitment to the making of rational and defensible distinctions between individuals and groups (i.e the "rational equality" approach); ii) a rejection of abusive and prejudiced forms of distinction (i.e. the "anti-discrimination" approach); and iii) some recognition of the role of the state in breaking down patterns of disadvantage and subordination (the "substantive equality" approach). Any narrower interpretation of the equality right would not sit well within the constitutional framework, or with most contemporary concepts of the appropriate role of the State.[59]

A multiplicity of approaches to equality could fit within this general framework, which represents the lowest credible common denominator interpretation of the equality guarantee. Arguably, most if not all of the mainstream of Irish political and legal life could operate comfortably within it. However, it is also important that *effective* respect is given to the constitutional equality principle. The Constitution sets out a system of norms and values, which is supposed to be respected and implemented in practice by the state institutions. The Supreme Court has often held that formalistic legal distinctions, or outdated legacies of the pre-1922 legal system, or considerations of executive convenience cannot be used to suspend or defer the application of constitutional rights.[60] Equality as a core constitutional right should be treated no differently. However, the fact that its exact content is so contested makes it more difficult to define with precision what giving effect to this right

[58] For this concept of "best fit", see R Dworkin, *Taking Rights Seriously* (Harvard University Press, Cambridge, MA, 1977), Ch. 4. This "equality of respect" approach would be similar in very general terms to that mapped out by Dworkin.

[59] Doyle suggests that the Supreme Court initially viewed the constitutional equality guarantee as solely applying to the civil and political context, but not to the wider social context, a "tripartite" concept of equality that can be seen as also implicit in some of Eamon De Valera's comments on Article 40.1 in the Dáil debates: he considers however that this conception of the effect of the equality right has been abandoned by the courts. See Doyle, *Constitutional Equality Law*, 11–13.

[60] See e.g. *Byrne v Ireland* [1972] IR 241; *Attorney-General (S.P.U.C. (Ireland) Ltd.) v Open Door Counselling Ltd.* [1988] IR 593; *Buckley v Attorney-General* [1950] IR 67.

should require in practice. Doyle argues that securing effective respect for the equality principle should involve the application of the "substantive equality" approach, where particular social groups are subject to clear and distinct forms of *de facto* subordination. He argues that the adoption by the Irish courts of such a substantive equality approach would be compatible with the history, design and text of the Constitution.[61] There is considerable force in this argument. If particular groups, such as Travellers, women or persons with disabilities are in practice subject to high levels of disadvantage, then giving effect to their constitutional entitlement to equality of respect in practice may justify special measures to remove the obstacles to which they are subject.[62] It may also justify more intense review of any legislative measures that might contribute to this *de facto* "second-class" status.

Nevertheless, even if one cavils at this argument, or would question how far this "equality of respect"/"substantive equality" approach should be applied, it is apparent that at a minimum, guaranteeing effective protection of the equality right should mean that individuals and groups are given the possibility of launching challenges to forms of exclusion that deny them "equality of respect".[63] For the equality right to have any "bite" or impact, there has to be a mechanism to assess the constitutionality of (and justification for) measures that expose particular individuals and groups to particular disadvantage. This mechanism should be accessible and effective: it should also be applied consistently and coherently, and reflect the structure and values of the Irish constitutional system as a whole. Even if substantial disagreement exists as to what exact approach should be adopted to flesh out the equality right, the mechanism for asserting this right should meet these basic requirements.

Article 40.1 and the Right to Equality

In the Irish constitutional framework, the mechanism that is supposed to perform this supervisory role is judicial enforcement of the Article 40.1 right to equality. However, how this equality right has been applied has been problematic both in terms of how it is defined, and also in the protection it confers. The constitutional logic discussed above, which points towards a relatively strong application of an "equality of respect" approach, has only rarely surfaced in the jurisprudence of the Supreme Court. Irish constitutional law has rarely benefited disadvantaged or unpopular minority groups in society. Homosexuals, non-nationals, members of the Traveller community and the disabled have found it difficult to secure any

[61] See Doyle, *Constitutional Equality* Law, ch 12.

[62] Irish constitutional law recognises the existence of positive obligations upon the State to take steps to protect fundamental rights: see e.g. *State (Healy) v Donoghue* [1976] IR 325.

[63] Judy Walsh has made a powerful argument that the Irish courts need to develop new approaches to conceptualising social relationships and their link to rights discourse, and to play a greater role in opening new terrain for political debates and alternative perspectives on equality: see J Walsh, "Unfamiliar Equalities" (2006) 57(1) *Northern Ireland Legal Quarterly* 156–185.

constitutional foothold to challenge discriminatory legislation or policy. This is not an uncommon feature of constitutional jurisprudence in many countries.[64] However, given the range and development of other areas of constitutional rights in Irish law, in particular the personal rights protected under Article 40.3 of the Constitution, the restraint of the Court in interpreting and applying Article 40.1 is all the more striking. The equality jurisprudence has also not always been very coherent in terms of its logic and consistency: the leading commentators on the case-law of the Court have been mainly unified in critiquing its application of Article 40.1.[65]

The text of Article 40.1 has been identified by some commentators as the source of the uncharacteristic reticence and unsure touch of the Supreme Court in this area. The text of Article 40.1 resembles many other constitutional equality clauses in being opaque in defining the equality right:

> "All citizens shall, as human persons, be held equal before the law. This shall not be held to mean that the State shall not in its enactments have due regard to differences of capacity, physical and moral, and social function".

The basic right to equality is therefore subject to the wide qualification clause inserted in the second sentence of Art. 40.1, as well as the apparently limiting proviso that "citizens" shall be held equal before the law "as human persons". Both these qualifiers were inserted to reflect Catholic social teaching, but also to give some tangible content to the abstract equality guarantee.[66] Article 40.1 does not set out a precise vision of how the equality principle should be applied, and these qualifications built into the text are important in that they constrain the scope of possible application of this principle. However, as Doyle has argued, the negative impact of these qualifying provisions can be greatly overestimated.[67]

The second sentence, which does permit the State to have due regard for differences in capacity and social function, is not so different from the general qualifying clauses contained in s 1 of the Canadian Charter of Fundamental Rights and Freedoms, or s 36 of the South African Constitution. States invariably must take account of differences in position in formulating legislation and policy: the role of the equality right is precisely to give protection against abuses of this function, but not to preclude its application where appropriate. By giving room to the Irish State

---

[64] See A McColgan, "Women and the Human Rights Act" (2000) 51(3) *Northern Ireland Law Quarterly* 417; also by the same author, *Women Under The Law: The False Promise of Human Rights* (Longman, London, 1999).

[65] See A Connelly, "The Constitution" in A Connelly (ed.) *Gender and the Law in Ireland* (Oak Tree Press, Dublin, 1993); G Hogan and G Whyte, *The Irish Constitution* (4th ed.) (Butterworths, Dublin, 2003) 1343; J Casey, *Constitutional Law in Ireland* (3rd ed.) (Sweet & Maxwell, Dublin 2000), 450–452; G Hogan, "The Supreme Court and the Equality Clause" (1998) *Bar Review* 116–120; O Doyle, *Constitutional Equality Law* (Round Hall, Dublin, 2004). For a more positive assessment, see John T O'Dowd, "The Principle of Equality in Irish Constitutional and Administrative Law" (1999) 11 *European Review of Public Law* 769.

[66] Doyle, *Constitutional Equality Law*, 51–66.

[67] *ibid*, Ch. 6.

to take into account differences of capacity, the Article 40.1 equality right could and has at times served as a justification for a highly deferential review of state-mandated distinctions.[68] However, it could also be interpreted as opening the door to the possibility of a substantive equality approach, requiring "due regard" to be given to the needs of disadvantaged groups in particular circumstances. This provision does not foreclose any particular approach to equality.

Similarly, the "human persons" proviso has been used in the equality jurisprudence of the Supreme Court to read down or restrict the scope of application of Article 40.1 to instances where discrimination impacts upon an essential feature of a person's personality, most notably in the judgments of Kenny J in *Quinn"s Supermarket v Attorney General*[69] and *Murtagh v Cleary*.[70] This approach can substantially narrow the field of application of the equality right to basic civil and political entitlements, as the equality analysis (or to be more precise, the lack thereof) in *Murtagh* demonstrates.[71] However, an alternative interpretation of the phrase exists, which Doyle has characterised as the "basis of discrimination" approach.[72] This treats the reference to "human persons" as precluding forms of discrimination and differentiation that were based upon the presumed inferiority of certain individuals or groups. Originally outlined by Walsh J in *Quinn's Supermarkets*,[73] Whyte suggests that this approach has come to the fore in constitutional jurisprudence.[74] As discussed by Doyle, it is certainly in play in the decision of the Supreme Court in the *Employment Equality Bill 1996*[75] and the decision of O'Higgins J in the High Court in *Equality Authority v Portmarnock Golf Club*[76] where it was used to affirm the State's

68 See e.g. *Murphy v Attorney-General* [1982] IR 241, 284; *Lowth v Minister for Social Welfare* [1994] 1 ILRM 378; *Norris v Attorney-General* [1984] IR 36.

69 [1972] IR 1.

70 [1972] IR 330: Kenny J considered that the equality guarantee had no relevance in relation to employment terms.

71 For criticism of this interpretation of Article 40.1, see FX Beytagh, "Equality under the Irish and American Constitutions: A Comparative Analysis" (1983) 18 *Irish Jurist (n.s.)* 56, 70; Casey, *Constitutional Law in Ireland* (3rd ed.), 457–458; K Lynch and A Connelly, "Appendix 18 to the Report of the Constitution Review Group", in the *Report of the Constitution Review Group* (Stationery office, Dublin, 1996), 586; G Hogan and G Whyte, *The Irish Constitution* (4th ed.) 1343; Y Scannell, "The Constitution and the Role of Women", in B Farrell (ed.) *De Valera's Constitution and Ours* (Gill and Macmillan, Dublin, 1988), 132. The Constitution Review Group recommended the deletion of the reference to "human persons": *Report of the Constitution Review Group*, 224.

72 Doyle, *Constitutional Equality Law*, 128–129.

73 [1972] IR 1, 13–14.

74 G Whyte, "A Comment on the Constitution Review Group's Proposals on Equality", in W. Duncan and R Byrne (eds.), *Discrimination law in Ireland and Europe* (ICEL, Dublin, 1997), 101–102.

75 *In the matter of Article 26 of the Constitution of Ireland and in the Matter of the Employment Equality Bill* [1997] 2 IR 321.

76 For the judgment of O'Higgins J, see *Equality Authority v Portmarnock Golf Club* [2005] IEHC 235 (10 June 2005). In its recent decision on appeal in this case, the Supreme Court, while sharply divided on how the relevant legislative provisions were to be interpreted and applied, considered that it was not necessary to comment on the constitutional background to the case: see *Equality Authority v Portmarnock Golf Club* (2009) IESC 73 (3 November 2009).

ability to introduce strong anti-discrimination legislation to protect individuals against unfair discrimination. It is also present in the *Blascaod Mór* decision,[77] where it was used to preclude reliance upon "pedigree" as a legitimate form of distinction in the circumstances.[78] This approach reflects the "anti-discrimination" and "equality of respect" approaches discussed earlier, could open the door to a "substantive equality" analysis, and echoes the emphasis on interpreting the equality right as a tool to protect human dignity in the jurisprudence of the Canadian and South African courts.[79] As Doyle has convincingly argued, criticism of the "human persons" qualification overlooks its potential use to intensify and focus the protection offered by Article 40.1, even if it can also be used to limit and narrow its scope of application. Again, no approach is ruled out by the bare language of Article 40.1.

Therefore, the text of Article 40.1 permits a range of possible equality approaches, provided that they can be justified by reference to its specific text, the overall structure of the Constitution, and the application of defensible methods of judicial reasoning. De Valera's insertion of Article 40.1 into the *Bunreacht* placed the recognition of equality of the person at the core of the Irish constitutional order, and also recognised that this provision would be interpreted and applied through an interpretative process by the organs of the state, including the judiciary.[80] As Doyle has argued, it allows for the equality principle to be given an interpretation that best fits with the constitutional logic and values of a rights-based democratic polity such as Ireland, as it develops over time. There is nothing inherent in the text of Article 40.1 that limits its capacity to be developed as an effective and constitutionally coherent equality guarantee.

However, the ambiguous, uneasy and muted status of equality in the Irish social and political order has seeped to an extent into the interpretation of Article 40.1 by the courts. After an initial flirtation with a purely formal approach, whereby there

---

[77] *An Blascaod Mór Teoranta v Commissioners of Public Works* [2000] 1 IR 6.
[78] Doyle also correctly notes that judicial endorsements of this approach have not always subsequently been reflected in actual decisions: see Doyle, *Constitutional Equality Law*, 129–132.
[79] For an excellent (and detailed) summary of the Canadian equality jurisprudence, see "Charter Equality Rights: Interpretation of Section 15 in Supreme Court of Canada Decisions", prepared by Mary C Hurley, Law and Government Division, Parliamentary Research Branch, Canadian Parliament, August 1995, revised March 2007, available at http://www.parl.gc.ca/information/library/PRBpubs/bp402-e.htm (last accessed 2 September 2008). See also E Grabham, "*Law v Canada*: New Directions for Equality Under the Canadian Charter?" (2002) 22 (4) *Oxford Journal of Legal Studies* 641–66. For a representative sample of the extensive South African jurisprudence, see *National Coalition for Gay and Lesbian Equality v Minister for Justice* [1999] (1) SA 6. As with the Canadian jurisprudence, this approach could also limit the primary focus of the constitutional equality guarantee to circumstances where human dignity was at issue, and therefore prevent over-broad applications of the equality guarantee: see Doyle, 131–132, and the Canadian Supreme Court decisions in *Andrews v Law Society* [1989] 1 SCR 143 and *Law v Canada (Minister of Employment and Immigration)* [1999] 1 SCR 497. See also the similar (if underdeveloped) approach taken by the House of Lords in interpreting Article 14 of the ECHR in *R v Secretary of State for the Home Department, ex p Carson* [2005] UKHL 37.
[80] See Doyle, *Constitutional Equality Law*, Ch. 3.

would be no breach of Article 40.1 if everyone in a class of person defined by legislation or executive policy was treated alike, the Supreme Court has adopted what Doyle describes as a "process conception" of equality.[81] A distinction made in law between individuals and groups will be contrary to Article 40.1 if it is arbitrary, or not reasonably capable of being supported by reference to the difference of capacity that is cited as justification, or is unrelated to the purpose of the legislation in question.[82] The focus of this approach is ensuring that the process of differentiating between individuals and groups is legitimate. It does not concentrate upon the potential for legislation or executive action to contribute to group subordination, nor does it make reference to an overarching standard of how citizens should be treated with equal respect. The Supreme Court's approach is built around securing equality of concern in how law is made and applied, not in securing "substantive equality" or "equality of respect" as an ultimate good.

This approach sidesteps any need on the part of the judiciary to nail their colours to a particular approach to equality.[83] This could be seen as a praiseworthy step, reflecting proper judicial caution in a contested and controversial area. However, the opposite critique could also be made that by avoiding the adoption of a more substantive approach, this approach has deprived the equality right of much substantial content. Irrespective of which perspective is adopted, it is clear that this test as currently framed is riddled with uncertainty. The Supreme Court does appear to regard distinctions that may cause arbitrary or unreasonable forms of indirect discrimination to particular groups as potentially covered by Article 40.1.[84] However, it is not clear what types of indirect discrimination will be prohibited. Nor is it clear whether or to what extent is affirmative action permitted,[85] or where the onus rests in an equality challenge to legislation or executive action,[86] or whether corporate bodies can bring an action,[87] or when the equality right can have direct horizontal effect.[88] The standard of review to be applied is also unclear: various alternative formulations as to what would qualify as an unconstitutional distinction

[81] Doyle, *Constitutional Equality Law*, 67–75; 201–211.

[82] See the judgment of Barrington J in *Brennan v Attorney General* [1983] ILRM 449, 480 (HC): "the classification must be a legitimate legislative purpose…it must be relevant to that purpose, and that each class must be treated fairly". See also *Dillane v Attorney-General* [1980] ILRM 167, 169; *O"B v S* [1984] IR 316, 335.

[83] Fiss has suggested that the judicial preference in the United States for "process" approaches reflects a desire to adopt a group-neutral, individualist approach that stays close to prevailing judicial practices and avoids some of this controversy: see Fiss, "Groups and the Equal Protection Clause", 118–128. Doyle makes a similar suggestion about the approach of the Irish judiciary: Doyle, *Constitutional Equality Law*, 18.

[84] See e.g. *In re Article 26 and the Illegal Immigrants (Trafficking) Bill 1999* [2000] 2 IR 360; Doyle, *Constitutional Equality Law*, 79–81.

[85] See Doyle, *Constitutional Equality Law*, 82–83.

[86] *ibid*, 113.

[87] *ibid*, 89–90.

[88] See Casey, *Constitutional Law in Ireland*, 474–475; note John Kelly's sceptical view, in J Kelly, "Equality Before the Law: Three European Jurisdictions" (1983) XVIII *Irish Jurist* (n.s.) 259, 266–267.

exist, such as "invidious discrimination", irrationality, "over- or under-inclusivity", or a "disproportionate" reliance upon the existence of a difference of capacity.[89]

This uncertainty is not unusual: equality tests are difficult to define in constitutional law. However, where this test has been applied, considerable deference has been shown to distinctions made between individuals and groups by the Oireachtas, as well as by the executive.[90] Doyle suggests that "double deference" has been in play in the jurisprudence, with the courts both reluctant to challenge why a distinction has been made, and also slow to challenge the assessment by the legislature or the executive as to what standard of equal treatment should be provided in general.[91] The courts have also been willing to give generous scope to the legislature and executive in ascertaining the purpose of legislation, and in linking that purpose to a legitimate aim.[92]

However, more significantly than this, the courts have often been consistent in privileging other constitutional values over the equality right, when they come into conflict. Repeatedly, equality claims have been deemed to be clearly outweighed by other constitutional claims, such as the interest in protecting family or married life, or by other state interests.[93] As Doyle argues, the Supreme Court has been very slow to recognise the equality right as having any "substantive, egalitarian content which could weigh against other...provisions of the Constitution".[94] The Supreme Court has also been slow to grant relief even in circumstances where a case under Article 40.1 could be made out, on the somewhat dubious grounds that no meaningful relief would be available in the circumstances.[95] Casey has suggested that the case-law has demonstrated a judicial "reluctance to invoke" equality as a substantive constitutional right in determining cases.[96] This represents a downgrading of the equality right in the constitutional hierarchy, and treats it as if it lacked any real substance. This is difficult to reconcile with the rhetoric that claims equality as a central value of the Irish state, and with the "equality of respect" approach that perhaps represents the most appropriate reading of the equality right.

---

[89] See Doyle, *Constitutional Equality Law* 113–124; Casey, 461–471.

[90] In particular, see the rejection of the equality arguments in *Murphy v Attorney-General* [1982] IR 241, described by Casey as the "low-water mark" of the equality guarantee: see Casey, 456. See also the acceptance of the link between protecting the family and discriminating against illegitimate children in *O'B v S* [1984] IR 316, and the acceptance of the government's link between sexual orientation and health problems in *Norris v Attorney-General* [1984] IR 36.

[91] Doyle, *Constitutional Equality Law*, 104–105.

[92] *ibid*, 113–122.

[93] *ibid*, 83–85. This trend can be clearly seen in the decisions in *O'B v S* [1984] IR 316, *Murphy v Attorney-General* [1982] IR 241, and in the privileging of property rights over the equality rights of disabled persons in *In the matter of Article 26 of the Constitution of Ireland and in the Matter of the Employment Equality Bill* [1997] 2 IR 321.

[94] Doyle, *Constitutional Equality Law*, p 75.

[95] See *Samjee v Minister for Justice* [1981] ILRM 324. Doyle notes inconsistencies in the case-law on this point: see Doyle, 86–88.

[96] See Casey, *Constitutional Law in Ireland*, 458–460.

However, recent decisions have seen notable shifts in the stance of the courts. In the *Employment Equality Bill* decision, the Supreme Court recognised that preventing discrimination on the grounds listed in the Bill gave effect to important constitutional objective, even if property rights were allowed to out-weigh the objective of removing obstacles faced by disabled persons to equal participation.[97] Perhaps more significantly, in the *Portmarnock* decision, O'Higgins J held that the Oireachtas was "entitled to legislate positively to vindicate and promote the value of equality", and affirmed the centrality of equality as a prime constitutional value, citing Barrington J in *An Blascaod Mór*[98] to the effect that Ireland "is a democratic society committed to the principle of equality".[99] In so doing, he considered that the constitutional interest in preventing unjust discrimination could outweigh freedom of association rights, which is a very important finding that equality does have some constitutional "weight", even where other constitutional rights are in play. A series of cases concerning the electoral process have seen the courts more ready to uphold equal treatment in the political arena,[100] while the *Blascaod Mór* and *Howard* decisions saw the Supreme Court ready to over-turn categorisations based upon "pedigree" and the special status of the State.[101]

Doyle suggest that these cases demonstrate a willingness on the part of the Irish courts to adopt a "strong process" model of equality, whereby particular forms of "suspect" distinctions are subject to higher levels of scrutiny, and state action to combat discrimination on these suspect grounds is seen as serving a valuable constitutional objective. They certainly signal a shift towards an "anti-discrimination" approach, in particular in the civil-political sphere. How far this new tendency will extend is unclear.[102] The judgments in *Employment Equality* Bill and *Portmarnock* are both *permissive* in nature: the constitutional value in protecting individuals against particular forms of discrimination was invoked to uphold legislation passed by the Oireachtas. Whether a similar emphasis on the "anti-discrimination" approach will be taken in challenges to legislation or executive

[97] *In the matter of Article 26 of the Constitution of Ireland and in the Matter of the Employment Equality Bill* [1997] 2 IR 321: see in particular Hamilton CJ's comments at 347.
[98] [2000] 1 IR 6.
[99] *ibid*, at p 19.
[100] See Doyle, *Constitutional Equality Law*, 90–93, citing in particular *McKenna v An Taoiseach (No. 2)* [1995] 2 IR 10, *Coughlan v Broadcasting Complaints Commission* [2000] 3 IR 1, *Kelly v Minister for the Environment* [2002] 4 IR 1, *Redmond v Minster for the Environment* [2001] 4 IR 61. It should be noted, as Doyle does, that some of the equality reasoning in these cases, in particular *McKenna*, is lacking in rigour.
[101] *An Blascaod Mór Teoranta v Commissioners of Public Works* [2000] 1 IR 6; *Howard v Commissioners for Public Works* [1994] 1 IR 101. Both these decisions, like *McKenna*, could perhaps have benefited from a more rigorous analysis of the positions of the different comparators on the face of the judgments: in all three decisions, rhetoric about equality of status substitutes for close analysis.
[102] For example, see Doyle at 210, where he speculates whether distinctions that have an indirect negative impact upon groups historically affected by "suspect" distinctions will be subject to extra constitutional scrutiny, even where the distinction *disproportionately* affects these groups rather than *only* affects those groups as a distinct category.

action remains to be seen. The detailed and context-sensitive judgment by the High Court in the case of *Foy (No. 1)* found no breach of Article 40.1, evidencing again a reluctance to push the envelope of the equality principle.[103] As discussed below, the incorporation of the ECHR may transform the situation, especially now that the case-law of the European Court of Human Rights is beginning to adopt a more developed "substantive equality" approach.[104] This may provide a strong impetus to the evolution of the Irish constitutional jurisprudence, perhaps in combination with the gradual trend in favour of a more substantive equality approach that Doyle has identified in recent Supreme Court case-law. However, it remains to be seen how far the influence of the ECHR will impact upon constitutional jurisprudence, or whether the Supreme Court may be willing to depart from its historically cautious approach to equality.[105]

Equality in Irish Public Law

Equality concerns have also rarely featured either in other areas of constitutional and administrative law. In his groundbreaking analysis of public interest litigation in Ireland, Gerry Whyte has traced the limited success of attempts to use law to combat the social exclusion faced by members of the Traveller community and other disadvantaged groups.[106] Similarly, attempts by non-citizens to invoke the protection of constitutional rights have yielded some results, but much of the spectrum of constitutional rights protection remains confined to citizens, including possibly the scope of the equality clause itself.[107]

Irish public law has a very limited vocabulary when it comes to equality issues: its lacks the constitutional language, case-law precedents, conceptual framework or sensitivity to concerns about group disadvantage that may be necessary to address equality claims in a fully coherent manner. It has given a muted role to equality values, both in the application of the equality clause itself and in providing avenues for disadvantaged groups to use the law as a lever for change. This reluctance to give "bite" to the equality principle might not be an issue in constitutional systems such as that of the UK (at least, before the introduction of the Human Rights Act 1998), which chose to place decision-making in controversial areas such as equality

---

103 *Foy v An t-Ard Chlaraitheoir & Ors* [2002] IEHC 116 (9 July 2002).

104 See e.g. the recent decision in *D.H. v Czech Republic*, Application No. 57325/00 (13 November 2007).

105 For an analysis of the potential impact of the Convention upon Irish constitutional law in general, see C O'Cinneide, "The European Convention on Human Rights and the Irish Constitutional System of Rights Protection: Complementary or Divergent?", in E Carolan and O Doyle, (eds.) *The Irish Constitution: Governance and Values* (Thomson Round Hall, Dublin, 2008).

106 G Whyte, *Social Inclusion and the Legal System: Public Interest Law in Ireland* (IPA, Dublin, 2002), especially 215–245.

107 Doyle suggests that notwithstanding the express wording of Art. 40.1, which appears to confer the equality right on citizens only, it is now established that the equality guarantee is not limited in scope to citizens. See Doyle, *Constitutional Equality Law*, 87, citing the readiness of the Supreme Court to let non-citizens bring an action under Art. 40.1 in *State (Nicolaou) v An Bord Uchtála* [1966] IR 567 and *In re Article 26 and the Illegal Immigrants (Trafficking) Bill 1999* [2000] 2 IR 360 in support of this proposition.

firmly in the political sphere. However, it does not sit comfortably in a constitutional system like Ireland, which is committed to maintaining protection for core constitutional values through an enforceable bill of rights, and gives considerable rhetorical weight to equality as a prime constitutional virtue.

This tentative approach to the equality principle reflects the reality that a fundamental ambiguity exists about the place of equality in Irish society. Equality as a core constitutional value is rhetorically significant, but when it comes to the specifics of how it should be applied, it remains a highly contested and controversial concept. This in turn inevitably generates reluctance on the part of legal actors, including the courts, to give firm content to the constitutional equality right, or to adopt equality-based perspectives in other areas of constitutional and administrative law. The same problem could be said to apply throughout the political system: equality as a value is underdeveloped in Irish political discourse, and other values, such as market efficiency, tend to be given semi-automatic priority as a consequence.

Judy Walsh has recently argued that Irish constitutional and administrative law has consistently neglected or impeded the attainment of what she describes as "affective equality" in social and family relationships of care.[108] She also suggests that the lack of commitment to an anti-subordination approach, when combined with the non-enforceability of socio-economic rights, means that the Court"s equality jurisprudence is inherently "flawed" and unable to give any meaningful content to the equality principle.[109] The type of egalitarian anti-subordination approach called for by both Walsh and Doyle has considerable attractions. However, it may take a fundamental conceptual leap on the part of the Supreme Court and the emergence of a new political and social consensus before it can be realised.

Rights review rarely advances too far ahead of prevailing social norms and expectations.[110] The concept of equality is so politically contested that the more neutral language of process review has obvious attractions for a court. There is scope for the development of a stronger "equality of respect" and "anti-discrimination" stance within the existing parameters of the text of Article 40.1 and the case-law, just as a similar scope exists within the parameters of the ECHR. There are legitimate grounds for concern about the extent of judicial activism in certain areas of Irish constitutional law over the last few decades.[111] Nevertheless, the equality jurisprudence has been if anything under-developed and excessively

---

[108] J Walsh, "Unfamiliar Equalities" (2006) 57(1) *Northern Ireland Legal Quarterly* 156–185.

[109] J Walsh, "Unfamiliar Equalities" (2006) 57(1) *Northern Ireland Legal Quarterly* 156–185, 176.

[110] See R Dahl, "Decision-Making in a Democracy: The Supreme Court as a National Policy-Maker" (1957) 6 *Journal of Public Law* 279; see also M Tushnet, *Taking the Constitution Away from the Courts* (1999) 153.

[111] See D Gwynn Morgan, *A Judgement Too Far? Judicial Activism and the Constitution* (Cork University Press, Cork, 2001). See also See CA Gearty, "Democracy and a Bill of Rights: Some Lessons From Ireland", in KD Ewing, CA Gearty and BA Hepple (eds.) *Human Rights and Labour Law: Essays for Paul O'Higgins* (Mansell, London, 1994) 188.

passive: it certainly is out of step with the extent of existing protection for other fundamental rights. It is time that the equality guarantee was given more "bite", and equality analysis began to feature in the application of other aspects of constitutional and administrative law.

Equality and Anti-Discrimination Legislation

The major area of exception to the prevailing underdevelopment of the equality principle in Irish law has been the introduction of Ireland's comprehensive anti-discrimination legislation, the Employment Equality Act 1998 and the Equal Status Act 2000. This legislation was at the time, and remains, a real achievement, and is one of the tangible achievements of the social partnership-based consensus that shaped much of Irish policy in the 1990s.[112] It was a major advance on existing legislative protection against discrimination, and prohibited direct and indirect discrimination, as well as victimisation and harassment, on the grounds of any of nine "equality strands", race, sexual orientation, gender, religion, gender, family status, disability, membership of the Traveller community and age. In covering a wide scope of activity, both Acts were very broad-ranging in comparison to anti-discrimination legislation in many other European countries, at least at the time of their introduction.

The legislation also established the Equality Authority, a single equality commission with the functions of promoting adherence to equality and anti-discrimination values and enforcing the legislation, which it does by either supporting individual complainants or through the use of its own audit and litigation powers.[113] The Authority has more powers than comparable institutions in the UK or elsewhere in Europe.[114] Through effective use of these powers and active leadership, it initially established a significant role for itself in the Irish legal and political landscape, playing an important role in generating debate on equality issues and enforcing the legislation through its litigation support strategy (however, recent budget cuts have effectively strangled the Authority, as discussed below).[115]

The legislation has also proved effective in providing remedies against instances of direct discrimination, and more straightforward examples of indirect discrimination. A considerable case-law has been generated by the Equality Tribunals, in particular in the areas of race discrimination, discrimination against

---

[112] See N Crowley, *An Ambition for Equality* (Irish Academic Press, Dublin, 2006), xi–xxi, for an account of the genesis of the legislation.

[113] See N Crowley, *An Ambition for Equality*, Ch. 2, for an account of the functioning and powers of the Authority.

[114] See C O'Cinneide, *Single Equality Bodies: Lessons from Aboard* (Equal Opportunities Commission Research Paper Series, Manchester, 2002).

[115] For an example of a successful and high-profile case brought by the Authority, see *Equality Authority v Ryanair*, DEC-E/2000/14. The frequency of the attacks on the Authority in much of the Irish media constituted a backhanded compliment to its success and profile: for an account of some of these media barbs, see N Crowley, *An Ambition for Equality*, 182–183.

[116] For information on the evolution of this case-law, see the Annual Legal Reviews prepared by the Equality Tribunal, available at http://www.equalitytribunal.ie/index.asp?locID=77&docID=-1 (last accessed 20 May 2006). See also N Crowley, *An Ambition for Equality*, 74–89.

members of the Traveller community, age discrimination and sex discrimination.[116] Community groups have used the legislation to challenge prejudicial behaviour, and it appears to be having some impact in reducing or eliminating certain overt forms of discrimination and prejudice, as well as having a considerable educative impact.[117]

However, as considerable an achievement as the legislation was, it is important that its limits are also recognised. The fact that Ireland's anti-discrimination legislation was considerably in advance of most of the rest of Europe in 2000 has generated a degree of complacency, best reflected in Minister Willie O'Dea TD's statement that in May 2004 that Irish equality legislation, and therefore Irish equality policy, was more advanced than that of most other European states.[118] Following the introduction of the Framework Equality and Race Equality Directives in 2000 and subsequent legislation throughout the EU member states, Ireland's anti-discrimination legislation is no longer far ahead of the pack.[119] Both the EEA and ESA have wide exemptions built into their scope: some of these were closed to comply with the requirements of the 2000 Directives in the Equality Act 2004, but others remain, some of which may not be in conformity with the requirements of the 2000 Directives.[120]

It remains unclear whether the provisions of the legislation apply to the performance of public functions by state authorities, in particular in the area of welfare and education provision: this is a substantial area of uncertainty.[121] Due to the Supreme Court's decision in the employment equality legislation reference[122] that private employers could not be required to bear "excessive burdens" in making reasonable accommodation for disabled persons, the EEA and ESA only required employers and service providers to incur "nominal costs" to satisfy these requirements.[123] Section 9 of the recent Equality Act 2004 now obliges employers to

---

[117] N Crowley, *An Ambition for Equality*, 185–186.

[118] See *The Irish Times*, 8 May 2004.

[119] For example, following the Equality Act 2006, UK anti-discrimination legislation has a similar scope as the Irish legislation, with the exception of the prohibition in the ESA of age discrimination in access to goods and services: this may be removed in the forthcoming Equality Bill. See C O'Cinneide, "Fumbling Towards Coherence: The Slow Evolution of Equality Law in England and Wales" (2006) 57(1) *Northern Ireland Legal Quarterly*, 65–73. Comprehensive cross-ground anti-discrimination legislation extending beyond the scope of the Directives have been introduced since 2000 in several European countries, such as Belgium, the Czech Republic and the Netherlands.

[120] See the Irish Human Rights Commission, *Observations on the Equality Bill 2004* (IHRC, Dublin, 2004), available at http://www.ihrc.ie/_fileupload/banners/obs1.doc (last accessed 22nd May 2006); see also N Crowley, *An Ambition for Equality*, 96–100.

[121] For an example of how a statutory prohibition on discrimination in the performance of public functions may have a tangible impact on the conduct of immigration and asylum procedures, see the UK House of Lords decision in *R v Immigration Officer at Prague Airport, ex parte European Roma Rights Centre* [2004] UKHL 55.

[122] *In the matter of Article 26 of the Constitution of Ireland and in the Matter of the Employment Equality Bill* [1997] 2 IR 321.

[123] See s 16(3) (c) of the Employment Equality Act 1998, and s 4(2) Equal Status Act 2000.

make reasonable accommodation, except where to do so would impose a "disproportionate burden": this was done to comply with the requirements of the 2000 Framework Equality Directive. This obligation does not extend to service providers, who are not covered by the Directive, unlike the case in the UK: this remains another substantial gap.[124] In addition, the remedies available under the legislation remain limited by the existence of a restrictive upper cap on damage awards outside the area of gender equality: this is again out of line with legislation in other countries, including the UK, and may be incompatible with the 2000 Directives.[125] The *Portmarnock* decision also revealed real problems with the wording and scope of certain of the ESA's provisions.[126]

It is also worth noting that elements of the legislation have been diluted since 2000. The Intoxicating Liquor Act 2003 transferred jurisdiction for discrimination cases involving licensed premises away from the Equality Tribunal to the District Court, following successful cases having been brought by Traveller groups before the Tribunal in respect of access to pubs. While enhancing the scope of some of the possible remedies available, this legislation has put extra cost and procedural impediments in the way of challenging discrimination by publicans.[127] The Equality Act 2004 also introduced some new exemptions in respect of non-nationals, again accentuating the national/non-national distinction in Irish law, as did steps in 2004 to restrict homosexual couples from accessing benefits granted under administrative schemes.[128] The provisions of the legislation have also not been built upon by further legislation: the Irish government has been slow in introducing legislation conferring partnership rights upon homosexual couples and comprehensive needs-based provision for disabled persons, in the face of considerable criticism from pressure groups and activists.[129] More seriously, slashing budget cuts were inflicted on the Equality Authority in 2008, which lead to the resignation of its Chief Executive Officer, Niall Crowley, on the grounds that he considered that the work of the Authority had been "fatally compromised".[130] The 43% cut in the Authority's budget was dramatically out of proportion to the budget cuts inflicted on similar state bodies and was accompanied by a cack-handed

---

[124] See C O'Cinneide, *Equivalence in Promoting Equality* (Equality Authority, Dublin, 2006), 42–43.

[125] See the Irish Human Rights Commission, *Observations on the Equality Bill 2004* (IHRC, Dublin, 2004), p 4. See also C O'Cinneide, *Equivalence in Promoting Equality* (Equality Authority, Dublin, 2006), 47–48.

[126] In *Portmarnock*, the majority of the Supreme Court adopted what could be described (with respect) as a strained and highly artificial interpretation of the provisions of the legislation governing discrimination in club membership: *Equality Authority v Portmarnock Golf Club* (2009) IESC 73 (3 November 2009).

[127] See N Crowley, *An Ambition for Equality*, 192.

[128] *ibid*, 192–193.

[129] See Irish Human Rights Commission, *Observations on the Disability Bill 2004* (IHRC, Dublin, 2004). See also G Quinn, "Towards Free and Inclusive Societies for People with Disabilities", in S Quin & B Redmond (eds.) *Disability and Social Policy in Ireland* (UCD Press, Dublin, 2003), 182–198.

[130] See *The Irish Times*, "Equality Authority chief resigns over budget cutbacks", 12 December 2008.

attempt to decentralise much of the Authority's work to Co. Tipperary. This has amounted to an effective evisceration of the Authority's ability to function as the primary enforcement body charged with ensuring the effective implementation of the equality legislation. The cuts have been widely attributed to political hostility towards the Authority and its work: at the very least, they illustrate how enforcing anti-discrimination law is not treated seriously in Irish public life.

The Irish legislative framework also shares the common structural limitations of anti-discrimination legislation in general: it is focussed upon providing retrospective redress for individuals brave enough to bring litigation who are subject to specific forms of clearly delineated discrimination in particular social and economic contexts.[131] It imposes no obligation on public or private bodies to change their policies and practices to reduce the impact of inequalities, or to take active steps to break down identified patterns of treatment that can contribute to the disadvantages faced by particular groups.[132] This form of equality legislation is possible, and limited variants of it have been introduced in fellow "trans-Atlantic" neo-liberal economies, such as Canada and the UK.[133] However, in the absence of such positive duties, which would require some degree of commitment to a "substantive equality" approach, Irish legislative provision adheres to a basic "anti-discrimination" approach.

Walsh critiques this type of limited anti-discrimination legislation as largely "remedial" in effect and incapable of bringing about wider social transformation. It certainly lacks the capacity to shift the fundamentals of Irish society, and in particular to do much about social inequalities.[134] However, within its circumscribed field of operation, it can play and has played a crucial important role in breaking down particular forms of discrimination and prejudice, or at least redirecting them into less harmful channels. For example, forty years of sex discrimination legislation has played an important role in transforming gender roles in society. Nevertheless, the current legislation is limited in scope and impact. Its existence should not generate complacency about the level of equality protection in Ireland.

---

[131] S Fredman, *Discrimination Law* (OUP, Oxford, 2001), 163–168; C McCrudden, "Anti-Discrimination Goals and the Legal Process" in N Glazer and K Young (eds.) *Ethnic Pluralism and Public Policy* (Treasury, London, 1983); B Hepple, "Judging Legal Rights", 33 *Current Legal Problems* (1983) 71.

[132] See C O'Cinneide, "Making Use of Positive Equality Duties: The UK Experience", in C Costello and E Barry (eds.) *Equality in Diversity: The New Equality Directives* (Irish Centre for European Law, Dublin, 2003), 75–99, 77–90.

[133] *ibid*, 91–97.

[134] See Walsh, "Unfamiliar Equalities", 167–169. For a non-legal but interesting critique, see MG Cronin, ""He"s My Country": Liberalism, Nationalism, and Sexuality in Contemporary Irish Gay Fiction", (2004) 39(3 & 4) *Éire-Ireland* 254: "Significantly, the primary source of inequality in any capitalist society, poverty, is not among the nine grounds on which the equality legislation rests. Therefore, a key effect of both the "social partnership" and "equality" discourses has been a conception of society in which class and class struggle have been replaced by the notion of equally positioned identities and interests, with the disinterested agents of the state mediating between them."

The political choice has been taken to confine the scope of anti-discrimination legislation, which reflects uncertainty and scepticism about how much further the equality principle can or should be pushed through state action. Combined with the "process" approach to the equality guarantee taken at present by the Supreme Court, this means that the equality principle in Irish law in general takes the form of a combination of "formal equality" and "anti-discrimination" approaches, with a garnishing of "equality of respect" rhetoric, which has the possibility of being given more tangible shape through developments in the case-law. This could be critiqued as falling short of constitutional aspirations: however, given the contested nature of equality in Irish political debate, further development may be slow in coming. The budget cuts inflicted on the Equality Authority, taken together with the approach adopted by the majority of the Supreme Court in *Portmarnock Golf Club*, demonstrate that there appears to be little real appetite within the legislative, executive or judicial branches of government for giving effective, far-reaching and substantive effect to the equality principle.

Alternative Avenues — Equality and Ireland's International Human Rights Commitments

However, legal influences percolating through Irish law from the international human rights frameworks of which Ireland is a member may generate change in unexpected ways. Ireland is embedded in a framework of overlapping and mutually influencing legal orders, which in both direct and indirect ways can substantially shape and influence the development of Irish law.[135] Within the confines of international law, Ireland is a signatory to the major UN human rights instruments, including the two UN Covenants, the Convention on the Elimination of Racial Discrimination, the Convention on the Elimination of Discrimination Against Women and the Convention on the Rights of the Child. Presumably Ireland will also sign and ratify the newly agreed Convention on the Rights of Persons With Disabilities (CRPD). These instruments commit Ireland to implementing the "anti-discrimination" approach in its domestic law, as well as imposing positive obligations upon states to take positive action in certain circumstances to secure meaningful and real equality for disadvantaged groups.[136] Article 2(2) of CERD for example provides that signatory states "shall...take...special and concrete measures

[135] For a general theoretical analysis of this concept of overlapping legal orders, see N Walker, "The Idea of Constitutional Pluralism" (2002) 65 *Modern Law Review* 317–359 See also G Anthony, "Clustered Convergence? European Fundamental Rights Standards in Irish and UK Public Law' (2004) *Public Law* 282.

[136] See Article 1 and 2 UDHR, Article 2(1) ICCPR and Article 2(2) ICESCR; see also U O'Hare, "Equality and Affirmative Action in International Human Rights Law and its Relevance to the European Union" (2000) 4 *International Journal of Discrimination and the Law* 3, 10, 18–20. O'Hare also argues that these two complementary obligations, the negative requirement to refrain from discrimination and the positive requirement to take the necessary action to remove obstacles to the equal participation of disadvantaged groups in society, have become part of customary international law, citing *inter alia* Judge Tanaka's opinion in the *South West Africa Case*: see O'Hare, p 11. This argument would appear to be a little stretched: if there is a customary international law obligation to respect both these principles, it is so diffuse and open-ended as to be meaningless.

to ensure the adequate development and protection of certain racial groups...", and "to bring to an end, by all appropriate means, racial discrimination..." [137]

International human rights law therefore adopts a combination of the "anti-discrimination" and "substantive equality" approaches, with the latter particularly emphasised.[138] As ever with international law obligations, exactly how these obligations should be implemented in practice remains a source of controversy and disagreement. As legal norms, they lack firm definition, even if they are valuable tools to use in political argument in pressing for a greater focus on the need for some positive action to redress persistent inequalities.[139] However, the emphasis on the "substantive equality" approach in these instruments is significant, because it ensures that there is a growing acceptance that the equality principle should be interpreted as necessarily containing some elements of this approach. For example, the European Committee of Social Rights in its recent case-law has recognised that signatory states to the European Social Charter should take positive steps to make special provision for disadvantaged groups.[140] With Ireland's dualist system, these developments may have little immediate influence on Irish domestic law, in the absence of creative judicial interpretation and intelligent use of international human rights law by lawyers before the courts. However, over time, they may exercise a considerable indirect influence.

EC law in contrast imposes definite requirements that have direct effect, which Ireland must implement through its domestic legislation. Until 2000, the scope of EC legislation did not extend beyond gender equality. Now, with the 2000 Directives and the introduction of the subsequent Gender Equality Directive in 2003, EC law requires the prohibition of direct and indirect discrimination in employment on the grounds of race, sex, disability, sexual orientation, religion and age, and discrimination in goods and services and the provision of "social advantages" on the grounds of race and gender. The Equality Act 2004 made some necessary changes to the EEA and ESA to comply with these requirements, but areas of potential lack of compliance remain, as discussed above. More significant is the gradual shift in the equality jurisprudence of

---

[137] See also Article 2(d) CERD, where State parties are required "to bring to an end, by all appropriate means...racial discrimination by any persons, groups or organisations." Other international instruments and bodies have adopted similar positions. The ILO Discrimination (Employment and Occupation) Convention (No. 111) classifies special measures for those needing special assistance as falling outside the definition of discrimination. A series of UN policy documents have also adopted similar views, such as The Mexico Declaration on the Equality of Women and the 1995 Copenhagen Declaration. The HRC's General Comment No. 27 supports this position, as has the UN Special Rapporteur on Minorities. See F Capotorti, *Study on the Rights of Persons Belonging to Ethnic, Religious and Linguistic Minorities* (UN, New York, 1991). See also O'Hare, 17–18.

[138] De Schutter notes that international human rights norms tend to actively encourage the adoption of special measures to promote equality: see O De Schutter, "Three Models of Equality and European Anti-Discrimination Law" (2006) 57(1) *Northern Ireland Legal Quarterly* 1, 46–49.

[139] See the submissions of the Irish Human Rights Commission to the various UH human rights monitoring committees, available at http://www.ihrc.ie/documents/.

[140] See *Autism-Europe v France*, Collective Complaint (No. 13/2002), 4 November 2003; *European Roma Rights Center v Greece*, Collective Complaint (No. 15/2003), 4 December 2004.

the European Court of Justice (ECJ) towards combining the "anti-discrimination" and "substantive equality" approaches. The ECJ had adopted a group disadvantage approach in applying the prohibition against indirect discrimination in the area of sex discrimination,[141] but outside of this context had been cautious about departing from a formal equality approach.[142] However, recent decisions have seen a cautious move towards acceptance of the legitimacy and necessity of substantive equality approaches based upon addressing group disadvantage.[143] These decisions have largely been permissive in nature, and confined to situations involving the use of positive action measures by member states. Nevertheless, this shift in the approach of the Court may have implications in future for how the Equality Directives are interpreted, as well on how future legislative proposals may be shaped and framed by the European institutions.[144] This may obviously have implications for Ireland: as happened with sex discrimination in the 1980s, the European train may yet pull Ireland towards a substantive equality approach of some sort, albeit one confined to the "obvious" inequalities recognised at present in the EC Directives.

Of more immediate relevance (as already mentioned) is the potential impact of the European Convention on Human Rights (ECHR) and the jurisprudence of the European Court of Human Rights, as incorporated into Irish law by the European Convention on Human Rights Act 2003. Highlighting the potential impact of the ECHR may appear strange. The limits of the 2003 Act in general have been extensively discussed,[145] and it appears to have had a moderate impact in its first few years of being

---

[141] See the decisions in Case 170/84 *Bilka-Kaufhaus v Weber von Hartz* [1986] ECR 1607; Case 109/88 *Danfoss* [1989] ECR 3199; Case 127/92 *Enderby v Frenchay Health Authority* [1993] ECR 5535; Case C-317/93, *Nolte* [1995] ECR I-4625; Case C-167/97, *R. v Secretary of State for Employment, ex p. Seymour-Smith* [1999] ECR I-0623.

[142] Case 450/93 *Kalanke v Bremen* [1995] ECR I-3051. Mark Bell has argued that a "patchwork of models" of equality has developed within EU equality law and policy, made up of three main strands: the standard anti-discrimination approach, a newer attachment to substantive equality, and a desire to manage diversity. See M Bell, "The Right to Equality and Non-Discrimination", in T Hervey and J Kenner (eds.) *Economic and Social Rights under the EC Charter of Fundamental Rights: A Legal Perspective* (Hart Publishing, Oxford, 2003), 91.

[143] Case 79/99 *Julia Schnorbus v Land Hessen* [2000] ECR I-10997; Case 319/03 *Briheche v Ministre de l"Intérieur,* Judgment of 30 September 2004, not yet reported. See the excellent analysis by Cathryn Costello in "Positive Action", in C Costello and E Barry (eds.) *Equality in Diversity: The New Equality Directives* (Irish Centre for European Law, Dublin, 2003), 177–212; see also C Tobler, "Positive Action under the Revised Second Equal Treatment Directive", in AFFA and EWLA (ed.) *L'égalité entre femmes et hommes et la vie profesionnelle; Le point sur les développements actuels en Europe* (Dalloz, Paris, 2003) 59–92.

[144] See the comments of the European Commission on the need for positive action to break patterns of disadvantage, in the Communication, "Non-Discrimination and Equality of Opportunities To All — A Framework Strategy", COM(2005)224 final, 1 June 2005, especially at para. 3.3. See also O De Schutter, "Three Models of Equality and European Anti-Discrimination Law" (2006) 57(1) *Northern Ireland Legal Quarterly* 1.

[145] See D Connell, "The ECHR Act 2003: A Critical Perspective", in U Kilkelly (ed.) *ECHR and Irish Law* (Jordans, Bristol, 2004) 1–11; R Murphy, "The Incorporation of the ECHR into Irish Domestic Law"(2001) 6 *European Human Rights Law Review* 640.

in force.[146] In any case, there is no great anticipation that incorporation of the Convention will have a major impact in the field of equality and anti-discrimination.[147] Unlike other national or international human rights instruments, the ECHR contains at present no free-standing right to equality: Article 14 of the Convention, its "equality clause", only guarantees equality of treatment in the enjoyment of other Convention rights. [148] It can only be applied where the facts in question falls within the "ambit" of one or more of the other rights of the Convention, that is, when they fall within the range of issues which relate to the enjoyment of the other Convention rights.[149]

Protocol 12 to the Convention is intended to supplement Article 14 with a free-standing guarantee of equality similar to that contained in Article 40.1 and other constitutions.[150] However, the Irish government has not as yet ratified the Protocol, which has entered into force, but only in respect of ratifying states.[151] Pending any future shift in Irish foreign policy, Article 14 with its circumscribed scope will remain the only equality guarantee recognised in the Convention. This may not be a substantial deficiency: the restricted scope of Article 14 can be exaggerated. However, the case-law of the European Court of Human Rights on Article 14 has been until recently largely underdeveloped. The Strasbourg court has historically tended to shy away from the complexities of Article 14, preferring instead to base its decisions on other articles of the Convention.[152] This historical discomfort with

[146] For a view that few issues of incompatibility would arise, and those that did arise would be subsumed into general constitutional litigation, see G Hogan, "Incorporation of the ECHR: Some Issues of Methodology and Process", in U Kilkelly (ed.) *ECHR and Irish Law* (Jordans, Bristol, 2004) 12–34. For the suggestion that the Convention has been historically under-utilised by Irish lawyers due to a lack of knowledge of its provisions and potential impact, see D O'Connell, "Ireland", in Blackburn and Polakiewicz (eds.) *Fundamental Rights in Europe: The European Convention on Human Rights and its Member States, 1950–2000* (OUP, Oxford, 2001), 68.

[147] See D Mullen, "Discrimination Law", in U Kilkelly (ed.) *ECHR and Irish Law* (Jordans, Bristol 2004) 217–242, 240. For similar views prior to incorporation of the ECHR into UK law, J Wadham and H Mountfield, *Blackstone's Guide to The Human Rights Act 1998* (Blackstone, London, 1999), 113: "the incorporation of Article 14 into United Kingdom law is, in itself, unlikely to add much to existing anti-discrimination law."

[148] S Livingstone, "Article 14 and the Prevention of Discrimination in the European Convention on Human Rights" (1997) 1 EHRLR 25.

[149] *Belgian Linguistic Case* (1979–80) 1 EHRR 252; *Abdulaziz, Cabales and Balkandali v The United Kingdom* (1985) 7 EHRR 471; see also L Wildhaber, "Protection Against Discrimination under the European Convention on Human Rights: A Second-class Guarantee?" (2002) 2 *Baltic Yearbook of International Law* 71.

[150] See U Khan, "Protocol 12 to the European Convention on Human Rights: A Step Forward or a Step Too Far?" (2001) *Public Law* 457.

[151] This stance can be criticised: the Protocol on its face appears to guarantee the same rights as are protected under Article 40.1, and non-ratification sends bad signals about the importance of this Protocol to other member states. For criticism of the UK's reluctance to sign and ratify Protocol 12, see N Grief, "Non-Discrimination under the European Convention on Human Rights: A Critique of the United Kingdom Government's Refusal to Sign and Ratify Protocol 12" (2002) *E.L.Rev.* 3.

[152] See e.g. the decision in *Dudgeon v UK* (1982) 4 EHRR 149, where the case was decided on the Article 8 arguments, with the majority of the Court finding that the Article 14 arguments did not require further analysis. See also Madden, "Discrimination Law", 221–222.

adjudicating on equality issues is remarkably similar to similar trends in Irish constitutional law. As discussed above, the Irish reluctance is probably attributable to the uncertain and muted role equality has in Irish political and legal debate in general: in the case of the Strasbourg court, it may reflect the diverse range of approaches across Europe to issues of equality.

This in turn, as with the Article 40.1 jurisprudence, has left important issues unresolved, or lacking clear definition. The test adopted by the Strasbourg court in adjudicating an Article 14 claim, where it is necessary for it do so, is to ask: a) whether the claim in question relates to an issue that comes within the "ambit" of one of the other Convention rights; b) whether there has been a difference in treatment of persons in similar situations; c) whether this difference in treatment is on one of the "suspect" grounds outlined in Article 14, that is, sex, race, colour, language, religion, political or other opinion, national or social origin, minority status, property, or birth, on the grounds of "other status"; and d) whether this difference of treatment was objectively justified, in the sense of satisfying the well-established Strasbourg proportionality analysis. What constitutes the "ambit" of another Convention right is notoriously unclear, and what remains hard to define: the Court's pronouncements on the point have often lacked precision.[153] Which individuals or groups will be deemed to be in a "similar situation" is also often uncertain, as is the extent to which indirect discrimination is covered.[154]

The grounds of discrimination that can trigger Article 14 are also unclear, in particular what constitutes "other status": the Strasbourg court has stated that Article 14 is a "non-exhaustive" guarantee, in that it is not confined in scope to a set amount of equality grounds, but has at times spoken of discrimination on the basis of a "personal characteristic".[155] This has periodically been interpreted by national courts as substantially restricting the scope of the guarantee, in the same way that the "human persons" phrase has been used at times in the Article 40.1 jurisprudence to narrow its scope.[156] In general, the trajectory of the Strasbourg equality jurisprudence has until recently quite similar to that of the Irish courts: a "process" approach is generally adopted, combining elements of the "formal equality" and "anti-discrimination" frameworks, but with some reluctance to invoke or to give real teeth to the equality guarantee.

Notwithstanding these limitations, it would be premature to write off the potential of the Convention to open up new avenues for challenging inequalities in the Irish legal context. To start with, the case-law of the Strasbourg court has given more

[153] For example, see the vague attempt to define the ambit of a right in *Petrovic v Austria* (1998) 4 BHRC 232, para. 28, "the subject matter of the disadvantage...constitutes one of the modalities of the exercise of a right guaranteed", or in the alternative, the measures complained of are "linked to the exercise of a right guaranteed".

[154] See Madden, 222–226.

[155] See e.g. *Magee v UK* [2000] ECHR 216, para. 50.

[156] See the decision of the UK House of Lords in *R (S) v Chief Constable of South Yorkshire* and *R (Marper) v Chief Constable of South Yorkshire* [2004] UKHL 39.

substantial content to other rights with considerable relevance in the equality context than has the Irish constitutional jurisprudence, in particular the Article 8 guarantee of personal privacy, home life and family life, as illustrated by *Norris v Ireland*.[157] Even with the underdeveloped state of the Convention equality jurisprudence, it is also apparent that more substantive weight is also placed upon the Article 14 equality right than has been the case with the Article 40.1 jurisprudence. This constitutes a substantial departure from the Irish case-law. It means that when it comes to balancing these rights against other values, the Convention scheme adopts a different weighing system than the Irish constitutional case-law, and existing Irish law may not fully comply with the Convention requirements.

For example, the decision in *Goodwin v UK*[158] has established that transsexuals have a right to official recognition of their gender change and therefore an entitlement to marry. This decision has already had an impact in Irish law, having been applied in the recent High Court decision in *Foy (No. 2)*, where the first declaration of incompatibility under the ECHR Act 2003 was issued in respect of the failure by the State to issue an amended birth certificate recognising Linda Foy's change of gender. Similarly, in *Karner v Austria*,[159] the Strasbourg court held that the denial of equal housing rights to lesbian and gay couples constitutes a breach of Articles 8 and 14, a decision followed by the House of Lords in applying the ECHR in *Ghaidan v Mendoza*.[160] Ireland may therefore be out of step by not giving some degree of legal recognition to same-sex couples, even if there is as yet no Convention requirement to introduce civil partnership legislation or the equivalent.[161]

The weight attached to the Article 8 right is also important in the equality context because of how the scope of this right can extend to protect against state interference with family life. For example, the European Court of Human Rights in *Connors v UK* held that public authorities may be obliged to take in account and give special consideration to the special needs of the Traveller community in exercising eviction powers.[162] The Court of Appeal in *First Secretary of State v Chichester District Council* applied this decision to restrain eviction proceedings being brought against a group of Travellers.[163] The subsequent House of Lords decision in *Price v Leeds* held that Article 8 of the Convention did not establish a right to a home *per se*,[164] but the

---

[157] See also the decisions in *Dudgeon v UK* (1981) 4 EHRR 149; *Smith and Grady v UK* (2000) 29 EHRR 493.

[158] *Goodwin v UK* (2002) ECHR 583

[159] (2003) 38 EHRR 528

[160] [2004] UKHL 30.

[161] See the analysis in J Walsh and F Ryan, *The Rights of* De Facto *Couples* (IHRC, Dublin, 2006), especially at 44–62.

[162] [2004] ECHR 223 (27 May 2004). For an analysis of the scope of positive obligations under the ECHR in general, see A Mowbray, *The Development of Positive Obligations under the European Convention on Human Rights by the European Court of Human Rights* (Hart, Oxford, 2004).

[163] [2004] EWCA Civ 1248. See also *Clarke v Secretary of State for the Environment* [2001] EWHC Admin 800.

[164] [2005] EWCA Civ 289.

Connors decision remains important in providing a degree against interference with the home life of members of the Traveller community. This shows the potential reach of Article 8, and how it could be used in the Irish context with some effectiveness.[165] Article 8, along with Article 3, is also been utilised in UK litigation to push for the provision of basic social services to disabled persons where extreme instances of state neglect are at issue.[166] It has also made its appearance in Irish law, with Laffoy J's decision in the recent case of *O'Donnell v South Dublin County Council*[167] that the living conditions of certain disabled members of the Traveller community violated Article 8.[168] These cases illustrate that the outer boundaries of the Convention rights remain to be explored through litigation, and real possibilities exist for new and innovative legal strategies to be deployed in using Convention rights to challenge unequal treatment.

It is also significant that forms of blatant discrimination rooted in a fundamental denial of equality of respect may fall foul of Article 3 of the Convention, with its prohibition on "inhuman and degrading treatment", even without coming within the ambit of another Convention right.[169] This remains a potential remedy in the case of serious discrimination. It may seem unlikely that Ireland would fall foul of an Article 3 finding in this context. However, note the English Court of Appeal decision in *R (Gezer) v Secretary of State for the Home Department*, where the Court of Appeal was prepared to consider that the severe racial abuse suffered by an asylum-seeker when moved to a Glasgow housing estate could constitute "inhuman and degrading treatment" for the purposes of Article 3, while being unwilling to find a breach by the state of its positive obligation to refrain from exposing individuals to such degrading treatment.[170] An Article 3 finding of discrimination amounting to degrading treatment would be a worst-case scenario, but it remains a fallback possibility.

---

[165] Connors will supplement and reinforce some existing approaches in Irish law: See the discussion in Whyte, *Social Inclusion and the Legal System*, Ch. 6.

[166] See e.g. *R (Bernard) v London Borough of Enfield* [2002] EWHC Admin 2282. See also the discussion in C O'Cinneide, "Socio-Economic Entitlements and the UK Rights Framework", paper delivered at the Conference on Economic, Social and Cultural Rights, 9 and 10 of December 2005, Croke Park, Dublin, available at http://www.ihrc.ie/_fileupload/banners/ESCRColmOCinneide1.doc (last accessed 10 January 2008).

[167] Unreported, Laffoy J, High Court, 22 May 2007.

[168] However see in contrast *Doherty v South Dublin County Council* [2007] IEHC 4, (22 January 2007).

[169] The European Commission for Human Rights established in the *East African Asians* case (1981) 3 EHRR 76 that the use of clear-cut racial or ethnic distinctions could constitute "inhuman and degrading treatment" and therefore violate Article 3. See also the recent decision of *Moldovan v Rumania*, App. No. 41138/98 and 64320/01, 12 July 2005.

[170] [2004] EWCA Civ 1730. The European Court of Human Rights has recognised that singling out of particular groups on the basis of their racial or ethnic origin can constitute degrading treatment in violation of Article 3: see *Moldovan v Rumania* (Application Nos. 41138/98 and 64320/01 (12 July 2005), *East African Asians v UK* (1973) 3 EHRR 76.

The European Court of Human Rights has also recently begun to expand and develop its Article 14 jurisprudence, and to place it on a firmer and more developed footing, due partially to new claims relating to discrimination against Roma in Eastern Europe. The Court has increasingly taken a wide interpretation of the "ambit" requirement.[171] The Strasbourg court in its case-law has also shown an increasing readiness to recognise indirect forms of discrimination as covered by Article 14, and to examine the effects of measures, rather than just the formal classifications used.[172] It also has established that the use of certain grounds of differentiation to distinguish between individuals and groups, such as race and gender would have to satisfy a very high threshold of justification: sexual orientation is one such "suspect" ground.[173] The Court is therefore developing a reasonably strong "anti-discrimination" approach in its jurisprudence. In *Connors v UK*, it even recognised that certain groups may require special treatment to reflect their special needs, which can be seen as representing the first glimmerings of a "substantive equality" approach. This shift in approach has been confirmed by the very significant recent decision of *D.H. v Czech Republic*, where the Grand Chamber of the Court held that the *de facto* segregation of Roma children in special schools violated Article 14, potentially opening up the scope of the Convention in new and dynamic ways.[174]

This gradual and tentative expansion of the Court"s Article 14 jurisprudence creates new room for legal challenges to inequalities. In the UK, Article 14 has generated a considerable volume of litigation, and taken with other articles of the Convention it has generated some very significant shifts in English and Scottish law. In particular, cases such as *Ghaidan v Mendoza*,[175] *Westminster City Council v Morris*[176] and *A v Secretary of State for the Home Department* (the "*Belmarsh*" decision)[177] have seen discriminatory distinctions which were deeply embedded in legislation found

---

171 In *Sidabras and Dziautas v Lithuania*, Application Nos 55480/00 and 59330/00, (27 October 2004), the ECHR considered that the imposition of severe and wide-ranging restrictions upon individuals taking up employment in the private sector could come within the ambit of Article 8, and therefore Article 14 could be triggered. Mantouvalou has suggested that this decision shows that the Strasbourg court "feels more competent to tackle discrimination". See V Mantouvalou, "Work and Private Life: *Sidabras and Dziautas v Lithuania*" (2005) 30(4) ELR 573, 581–82. See also the admissibility decision of *Stec v UK*, Application nos. 65731/01 and 65900/01, judgment of 5 September 2005, where the Grand Chamber of the European Court of Human Rights held that non-contributory social welfare benefits did come within the ambit of the right to property in Article 1 of Protocol 1, and therefore Article 14 could apply in this area, widening the potential applicability of the Convention's equality guarantee.

172 See *Thlimmenos v Greece* (2000) 29 EHRR 162.

173 See also the House of Lords decision in *R v Secretary of State for the Home Department, ex p. Carson* [2005] UKHL 37.

174 Application No. 57325/00 (13 November 2007).

175 [2004] UKHL 30.

176 [2005] EWCA Civ 1184.

177 [2004] UKHL 56.

to be incompatible with the Convention.[178] *Ghaidan* has been discussed above. However, *Morris* and *Belmarsh* are also significant decisions from an Irish perspective. In these cases, distinctions between national and non-nationals were subject to strict scrutiny under Article 14, and the UK public authorities maintaining these distinctions were unable to demonstrate objective justification for the discrimination against non-nationals. In general, Article 14 has proved to have more impact than was originally anticipated in the UK when the Human Rights Act 1998 was first introduced.

Therefore, while essentially running in parallel tracks to the Irish constitutional jurisprudence, the Convention case-law may offer new methods and routes for subjecting forms of inequality to close judicial scrutiny. In particular, by placing more substantive weight on the equality right and other equality-associated rights, it may complement and enhance the constitutional guarantees to a greater degree than currently expected, and give more tangible heft to the equality principle in Irish domestic law. In the recent decision of *G*, McKechnie J applied the right to family life protected in Article 8 of the ECHR and the prohibition on discrimination between married and unmarried parents recognised in the Convention case-law on Article 14 in finding that an unmarried father may have inchoate custody rights in relation to his children.[179] This decision flowed directly from the incorporation of the Convention into Irish law: the Irish constitutional jurisprudence does not at present require the recognition of such inchoate parental rights.[180] This decision, taken together with the *Foy (No. 2)* and *O'Donnell* judgments, may mark the moment at which the equality provisions of the ECHR begin to have a more active role within the Irish legal system.[181]

Equality and the Belfast Agreement — Equivalence or Footdragging?

One other important international obligation also needs to be considered. The Belfast Agreement contains significant commitments on the part of both the UK and Irish governments, as well as the other parties to the document, to implement

---

[178] The picture is not all positive. The UK courts are still struggling with Article 14, and the case-law that has emerged thus far has again been less than coherent. Often, some of the problems that have bedevilled the Article 40.1 jurisprudence, such as an excessive focus upon the purpose of the legislation rather than its actual effects, have surfaced in the UK's equality jurisprudence. See A Baker, "Comparison Tainted by Justification: Against A "Compendious Question" in Article 14 Discrimination" (2006) *Public Law* forthcoming; C O'Cinneide, "Fumbling Towards Coherence: The Slow Evolution of Equality and Anti-Discrimination Law in Britain" (2006) 57(1) *Northern Ireland Legal Quarterly* 57–101, 83–88.

[179] McKechnie J, High Court, Unreported, 11 September 2007.

[180] See *H.I. v M.G. (Child Abduction: Wrongful Removal)* [2000] 1 IR 110. For further analysis, see Geoffrey Shannon, "Unmarried Fathers" Stable Relationship with Children Must be Reflected in Law", *The Irish Times*, 13 October 2007.

[181] However, note the recent decision of the Supreme Court in *McD v L* [2009] IESC 81 (10 December 2009) and in particular the judgment of Murray CJ, who emphasised the "dualist" nature of the Irish legal system and concluded that the Convention itself was not directly applicable in Irish law, save for the limited remedies available against state bodies under the European Convention on Human Rights Act 2003.

measures to ensure the protection of human rights.[182] Some of these core human rights obligations relate to the equality principle that occupies an important place in the overall framework of the Agreement.[183] Both governments have entered into several binding commitments in the Agreement to enhance existing equality legislation. These commitments are reinforced by the Irish government's commitment in the Agreement to "further strengthen the protection of human rights in its jurisdiction", by bringing forward measures "to strengthen and underpin the constitutional protection of human rights", drawing upon the ECHR and other "international legal instruments in the field of human rights" to ensure "at least an equivalent level of protection of human rights as will pertain in Northern Ireland".[184] Therefore, Ireland is obliged to ensure equivalence in the effective protection of the spectrum of core fundamental rights that are set out in ratified international human rights instruments, including equality rights.[185]

It is possible to identify several areas where the equality principle is given higher levels of statutory protection in Northern Ireland than in the Republic, and therefore an issue of equivalence arises.[186] Some of the defects in the Republic's anti-discrimination legislation discussed below, in particular the cap on damages and the constitutional prohibition on service providers having to sustain more than "nominal" costs in making reasonable accommodation for disabled people, are not present in the Northern Irish legislation (which is narrower in scope in certain respects, but can be described as deeper in impact in others). The lack of civil partnership legislation in the Republic also raises an issue of lack of equivalence.[187]

However, the single most obvious lack of equivalence arises in respect of the absence in Ireland of any real equivalent to the adoption in Northern Ireland of a "substantive

[182] These commitments were reiterated in para. 8 and Annex B of the multi-party Agreement at St. Andrews, 13 October 2006, available at http://www.nio.gov.uk/st_andrews_ agreement.pdf (last accessed 21 November 2007).
[183] This is recognised in the general commitments made by the parties to respect "the right to equal opportunity in all social and economic activity, regardless of class, creed, disability, gender or ethnicity" and "the right of women to full and equal political participation". See Multi-Party Agreement, *Rights, Safeguards and Equality of Opportunity*, para. 1. See also Multi-Party Agreement, *Constitutional Issues*, (v). Colin Harvey has argued that "equality underpins any dialogic model of constitutionalism, for the existence for inequality has distorting effects…if there is a core value which underpins the Agreement, it is equality". See C Harvey, "Governing After the Rights Revolution" [2000] 27 (1) *Journal of Law and Society* 61–97, 81.
[184] Multi-Party Agreement, *Rights, Safeguards and Equality of Opportunity*, para. 9.
[185] In a Seanad debate, Minister Willie O'Dea TD expressed the view that Ireland's commitment to ensure an equivalence of human rights protection as applying in Northern Ireland did not extend to ensuring an equivalence of "equality provisions": see the Equality Bill 2004 [Seanad]: Report and Final Stages (1 July 2004). This interpretation would appear to be inconsistent with the Agreement's purpose and provisions. See C O'Cinneide, *Equivalence in Promoting Equality* (Equality Authority, Dublin, 2006), 32–34. For an excellent discussion of the Agreement's provisions concerning a potential charter of rights for the whole island of Ireland, see S Egan and R Murray, "A Charter of Rights for the Island of Ireland: An Unknown Quantity in the Good Friday/Belfast Agreement" (2007) 56 ICLQ 797–835.
[186] See O"Cinneide, *Equivalence in Promoting Equality*, Ch. 7 for more detail.
[187] *ibid.*

equality" approach to equality, by means of the introduction of positive equality duties upon public and private sector bodies.[188] It is increasingly recognised that individual-orientated reactive complaint procedures need to be reinforced by proactive steps to remove group disadvantages and of breaking down structural forms of discrimination.[189] Mainstreaming is the policy tool that has been extensively used in Ireland to implement this type of equality strategy in the public sector: various types of "proofing" initiatives have been used to attempt to address gender, ethnic, disability and poverty inequalities.[190] However, implementation of equality and poverty proofing in Ireland has suffered from a degree of lack of commitment, resources and follow-through.[191] The introduction of positive duties in Northern Ireland was intended to play a role in overcoming similar problems north of the border.[192]

Section 75 of the Northern Ireland Act 1998 now imposes a positive duty upon public bodies to implement measures to promote equality of opportunity across the anti-discrimination grounds. Similar duties have been introduced in Britain.[193] This relatively new form of positive action strategy involves the imposition of a statutory duty on public authorities to: a) eliminate unlawful discrimination; and b) to promote equality of opportunity in the performance of their functions.[194] In discharging this duty, public authorities are supposed to assess the impact that their practices and policies are having upon the goal of promoting equality of opportunity, and to take remedial action when necessary. Consultation with affected groups should also form a central part of this assessment process.[195] In contrast, equality proofing in Ireland lacks any real legal basis or enforcement dimension. This represents a significant lack

[188] See the Irish Human Rights Commission, *Observations on the Equality Bill 2004* (IHRC, Dublin, 2004), 6–7.

[189] For more on this, see S Fredman, "Equality: A New Generation?" (2001) 30 *Industrial Law Journal* 145–168.

[190] For some of the literature on this, see in particular Siobhan Mullally's analysis, in S Mullally, "Mainstreaming Equality in Ireland: A Fair and Inclusive Accommodation?" (2001) *Legal Studies* 99; *The National Anti-Poverty Strategy* (Stationery Office, Dublin, 1997); Government of Ireland (2002), *Building an Inclusive Society: Review of the National Anti-Poverty Strategy under the Programme for Prosperity and Fairness* (Department of Social, Community and Family Affairs, Dublin, 2002); S Mullally and O Smith, *Equality Proofing: Report of the Partnership 2000 Working Group* (Department of Justice, Equality and Law Reform, Dublin, 1999); The National Economic and Social Forum, *Partnership 2000: Development of the Equality Provisions*, Forum Opinion No. 1 (Stationery Office, Dublin, 1997); National Economic and Social Forum, *A Strategic Policy Framework for Equality Issues* (NESF Report No. 23, Dublin, March 2002).

[191] Equality Authority and Combat Poverty Agency, *Poverty & Inequality: Applying an Equality Dimension to Poverty Proofing* (Equality Authority and Combat Poverty Agency, Dublin, 2003), p 6.

[192] See C McCrudden, "Equality" in C Harvey (ed.), *Human Rights, Equality and Democratic Renewal In Northern Ireland*, (Hart, Oxford, 2001).

[193] C O'Cinneide, "Fumbling Towards Coherence: The Slow Evolution of Equality and Anti-Discrimination Law in Britain" (2006) 57(1) *Northern Ireland Legal Quarterly* 57–101, 89–94.

[194] See S Fredman, *Discrimination Law*, 176–195. See also C O'Cinneide, "Positive Duties and Gender Equality", *International Journal of Discrimination and the Law* (2005), 91–119; by the same author: "A New Generation of Equality Legislation? Positive Duties and Disability Rights", in A Lawson and C Gooding (eds.), *Disability Rights in Europe* (Hart, Oxford, 2005) 219–247.

[195] Fredman, *Discrimination Law*, 181–182.

of equivalence.[196] As legal duties, the Northern Irish duty and its British equivalents have some "bite", and are supported by enforcement mechanisms which involve the Northern Irish and British equality commissions. In contrast, the Irish "proofing" initiatives are just administrative guidelines.[197]

Positive duties can also be applied to the private sector, in the form of legislative duties requiring action on the part of certain private sector employers to monitor the composition and pay of their workforce and to take steps to remove any inequalities that arise. Such equality duties have been introduced with some success in the USA,[198] Canada,[199] Norway,[200] Sweden[201] and Northern Ireland,[202] often via "contract compliance" requirements, where private sector bodies contracting with public bodies are obliged as part of their contractual conditions to give effect to a positive duty approach.[203] It could be argued that no direct issue of relevance arises in respect of these duties as between Ireland and Northern Ireland, due to the Northern Irish private sector duty being concentrated upon securing equality between the Nationalist and Unionist communities.[204] However, the Equality Authority has called for some form of public and private sector duties to be introduced south of the border, both as a fulfilment of the need to ensure equivalence in respect of the public sector, and also because both sets of duties offer the possibility of encouraging positive action to break down patterns of inequality and exclusion.[205]

The positive duty mechanism is not a panacea. The Northern Ireland and British duties can give little guidance as to how important promoting equality of opportunity should be when competing considerations and values come into play, or what precisely constitutes promoting equality of opportunity. There is also a danger that complying with the duties will become a purely bureaucratic process, where public authorities and employers treat the duty as merely involving complying with a set of bureaucratic "tick-box" requirements, while maintaining

---

196 C O'Cinneide, *Equivalence in Promoting Equality* (Equality Authority, Dublin, 2006), 50–55.

197 Note however the uncertain extent of the legal obligation that the duties actually impose upon public authorities, and the inherent difficulties of enforcing these duties, discussed in C O'Cinneide, "Fumbling Towards Coherence: The Slow Evolution of Equality and Anti-Discrimination Law in Britain", 89–94.

198 For an analysis of the US use of contract compliance initiatives in the race context, see PE Morris, "Legal Regulation of Contract Compliance: An Anglo-American Comparison" (1991) 19 *Anglo-American Law Review* 87–144, 87–90.

199 See HC Jain, PJ Sloane and FM Horwitz, *Employment Equity and Affirmative Action: An International Comparison* (ME Sharpe, London, 2003), 22–27.

200 See K Mile, "Mainstreaming Equality – Models for a Statutory Duty", in *Mainstreaming Equality: Models for a Statutory Duty – Conference Report* (Equality Authority, Dublin, 2003), available at www.equality.ie.

201 Equal Opportunities Act 1991: see http://www.ilo.org/public/english/employment/gems/eeo/law/sweden/l_eoas.htm (last accessed 22 November 2003).

202 C McCrudden, R Ford, A Heath, "Legal Regulation of Affirmative Action in Northern Ireland: An Empirical Assessment" (2004) 24 (3) OJLS 363–415.

203 See also See C McCrudden, "Using Public Procurement to Achieve Social Outcomes" (2004) 28(4) *Natural Resources Forum* 257–267.

204 See O'Cinneide, *Equivalence in Promoting Equality*, 55–58.

205 See Crowley, *An Ambition for Equality*, 108–114.

the illusion of real change.[206] The duties may become no more than a technocratic tool in policymaking and human resources, which can be readily co-opted to maintain existing practices.[207] The positive duty mechanisms that exist concentrate upon "discrimination" grounds of inequality: poverty-related inequalities are often not directly targeted, although there is some discussion as to how the duty mechanism could be utilised to combat socio-economic based exclusion.[208]

Nevertheless, positive duties could have considerable symbolic and educative potential. Designed to give effect to a "substantive equality" approach, the duty mechanism recognises that unconscious, structural or institutional forms of discrimination exist, and that some form of special and directed action is needed to minimise these forms of inequality.[209] They also can serve as useful "pressure points" to demand greater focus upon equality issues from public authorities: public authorities and employers can be called to account for how they have complied with the duty, and pressed to demonstrate progress.[210] On balance, the duty mechanism has considerable potential.

The equivalence requirement contained in the Belfast Agreement opens the door for a strong political case to be made for the introduction of some form of positive public sector duty, at least. It also highlights some of the deficiencies that exist in Irish legislation, and most importantly, demonstrates the need for a serious look at whether Ireland needs to introduce an element of "substantive equality" in how it conceptualises and gives effect to the equality principle in law. As with international human rights law, the Agreement's equivalence provisions could play an indirect role in litigation in Ireland. The Supreme Court has been open to using the ECHR and other international instruments in interpreting the scope of constitutional rights:[211] this leaves open the possibility that the Agreement and international

---

[206] See O'Cinneide, "Positive Duties and Gender Equality", *International Journal of Discrimination and the Law* (2005) 91–119, 104.

[207] Maria Stratigaki has argued that at the level of the EU institutions, the adoption of mainstreaming measures is often used to neutralise or defer the adoption of other forms of positive action measures. See M Stratigaki, "Gender Mainstreaming Vs Positive Action", 12(2) *European Journal of Women"s Studies* 165–186.

[208] See G McKeever and F Ni Aoláin, "Thinking Globally, Acting Locally: Enforcing Socio-Economic Rights in Northern Ireland" [2004] *European Human Rights Law Review* 158. For a more sceptical perspective, see C McCrudden, "Mainstreaming Human Rights", in C Harvey (ed.) *Human Rights in the Community: Rights as Agents for Change* (Hart, Oxford, 2005).

[209] The existence of a duty may also serve to compel public authorities to adopt equality initiatives even where the perception exists that inequality is no longer a "real problem": for the dangers associated with this perception, see D Rhode, "The "No-Problem" Problem: Feminist Challenges and Cultural Change" (1991) 100 *Yale LJ* 1731.

[210] In an important judgment in the English case of *R(Elias) v Secretary of State for Defence* [2005] IRLR 788, Elias J held that a failure to consider whether a particular policy raised issues relating to racial equality, or to assess whether any adverse impact was possible, or to consider what steps might be necessary to eliminate any negative impact, would breach the duty to promote racial equality imposed upon British public authorities by the Race Relations (Amendment) Act 2000.

[211] See *State (Healy) v Donoghue* [1976] IR 325, 351; *O'Leary v Attorney-General* [1993] 1 IR 102.

human rights law could be used as persuasive authority in the process in interpreting and applying Article 40.1 and other legal provisions.[212] This could indirectly lead to a greater willingness to adopt "substantive equality" analysis in constitutional and administrative case-law.

However, perhaps more importantly, the equivalence requirement raises quite far-reaching questions for Ireland: if Northern Ireland has gone down the substantive equality route, why has the Republic remained committed to a more cautious combination of "formal equality" and "anti-discrimination" approaches to equality, notwithstanding its constitutional commitment to equality and the central place of equality in the national self-perception?[213]

Conclusion

How to give effect to the equality principle will always generate controversy. Contemporary Ireland is no exception to this rule. Equality has tended to be both venerated as a fundamental constitutional and political principle, and also often given a subordinate status to other values and principles. Irish law has rarely blazed a trail in the field of equality: the equality principle has been often subordinated in law and policy since 1922. However, this sidelining of equality sits uncomfortably with the central place formally given to equality in the Irish constitutional scheme of values, and the scope of the Article 40.1 equality guarantee. It is perhaps time to look again at how the equality principle should be defined and applied in Irish law.

Shifts in EC law, the requirements of international human rights law, the ongoing evolution of the ECHR jurisprudence, and the equivalence requirement built into the Belfast Agreement all suggest that it is perhaps time for more space to be given to "substantive equality" approaches to equality. Nor is this prodding solely a matter of external influences. Human rights norms are often presented both by their advocates and their detractors as alien arrivals into the Irish constitutional and political order. However, the inherent logic of the 1937 Constitution, its commitment to shaping a new constitutional order based upon human dignity and equality, and the type of state that Ireland aspires to be all point in a similar direction. Also, recent controversies about schooling places in Dublin and Garda headgear show that serious consideration has to be given quickly to how the equality principle should be given effect in a fast-changing society: equality is no longer an issue that can be left on the back-burner while more pressing issues of national development are given priority. It is time to reconsider anew what "cherishing all of the children of the nation equally" should mean in contemporary and fast-changing Ireland, and to contemplate moving beyond current approaches to equality in the Irish legal system.

---

[212] However, note that the Supreme Court in *O'Neill and Quinn v Governor of Castlerea Prison* [2004] IESC 7 (29 January 2004) reaffirmed their earlier decision in *Doherty v Governor of Portlaoise Prison* [2002] 2 IR 252 that the Agreement did not confer any individual rights in Irish law and was not incorporated within domestic law.

[213] Note also that the ongoing discussions about the proposed Bill of Rights for Northern Ireland may have considerable implications for Ireland due to the existence of the equivalence requirement, if a final text of the Bill is agreed and adopted. See O'Cinneide, *Equivalence in Promoting Equality*, 63–64.

Why is it so Difficult to Promote a Human Rights–Based Approach to Immigration?

Ciara Smyth*

Introduction

Ireland's swift transition from being a country of net emigration to a country of net immigration understandably caught policy-makers by surprise. The response was a flurry of legislation in the area of immigration control and the *ad hoc* development of administrative practice regulating labour migration into the country.[1] The result was somewhat chaotic: legislation that was piece-meal and reactive and leaned heavily towards the control (rather than the management) of immigration; and administrative practice that was difficult to navigate and characterised by legal uncertainty. This led to calls for a revised immigration system, to which the government has lately begun to respond.[2] In 2006, a new Employment Permits Act was passed, codifying some administrative practice regulating labour migration. Earlier this year, following a protracted gestation, the government published a new Immigration, Residence and Protection Bill, the aim of which is to consolidate or amend many aspects of existing immigration law.[3] Also, the first comprehensive piece of anti-trafficking legislation — the Criminal Law (Human Trafficking) Act 2008 — was passed.

---

* Lecturer in law, National University of Ireland, Galway. Visiting Researcher and Lecturer at the Institute of Immigration Law, University of Leiden, The Netherlands. I would like to thank Pieter Boeles for his comments on an earlier draft of this article.

[1] For immigration control legislation see the Immigration Acts 1999, 2003, 2004, the Illegal Immigrants (Trafficking) Act 2000 and the Employment Permits Act 2003; labour migration was facilitated through two administrative schemes, namely, the Employment Permit Scheme and the Work Visa / Authorisation Scheme. A skeletal legislative foundation for these schemes was provided in the Employment Permits Act 2003. Since entry into force of the Employment Permits Act 2006, these schemes have been replaced by a Green Card Scheme and a Work Permit Scheme.

[2] See Submissions on the Public Consultation on Immigration Policy, 2002, available on www.justice.ie.

[3] The current Immigration, Residence and Protection Bill was preceded by a bill of the same name which was published and lapsed in 2007. In 2005, a Discussion Document entitled *Immigration and Residence in Ireland, Outline Policy Proposals for an Immigration and Residence Bill* was published by the Department of Justice, Equality and Law Reform. This, in turn, was preceded by a Public Consultation on Immigration Policy conducted in 2002.

These legislative initiatives have elicited a robust response from a number of organisations with a mandate in or relating to the area of immigration.[4] In general, the initiatives have been welcomed but concern has been expressed about the need for, and apparent failure to adopt, a "human rights-based" approach to managing immigration. A rights-based approach can be broadly described as one that places a concern for the human rights of migrants at the centre of law and policy, although not necessarily to the exclusion of other legitimate factors, such as security or the maintenance of executive discretion or flexibility.[5] The difficulties in promoting a rights-based approach can be seen in the lack of discernible difference between the central features of prior existing law and policy and the new legislative package. In this regard, the new initiatives are noteworthy for their failure to grapple meaningfully with the concerns about human rights that have long been expressed in relation to the immigration system.

It would be to some extent proper to lay the blame at the government's door by asserting, in answer to the question posed by this article, that the reason it is so hard to promote a rights-based approach to immigration is precisely because the government is so resistant to such an approach. However, this is (rightfully so) well worn territory and hence not the primary aim of this article. The central aim is rather to examine to what extent human rights law *itself* is resistant to the particular needs of immigrants. The skepticism at work here is not novel: human rights law typically delivers less than the normative rhetoric underpinning such law would have us believe, drafted and agreed as it is by States that, predictably, seek to limit their sovereign powers as little as possible. Since immigration is a defining aspect of State sovereignty, if not *the* defining aspect, it should come as little surprise that human rights law and jurisprudence is rather muted when it comes to the treatment of immigrants. Moreover, contemporary forms of immigration and immigration regulation are new and human rights law is still catching up, both in terms of developing appropriate rights and in applying existing rights to new situations. Finally, some aspects of immigration management raise issues that are at the difficult and almost intractable edge of human rights law.

If it is the case that human rights in the immigration context are not as robust as might be supposed, this presents a challenge to advocates of a rights based approach,

[4] On the 2005 Employment Permits Bill (later enacted) see Immigrant Council of Ireland, *Briefing Note on the Proposed Employment Permits Bill 2005: All Change or Not Really Very Much?*; and Immigrant Council of Ireland, *Briefing Note 2 of the Employment Permits Bill 2005: Recommended Amendments for Committee Stage of Debate*. On the 2008 Immigration, Residence and Protection Bill see Immigrant Council of Ireland, *Analysis of the Immigration, Residence and Protection Bill 2008 (as initiated) And Suggested Amendments*, April 2008; Irish Human Rights Commission, *Observations of the Immigration, Residence and Protection Bill 2008*, March 2008. On the Bill which preceded the 2008 Bill, see Migrant Rights Centre Ireland, *Immigration, Residence and Protection Heads of Bill*, October 2006.

[5] See Irish Human Rights Commission and National Consultative Committee on Racism and Interculturalism, *Safeguarding the Rights of Migrant Workers and their Families, A Review of EU and International Human Rights Standards: Implications for Policy in Ireland*, April 2004.

because the problem is not so much non-compliance with the letter as with the spirit of human rights law. As can be readily appreciated, it is harder to advocate for immigrants on the basis of normative principles than positive law. This point will be dealt with in the conclusion. But first the article will test the ability of human rights law to provide a meaningful response to key immigration dilemmas. The recent and proposed immigration reforms provide the context for identifying those dilemmas. The article proceeds from a number of (sometimes overlapping) propositions about the shortcomings of human rights law in the context of immigration, namely that:

- The relevant right is too qualified to be helpful;
- A link to the relevant right is too hard to establish;
- A specific immigration exception has been carved into the relevant right;
- The standard set in relation to the relevant right is too low to be meaningful;
- The relevant right is too new to be useful;
- Only "soft law" governs the area;
- The relevant right or its violation is, arguably, another country or entity's responsibility.[6]

The Right is Too Qualified to be Helpful

A striking aspect of the Irish immigration system (and indeed the immigration systems of most countries in the "developed" world) is that it treats different groups of people differently. The central distinction, dealt with later, is between nationals and non-nationals. But a myriad of distinctions are made between different groups of non-nationals: between EU citizens who enjoy extensive rights of free movement throughout the union and "third country nationals" who do not;[7] between third country nationals who are family members of EU citizen migrants and are therefore privileged and third country nationals who have no such family connections;[8] between non-nationals on the visa "black list" and non-nationals who do not require a visa to come to Ireland[9]; between high-skilled migrants whom the system treats relatively well and lower-skilled migrants who are treated less well[10]; between

[6] The focus here is on immigration, as distinct from asylum, and the use of the terms "non-national" and "immigrant" are intended to connote "third country nationals", or non-EU/EEA nationals.

[7] Compare Title III of the Treaty establishing the European Community (TEC) and secondary legislation governing free movement of EU citizens with Title IV of the TEC and secondary legislation governing movement of third country nationals.

[8] See Directive 2004/38/EC on the right of citizens of the Union and their family members to move and reside freely within the territory of the Member States. "Family members" include third country national family members. See the judgment of the European Court of Justice in Case C-127/08, *Metock and Others v Minister of Justice, Equality and Law Reform.*

[9] The Immigration Act 2004 (Visas) (No.2) Order 2006 (SI No. 657 of 2006) establishes a visa "white list" – a list of countries whose citizens do not require a visa to enter the State. The "black list" is thereby established by default. It is determined by whether Ireland (or indeed the UK, given the Common Travel Area) is a destination country for migrants from that State, especially forced migrants and irregular migrants.

[10] Note, for example, the different family reunification rights of holders of Green Card Permits and holders of Work Permits, dealt with in section D below.

regular migrants, who certainly have rights, and irregular migrants, whose rights under the 2008 Bill are to be limited to core rights.[11]

To the uninitiated, these many distinctions might seem to offend the principle of non-discrimination, broadly defined as:

> "...any distinction, exclusion, restriction or preference which is based on any ground such as race, colour, sex, language, religion, political or other opinion, national or social origin, property, birth or other status, and which has the purpose or effect of nullifying or impairing the recognition, enjoyment or exercise by all persons, *on an equal footing*, of all rights and freedoms."[12]

Unfortunately, the non-discrimination principle is more complex than it appears and, as a result, its application to certain immigration decisions is limited. Furthermore, it has been developed jurisprudentially in a way that, advertently or inadvertently, has placed some immigration decisions beyond scrutiny, or, at best, difficult to argue.

On the complexity issue, it is important to note that there are actually two non-discrimination principles. First, there is the subordinate non-discrimination principle, found, for example, in Article 14 of the European Convention on Human Rights (ECHR) and Article 2 of the International Covenant on Civil and Political Rights (ICCPR). This right prohibits discrimination in the enjoyment of *other* convention rights, and has no independent existence. As there is no right to migrate in either the ECHR or the ICCPR (or any other internationally recognised document for that matter), decisions relating to entry and expulsion are beyond the reach of the subordinate non-discrimination principle, unless, of course, they also implicate another substantive right.

Second, there is the autonomous non-discrimination or free-standing equality principle found both in new Protocol 12 ECHR (which Ireland has not yet ratified) and in Article 26 ICCPR. This right requires that whenever a State regulates a particular area, even if that area is ostensibly unconnected to human rights, it must do so in a non-discriminatory manner. At first glance, this would appear to outlaw discrimination in the making or applying of immigration law. However, in the area of pre-entry decisions and border control, the right comes up against the territorial scope of human rights law, which generally applies to "everyone within the jurisdiction."[13] Visa applicants are, by necessity, outside the jurisdiction. Non-nationals who present at the border have not yet been admitted to the State, under

[11] See for example s 6 – *Non-entitlement to services of foreign nationals unlawfully present*.

[12] Human Rights Committee, General Comment 18, para.7. This definition is taken from the Convention on the Elimination of Racial Discrimination and applied by the HRC to Article 26 ICCPR. Emphasis added.

[13] The complex issue of the extraterritorial application of the ECHR has not been definitively settled by the court: compare the admissibility decision *Bankovic and others v Belgium*, ECtHR 12 December 2001, application no. 52207/99, with the judgment *Issa and others v Turkey*, ECtHR 16 November 2004, application no. 31821/96.

the legal fiction of the "international zone" — a fiction, incidentally, that has not been completely accepted by the European Court of Human Rights (ECtHR).[14] Therefore, the drawing up of visa black lists, the making of decisions about who on the black list should be granted a visa, and the refusal of permission to enter at the border are insulated from the non-discrimination principle.

As for the jurisprudential development of the non-discrimination right, it is useful to focus on the Article 14 case law of the ECtHR, since it is the most developed and has greatly influenced the interpretation of the relevant provisions of the ICCPR by its monitoring body, the Human Rights Committee (HRC). Three "hurdles" have to be jumped in order to successfully argue a case of discrimination.

First, the discrimination must be linked to a ground such as "sex, race, colour, language, religion, political or other opinion, national or social origin, association with a national minority, property, birth or other status." Although nationality/alienage is not listed, the grounds are indeterminate, so it is relatively straightforward to argue discrimination on the basis of having the status of a non-national.[15] It is, however, more difficult to argue that distinctions *between* different groups of non-nationals are based on race. This was the argument advanced in the landmark case of *Abdulaziz, Cabales and Balkandali v UK*.[16] In this case, three women resident in the UK sought to bring their husbands to live with them, but were unsuccessful because they fell into a category of non-national wives to which very strict rules regarding family reunification applied. On the question of whether this constituted racial discrimination, the Court held:

> "That mass immigration against which the rules were directed consisted mainly of would-be immigrants from the New Commonwealth and Pakistan, and that as a result they affected at the material time fewer white people than others, is not a sufficient reason to consider them racist in character: it is an effect which derives not from the content of the ... rules but from the fact that, among those wishing to immigrate, some ethnic groups outnumbered others."[17]

This outcome may be partially attributable to the fact that the case involved an allegation of indirect discrimination — always more difficult to establish, although the Court has dealt positively with indirect discrimination cases in other contexts.[18] In any event, *Abdulaziz* has effectively added to the legal difficulties in challenging visa black lists and other pre-entry decisions.

Second, as established by the Court in the *Belgian Linguistics* case,[19] not every difference in treatment amounts to discrimination, since states "are frequently

[14] See *Amuur v France* [1996] 22 EHHR 553.
[15] For example, *Gaygusuz v Austria* [1997] 23 EHHR 364.
[16] [1985] 7 EHRR 471.
[17] *ibid*, at para. 85.
[18] See, for example, *Thlimmenos v Greece* [2001] 31 EHRR 411. For commentary on the issue, see R. Wintemute, '"Within the Ambit': How Big Is the 'Gap' in Article 14 European Convention on Human Rights?" 4 *European Human Rights Law Review* 2004.
[19] [1979-80] 1 EHRR 252.

confronted with situations and problems which, on account of differences inherent therein, call for different legal solutions."[20] In other words, equals should be treated equally and unequals unequally. But, as Aristotle said: "equals and unequals *in what*?"[21] The risk is that the Court will use the very difference in treatment complained of to conclude that the allegedly equivalent situations are not equivalent at all and, hence, that there has been no discrimination.[22] This risk is particularly acute in the immigration context where categorisations abound, as the following case illustrates.

In *Moustaquim v Belgium*,[23] a non-national faced deportation from Belgium following a string of criminal offences committed while a minor. He successfully argued that his deportation would violate Article 8 in that it would interfere with his right to respect for family life. However, he also argued that because "third country nationals" were treated more harshly under Belgian law than EU citizens in deportation matters, this constituted discrimination contrary to Article 14 in conjunction with Article 8. The Court disposed summarily of the latter argument by stating:

> "...Article 14 safeguards individuals placed in similar situations from any discriminatory differences of treatment in the enjoyment of the rights and freedoms recognised in the Convention and its Protocols...As for the preferential treatment given to nationals of the other Member States of the Communities, there is objective and reasonable justification for it, as Belgium belongs, together with those States, to a special legal order."[24]

Apart from the objection that the Court confuses the question of whether there is a distinction between similarly situated individuals, with the separate question of whether the distinction is justified (see below), this finding can be criticised for failing to engage with the question of whether third country national migrants are *really* in an analogous or a different situation to EU citizen migrants.[25] The judgment would appear to place immigration classifications beyond scrutiny.

---

[20] *ibid,* at para 10.

[21] Aristotle, *Politics*, Book V.

[22] For more on this, see A. Bayefsky, "The Principle of Equality or Non-Discrimination in International Law", 11 *Human Rights Law Journal* 1990.

[23] [1991] 13 EHRR 802.

[24] *ibid,* at para 49.

[25] If we understand the applicant's argument as a syllogism, where X = EU citizens, Y = third country nationals, and Z = migrants, then the applicant's position is as follows:

> X and Y are in the same category Z
> The law governing Z treats X and Y differently
> Therefore the law governing Z is discriminatory

As a matter of logic, in order to refute this argument, it is necessary to show that X and Y are not in the same category Z, or that Z is not the correct category to assess. The court does neither explicitly, although it does the second implicitly. The lack of reasoning by the court is arguably not good enough in a context where discrimination is rife.

Third, the *Belgian Linguistics* case also established that a distinction will not amount to discrimination if it has an objective and reasonable justification, i.e. where there is a legitimate aim and a reasonable relationship of proportionality between the means used to achieve it and the aim itself. Since immigration is a defining aspect of state sovereignty today, the control of immigration for economic, social or security reasons is a justification likely to be readily accepted by the Court as objective and reasonable. So decisions turn mainly on the proportionality issue and in this regard states enjoy a considerable margin of appreciation. This is not to suggest that the Court never finds immigration distinctions to be disproportionate. In fact it demonstrates particular vigilance when a classically suspect ground of discrimination appears to be at issue, as illustrated by the *Abdulaziz* case, which succeeded on the ground of sex discrimination. But the apparent foreclosure of race as an arguable ground in the context of immigration decisions in the same case suggests that the Court may be less alert to disproportionality in the normal course of events.

A Link to the Right is Too Hard to Establish

Having discussed the difficulties in arguing discrimination in the context of distinctions between non-nationals, let us now turn to the question of equality between nationals and non-nationals. At one level, Ireland has made appreciable progress in enacting legislation to provide for the formal equality of nationals and non-nationals[26] and in establishing institutions to monitor and combat racism and xenophobia.[27] But simultaneously, it is possible to discern counter-productive actions on the part of the state that lead to racism and discrimination against non-nationals by the local population. Three aspects of the current/proposed immigration system will be used to illustrate this phenomenon — the exploitation of migrant workers; the lack of an integration policy; and the stereotyping and vilification of immigrants — before the human rights position is assessed.

On the first point, the exploitation of migrant workers is, to an extent, facilitated by the rules relating to work permits for low-skilled workers. Under the administrative scheme that pertained until 2007, the employment permit was granted to the employer for one year, was held by the employer and was renewable at the request of the employer.[28] The employee's legal status in the country was completely dependent on the permit and he/she was not free to move to another job even within the sector. This led to many documented cases of abuse, for example: passing the cost of the permit on to the employee; paying the employee below minimum wage or average industrial wage for the sector; forcing the employee to work long

[26] For example, the Employment Equality Act 1998 and the Equal Status Act 2000 as amended by the Equality Act 2004.

[27] The National Consultative Committee on Racism and Interculturalism was established in 1998, the Equality Authority was established in 1999 and the Irish Human Rights Commission was established under the terms of the Good Friday Agreement in 2001.

[28] This scheme had no statutory basis, except in the negative: under the Employment Permits Act 2003, it was an offence to employ a non-national or be employed as a non-national without an employment permit.

hours; refusing annual leave; refusing holiday pay etc.[29] The Employment Permits Act 2006 transfers ownership of the permit to the employee, a partial solution only as the person holding the permit is still generally tied to a particular employer.[30]

The exploitation of foreign workers is only one dimension of racial discrimination experienced by immigrants. Instances of racism at the hands of the local population, including racist violence, have been well documented over the years.[31] This brings me to the second point — the lack of an integration policy. A systematic response to exploitation and racism requires the development of a comprehensive integration policy, or package of measures designed both to help non-nationals adjust to life in Ireland and assist public bodies and the public in general to adjust to the presence of non-nationals in the State. A central criticism of the current immigration system is the lack of a coherent integration policy. The 2008 Bill is reminiscent of earlier immigration legislation it its failure to address *at all* the issue of integration.[32] Admittedly, a Minister of State with responsibility for integration, under the auspices of three Government departments, was appointed in 2007. However, while the Minister has responded *post hoc* to certain issues that relate to integration[33] there is no sign, to date, of the development of an overall integration policy. There has been no consultation document, White Paper or other document that would signal the development of a comprehensive or strategic policy.

On the third point, a key component of racism is the stereotyping of foreigners as behaving differently and having different moral qualities from the local population. The stereotype then legitimates treating foreigners differently. The fact that immigration law to date has leaned towards control and enforcement feeds into the stereotype of immigrants as "different" or even "undesirable". Documents that preceded the current version of the Immigration, Residence and Protection Bill also displayed a tendency to stereotype. For example, the 2005 Government Discussion Document on a proposal for an immigration and residence bill, stated:

> "[The immigration system] plays an important role in protecting the State and its citizens from those who seek to abuse our immigration systems, such as people

---

[29] See for example, Immigrant Council of Ireland, *Labour Migration into Ireland: Study and Recommendations on Employment Permits, Working Conditions, Family Reunification and the Integration of Migrant Workers in Ireland*, 2003.

[30] Only if the foreign national has applied for the employment permit him/herself, can he/she move employment within the sector; if — as is more likely to be the case — the application is made by the employer, the foreign national is tied to the particular employer for at least 12 months.

[31] See the National Consultative Committee on Racism and Interculturalism's *Six Monthly Incidents Reports* on www.nccri.ie.

[32] This omission is all the more striking because one of the key preparatory documents leading to the government's 2005 Discussion Document, namely IOM's *International Comparative Study of Migration Legislation and Practice*, 2002, contains a chapter on integration. However, this chapter was included on the insistence of IOM and was not requested by the Government when it commissioned the report from IOM.

[33] For example, the issue of whether the Department of Education and Science or individual school boards of management should devise a policy on the wearing of the hijab.

> traffickers with links to organised crime, and terrorists. The immigration system must therefore play the dual roles of being welcoming to bona fide visitors and also of deterring those with malevolent intentions in seeking to come to Ireland."[34]

This crude assertion that the immigrant population, stereotypically, includes criminals and subversives is not based on any known data and is likely to be no more or less true than any assumptions made about the general population. Indeed, those who engage in people-trafficking are not necessarily immigrants themselves. The supposed dichotomy between *bona fide* "visitors" (note the connotation of short-term presence) and those with malevolent intentions does not withstand scrutiny if the latter are supposed to denote irregular immigrants, since one-time regular migrants (or *bona fide* "visitors") can and do find themselves in positions of irregularity through no fault of their own. What is particularly unfortunate about statements of this kind is the conflation of immigrants with terrorists, something which is harder to contest since the UN Security Council passed Resolution 1373 in the immediate aftermath of "September 11".[35]

These three points illustrate the causal link between state action, on the one hand, and racism and xenophobia on the part of the local population, on the other. While this link may be evident from a common sense perspective, as a matter of law it is almost impossible to sustain an allegation that state action is itself racist.[36] As a leading Irish commentator has noted:

> "...the issue is no longer constructed purely as a "racial" conflict but is often portrayed as a clash between allegedly irreconcilable cultures. The substitution of a discourse of explicit racism by one of cultural exclusion and/or rejection has if anything further complicated the debate."[37]

Human rights law erects its own obstacles to counteracting state discrimination against non-nationals. First, there is a procedural obstacle. Human rights enforcement mechanisms are established primarily to deal with individual complaints. And while the institutionalised aspect of state discrimination may be introduced in evidence in support of a given complaint, there is little scope for group actions in which the institutionalised aspect is at the core of the complaint. There are, of course, monitoring mechanisms to investigate gross and widespread

[34] Discussion Document, *supra* n 3 at p 7.

[35] The resolution calls on all States to "(p)revent the movement of terrorists or terrorist groups by effective border controls and controls on issuance of identity documents and travel documents, and through measures for preventing counterfeiting, forgery, or fraudulent use of identity papers and travel documents." The link in the resolution between terrorism and asylum is even more damning.

[36] Also, as a matter of strategy, such an allegation may well be counter-productive. Recall the government and public reaction to the 2001 Amnesty International advertisement suggesting that the Taoiseach was racist. Furthermore, in the skewed politics of immigration, an allegation of racism is likely to be met by a counter-allegation of playing the "race card."

[37] P MacEinri, "The implications for Ireland the UK arising from the development of recent EU policy on migration", available on http://migration.ucc.ie/schengencta.htm.

violations of human rights but the threshold is usually too high to permit scrutiny of "ordinary" institutionalised discrimination (i.e. forms of institutionalised discrimination short of apartheid). Second, and perhaps more importantly, there is a substantive obstacle. Thus, what should be a hugely important treaty in context of immigration — the Convention on the Elimination of Racial Discrimination (CERD) — expressly excludes discrimination against non-nationals from its scope. Article 1(2) states that the Convention "shall not apply to distinctions, exclusions, restrictions or preferences made by a State Party to this Convention between citizens and non-citizens." This leaves the Committee on the Elimination of Racial Discrimination in the unenviable position of trying to interpret Article 1(2), *pace* its explicit wording, in the light of other, less exclusionary human rights obligations. Thus, in its *General Recommendation 30 on Discrimination Against Non-Citizens*, the Committee stated:

> "Article 5 of the Convention incorporates the obligation of States Parties to prohibit and eliminate racial discrimination in the enjoyment of civil, political, economic, social and cultural rights...States Parties are under an obligation to guarantee equality between citizens and non-citizens in the enjoyment of these rights *to the extent recognised under international law*."[38]

Essentially, there is a central contradiction at the heart of the Convention, i.e. the elimination of racial discrimination except in the area of nationality / alienage which, itself, is a source of contemporary racial discrimination recognised by the Committee.[39]

A Specific Immigration Exception has been Carved into the Right

Perhaps the single biggest criticism of the Irish immigration system — actual and proposed — is the lack of procedural guarantees it affords immigrants. Existing rules relating to the whole range of immigration decisions (pre-entry decisions about visas, decisions about permission to enter at the border, decisions about residence permits, decisions about Green Card Permits and Work Permits, decisions about family reunification and removal from the State) are either not specified in legislation or are drafted at such a broad level of generality as to be open-ended. Decision-makers are vested with wide-ranging discretionary powers. Decisions are

[38] CERD, General Recommendation 30, Discrimination against Non-Citizens, UN Doc. CERD/C/64/Misc.11/rev.3 (2004) at para 3. Emphasis added.

[39] The preamble to General Recommendation 30 recalls "the Durban Declaration in which the World Conference against Racism, Racial Discrimination, Xenophobia and Related Intolerance recognised that xenophobia against non-nationals, particularly migrants, refugees and asylum seekers, constitutes one of the main sources of contemporary racism and that human rights violations against members of such groups occur widely in the context of discriminatory, xenophobic and racist practices." Despite the textual limitations of the Convention, the Committee on the Elimination of Racial Discrimination recently criticized Ireland for fostering/failing to counter racism and discrimination by the general public. See Conclusions and recommendations of the Committee on the Elimination of Racial Discrimination, Ireland, U.N. Doc. CERD/C/IRL/CO/2 (2005).

either not reviewable or subject to internal review only and the power of the courts to review immigration decisions has been significantly curtailed by the legislature.[40] While the 2008 Bill consolidates the previous rules and elaborates on some of them, it contains little substantive change on what went before. The establishment of an independent body to review immigration decisions is resisted. Just as before, such decisions as are amenable to review are to be reviewed internally. There does not appear to be a principled distinction between those that are reviewable and those that are not.[41] Remarkably, the Bill provides for the summary removal of a foreign national from the State where he/she "appears" to be unlawfully present, without providing any procedural guarantees.[42]

The lack of procedural guarantees cannot be explained away by reference to the lack of a right to migrate. By analogy, one may have no right to a particular job, but one might legitimately expect fairness in the selection procedure. It goes without saying that due process guarantees are recognised in human rights law. In fact, certain procedural rights apply specifically to non-nationals, such as guarantees relating to the expulsion of lawful aliens found in Article 13 ICCPR and Protocol 7, Article 1 ECHR, and the prohibition of collective expulsion of aliens found in Protocol 4, Article 4 ECHR. In relation to the former, the Human Rights Committee recently criticised Ireland for the apparent incompatibility between the summary removal procedure envisaged in the 2008 Bill and Ireland's obligations under Article 13.[43]

However, Article 13 and the other rights relating to expulsion, while important *per se*, are of limited applicability to most immigration decisions since they relate only

---

[40] See s 5, Illegal Immigrants (Trafficking) Act 2000, which limits the time for instigating judicial review proceedings in the immigration context to 14 days from the issuance of the decision. Before enactment, s 5 of the bill was the subject of an unsuccessful Article 26 referral to the Supreme Court. For critical commentary, see S Mullally, "The Irish Supreme Court and the Illegal Immigrants (Trafficking) Bill 1999", 13 *International Journal of Refugee Law* 2002. This provision is replicated in s 118(3) of the Immigration, Residence and Protection Bill 2008.

[41] Contrast, for example, refusal to issue a visa, which is susceptible to an internal review, with refusal of permission to enter the State at port, which is not. Similarly, contrast refusal to renew a renewable residence permit or to issue a long term or qualified long term residence permit, both of which are susceptible to internal review, with refusal to issue a residence permit in the first place — on which the bill is silent.

[42] s 54(1) provides: "Where it appears to an immigration officer or a member of the Garda Siochana that a foreign national is unlawfully present in the State or at a frontier of the State, the officer or member may remove the foreign national from the State". Presumably, this provision is subject to the non-refoulement guarantee in s 53. The assumption seems to be that any potential refoulement would have been ruled out in the protection procedure. However, I have argued elsewhere that the protection procedure does not exhaust the possibilities for refoulement: Smyth, "Protection Aspects of the Scheme for an Immigration, Residence and Protection Bill", paper presented to the conference, *New Rules for the New Irish*, hosted by the Law Society on the Proposed Immigration, Residence and Protection Bill 2007, 27 January 2007.

[43] See *Concluding Observations of the Human Rights Committee on Ireland*, CCPR/C/ILR/CO/3, 22 July 2008 at para. 19.

to expulsion. Moreover, the guarantees relating to the expulsion of *lawful* aliens apply only to a small minority of persons faced with expulsion since expulsion usually follows a determination of illegality. It is, arguably, in relation to this prior determination that procedural guarantees are needed.[44] The collective expulsion of aliens prohibits collective decisions in relation to expulsion and therefore requires an individual decision in each case. Although there are positive signs that the ECtHR may be willing to infer a collective (and thereby improper) decision from a collective removal,[45] the Court has been unwilling to specify guidelines for the making of (proper) individual decisions.

What is really needed, therefore, is a set of procedural guarantees that would apply to immigration decisions *tout court*. On the face of it, Article 6 ECHR on the right to a fair trial, which has no equivalent in the ICCPR outside the criminal context, appears to supply just such a set of guarantees. It provides, *inter alia*:

> In the determination of his civil rights and obligations or of any criminal charge against him, everyone is entitled to a fair and public hearing within a reasonable time by an independent and impartial tribunal established by law.

Unfortunately, the words "civil rights" have been interpreted by the Court to mean private law rights, although the jurisprudence of the Court is confused and inconsistent on the point allowing for some consideration of what might be seen as "public law" situations.[46] Notwithstanding its confusion on the broad principle the Court is clear that Article 6 definitely does not apply to immigration proceedings. This long-held view of the Commission was affirmed by the court in the landmark case of *Maaouia v France*, where a non-national unsuccessfully challenged the excessive length of proceedings to rescind an exclusion order as being unreasonable and contrary to Article 6.[47] The Court justified the view that Article 6 does not apply to immigration proceedings by arguing that the addition of Protocol 7, Article 1 (procedural guarantees regarding the expulsion of lawful aliens) in 1984 signaled states" intention not to include such proceedings within the scope of Article 6 of the Convention. This is a strange interpretative ploy: a Convention signed by all states parties defined narrowly by reference to an additional and subsequent protocol signed by only some. Moreover, it offends against the general rule of treaty interpretation whereby a reservation must be express and cannot be incompatible with the object and purpose of the treaty.[48] Here, the restrictive interpretation of

---

[44] The ease with which States can avoid their obligations under these provisions (Art 13 ICCPR, Protocol 7, Art 1 ECHR) by simply rendering the person illegal (e.g. by terminating a residence permit) before expelling him/her was appreciated by the Human Rights Committee as early as 1986. Thus in its General Comment No. 15 the Committee recommends that Article 13 apply where the legality of entry/stay is in dispute. The ECtHR has been slower to respond. However, lately there have been some indications that the Court is not willing to give a literal interpretation to the terms "lawfully resident". See for example, the judgment in *Bolat v Russia*, ECtHR, 5 October 2006, application no. 14139/03.

[45] *Čonka v Belgium* [2002] 34 EHRR 1298.

[46] See Jacobs & White, *The European Convention on Human Rights* (4th ed., OUP, Oxford, 2006), ch 8.

[47] [2001] 33 EHRR 1037.

[48] See in particular Arts 19 & 23 of the Vienna Convention on the Law of Treaties 1969.

Article 6 constitutes an implied reservation to the personal jurisdiction of the Convention contained in Article 1, which encompasses *everyone* within the jurisdiction and is, arguably, incompatible with the object and purpose of the ECHR as set out in Article 1 and in the Preamble.

Despite these fundamental objections, *Maaouia* constitutes "good law" and is a prime example of where a specific immigration exception has been carved into a right that would otherwise be extremely useful to immigrants.[49] A further example, relevant in the Irish context, is the right to liberty (freedom from arbitrary arrest or detention). Immigration detention is currently permitted in Ireland at two points: where a person is refused permission to enter the State[50]; and where a person is subject to a deportation order but has failed to comply with provisions of the order or, controversially, is suspected of an *intention* to leave the State without permission or in order to avoid removal.[51] In both cases, detention cannot exceed eight weeks in total, but various periods are not reckonable, including if a person institutes court proceedings challenging the detention. These provisions have been roundly criticised by a variety of groups on a variety of grounds including the fact that, in practice, the average length of immigration detention is rising.[52] Yet the 2008 Bill appears to consolidate the above provisions into a single overarching provision that provides for detention for the purposes of removal of any person who "appears" to be "unlawfully present" subject to the same eight week limit.[53]

The right to liberty is protected by Article 5 ECHR and Article 9 ICCPR although the two provisions are differently framed: Article 5.1(f) ECHR expressly provides for an immigration-related limitation clause,[54] whereas Article 9 ICCPR (which prohibits arbitrary detention) contains no limitation clause whatsoever. Not too much should be made of this difference, however, since the prohibition of "arbitrary" detention in the ICCPR allows for immigration detention.[55] A more crucial difference lies in the jurisprudential approach of the ECtHR and the HRC to the right. The latter applies a balancing test in assessing the legality of immigration detention by weighing an individual's right to liberty against a state's legitimate interest in preventing unauthorised entry or in effecting deportation. There must be a

---

[49] The Court has also found that Article 6 ECHR does not apply to extradition proceedings. See *Mamatkulov and Askarov v Turkey*, ECtHR 4 February 2004, application nos. 46827/99 and 46951/99 (judgment).

[50] s 5 Immigration Act 2003.

[51] s 5 Immigration Act 1999, as amended by s 10, Illegal Immigrants (Trafficking) Act 2000. Before the latter was enacted, s 10 of the bill was the subject of an unsuccessful Article 26 referral to the Supreme Court. For critical commentary, see S Mullally, *supra* n 40.

[52] See M Kelly, *Immigration-related detention in Ireland, A research report for the Irish Refugee Council, Irish Penal Reform Trust & Immigrant Council of Ireland*, November 2005.

[53] See s 54 and s 55.

[54] Article 5(1) states: "Everyone has the right to liberty and security of the person. No one shall be deprived of his liberty save in the following cases and in accordance with a procedure prescribed by law:...(f) the lawful arrest or detention of a person to prevent his effecting an unauthorized entry into the country or of a person against whom action is being taken with a view to deportation or extradition".

[55] See for example, *A v Australia*, No. 560/1993, and *C v Australia*, No. 900/1000.

reasonable relationship of proportionality between a state's aim in preventing unauthorised entry or effecting deportation and the detention itself, an assessment that must be made in relation to the risks posed by the particular individual.[56]

Conversely, the ECtHR refuses to apply a proportionality test. Thus, in its seminal *Chahal* decision,[57] in which a non-national was in detention for more than six years pending deportation on national security grounds, the Court held that the right to liberty "does not demand that the detention of a person against whom action is being taken with a view to deportation be reasonably considered necessary, for example to prevent his committing an offence or fleeing."[58] The Court's refusal to apply a proportionality test cannot be explained by the existence of the Article 5.1(f) limitation clause because in reviewing other types of detention, such as detention of mental patients expressly permitted under Article 5(1)(e), the court has "read down" a proportionality test.[59] In the immigration context, the Court merely implements a much weaker "due diligence" test. Under this test, a state must proceed with the task of verifying the status of the immigrant seeking to enter and/or of processing the deportation with due diligence or the detention will become unlawful. What exactly "due diligence" means, especially since Chahal's detention of more than six years was deemed to be lawful, is an open question. Not surprisingly, the test has been criticised for being ambiguous and unduly permissive of delay on the part of the State.[60]

Even more worrying is the suggestion, apparently accepted by the Court, that immigration detention may not even constitute "detention" for the purposes of Article 5. In *Amuur v France*,[61] a group of Somali asylum seekers were arrested after disembarking from a flight from Syria and detained for twenty days in the international zone of Orly airport in Paris. France contended that the detention was not in fact detention falling under Article 5, but rather a "mere restriction on liberty of movement" dealt with by Article 2 of Protocol 2. France further contended that

---

[56] *ibid.*

[57] *Chahal v UK* [1996] 23 EHHR 413. It is perhaps ironic that on the central legal issue in Chahal —whether someone who is a threat to national security can be deported to a country where they face a risk of torture — the court refused to adopt a State-centred position and affirmed the absolute nature of the Article 3 non-refoulement guarantee.

[58] *ibid*, at para. 112.

[59] See *Winterwerp v Netherlands* [1979-80] 2 EHRR 387. A similar approach is taken to alcohol-related detentions.

[60] See D Wilsher, "The Administrative Detention of Non-Nationals Pursuant to Immigration Control: International and Constitutional Law Perspectives", 53 *International and Comparative Law Quarterly*, 2004. Notwithstanding these criticisms, the Court has recently confirmed the non-applicability of a proportionality test in the immigration detention context: *Saadi v UK*, ECtHR, 11 July 2006, 13229/03 (judgment). However, in a case involving the detention of an unaccompanied minor, the Court, finding itself constrained by its own jurisprudence on Article 5, introduced a proportionality test of immigration detention via Article 8 ECHR: *Mubilanzila Makeya and Kaniki Mitunga v Belgium*, ECtHR, 12 October 2006, 13178/03 (judgment).

[61] [1966] 22 EHRR 533.

the applicants had in effect consented to being detained because they were free to leave France at any time and return to Syria, and could not therefore "validly complain of a situation which they had largely created."[62] On the first point, the Court held that if a mere restriction on liberty is prolonged excessively then it may become a deprivation of liberty. On the second point, the Court held that the fact that applicants were free to return to Syria did not vitiate the detention given that Syria was not a signatory to the Refugee Convention. Thus, the Court stated "the possibility [of leaving] becomes theoretical if no other country offering protection comparable to the protection they expect to find in the country where they are seeking asylum is inclined or prepared to take them in."[63] The problem with this finding is that, arguing *a contrario*, the detention of an immigrant not seeking asylum and therefore not prevented from returning to a transit State or the country of origin is permissible. The Court has yet to rule squarely on this point, but the indications from *Amuur* are worrying.[64]

The Standard Set in Relation to the Right is Too Low to be Meaningful

A recurrent criticism of the Irish immigration system, and the one that most exercises immigrants themselves, is the lack of a right to family reunification. Family reunification has no legislative basis in Ireland,[65] but different administrative practice has emerged over the past ten years depending on whether the sponsor is in a low-skilled or high-skilled category of workers. New administrative arrangements, preserving the old distinction between high and lower skilled workers, came into force on 1 February 2007, following the entry into force of the Employment Permits Act 2006. The new arrangements comprise a Green Card Permits system for highly paid employees or those who work in strategically important occupations, and a Work Permits system for either employers or employees in generally lower paid sectors. Green Card Permit holders are entitled to apply for immediate family reunification. Work Permit holders are entitled to family reunification after 12 months of full-time employment if they earn more than the threshold that would quality the family for payment under the Family Income

---

[62] *ibid*, at para. 39.

[63] *ibid*, at para. 48.

[64] In an admissibility decision, the Court held that two Algerian asylum seekers who were held in the regular transit zone of Vienna airport for over a month were not deprived of their liberty contrary to Article 5. The case was distinguished from *Amuur* because in the instant case the applicants" asylum claims had been considered and rejected after three days, after which point they resisted deportation. Furthermore, they were not under strict police surveillance and they had access to legal and social assistance. See *Mahdid and Haddar v Austria*, ECtHR, 8 December 2005, application no. 74762/01. This decision bolsters the view that immigration detention is not considered to be detention proper.

[65] Ireland is not opting into EU Directive 2003/86/EC on the right to family reunification, which provides a limited right of family reunification to "third country nationals" in Member States.

Supplement Scheme.[66] If they earn less than this, they must have been in employment for at least 36 months before they can apply for family reunification. Little information is publicly available on how applications for family reunification are processed, how decisions are made in individual cases, whether a review of a negative decision is possible or how long the decision takes. The process has been the subject of sustained criticism.[67] Unfortunately, there is nothing in the 2008 Bill on family reunification.

There is no free-standing right to family reunification in human rights law. However, the right to respect for family life, contained in Article 8 ECHR, Article 17 ICCPR and Article 10 CRC, *may* imply a right of family reunification in certain circumstances. Unfortunately, the HRC has yet to develop jurisprudence on the question of whether the right to family life imposes on states a positive obligation to admit persons into a state to join family members already present, while the Committee on the Rights of the Child is constrained by the lack of an individual complaints mechanism and has yet to issue a General Comment on the right. That leaves Article 8 ECHR, which establishes a right to family life in the first paragraph and a limitation clause in the second.[68]

The Strasbourg court cut its teeth on the negative dimension of Article 8, namely the obligation not to interfere with family life already existing in a state by deporting one of its members. In such cases, the Court generally assumes that the deportation will cause an interference with family life and analyses the case according to whether the interference is permissible under the limitation clause. This involves balancing a state's legitimate interest in deportation — usually a function of immigration control or the criminal process — against an individual's right to family life. In practice, where the Court considers that it would be "unreasonable" for family members to accompany the deportee very strong reasons have to be adduced by the State to justify the deportation.[69]

---

[66] The Family Income Supplement Scheme is an income support scheme for families in which one or both parents is in full-time employment but has an average weekly family income of less than a defined amount, calculated on the basis of the number of children in the family. For example, if the family has one child, the limit is €490 per week; if the family has eight or more children, the limit is €1,170. The FIS payment is 60% of the difference between the family's average weekly income and the income limit for the family size.

[67] See, for example, website of Immigrant Council of Ireland (www.immigrantcouncil.ie) for various critical publications relating to family reunification.

[68] Article 8:

1. Everyone has the right to respect of his private and family life, his home and his correspondence.
2. There shall be no interference by a public authority with the exercise of this right except such as is in accordance with law and necessary in a democratic society in the interests of national security, public safety or the economic well being of the country, for the prevention of disorder or crime, for the protection of health or morals, or for the protection of the rights and freedoms of others.

[69] See for example, *Amrollahi v Denmark*, ECtHR, 11 July 2002, application no. 56811/00.

However, in *Abdulaziz, Cabales and Balkandales v UK*,[70] the question arose as to whether Article 8 might entail a positive obligation, namely a duty to facilitate family life by admitting a non-national to the State to join family members already present. Although the Court responded by stating that the article could encompass a positive obligation, it held that states have a wide margin of appreciation in determining the extent of the obligation. This is a rather strange use of the margin of appreciation doctrine, which is normally invoked as part of the proportionality test in the context of the limitation clause. In other words, the usual sequence of events is to first find a violation of a right under the substantive clause and then, in considering whether the violation is justified under the limitation clause, to balance the State's interest against the individual's interest, with the margin of appreciation perhaps tipping the balance in favour of the State (notwithstanding that the burden of proof in justifying the violation is on the State). The net result of the *Abdulaziz* approach is that in positive obligation cases, the odds are stacked against the individual: s/he bears the burden of proving that the right is violated *and* the State has a margin of appreciation in determining that it is not. This has resulted in a different standard than the one that pertains in negative obligation cases. Short of there being "obstacles" to family life elsewhere[71] or even of it being "impossible" to enjoy family life elsewhere,[72] the Court will find no interference with the right. Unsurprisingly, no family reunification cases have ever succeeded before the Court applying this arguably impossible standard.[73]

However, following sustained criticism from both inside and outside the Court of the difference in approach to negative and positive obligation cases, the Court appeared recently to revise its approach.[74] In *Sen v the Netherlands*,[75] which involved family reunification of a Turkish teenager with her parents and Dutch-born siblings in the Netherlands, the Court decided that it would be unreasonable to expect the parents and their Dutch children to relocate to Turkey. Although it began its analysis by stating that there were "major obstacles" to enjoyment of family life elsewhere (i.e. Turkey), the Court actually settled on a much lower threshold, namely, whether family reunification in the Netherlands was "the most adequate way" to develop family life — an expression that seems to be a euphemism for

[70] *Supra* n 16.
[71] *Gül v Switzerland*, [1996] 22 EHRR 93.
[72] *Ahmut v the Netherlands*, ECtHR, 28 November 1996, Reports 1996, p 2017.
[73] Possibly the only situation that would meet this standard would be a refugee-type situation. Most Council of Europe countries already operate some type of favourable family reunification regime for refugees. Under EU Directive 2003/86/EC on the right to family reunification, refugees enjoy enhanced family reunification rights. Ireland has not opted into this Directive. However, pursuant to the Refugee Act 1996, as amended, refugees enjoy favourable family reunification rights, although processing can still be susceptible to considerable delays.
[74] See Nicola Rogers, "Immigration and the European Convention on Human Rights: Are New Principles Emerging?", 1 *European Human Rights Law Review* 2003. From within the court, Judge Martens has been particularly outspoken in his dissenting opinions on family reunification cases.
[75] [2001] 33 EHRR 50.

reasonableness.[76] Thus the Court's reasoning is more akin to negative obligation cases, although the judgment is arguably facts-based and the Court was careful to affirm *Abdulaziz* and other similar cases. Following a spate of subsequent admissibility decisions either distinguishing or ignoring the ruling, *Sen* was recently affirmed by a judgment of the Court in *Tuqabo Tekle v the Netherlands*.[77] The discrepancy between the admissibility decisions and this recent judgment is hard to rationalise and leaves a lingering doubt over whether *Sen* constitutes the accepted test for family reunification cases. Pending a further endorsement of *Sen*, it is probably safe to assert that Article 8 ECHR sets a standard in relation to family reunification that is too low to be meaningful.[78]

The Right is Too New to be Useful

There is a growing awareness of the existence of trafficking in Ireland, particularly of women and children.[79] Until recently, there was a dearth of legislation dealing with the phenomenon. The Child Trafficking and Pornography Act 1998, which criminalises the trafficking of children for the purpose of sexual exploitation, was the only piece of anti-trafficking legislation on the statute book until earlier this year.[80] There was of course the Illegal Immigrants (Trafficking) Act 2000 which criminalises the *smuggling* (not trafficking) of irregular migrants into the country. The difference between smuggling and trafficking is, briefly, that the former involves transporting migrants irregularly from one country to another for economic gain while the latter, which may or may not involve smuggling, involves exploiting the migrant in the country of origin, in transit and / or upon arrival in the destination country typically by some form of bonded or forced labour situation.[81] This year has seen the enactment of the first comprehensive anti-trafficking

[76] The judgment, which is only available in French, provides "Dans ces conditions, la venue de Sinem aux Pays-Bas constituait le moyen le plus adéquat pour développer une vie familiale avec celle-ci d'autant qu'il existait, vu son jeune âge, une exigence particulière de voir favoriser son intégration dans la cellule familiale de ses parents." At para 40.

[77] ECtHR, 1 December 2005, application no. 60665 / 00.

[78] Furthermore, the Court has recently upheld a national rule conditioning family reunification on a certain level of income. See *Haydarie and others v the Netherlands*, ECtHR, 20 October 2005, application no. 8876 / 04 (decision).

[79] See for example, P Conroy, *Trafficking in Unaccompanied Minors in Ireland*, IOM, 2004. The phenomenon of trafficking in Ireland received high profile coverage in RTE's *Primetime Investigates* on 8 May 2006.

[80] There have been only a handful of successful prosecutions for child trafficking since the Act entered into force.

[81] The official definition of trafficking, provided in Article 3 of the Protocol to Prevent, Suppress and Punish Trafficking in Persons Especially Women and Children, supplementing the United Nations Convention against Transnational Organized Crime, 2000, is:

> [The] recruitment, transportation, transfer, harbouring or receipt of persons, by means of the threat or use of force or other forms of coercion, of abduction, of fraud, of deception, of the abuse of power or of a position of vulnerability or of the giving or receiving of payments or benefits to achieve the consent of a person having control over another person, for the purpose of exploitation. Exploitation shall include, at a minimum, the exploitation of the prostitution of others or other forms of sexual exploitation, forced labour or services, slavery or practices similar to slavery, servitude or the removal of organs.

legislation — the Criminal Law (Human Trafficking) Act 2008. Unfortunately, the Act adopts a criminal justice approach to trafficking to the exclusion of a human rights approach.

The difference between the two approaches can be understood in the following way. The criminal justice approach to trafficking emphasises the illegality of clandestine border crossings and focuses on the prosecution of the offender. From this point of view, the "victim" is the State whose borders, controls and, ultimately, sovereignty have been violated. This approach is more or less blind to the human victims of trafficking. They are effectively prevented from seeking the protection of the State since they are (generally) illegally present and therefore susceptible to being deported home. Inadvertently, the deportation of the victim can facilitate their re-trafficking. The human rights approach to trafficking considers the issue from the point of view of the human victim rather than the State, although it presents both interests as mutually compatible. Here, trafficking is regarded as a severe violation of fundamental human rights, in that it involves some or all of the following: violence, coercion, slavery, forced labour and forced prostitution. The human rights approach advocates extending temporary or longer term immigration benefits to trafficking victims, thereby enabling them to seek protection. Acquiring legal status may also be the only way victims can exercise their right to an effective remedy. A "compromise" between the criminal justice and human rights approaches entails extending immigration benefits only to those victims of trafficking who are willing to testify against their traffickers.[82]

The emergence of the human rights approach is a recent phenomenon, driven by developments at the international level. Thus, an Optional Protocol to the United Nations Convention against Transnational Organised Crime to Prevent, Suppress and Punish Trafficking in Persons, Especially Women and Children was adopted in 2000. It provides in Article 7 that "each State Party shall consider adopting legislative or other appropriate measures that permit victims of trafficking in persons to remain in its territory, temporarily or permanently, in appropriate cases." At the regional level, a Council of Europe Convention on Action Against Trafficking in Human Beings was adopted in 2005. It is more specific than the UN Convention, advocating a 30 day recovery and reflection period, followed by the issuance of a renewable residence permit: in one or other of the two following situations or in both: a) the competent authority considers that their stay is necessary owing to their personal situation; b) the competent authority considers that their stay is necessary for the purpose of their cooperation with the competent authorities in investigation or criminal proceedings".[83] While these two conventions envisage extending immigration benefits to victims of trafficking, it is clear from the wording that considerable discretion is left to States Parties to decide on the qualifying criteria. Ireland has signed both conventions but ratified neither.

---

[82] For a thorough discussion of the human rights approach to trafficking, see D Francesca Haynes, "Used, abused, arrested and deported: extending immigration benefits to protect the victims of trafficking and to secure the prosecution of traffickers", 26 *Human Rights Quarterly* 2004.

[83] Article 14.

At the EU level, a Directive relating to the treatment of victims of trafficking was passed in 2004 requiring that victims be afforded temporary stay on condition that they testify — the compromise approach referred to above.[84] Despite the fact that Ireland declined to "opt in" to this Directive at the time of its adoption, the intention seems to be to follow the approach it exemplifies.[85] Thus, the 2008 Immigration, Residence and Protection Bill contains a section providing for a 45 day recovery and reflection period for victims of trafficking, which may be extended to six months if necessary for the criminal investigation.[86] Two observations may be made on this. Firstly, it is unclear why this provision was not included in the Criminal Law (Human Trafficking) Act 2008, which, from the point of view of the tidiness and accessibility of the statute book, would seem to be its natural home. Secondly, while some provision for the victims of trafficking is to be welcomed, it is a pity that the Government does not intend to align Ireland more fully with the emerging international consensus on best practice in dealing with victims of trafficking.

However, it is difficult to make this argument from a legal point of view. The consensus is only still emerging. The qualified wording of the two conventions indicates that the reconceptualisation of trafficking as a human right violation and not solely a criminal justice issue has yet to be fully realised. It is certainly too early to predict the emergence of a norm of customary international law which would oblige states generally to protect the victims of trafficking for the sake of their human rights as distinct from for the sake of the criminal process. The human rights approach is, as yet, too new to be useful.

Only "Soft Law" Governs the Area

Immigration from so-called "developing" countries to "developed" countries, like Ireland, raises two major issues in the context of international development co-operation. The first is *"le colonialisme chez nous,"* a form of neo-colonialism which sees migrant workers from developing countries subjected to the same forms of labour exploitation as they suffered in their own countries under colonialism proper. The issue of labour exploitation has already been dealt with in this article. The second relates to the "brain- drain" phenomenon, whereby developed countries" demand for and inability to supply "indigenous" skilled labour causes a drain of human resources from developing countries. The phenomenon hardly needs explaining in Ireland in light of the hemorrhaging of educated young people from the country in the 1980s. The 2005 Discussion Document that preceded an earlier version of the Immigration, Residence and Protection Bill 2008 anticipates that, in future, Ireland's demand for labour from outside the EEA will be mainly in the high skills area and that Ireland will have to compete with other developed countries to attract this labour.[87]

---

[84] Council Directive 2004/81/EC of 29 April 2004 on victims of trafficking.

[85] For a description of the legal basis for opting-in to EU immigration legislation, see *infra*, section G.

[86] s 124.

[87] *Supra* n 3.

The migration-development nexus is a complex one. Disparities in development levels between countries create push and pull factors for international migration. International migration, in turn, has an impact on the development of both sending and receiving states. From the point of view of the sending state, the impacts are by no means all "bad." Emigration can have a positive influence on the economy, by way of migrant remittances which can make up a large proportion of GNP, and in terms of elevated skills levels of returned emigrants. However, the positive dimension of emigration is dependent on the existence of financial transaction networks which facilitate the transfer of remittances, on the ability of emigrants to acquire skills abroad, which involves training and education of immigrants in the host country, and on the fostering of pull-factors to draw emigrants home. The latter is not simply a matter for the home country because emigrants can be discouraged from returning home if they have to relinquish their immigration status in the host country by so doing.[88]

Conversely, emigration can also have a profoundly negative effect on sending countries. Among other things, it can entail the loss of highly skilled workers from essential areas of public service such as health and education, a lower return from investment in public education, a loss of tax revenue and an undesirable environment for the attraction of foreign direct investment. Developing a policy response to these issues is complex and lies beyond the scope of this article. It is worth noting, however, that recommended policy responses include identifying "hotspots" where emigration has a depleting effect, engaging in multilateral efforts to slow the flow from "hotspots" and bolstering training and retention in "hotspot" sectors.[89] The key point about maximizing the advantages of emigration to the sending state and minimising the disadvantages is that it requires management across the related areas of immigration policy, international development policy and economic policy.

However, the whole complex issue received scant attention in the 2005 Discussion Document. The protection and development of Ireland's international relations was flagged as one of the overall objectives of the proposed Bill. But when it came to substantive proposals for addressing the matter, a solitary paragraph entitled "Encouraging a brain drain?" simply stated:

> "These are not issues that are to be considered in each individual case but are to be considered in the development of policy in the area generally. They relate as much to the areas of development assistance policy and economic policy as they do to immigration policy. The fact is that there is international competition for these workers and that developments in Ireland alone will not change the systems currently in place internationally."

---

[88] In response, some countries of immigration have promoted "circular migration". The US "J" cultural exchange visa is an example, whereby the immigrant is required to return home for a specified period after the expiry of the visa and before re-applying for another.

[89] For a thorough treatment of these issues see, D Sriskandarajah, *Migration and Development: A paper prepared for the Policy Analysis and Research Programme of the Global Commission on International Migration*, September 2005. Available on www.gcim.org.

Unsurprisingly, there is no mention of the brain drain issue in the 2008 Bill. What is surprising, given the above statement, is that there is no mention of it in the 2006 White Paper on Irish Aid. The White Paper does provide for the establishment of an Inter-Departmental Committee for Development in order to ensure a coherent approach to development across government departments. However, the Committee, which has met five times since its establishment, does not include a representative of the Department of Justice, Equality and Law Reform and has discussed the issue of brain-drain only in the context of EU developments on policy coherence for development.

Although this state of affairs is clearly inadequate, the ability of human rights to supply a robust response is equally limited. There is a Declaration on the Right to Development,[90] Article 3 of which provides, *inter alia*, that "States have the primary responsibility for the creation of national and international conditions favourable to the realisation of the right to development [... and in particular] States have the duty to co-operate with each other in ensuring development and eliminating obstacles to development." However, this declaration, which failed to achieve consensus and was by and large rejected by the major industrialised countries — the US voted against, while the UK, Japan, Germany FR, Israel, Sweden, Denmark, Finland and Iceland abstained — was never transformed into a legally binding convention. Moreover, the State practice and *opinio juris* necessary to translate a nascent right into a norm of customary international law is undoubtedly lacking. As regards State practice, witness the failure of most industrialised countries, including Ireland, to commit to allocating 0.7% of GNP to development assistance by 2007. As for *opinio juris*, note the constant resistance by developed countries to the notion that they are under an international legal *obligation* to provide development assistance or that the content of any such obligation might extend beyond aid, to cover trade and debt relief.[91] At best, therefore, the right to development can be considered "soft law."

The Right or its Violation is Arguably another State or Entity's Responsibility

Immigration and asylum became matters of EC competence under the Treaty of Amsterdam, which shifted these issues from Title VI of the Treaty on European Union to Title IV of the Treaty Establishing the European Community (and thereby from the intergovernmental third pillar to the community first pillar). In order to retain the Common Travel Area with the UK, and owing to that country's particular difficulties in ceding sovereignty in this contentious area, Ireland secured an "opt-out" from Title IV legislation, with an option to "opt-in" to any particular measure under a protocol to the Amsterdam Treaty.[92] It is well known, and a matter of

[90] UN General Assembly Resolution 41/120 (1986).

[91] For more than a decade, discussions of the right to development in the Commission on Human Rights were highly divisive, with voting patterns on resolutions relating to the right indicating a cleavage between developing and developed countries.

[92] Protocol on the Position of the United Kingdom and Ireland.

considerable criticism, that Ireland tends to opt out of measures which secure rights to third country nationals and opt in to measures which relate to immigration control and enforcement.[93] In preferring the latter, it should be pointed out that a double jeopardy is involved because enhanced immigration control measures are themselves supposed to "flank" or compensate for the abolition of internal borders within the EU — something that Ireland has not done.

Based on documents preceding earlier versions of the 2008 Bill, it was anticipated that the bill would pre-empt Ireland's opt-in to various EU immigration control measures dealing with return of irregular migrants. Thus, the Government's 2005 Discussion Document stated:

> "The legislation should provide for Irish immigration officers and officials to work outside the State, for example to work as ... escorts in removal or deportation cases and to participate in international missions. This should allow Irish staff to participate in EU work in the area of border controls (such as with the European Border Management Agency), removals and combating trafficking in human beings."[94]

What is referred to here is measures flowing from the EU's Return Action Programme which was adopted in 2002. This Programme establishes a framework for Community actions relating to the return of irregular migrants in the short and longer term. In the short term, the Programme envisages enhancing existing operational cooperation in the area of return such as joint charter flights and joint return operations. This has already led to the adoption of a number of legal measures,[95] including the establishment of the above-mentioned European Border Management Agency (FRONTEX), which has a coordinating function in the area of return.[96] In the medium term, the operational cooperation is to be grounded in a legal framework establishing common standards for return procedures. At the time of writing, the Commission has produced a Proposal for a Directive on Common

---

[93] Ireland has not opted into Council Directive 2003/86/EC of 22 September 2003 on the right to family reunification, Council Directive 2003/109/EC of 25 November 2003 concerning the status of third country nationals who are long term residents or Council Directive 2004/81/EC of 29 April 2004 on victims of trafficking. See *infra*, n 95 for an illustrative list of EU control/enforcement measures which apply to Ireland.

[94] *Supra* n 3, p 125.

[95] For example, Council Decision 2005/267 of 16 March 2005 on information and coordination network for Member States" migration management services (ICONET — platform for the exchange of strategic , tactical and operational information concerning illegal migratory movements); Council Regulation 2004/377 of 19 February 2004 on the immigration liaison officers" network (see also in this regard Council doc. 8418/06, 25 April 2006, a draft common manual for immigration liaison officers posted abroad by the member States of the EU); Council Decision 2004/573 EC of 29 April 2004 on the organisation of joint flights (an annex contains common guidelines on security provisions for joint removals by air); Council Directive 2003/110/EC of 25 November 2003 on assistance in cases of transit; Council Directive 2001/40 of 28 May 2001 on the mutual recognition of decisions on the expulsion of third country nationals.

[96] Council Regulation 2007/2004 of 25 November 2004, OJ L 349/1. Article 9 relates to the provision of support in joint return operations.

Standards and Procedures in Member States for Returning Illegally Staying Third-Country Nationals.[97] Ireland is not participating in the negotiations on the proposed Directive which are ongoing although it may decide to apply the Directive once the text is finalised and approved.

Surprisingly, despite the clear commitment in the 2005 Discussion Document to cooperation with other EU Member States in returning irregular migrants, the 2008 Bill is silent on the matter. It would be unwise to infer from this that Ireland has shunned EU cooperation on returns, since it already participates in a number of measures.[98] What is worrying is that the Government may be considering informal operational cooperation without a legislative basis. Such an approach is worrying on two grounds: it lacks transparency and accountability but, perhaps more importantly, the EU return structures are themselves problematic from a human rights viewpoint. There are three central difficulties. First, while the return procedure has the potential to violate human rights, the law governing the area is relatively underdeveloped. Second, it is not clear who would be accountable for any human rights violations that might occur. Third, the international legal rules relating to State responsibility, which could offer guidance on the matter, are both contentious and underdeveloped.

On the first point, while human rights law is relatively well developed on the concept of *non-refoulement*,[99] and less so (as we have seen in section C) in the area of expulsion of aliens, it is underdeveloped on standards regarding the method of expulsion.[100] Carrying out return, particularly forced return, raises such matters as detention, restraint, use of force and the parameters of self-defence. States are clearly under an obligation to respect the right to life and the prohibition of torture and cruel, inhuman or degrading treatment when effecting returns. But there is little guidance in human rights law about when the kinds of actions that are used during forced returns meet the threshold for cruel, inhuman or degrading treatment, or

---

[97] COM/2005/391.

[98] Of the measures listed in footnote 98, the only measure which does not apply to Ireland is Council Directive 2003/110/EC of 25 November 2003 on assistance in cases of transit. As regards Council Directive 2001/40 of 28 May 2001 on the mutual recognition of decisions on the expulsion of third country nationals, the situation is somewhat complicated. Ireland did not opt into the Directive at the time of its adoption. However, by way of Council Decision (2002/192/EC) of 28 February 2002 concerning Ireland's request to take part in some of the provisions of the Schengen acquis, it was agreed that Ireland would participate in the Directive. However, the Council has not yet put the relevant provisions of the acquis into effect for Ireland.

[99] Article 3 European Convention on Human Rights and its jurisprudence; Article 3 Convention against Torture and its jurisprudence; Article 7 International Covenant on Civil and Political Rights and its jurisprudence; Article 33 Convention relating to the Status of Refugees and relevant United Nations High Commissioner for Refugees Guidelines and Executive Committee Conclusions.

[100] For more on relevant standards see C Phuong, Minimum Standards for Return Procedures and International Human Rights Law, *European Journal of Migration and Law* 9 (2007).

when a death during a return operation can be justified by self-defence.[101] Only soft-law instruments provide detailed guidance on the matter.[102] This dearth of guidance is exploited in the EU draft return Directive. Article 10 of the draft contains the rather bald statement that coercive measure shall be proportional, shall not exceed reasonable force, and shall be implemented "in accordance with fundamental rights and with due respect for the dignity of the third country national concerned."

On the second point, return constitutes the enforcement of a deportation decision (variously called deportation/expulsion/removal decision). While there is an, as yet un-invoked Directive on the mutual recognition of deportation decisions,[103] there is no harmonisation of Member State laws relating to *how* deportation decisions are made. In other words, it is fully within Member State jurisdiction to decide when and how the stay of an immigrant becomes illegal warranting removal from the State. Consequently, it is up to each state to assess and dispel any potential *refoulement* issues. If a deportation decision is made in contravention of the right of *non-refoulement* and return is affected by or with the assistance of another state, is that state jointly responsible for the human rights violation? Similarly, as has already been pointed out, carrying out return (particularly forced return) raises such matters as detention, restraint, use of force and the parameters of self-defence. Pending the adoption of the draft return Directive, the security aspects of joint return by air are governed by non-legally binding guidelines.[104] But what external standard provides an answer to the question of which Member State is responsible for human rights violations that occur in the course of a joint operation? These questions are further complicated where FRONTEX is involved in the operation.

These are complex issues not purely of human rights law but of public international law and, specifically, the law relating to state responsibility. As regards joint state responsibility, some guidance can be found in the United Nations International Law Commission's (ILC) Articles on State Responsibility 2001, which both codify existing customary international law and develop the law. Article 16 relates to aid or assistance in the commission of an internationally wrongful act and provides:

> "A State which aids or assists another State in the commission of an internationally wrongful act by the latter is internationally responsible for doing so if:
> (a) That State does so with knowledge of the circumstances of the internationally wrongful act; and

[101] The Human Rights Committee in its 1998 Concluding Observations to Belguim, noted: "Procedures used in the repatriation of some asylum seekers, in particular the placing of a cushion on the face of an individual in order to overcome resistance, entails a risk to life. The recent case of a Nigerian national who died in such a manner illustrates the need to re-examine the whole procedure of forcible deportations." Concluding Observations on Belgium, CCPR/C/79/Add.99, 19 November 1998, para 15.

[102] See Committee of Ministers of the Council of Europe, "Twenty Guidelines on Forced Return", May 2005; See also the Council of Europe Recommendation 1547 (2002) on expulsion procedures in conformity with human rights and enforced with respect of safety and dignity.

[103] Council Directive 2001/40 of 28 May 2001 on the mutual recognition of decisions on the expulsion of third country nationals.

[104] Council Decision 2004/573 EC of 29 April 2004 on the organisation of joint flights contains an annex providing common guidelines on security provisions for joint removals by air.

(b) The act would be internationally wrongful if committed by that State."[105]

The knowledge requirement, which in no way undermines the maxim that ignorance of the law is no excuse, nevertheless provides that ignorance of the facts surrounding a violation may exclude liability. Therefore, from the perspective of cooperating States it would be better to remain ignorant of each other's deportation proceedings. As for the actual removal, it would seem that if officers of one state witnessed the commission of a human rights abuse by officers of another state the former would be regarded as being complicit and therefore jointly responsible.

As regards the responsibility of FRONTEX, there is a real accountability deficit.[106] As an EU agency, FRONTEX is not a State and therefore not party to any of the relevant human rights instruments such as the ECHR or the ICCPR. The thorny issue of the responsibility of Member States for internationally wrongful acts committed by international organisations was considered by the ILC when drafting its Articles on State Responsibility but ultimately excluded due to lack of agreement. There are two well known albeit contradictory standards for imputing the actions of non-State actors to States which could be applied, by analogy, to FRONTEX. The "effective control" standard, elaborated by the International Court of Justice in the famous *Nicaragua* case,[107] provides that a state must exercise control over each and every operation that the non-state actor conducts in order for the wrongful acts of the latter to be imputed to the state. This standard was effectively "overruled" by the International Criminal Tribunal for the former Yugoslavia (ICTY) in the *Tadic* case as being too high.[108] The proper test, according to the ICTY, is whether a State exercises "overall control" over operations but "it is not necessary that, in addition, the State should also issue, either to the head or to members of the group, instructions for the commission of specific acts contrary to international law."[109]

Although the *Nicaragua* test is endorsed by the ILC in Article 8 of the Articles on State Responsibility, this cannot be regarded as reflecting customary international law given the debate that still rages. The confused state of international law in this

---

[105] Article 17 provides that the same rules apply when a State directs and controls another State in the commission of an internationally wrongful act.

[106] This deficit exists not only under public international law but under EU public law also. Hence, it has been said that "the Agency resembles the model of EC Regulatory Agencies set up to facilitate the implementation of EC policies. However, unlike other Community agencies, it appears to have a very strong operational function which is inextricably linked with the exercise of State powers and may have a huge impact on civil liberties. Is the form of an Agency an appropriate choice for the development of EU policy in this sensitive field?" — V Mitsilegas, "The European Border Agency", paper presented to the ILPA/Justice Conference, *How Much Freedom, Security and Justice? Developments in EU Asylum and Immigration Law*, 13 and 14 May 2005. On file with author.

[107] *Military and Paramilitary Activities in and Against Nicaragua (Nicaragua v United States of America)*, Judgment of 27 June 1986.

[108] *Prosecutor v Tadic* (IT-94-1), Appeals Chamber, 15 July 1999. The ICTY considered that the Nicaragua test was a) not consonant with the logic of the law on State responsibility, and b) at variance with jurisprudence and State practice.

[109] *ibid*, at para.131.

area provides a taste of the difficulties in holding States responsible for joint, multiple and delegated operations in the area of immigration control and enforcement.

Conclusion

I have used a cross-section of the key criticisms of the current and proposed immigration system in Ireland to examine the ability of human rights law to provide a meaningful response. Naturally, this has involved a certain selectivity and there are doubtless other areas where human rights would not be found wanting.[110] There are, however, many other areas of immigration law and policy where human rights are weak or underdeveloped that have not been considered here for reasons of space.[111] The picture that emerges from this review is that human rights law is habitually deficient when it comes to protecting immigrants. This raises uncomfortable questions about human rights advocacy and lobbying: why argue for a human rights-based approach to immigration policy when this approach so regularly fails to deliver? Why bang the same old drum? Is it worth searching for new or alternative tools to instigate change and protect the most vulnerable in society? Or should greater energies be directed towards changing the content of human rights law itself, through such tactics as public interest litigation or *amicus curiae* interventions in relevant cases at the domestic, EU, Council of Europe and UN levels?

Another mainstay of the rights-based approach is to decry Ireland's failure to either ratify relevant human rights instruments, such as the International Convention on the Protection of the Rights of All Migrant Workers and Members of their Families, or to incorporate into Irish law those that the State has ratified, such as the ICCPR. On the first point, while ratification of the Migrant Workers Convention is often offered as a panacea to the human rights problems of migrants, it does not substantially alter the content of rights that immigrants already have under more enforceable treaties such as the ECHR. For this reason, and also because the possibility of ratification appears so remote, the Migrant Workers Convention has not been dealt with in this article.

The second point — habitual failure to incorporate ratified human rights treaties into domestic law — is a valid complaint that underpins what is known as the problem of *authentic enforcement*. It reveals a critical weakness of international human rights law (beyond the substantive weaknesses outlined in this article), namely, its frequent lack of justiciability on the ground. It also reveals a deep cynicism on the part of a government that derives substantial international acclaim from its general eagerness to ratify international human rights instruments but that fails to deliver on them back home. However, outing this cynicism will only

[110] For example, the Article 8 jurisprudence of the ECtHR in the area of family life may ultimately have a very positive impact on family reunification of "non-traditional" families.

[111] For example, the ability of the right to privacy to meaningfully counteract developments in biometrics or the ability of the law on the extraterritorial application of human rights to keep up with the new EU trend towards exporting immigration control to buffer countries.

advance the rights-based lobby so far. Further questions have to be asked: why, in attempting to influence policy, cite conventions that have not been incorporated and therefore have no domestic legal standing? Is it for their moral authority? Can the moral authority of such treaties trump their lack of legal authority in the minds of the very people who have not been sufficiently persuaded by their moral authority to give them legal force in the first place?

I pose these questions not (unhappily) with any particular solutions in mind, but rather to prompt debate. In doing so, I do not wish to undermine the rights-based approach but to strengthen it or replace it with something better. As a well-known human rights skeptic-advocate has said: "…[T]o deplore such defective means [is] to be more of a human rights enthusiast than those who promote their mere existence as sufficient in itself to warrant celebration."[112]

[112] C Gearty, *Can Human Rights Survive?* The Hamlyn Lectures 2005, (Cambridge University Press, Cambridge, 2006) p 4.

Local Authorities and the European Convention on Human Rights Act 2003

Dr Padraic Kenna*

Introduction

This article discusses the impact of the European Convention on Human Rights Act 2003 (ECHR Act) on local authorities in Ireland. The Act creates a new framework for the representative, regulatory, agency and service provision roles of these "organs of the State". Judicial review — with its many limitations — remains the ultimate legal method of evaluating compliance with these obligations. Interpreting the concepts of respect for human rights, positive obligations, reasonableness and proportionality from European Court of Human Rights precedents within Irish jurisprudence may bring some interesting outcomes. The Irish courts have already held that some local authorities failed to comply with their obligations under the ECHR Act. The Act could yet have a significant impact on the actions, obligations and judicial review of local authorities, but there are significant political, cultural, social and other barriers to its implementation.

The European Convention on Human Rights Act 2003

The ECHR Act has created a new framework for the operation of organs of the State in Ireland since 31 December 2003,[1] arising from the commitments in the Good Friday / Belfast Agreement.[2]

The main Articles of the European Convention on Human Rights are reproduced in Schedule 1 of the ECHR Act[3]:

Article 1 — obligation to respect human rights;
Article 2 — right to life;
Article 3 — prohibition of torture;
Article 4 — prohibition of slavery;
Article 5 — right to liberty and security;
Article 6 — right to a fair trial;

---

* Member of FEANTSA Expert Group on Housing Rights, Lecturer in Law, School of Law, NUI Galway.

[1] See U Kilkelly (ed.) *ECHR and Irish Law*, (2nd ed, Bristol, Jordans, 2008). See also: D O'Connell, S Cummiskey and E Meeneghan with P O'Connell, *ECHR Act 2003: A Preliminary Assessment of Impact* (Law Society of Ireland and Dublin Solicitors' Bar Association, 2006).

[2] Under the Good Friday / Belfast Agreement of 1998, two Human Rights Commissions have also been established, charged with promoting and protecting human rights in their respective jurisdictions. See Harvey, "Governing after the Rights Revolution" (2000) 27(1) *Journal of Law and Society* 61.

[3] Council of Europe, The European Convention on Human Rights, Rome, 4 November 1950. Available at http: / / www.hri.org / docs / ECHR50.html.

Article 7 — no punishment without law;
Article 8 — right to respect for private and family life, home and correspondence;
Article 9 — right to freedom of thought, conscience and religion;
Article 10 — right to freedom of expression;
Article 11 — right to freedom of assembly and association;
Article 12 — right to marry;
Article 13 — right to an effective remedy;
Article 14 — prohibition of discrimination;
Article 15 — derogations;
Article 16 — exemption for political activities of aliens;
Article 17 — prohibition of abuse of rights;
Article 18 — limitations on permitted restrictions of rights;
Article 1 of Protocol 1 — right to property;
Article 2 of Protocol 1 — right not be denied education.

A person who has suffered injury, loss or damage as a result of a breach of this statutory obligation may, if no other remedy in damages is available, institute proceedings in the High Court and the Court may award damages as it considers appropriate.[4] It remains to be seen what other forms of relief, if any, are available for breaches of the statutory duty contained in s 3.[5]

However, there is a provision for courts to make a declaration of incompatibility where existing law is incompatible with the Act. Section 5 states:

> "(1) In any proceedings, the High Court, or the Supreme Court when exercising its appellate jurisdiction, may, having regard to the provisions of s 2, on application to it in that behalf by a party, or of its own motion, and where no other legal remedy is adequate and available, make a declaration (referred to in this Act as "a declaration of incompatibility") that a statutory provision or rule of law is incompatible with the State's obligations under the Convention provisions.
>
> (2) A declaration of incompatibility—
> (a) shall not affect the validity, continuing operation or enforcement of the statutory provision or rule of law in respect of which it is made, and (b) shall

---

[4] ECHR Act, s 3(2). In *O'Donnell v South Dublin County Council* [2007] IEHC 204, Laffoy J awarded damages of €58,000 to cover the cost of providing a mobile home, where a breach of the ECHR Act was found.

[5] It was held in *Pullen v Dublin City Council,* High Court, 28 May 2009, that even where a local authority did not comply with its obligations under the ECHR Act in performing its functions in a manner compatible with the State's obligations under the Convention, nevertheless, the court had no jurisdiction to grant relief other than an award of damages, and not the injunctive relief sought. Irvine J stated: "To grant an injunction would be to grant relief not provided for in s.3(2) of the ECHR Act 2003 and would be an order that would conflict with the clear provisions of s.3(2), would offend the doctrine of the separation of powers and would be against the canons of construction already referred to." Previously, in *Byrne v Dublin City Council* [2009] IEHC 122 an interlocutory injunction (with conditions as to the family members who could occupy the property) was granted by Murphy J to restrain a breach of the s 3 duty.

not prevent a party to the proceedings concerned from making submissions or representations in relation to matters to which the declaration relates in any proceedings before the European Court of Human Rights.

(3) The Taoiseach shall cause a copy of any order containing a declaration of incompatibility to be laid before each House of the Oireachtas within the next 21 days on which that House has sat after the making of the order."

Thus, the ECHR Act will only generate a declaration of incompatibility where no other remedy exists.[6] Where a declaration of incompatibility is made the Government in their discretion may make an *ex gratia* payment of compensation to that party who has suffered loss as a result of the incompatibility. Clearly, this will not lead to any rewriting of laws by the courts, but requires the Government to amend the law as they see fit.

Domestication of the ECHR

The domestication or "patriation" of an international human rights instrument, like the ECHR, though legislation such as the ECHR Act, presents novel challenges to the legal system, as well as to political and administrative culture.[7] The Convention has been incorporated into Irish law at sub-constitutional level, and the long title of the Act describes it as an Act "to enable further effect to be given, subject to the Constitution, to certain provisions of the European Convention on Human Rights and Fundamental Freedoms....". Those familiar with the Convention viewed it as a welcome addition to the corpus of Irish law.[8] Others have been critical of the minimalist approach of the legislation.[9] Hogan points out that there is a vast and continuing constitutional jurisprudence in Ireland involving fundamental rights, aside from any references to the ECHR Act.[10] He points out that a proper comparison of its constitutional relevance is to be found in the German context. There, the ECHR has the status of a federal law at sub-Constitutional level, but is

---

[6] At the time of writing a number of High Court cases have found that organs of the State have been in breach of the ECHR Act and three cases have resulted in declarations of incompatibility. See *Foy v An t-Ard Chláraitheoir & Ors* [2007] IEHC 470; *Donegan v Dublin City Council,* [2008] IEHC 288; *Dublin City Council v Gallagher* [2008] IEHC 353.

[7] See *Celebrating the European Convention on Human Rights Act 2003* (Independent Law Centres Network, Dublin, 2004).

[8] See Keane, CJ "Issues for the Judiciary in the application of the ECHR Act 2003". Paper to the Human Rights Commission and Law Society of Ireland Conference on New Human Rights Legislation. October 2003.

[9] See, for example, D O'Connell, "The ECHR Act 2003: A Critical Perspective", ch 1, in U Kilkelly, (ed.) *The ECHR and Irish Law,* (Jordans, Bristol, 2004); S Egan, "The European Convention on Human Rights Act 2003: A Missed Opportunity for Domestic Rights legislation" (2003) 25 DULJ 230.

[10] G Hogan, "The European Convention of Human Rights Act 2003," *European Public Law,* Volume 12, Issue 3. 331-343. These are cases largely in relation to traditional liberal civil and political rights, rather than socio-economic rights, except in the family and property related cases. Some of the positive obligations on the State, such as to respect human rights, to prohibit discrimination and to protect and vindicate certain minimum Convention rights have no directly corresponding base in the Irish Constitution, except perhaps in relation to a very limited number of precedents developed before 2000 under Articles 40-43.

treated as a guide to the interpretation of the Basic Law or Constitution. A similar approach in Ireland might cross-fertilise the constitutional jurisprudence here with developing Strasbourg interpretations of human rights.[11]

However, Mr Justice McKechnie pointed out in the *Foy* case, where a declaration of incompatibility was issued that:

> "It is misleading to say that the Convention was incorporated into domestic law. It was not. The rights contained in the Convention are now part of Irish law. They are so by reason of the 2003 Act. That is their source. Not the Convention. So it is correct to say, as I understood in this way, that the Convention forms part of the law. The method employed by the Oireachtas was the interpretative method. S 2 of the 2003 Act, compels this court to interpret and apply any and every statutory provision and rule of law, insofar as is possible in a manner compatible with Ireland's obligations under the Human Rights Convention.[12]

However, in the first study of the early impact of the ECHR Act in 2006, O'Connell *et al* point out that: "it would be incorrect to say that the Convention has in any sense displaced the Constitution or other sources of Irish law as the main basis upon which actions in judicial review are maintained."[13] It remains to be seen how the Irish Constitution, with its inherent difficulties in relation to equality and other matters will become a barrier to the development of a rights culture, arising from the ECHR Act, in the courts and in public administration generally."[14]

Local Authorities and Statutory Provisions

The ECHR Act is an important legal development for local authorities in Ireland.[15] It integrates a human rights perspective within the legal, policy-making and operational functions of Irish local authorities.[16]

---

[11] See G Hogan, "The Value of Declarations of Incompatibility and the Rule of Avoidance", (2006) DULJ 408a Cases and Comment.

[12] *Foy v An t-Ard Chláraitheoir & Ors* [2007] IEHC 470 at para. 93. This case is on appeal to the Supreme Court at time of writing.

[13] See D O'Connell *et al, ECHR Act 2003:– A Preliminary Assessment of Impact* (Law Society of Ireland and Dublin Solicitors' Bar Association) *op cit* at p 15.

[14] See O Doyle, *Constitutional Equality Law*. (Thomson Round Hall, Dublin, 2004).

[15] While the planning function is topically high on the local authority and public agenda, there is insufficient space to deal fully with this here. See P Kenna, "Land Law, Property, Housing and the Environment" in U Kilkelly, (ed.) *ECHR and Irish Law*. (2nd ed, Jordans, Bristol, 2008). See also A Quinn, (2001) "Third-Party Appeals and the Human Rights Convention," *Irish Planning and Environmental Law Journal* – Vol. 8, No. 3, pp. 96-102; P McGarry, "The European Convention on Human Rights Act 2003; Implications for local planning and housing authorities." 2006 13 (1) IPELJ, 3-14.

[16] See P Kenna, "Will the European Convention on Human Rights Act 2003 affect Local Government in Ireland", *The Irish Journal of European Law*, Vol. 11, No. 2, 2004. In *O'Reilly and Others v Ireland*. Application No. 54725/00, Judgment, 29 October 2004, where the applicants had brought proceedings in the Irish courts to compel the local authority to repair public roads, the European Court of Human Rights (ECtHR) held that the delay in processing their claims, and the failure to resolve the issue of costs, constituted a failure on behalf of the State to deal with the case in a reasonable time, contrary to Article 6.

Section 3(1) of the Act provides:

> "Subject to any statutory provision (other than this Act) or rule of law, every organ of the State shall perform its functions in a manner compatible with the State's obligations under the Convention provisions."[17]

An organ of the State includes:

> "[A] tribunal or any other body (other than the President or the Oireachtas or either House of the Oireachtas or a Committee of either such House or a Joint Committee of both such Houses or a court) which is established by law or through which any of the legislative, executive or judicial powers of the State are exercised."[18]

This amounts to a new tortious action (where no other remedy exists) for breaches of statutory duty by organs of the State, for which damages can be granted.[19] There is also the provision for a declaration of incompatibility described above, which may lead to an *ex gratia* award of damages, in line with the moderate levels awarded by the Strasbourg court.

Local authorities in Ireland are clearly within the range of organisations termed "organs of the State". Article 28A of the Constitution, introduced by way of constitutional amendment in 1999 recognises "the role of local government in providing a forum for the democratic representation of local communities, in exercising and performing at local level powers and functions conferred by law and in promoting by its initiatives the interests of such communities."[20]

Local authorities in Ireland carry out their delegated, agency and inherent regulatory, representative and service provision functions under many statutory provisions.[21] A statutory provision is defined in the ECHR Act as:

> "any provision of an Act of the Oireachtas or of any order, regulation, rule, licence, bye-law or other like document made, issued or otherwise created

---

[17] Hogan states that ultimately the State's only obligations are set out under Art 46(1) ECHR "to abide by the final judgement of the Court [ECtHR] in any case to which they are the parties". But s 4 of ECHR Act, on the requirements of judicial notice of the Convention provisions and any declaration, decision, advisory opinion or judgment of the ECtHR, effectively binds the Irish courts to the corpus of ECtHR case law. See G Hogan "The Value of Declarations of Incompatibility and the Rule of Avoidance", (2006) DULJ 408a Cases and Comment.

[18] ECHR Act, s 1.

[19] See *O'Donnell v South Dublin County Council* [2007] IEHC 204; See also A Lowry "Practice and Procedure under the European Convention on Human Rights Act 2002", *Bar Review*, November 2003, 183–185.

[20] Twentieth Amendment of the Constitution Act, 1999.

[21] Local Government Act, 2001 (No. 37 of 2001), s 10(1). Schedule 12 of the 2001 Act sets out some eighty areas of legislation which establish various local authority functions. These encompass such diverse areas as housing, planning, air pollution, control of horses, sanitary services, gaming, lotteries and air raid precautions. See J Canny *The Law of Local Government*. (Round Hall, Dublin, 2000).

thereunder or any statute, order, regulation, rule, licence, bye-law or other like document made, issued or otherwise created under a statute which continued in force by virtue of Article 50 of the Constitution."[22]

Significantly s 2(1) of the Act provides that:

"In interpreting and applying any statutory provision or rule of law, a court shall, in so far as is possible, subject to the rules of law relating to such interpretation and application, do so in a manner compatible with the State's obligations under the Convention provisions".

This effectively means that in a judicial review of a local authority action under a statutory provision (which covers practically all local authority actions), the interpretation and obligations of that provision must be in line with Convention provisions. These are defined in the Act as Articles 2 to 14 of the ECHR and its protocols (subject to any derogation which the State may make pursuant to Article 15 of the Convention). Clearly, there is now a new standard in the implementation of statutory provisions by local authorities influenced by this overarching interpretative obligation.

But even in the absence of a statutory provision, there may still be a breach of the ECHR. This was highlighted in *O'Donnell v South Dublin County Council,*[23] where Laffoy J pointed out that:

"[I]f there is no statutory protection for the plaintiffs in their current predicament which ensures suitable and appropriate accommodation for them having regard to their age, mental condition, disability, dependency and family circumstances, the interstices into which they have fallen must represent a failure of the State and its organs to function in a manner compatible with Article 8."[24]

The Local Government Act 2001

The Local Government Act 2001,[25] comprising some 240 sections, represents a complete restatement of local government law in Ireland. This encompasses the representative, regulatory, agency and service provision roles of local authorities.[26] It also consolidated into law many recent developments in "participatory democracy,"[27] as well as "new public management" (NPM) approaches to local

---

[22] ECHR Act, s 1(d).

[23] [2007] IEHC 204.

[24] *O'Donnell v South Dublin County Council* [2007] IEHC 204.

[25] No. 37 of 2001.

[26] See M Callanan "The Role of Local Government" chapter 1 of M Callanan and JF Keogan (eds.) *Local Government in Ireland — Inside Out*. (IPA, Dublin, 2003).

[27] See Parts 7 and 13 of the 2001 Act. Part 13 provides that "a local authority may take such steps as it considers appropriate to consult with and promote effective participation by the local community in local government."

government.[28] Part 9 of the 2001 Act contains a general statement of the functions of local authorities, while s 63 sets out the general functions of local authorities.

Section 63(3) of the Act of 2001 states that "[s]ubject to law, a local authority is independent in the performance of its functions".[29] Thus, while many local authority operations are guided by Government Department Guidelines and Circulars, the local authority must perform its functions in a manner compatible with the Convention. Indeed, in circumstances where there is no statutory obligation to act, or where it does not breach other existing legislation, an indifferent local authority can breach the ECHR Act, in circumstances which give rise to a positive obligation.[30] Indeed, vicarious and or joint liability may also attach to a Government Department, where the local authority in breach of the ECHR Act is carrying out a delegated Departmental function, or acting according to Departmental Circulars or Guidelines.

Corporate Plans

The Local Government Act 2001 also requires each local authority manager to prepare a corporate plan.[31] In preparing its corporate plan a local authority shall comply with sections 69, 71 and 129 of the Act and:

> "... shall take account of such policies and objectives in relation to any of its functional programmes as are set out in any other plan, statement, strategy or other document prepared by it under any other provision of this or of any other enactment."[32]

Clearly, the ECHR Act is a relevant enactment for the purpose of the preparation of the corporate plan under the Local Government Act. It is therefore incumbent on local authority managers and, indeed, local councillors, to take account of the requirements of the ECHR Act in preparing corporate plans. It is significant, therefore, that after the ECHR Act came into force Ministerial Guidelines on the preparation of local authority corporate plans for 2004-2009 make no reference to the obligations on local authorities under that Act.[33] The "core values" or key principles proposed in the Guidelines emphasise corporate governance and other approaches, but there is no explicit reference to human rights or the provisions of the ECHR Act:

> "Some values identified in existing local authority corporate plans in Ireland which may be relevant, have included: supporting the democratic process and

[28] See M Barzelay, *The New Public Management*, (University of California, 2001). NPM is widely accepted as a form of economic rationalisation or "economism" in public service provision.

[29] See *Keane on Local Government* (PA Butler, (ed.) (First Law, Dublin, 2003).

[30] See *O'Donnell v South Dublin County Council* [2007] IEHC 204; P Kenna "Housing Rights: Positive Duties and Enforceable Rights at the European Court of Human Rights", EHRLR 2008, 2, 193–208.

[31] Local Government Act 2001, s 134(3)(a).

[32] Local Government Act 2001, s 134(7).

[33] Department of the Environment, Heritage and Local Government, *Guidelines of Local Authorities in the Preparation of Corporate Plans for 2004-2009*, (The Stationery Office, Dublin, 2004).

> civic leadership; a customer and citizen focus; partnership, participation and inclusiveness; community development; empowerment of staff to improve potential; and corporate governance issues such as openness and transparency, accountability, ethics, probity and risk management."[34]

Clearly, a local authority's obligations to carry out its functions in a manner compatible with the Convention should be reflected as a core value in the Corporate Plan.

Contracting Out of Functions

Contacting out of services and operational functions is a common feature of local government practice in Ireland. Indeed, the Local Government Act 2001 provides that:

> "A local authority may enter into an agreement in writing with a recognised association for the carrying out by the association on behalf of the local authority of certain functions of the authority which in its opinion may be satisfactorily carried out by the recognised association, subject to such terms, conditions, restrictions and other requirements as the authority considers necessary and specifies in the agreement."[35]

This NPM approach is growing in all areas of local authority activity and poses major difficulties for judicial review and rights enforcement.[36] The role of the local authority is to be an "enabling authority", mobilising, guiding and stimulating other public, private and voluntary agencies to provide services and carry out the functions of the authority.[37] The focus has shifted from probity and due process in meeting statutory and other obligations, to performance, (financial) competitiveness, contractual and managerialist approaches in public services.[38] One of the consequences of this has been to blur the distinction between the role and responsibility of the State and those of other organisations that may be carrying out some local authority functions.

The Minister who introduced the ECHR Bill in 2001 argued that the definition of "organ of the State" for the purpose of s 2 of the Bill was drawn as widely as possible

---

[34] *ibid*, p 22.

[35] Local Government Act 2001, s 128(2)(d).

[36] The Strategic Management Initiative (SMI) for the Irish Public Service of 1994 has created significant changes in public service management. Major developments at local government level include the launching of *Better Local Government: A Programme for Change* (1996), a major initiative on local government and local development leading to the creation of county/city development boards; and the publication of the Local Government Act, 2001. See R Boyle and P Humphries, *A New Change Agenda for the Irish Public Service*, (IPA, Dublin, 2003).

[37] See M Callanan and JF Keogan, (eds.) *Local Government in Ireland - Inside Out*, (IPA, Dublin, 2003).

[38] See S Halliday *Judicial Review and Compliance with Administrative Law*, (Hart Publishing, Oregon, 2004), ch 6.

to ensure that the maximum number of organisations would be embraced by it.[39] Clearly, local authorities are included in the definition but, under an NPM approach, integrating ECHR Act obligations into the duties of contracted-out operations will not be without difficulty. The equivalent definition in the UK Human Rights Act 1998 of a "public body" has led to some litigation, especially in establishing whether non-government, private and charitable bodies providing government services are acting as public bodies.[40] There is still considerable uncertainty in England and Wales in relation to the extent of the obligations under the Human Rights Act 1998 where an organisation "stands in the shoes of the State".[41]

In *YL v Birmingham CC, Southern Cross Healthcare, OL, VL and Secretary of State for Constitutional Affairs*[42] the House of Lords in a 3:2 split, held that a private care home, providing care and accommodation to the elderly, which had been arranged by the local authority under the National Assistance Act 1948, was not carrying out functions of a public nature. Lord Neuberger listed seven factors to determine if a non-State body under a contract with the State was performing a "function which is public in nature".[43]

It is established in Strasbourg jurisprudence, to which the Irish Courts must pay "due regard", that the State cannot evade its obligations to safeguard Convention rights by delegation to private bodies or individuals.[44] A State or public body cannot escape liability simply by asserting that an individual or body entrusted with public

[39] The then Minister for Justice, Equality and Law Reform, Mr. John O'Donoghue, TD, introducing the *European Convention on Human Rights Bill*, Second Stage. *Dail Debates*, 2001, Vol. 538. para. 303 said: "It includes tribunals or any other body — other than the President, the Oireachtas, either House of the Oireachtas, a committee of either House, a joint committee of the Houses or a court — which is established by law, or through which any of the legislative, executive or judicial powers of the state are exercised. The courts are excluded from the definition on the basis that they are already under a duty to administer justice in accordance with the law and the Constitution. The definition of organ of the state is drawn as widely as possible to ensure that the maximum number of organisations will be embraced by it."

[40] See, for example, *R (on the application of Heather) v Leonard Cheshire Foundation* [2002] EWCA. Civ. 366. 2 All ER 936 (CA); *Parochial Church Council of the Parish of Aston Cantlow, Warwickshire v Wallbank* [2004] 1 AC 546. See also V Sachdeva "The Scope of Hybrid Public Authorities within the HRA 1998," *Judicial Review* [2004] 43-48; A Denney "Utility Companies and the Public/Private Divide," *Judicial Review* [2005] 65-71.

[41] House of Lords, House of Commons, Joint Committee on Human Rights, *The Meaning of Public Authority under the Human Rights Act* (HMSO, London, 2004), p 16.

[42] [2007] UKHL 27.

[43] [2007] UKHL 27 at para. 154. Neuberger considered that each factor, at least if taken individually, would be insufficient to render the provision of care and accommodation by Southern Cross in its care home to Mrs YL a "function of a public nature". However, it must be right to consider the effect of the various factors together, and, indeed, in the broader policy context.

[44] See, for example, *Van der Musselle v Belgium* (1983) 6 EHRR. 163; *Costello-Roberts v UK* (1993) 19 EHRR 112.

functions acted *ultra vires,*[45] or where the State has facilitated or colluded in acts breaching the ECHR.[46] In the case of *A v France*[47] the Commission observed that the responsibility of the State under Convention law may arise for acts of all of its organs or servants.[48]

Judicial Review and the ECHR Act

The ECHR Act could lead to some important changes in the nature and practice of judicial review.[49] Section 2(1) of the Act requires — in so far as is possible and subject to any other rule of interpretation — all courts to interpret and apply any statutory provision or rule of law in a manner compatible with the State's obligations under the ECHR. Traditional approaches to judicial supervision of administrative bodies in the common law, such as local authorities, are widely attributed to the influence of Dicey.[50] Indeed, nineteenth-century legal theorists may have had more than a passing experience of public administration based on undue political influence, discriminatory and discretionary administrative decisions and the "contracting" out of public functions to private corporations and companies. Some would see the recent growth of quasi-autonomous, non-government organisations or "quangos" as something of a return to this type of public magisterial or "grand jury" type of governance with Ministers appointing members of bodies through patronage with these bodies in turn being accountable only to the Minister.[51] It has been shown that one-third of the quangos in the Irish State do not have a statutory basis, which may enable them to evade judicial review.[52]

---

[45] See D Oliver "The Frontiers of the State: Public Authorities and Public Functions under the Human Rights Act," *Public Law,* Autumn 2000, 477–493.

[46] *Lopez-Ostra v Spain* (1995) 20 EHRR 277.

[47] (1993) 17 EHRR 462.

[48] The UK Audit Commission in Human Rights — Improving Public Service Deliver (Audit Commission, London, 2003) states (at p 12): "In order to minimise breaches of human rights by service providers, public bodies should, when negotiating contracts, require the service provider to undertake to protect the human rights of service users. This will bind service providers to the Act. If an individual's human rights are breached by a service provider who has entered into a contract that guarantees service users rights, an individual may bring a claim directly against the service provider using the Act. If a public body enters into a contract in this way it will have endeavoured to protect the rights of service users".

[49] See M de Blacam *Judicial Review,* (Tottel Publishing, Dublin, 2007); H Delany "Significant Themes in Judicial Review of Administrative Action", (1998) 5(1) DULJ 73.

[50] See generally: G Hogan and D Morgan (1998) *Administrative Law in Ireland,* (Round Hall, Dublin, 1998); C Bradley, *Judicial Review,* (Round Hall, Dublin, 2000); H Delany, *Judicial Review of Administrative Action — A Comparative Analysis.* (Round Hall, Dublin, 2001); M de Blacam, *Judicial Review,* (Butterworths, Dublin, 2007). See also Law Reform Commission, *Consultation Paper of Judicial Review Procedure* (LRC CP 20-2003).

[51] The growth of agencies in Ireland established by the Executive, some with statutory basis and some without, where a Minister controls their objectives, selects the members of the "Board", defines the contacts and consultation processes etc. outside the control of the Parliament and creating a major dilemma as to the legal obligations of such agencies acting as "organs of the State". See C Clancy and G Murphy, *Outsourcing Government: Public Bodies and Accountability,* (TASC, Dublin, 2006).

[52] See AM McGauran *et al, The Corporate Governance of Agencies in Ireland Non-Commercial Agencies* (IPA, Dublin, 2005).

The actions of public bodies must not be *ultra vires*, i.e., they must not exercise powers beyond those which they are legally or statutorily entitled to exercise.[53] The Government cannot make regulations giving powers which are not within the "principles and policies" contained in the parent statute,[54] but, of course, many Statutory Instruments are transpositions of EU law and these can amend existing statutes.[56]

Administrative discretion by State agencies must be exercised fairly and reasonably in line with *Wednesbury* principles.[56] This concept of "unreasonableness" was developed by the Irish courts in *State (Keegan) v Stardust Compensation Tribunal*.[57] Henchy J set out the situations where administrative decisions would be quashed by the court as "irrational". This involved situations where the decisions were fundamentally at variance with reason and common sense, or indefensible for being in the teeth of "plain reason and common sense". A court must be satisfied that the decision-maker had breached his obligation, where it must not flagrantly reject or disregard fundamental reason or common sense in reaching the decision. The scope of judicial review on administrative discretion in decision-making was considerably limited in the case of *O'Keeffe v An Bord Pleanala* [58] where Finlay CJ stated:

> "I am satisfied that in order for an Applicant for Judicial Review to satisfy a Court that the decision making authority has acted irrationally in the sense which I have outlined above so that the Court can intervene and quash it's decision, it is necessary that the Applicant should establish to the satisfaction of the Court that the decision making authority had before it *no relevant material* which would support it's decision."[59] (author's emphasis)

This means, effectively, that if a local authority has any relevant material before it, on which to base a decision, it will not be found by a court to be unreasonable.

The orthodox grounds of judicial review based on illegality, unconstitutionality, irrationality or procedural impropriety have now, however, been supplemented by

---

[53] But the Local Government Act 2001 s 65 gives a local authority power to do anything which is "ancillary, supplemental or incidental to or consequential on or necessary to give full effect to, or is conducive to the performance of, a function conferred on it by this or any other enactment". Section 66 permits a local authority to provide assistance in money or in kind as it considers necessary or desirable to promote the interests of the local community.

[54] *Cityview Press Ltd v An Comhairle Oiliuna* [1980] IR 381.

[55] As a result of Article 29.4.10 of the Constitution. See *Meagher v Minister for Agriculture* [1994] 1 IR 329. There are some 300-600 Statutory Instruments each year, with a significant proportion derived from EU law.

[56] See *Associated Picture Houses Ltd v Wednesbury Corporation* [1948] 1 KB 223; *East Donegal Co-op v A.G* [1970] IR 317.

[57] [1986] IR 642.

[58] [1993] 1 IR 39.

[59] [1993] 1 IR 39, at p 72.

another set of grounds for the review of administrative action. These derive from the ECHR Act. Section 4 provides:

> "Judicial notice shall be taken of the Convention provisions and of—
> (a) any declaration, decision, advisory opinion or judgment of the European Court of Human Rights established under the Convention on any question in respect of which that Court has jurisdiction;
> (b) any decision or opinion of the European Commission of Human Rights so established on any question in respect of which it had jurisdiction;
> (c) any decision of the Committee of Ministers established under the Statute of the Council of Europe on any question in respect of which it has jurisdiction, and a court shall, when interpreting and applying the Convention provisions, take due account of the principles laid down by those declarations, decisions, advisory opinions, opinions and judgments".

Clearly, the curial examination of discretion and local authority decision-making in the form of judicial review requires a fresh perspective in the light of the ECHR Act. An authoritative English case highlights this contemporary situation:

> "The Wednesbury, test, for all its defects, had the advantage of simplicity, and it might be thought satisfactory that it must now be replaced (when human rights are in play) by a much more complex and contextually sensitive approach. But the scope and reach of the [UK] Human Rights Act is so extensive that there is no alternative."[60]

Bamforth points out, in reviewing the UK Human Rights Act 1998 after five years, that it has brought about some significant changes in the methods in which cases are determined. This is most obvious in the open recognition by the UK courts that proportionality is now to be used in judicial review or statutory interpretation cases where Convention rights are involved. But the use and impact of ECHR arguments has been relatively tightly controlled and there has been no explosion of human rights litigation.[61] Other UK writers have pointed out that the unreasonableness test in judicial review is now outdated and:

> "... struggling to survive as a coherent and useful ground of review. Its days are surely numbered as a tool for dealing with Convention rights claims; proportionality or merits review look set to step in (according to the nature of the Convention right engaged)."[62]

What is Judicially Reviewable?

While the contemporary contours of what amounts to a body administering justice have been examined recently in the Irish cases arising from Tribunals of Inquiry

---

[60] Lord Walker in *R (Pro-life Alliance) v BBC* [2003] UKHL 23.

[61] N Bamforth, "Understanding the Impact and Status of the Human Rights Act 1998 within English Law", *Global Law Working Paper 10/04*. Hauser Global Law Program, NTU School of Law, New York. p vi.

[62] A Le Sueur, "The Rise and Ruin of Unreasonableness," [2005] *Judicial Review*, 25-51 at p 43.

such as *Goodman International v Hamilton (No. 1)*,[63] *Haughey v Moriarty*,[64] *Lawlor v Flood*,[65] *F Murphy v Flood*[66] and *Maguire v Ardagh*,[67] a more complex question arises in relation to what is actually justiciable, or open to judicial review.

Which actions of the State, as carried out by local authorities, are subject to judicial review? Setting budgets, acting as agents of the central Departments of State, making corporate plans, making payments, grants and fines, awarding contracts, dealing with appeals and allocating through licensing and other non-financial means the largesse of the State, are all part of the work of local authorities.[68] Indeed, local authorities in Ireland operate under a myriad of statutes and statutory instruments on a daily basis. Most of the policies and established practices of local authorities have never been judicially reviewed. Judicial review cases appear to largely involve planning, licensing and issues connected with the compulsory purchase of land, although the housing of members of the Traveller Community also generates many cases.[69]

In order to establish a right of action for an alleged breach of the ECHR Act a plaintiff must frame the issue as a legal issue. Thus, it must be distinguished from a political issue which would be within the exclusive remit of the Legislature or, in limited cases, the elected body of the local authority itself. Secondly, the matter must not be a purely bureaucratic one that is seen as, essentially, a management issue, or one that is entirely within the area of administrative discretion. Defining what is justiciable has been based, among other things, on the criteria required for something to be a "justiciable controversy." Kenny J, in *McDonald v Bord na gCon*[70] stated that a justiciable controversy was one which as a matter of history has been capable of litigation in the courts, but that is a rather circular formulation of justiciability.

The courts have eschewed judicial intervention on such issues as State spending on Traveller accommodation,[71] binding a Minister to published timescales for the

[63] [1992] 2 IR 542; [1992] ILRM 145.
[64] [1999] 3 IR 1.
[65] [1999] 3 IR 107.
[66] [1999] 3 IR 97.
[67] [2002] 1 IR 385.
[68] In *Hempenstall v Minister for the Environment* 1994 2 IR 20 at 28, Costello J pointed out that licences by State bodies can be revoked or reduced in value. "Property rights arising in licences created by law (enacted or delegated) are subject to the conditions created by law and to an implied condition that the law may change those conditions. … an amendment of the law which by changing the conditions under which a licence is held cannot be regarded as an attack on the property right in a licence-it is the consequence of the implied condition which is an inherent part of the property right in the licence".
[69] Reasons for the lack of development of judicial review of other local authority functions in Ireland may be based on the very limited access to legal aid, the nature of local authority functions historically, and perceptions of judicial deference to State bodies generally. See *Access to Justice: A Right not a Privilege*, (FLAC, Dublin, 2005).
[70] [1965] IR 217.
[71] *O'Reilly and Others v Limerick Corporation* [1989] ILRM 181.

provision of services for homeless children,[72] requiring a local authority to repair roads in County Cavan,[73] requiring a Minister to provide education for persons with disabilities over 18 years,[74] obliging the State to implement international legal instruments signed by the State[75] and reviewing the nomination of a former judge to the European Central Bank.[76]

There is clearly a reluctance to tread too closely to some "recognised" demarcation set out in the separation of powers doctrine, enshrined in a limited and rather descriptive form in Article 6.1 of the Constitution which provides:

> "All powers of government, legislative, executive and judicial, derive, under God, from the people, whose right it is to designate the rulers of the State and, in final appeal, to decide all questions of national policy, according to the requirements of the common good".

However, while the courts have treated all constitutional provisions as *prima facie* justiciable,[77] embedding a breach of human rights, as defined by the ECHR Act, into the criterion of a justiciable controversy has not yet developed to any great degree in constitutional case law.

The courts have sought to examine closely the decisions of public bodies to differentiate issues of public law, which are reviewable (by way of judicial review), in contrast to issues of private law, such as contractual relations, which are not. However, there is much judicial deference to the operations of local authorities and the tests of reasonableness just discussed can operate as a proverbial litigation "wet blanket". Writers such as Hogan and Morgan describe the historical difficulties in developing administrative law in Ireland and in trying to reconcile classical separation of powers doctrines with the "fused executive-legislature" system in Ireland.[78] There has been a notable reluctance by the Irish courts to compel the Executive to comply with constitutional or statutory obligations for the benefit of citizens.[79] This has been justified — sometimes interchangeably — by reference to a particular understanding of the doctrine of separation of powers, Aristotlean

---

[72] *DB (A minor, suing by his Mother and Next Friend) v The Minister for Justice, the Minister for Health, the Minister for Education, Ireland and the Attorney General and the Eastern Health Board* [1999] 1 IR 29; [1999] 1 ILRM 102.

[73] *Brady v Cavan County Council* [1999] 4 IR 99.

[74] *TD v Minister for Education and Others* [2001] 4 IR 259.

[75] *Re O'Laighleis* [1960] IR 183; *Kavanagh v Governor of Mountjoy Prison* [2002] 2 ILRM 81; *Horgan v An Taoiseach* [2003] 2 ILRM 357.

[76] *Riordan v Ireland* [2000] 4 IR 537.

[77] See G Hogan and G Whyte (2004) *Kelly's — The Irish Constitution.* (Butterworths, Dublin, 2004) at 6.1.42.

[78] Hogan and Morgan, *Administrative Law in Ireland* (3rd ed, Round Hall, Dublin, 1998), p 10.

[79] "The really troubling area is where the Court is called on to make an order against the State or its legislative or executive organ which carries with it financial implications". See Byrne and Binchy, *Annual Review of Irish Law 2001*, (Round Hall, Dublin, 2002), p 110.

conceptions of commutative and distributive justice and the almost sacrosanct but largely symbolic status of Dáil approval of the annual Finance Acts.[80] This model of judicial deference was exemplified by Hardiman, J in the seminal 2001 Supreme Court decision of *Sinnott v Minister for Education and Others.*[81] Referring to the possibility that a court could order a State body to carry out a constitutionally guaranteed education service he said:

> "Such an order... could only be made as an absolutely final resort in circumstances of great crisis and for the protection of the constitutional order itself. I do not believe that any circumstances which justify the granting of such an order have occurred since the enactment of the Constitution sixty-four years ago."[82]

Standard justifications by the State for failure to meet legal and human rights obligations include local budgetary constraints, lack of funds from the Government and the questionable justification of such expenditure.[83] However, in *Hoey v Minister for Justice*,[84] the lack of resources argument, preventing a Minister from carrying out a statutory duty (repair and maintenance of a court house), was found to be based on "a misconception of powers, duties and functions of the executive in regard to the implementation of legislation enacted by the Oireachtas".[85]

ECHR Act and Local Authorities

In relation to judicial review s 3(1) of the ECHR Act integrates the jurisprudence on the European Court of Human Rights (ECtHR) into the relevant law relating to the functions of local authorities as "organs of the State". It provides:

> "Subject to any statutory provision (other than this Act) or rule of law, every organ of the State shall perform its functions in a manner compatible with the State's obligations under the Convention provisions".

[80] See *O'Reilly and Others v Limerick Corporation* [1989] ILRM 182: *TD v Minister for Education and Others* [2001] 4 IR 259: *Sinnott v The Minister for Education, Ireland and The Attorney General,* [2001] 2 IR 545. The State has of course, bound itself to many multi-annual funding agreements, such as public private partnerships and leases over 20 or more years, which would seem to conflict with the doctrine that all State expenditure must be approved annually, espoused by some commentators on the separation of powers doctrine. The archaic nature of this legal reasoning is apparent from the legally enforceable but unknown commitments given by the State in the NAMA legislation, which bind future Oireachtas fiscal and spending decisions into the future, as well as the EU Stability and Growth Pact, whereby Members of the Eurozone countries have committed to an annual budget deficit no higher than 3% of GDP and a national debt lower than 60% of GDP or approaching that value.

[81] [2001] 2 IR 545.

[82] *Sinnott v The Minister for Education, Ireland and The Attorney General* [2001] 2 IR 545 at 559.

[83] See, for instance, *Brady v Cavan County Council* [1999] 4 IR 99.

[84] [1994] 3 IR 329.

[85] *ibid*, at 343.

There are a number of areas of European Court of Human Rights (ECtHR) jurisprudence that are particularly relevant.[86] Clearly, the representative, agency, regulatory and service provision roles of local authorities will need to be carried out in a manner compatible with Convention obligations. The machinery of decision-making, appeals and policy-making must also be Convention-compatible, with the concept of proportionality which already existed in Irish law gaining new importance.[87] However, the major impact of the ECHR Act is likely to be in the culture shift required to accept that local authorities now have "positive obligations" to ensure that Convention rights are secured. The doctrine of positive obligations requires States to protect individual persons from threats to their Convention rights or to assist them to achieve full enjoyment of those rights.[88] Under Article 1 ECHR there is an obligation to respect human rights and to secure to everyone within the jurisdiction the rights and freedoms contained in the Convention. Equally, it is long established that Convention rights must be guaranteed not in a theoretical or illusory way, but in a practical and effective manner.[89]

Article 3 Issues Relating to "Inhuman and Degrading Treatment" and Local Authorities

In relation to Article 3 ECHR which states in quite absolutist terms that "no one shall be subjected to torture or to inhuman or degrading treatment or punishment" there are specific obligations on organs of the State encompassing a wide range of matters.[90] While this applies to local authorities in their dealings with people there is also an obligation on all State organs to prevent such treatment by others. The ambit of such treatment has been clarified in *Pretty v United Kingdom*:

> "Where treatment humiliates or debases an individual showing lack of respect for, or diminishing his or her human dignity arouses feelings of fear, anguish or inferiority capable of breaking an individual's moral and physical resistance it may be characterised as degrading and also fall within the prohibition of Article 3.[91]

[86] See S Barton, "The ECHR Act 2003 — A Practitioner's Perspective", Paper presented to Irish Human Rights Commission and Law Society of Ireland Conference on European Convention on Human Rights Act 2003 Review and Human Rights in Committed Relationships, Conference, 16 October 2004. See also Kenna, "Implications for Local Authorities of the ECHR Act 2003," Paper presented to Irish Human Rights Commission and Law Society of Ireland Conference on European Convention on Human Rights Act 2003 Review and Human Rights in Committed Relationships, Conference, 16 October 2004.

[87] See I Leigh, "Taking Rights Proportionately: Judicial Review, The Human Rights Act and Strasbourg" [2002] *Public Law*, Summer, 265-287.

[88] See P Kenna, "Housing Rights: Positive Duties and Enforceable Rights at the European Court of Human Rights", *EHRLR* 2008, 2, 193-208; A Mowbray, *The Development of Positive Obligations under the European Convention on Human Rights by the European Court of Human Rights*, (Hart, Oxford, 2004).

[89] *Airey v Ireland* [1979] 2 EHRR 305; [1981] 3 EHRR 592.

[90] *Price v United Kingdom* (33394/96) [2001] ECHR 453 (10 July 2001); *R (Q) v Secretary of State* [2003] 2 All ER 905.

[91] *Pretty v UK* (2002) 35 EHRR 1. at para. 52. It should be noted, however, that no violation of Article 3 ECHR was declared in this case.

In the case of *Limbuela*[92] a homeless asylum-seeker sought State assistance, citing Article 3 ECHR in support of this claim.[93] The House of Lords found that the State had positive obligations to such destitute asylum-seekers.[94] The case raised, in its starkest form, to the question of what level of abject destitution to which individuals must sink before their suffering or humiliation reached the minimum level of severity to amount to "inhuman or degrading treatment" under Article 3 ECHR.[95] Lord Bingham stated that the answer must be:

> "... when it appears on a fair and objective assessment of all relevant facts and circumstances that an individual applicant faces an imminent prospect of serious suffering caused or materially aggravated by denial of shelter, food or the most basic necessities of life. Many factors may affect that judgment, including age, gender, mental and physical health and condition, any facilities or sources of support available to the applicant, the weather and time of year and the period for which the applicant has already suffered or is likely to continue to suffer deprivation."[96]

In *Marzari v Italy*[97] Article 3 obligations were considered to place an obligation on public authorities to provide assistance to an individual suffering from a severe disability because of the impact of such refusal on the private life of the individual. The ECtHR stated that: "State has obligations of this type where there is a direct and immediate link between the measures sought by the applicant and the latter's private life". [98]

Although the emphasis in Article 3 cases is on minimum levels of State support for individuals in adverse circumstances, combined with the obligations under Article 8 ECHR this may lead to significant positive obligations for the State of a nature completely unfamiliar to Irish local authorities, particularly for people with disabilities.

Article 6 ECHR and Local Authorities

Article 6 obligations in relation to fair hearings by independent and impartial tribunals involved in the determination of civil rights and obligations will create many difficulties for Irish local authorities.[99] The range of civil rights and obligations

---

[92] *R. (on the application of Limbuela) v Secretary of State for the Home Department* [2005] UKHL 66; [2006] 1 AC 396.
[93] See also *Anufrijeva v Secretary of State* [2003] EWCA 1406.
[94] *R. v Secretary of State for the Home Department ex parte Adam (FC) and others.* [2005] UKHL 66.
[95] Same case as *Limbuela* at Court of Appeal. *R. ex parte Adam and others v Secretary of State for the Home Department* [2004] EWCA Civ. 540. at para 84.
[96] [2005] UKHL 66, at para. 8.
[97] *Marzari v Italy* (1999) 28 EHRR CD 175.
[98] *ibid*, at 179.
[99] See A Lowry, "Practice and Procedure under the European Convention on Human Rights Act 2002", *Bar Review*. November 2003, pp 183–185.

involving local authorities is broad and largely indeterminate.[100] Local authorities exercising statutory functions are involved in dispensing the largesse of the State in zoning development land; awarding grant funding and licences; appointing selected providers and suppliers; and enhancing the value of property through "betterment" of certain locations.[101]

In exercising such statutory and regulatory powers all public bodies must comply with the substantive and procedural requirements flowing from Article 6 ECHR, such as hearing both sides within a reasonable time, "equality of arms," offering an independent and impartial tribunal established by law for appeals, procedural protection, adequate time and facilities for preparation of defence, etc.[102]

The summary possession procedures under s 62 of the Housing Act 1966 have already been found to breach Article 6 ECHR.[103] The absence of any opportunity to defend summary possession proceedings in relation to the home was considered by the ECtHR in *Connors v UK* in 2004.[104] The Court held that Article 6 was breached where the applicant was unable in the summary possession proceedings to challenge the Council's allegations whether by giving evidence himself or calling witnesses. There was no equality of arms and he was denied any effective access to Court against this very serious interference with his home and family.

Historical judicial deference to the Executive and Legislature in these areas will not be sufficient to ensure compatibility with the ECHR Act.[105] In judicial supervision of the operation of public and housing legislation, there is now a new climate.

> "That a court should presume that the myriad of rules of domestic landlord and tenant law can be given a clean bill of jurisprudential health for Article 8 purposes seems in one sense a cavalier approach to judicial law-making, in that the court is eschewing its traditional role to reach legal conclusions in reaction to specific, micro-problems posed by litigants in favour of making sweeping macro-level policy statements."[106]

Article 8 ECHR and Local Authorities

Article 8(1) protects the right of individuals to "respect" for their private life, family life, "home" and correspondence. There is a right of access to, occupation of, and

---

[100] See *König v Germany,* (judgment of 28 June 1987, Series A. No. 27, p 30, § 89). Whether or not a right is to be regarded as civil within the meaning of that term in the Convention must be determined by reference not only to its legal classification but also to its substantive content and effects under the domestic law of the State concerned.

[101] See P Kenna "Land Law, Property, Housing and Environment" in U Kilkelly (ed.) *ECHR and Irish Law,* (2nd ed, Jordans, Bristol, 2008).

[102] Council of Europe, *Short Guide to the European Convention on Human Rights* (1998) pp 38–50.

[103] *Pullen v Dublin City Council* [2008] IEHC 379.

[104] *Case of Connors v UK.* (2004) 40 EHRR 189.

[105] See R Edwards, (2002) "Judicial Deference under the Human Rights Act", 65 MLR. 859.

[106] See I Loveland, "The Impact of the Human Rights Act on Security of Tenure in Public Housing", [2002] *Public Law,* Autumn, pp 594–601 at p 608.

peaceful enjoyment of the home. "Home" is an autonomous concept under the ECHR and does not depend for classification by domestic law.[107] Article 8(2) provides that there shall be no interference by a public authority with the exercise of the right set out in Article 8(1) except in accordance with law and necessary in a democratic society. There is extensive jurisprudence on the nature and extent of such permitted restrictions on Article 8 rights.[108]

Although there is a margin of appreciation allowed to States in the interpretation and application of Convention rights, the ECtHR jurisprudence in relation to evictions from home affords States a narrow margin of discretion. In *Buckley v United Kingdom* where a Traveller family was evicted from an unauthorised site, the offer of alternative accommodation, even where there was a fear of violence, was held to justify the interference with the applicants' Article 8 rights.[109]

But in *Stankova v Slovakia,*[110] the eviction by the relevant municipality interfered with the applicant's "home" but was found to be in accordance with law. The only point at issue was whether that interference was justifiable as "necessary in a democratic society" to achieve the legitimate aim pursued by the eviction. This notion of necessity implies a "pressing social need". In particular, the measure employed must be proportionate to the legitimate aim pursued. The municipality was in charge of public housing, and under an obligation to assist the town's citizens in resolving their accommodation problems. These considerations were sufficient for the ECtHR to conclude that the interference complained of was not "necessary in a democratic society" and accordingly there was a violation of Article 8 ECHR.

In the case of *Cosic v Croatia,*[111] involving the eviction of a teacher tenant from the State flat where she had lived for 18 years the ECtHR stated that the central question was whether the interference complained of was proportionate to the aim pursued and thus "necessary in a democratic society".[112] The ECtHR again pointed out that the loss of one's home is a most extreme form of interference with the right to respect for the home.

> "Any person at risk of an interference of this magnitude should in principle be able to have the proportionality and reasonableness of the measure determined by an independent tribunal in the light of the relevant principles under Article 8 of the Convention, notwithstanding that, under domestic law, his or her right of occupation has come to an end (see *McCann v the United Kingdom*, no. 19009/04, § 50, 13 May 2008)."[113]

---

[107] *Chapman v UK* (2001) 33 EHRR.

[108] See C Ovey, and R White, Jacobs and White, *The European Convention on Human Rights,* (4th ed, OUP, Oxford, 2006).

[109] *Buckley v UK* (1996) 23 EHRR 101. In *Connors v UK* 40 EHRR 189 the ECtHR held that a state's margin of appreciation is narrower where an applicant's home is at risk. See further: *McCann v UK,* judgment of 13 May 2008.

[110] 7205/02 [2007] ECHR 795 (9 October 2007).

[111] *Cosic v Croatia,* (Application No 28261/06) European Court of Human Rights, Judgment of 15 January 2009.

[112] *ibid,* para. 20

[113] *ibid,* para. 22.

The landmark ECtHR decision under Article 8 is *Botta v Italy.*[114] Mr Botta, who was physically disabled, was on holiday at a seaside resort in Italy in 1990 when he discovered that the bathing establishments were not equipped with the facilities to allow people with disabilities to access the beach and the sea. Specifically, the resort lacked special access ramps, lavatories, and washrooms in breach of Italian legislation. In March 1991, Mr. Botta asked the local mayor to remedy these shortcomings and when he returned to the resort later in 1991, he found no changes. Taking legal action, he claimed the impairment of his private life and development of his personality resulting from the Italian State's failure to remedy the omissions at this private bathing establishment breached the Convention obligations on the Italian State. Before the ECtHR it was established that a State had a positive obligation towards people with disabilities to enable them to enjoy, so far as possible, a normal private and family life. The ECtHR, in defining the scope of the positive obligation, stated that there "must be a direct and immediate link between the measures sought by the applicant and the latter's private and family life".[115]

Under the UK Human Rights Act 1998 damages of £10,000 were awarded against a local authority in relation to the provision of inadequate housing. In *R. (Bernard) v Enfield L.B.C.*[116] the High Court found that the authority had acted unlawfully and incompatibly with Article 8 ECHR in failing for over two years to provide suitable accommodation for a family. The mother was severely disabled and confined to a wheelchair and was housed in temporary accommodation by the authority which meant that she was effectively confined to a single room. The conduct of the authority not only engaged, but breached Article 8 obligations, since it condemned the claimants to living conditions which made it virtually impossible to have any meaningful private or family life in the sense in which that right was protected by that article. However, the part of the claim for breach of Article 3 ECHR failed on the ground that the authority's "corporate neglect" was not intended to deliberately inflict such suffering. The judgment relied on the abovementioned *Botta* case and reasoned:

> "... Respect for private and family life does not require the State to provide every one of its citizens with a house. However, those entitled to care under section 21 [of the relevant UK Act] are a particularly vulnerable group. Positive measures have to be taken (by way of community care facilities) to enable them to enjoy, so far as possible, a normal private and family life. The Council's failure to act... showed a singular lack of respect for the claimants' private and family life. It condemned the claimants to living conditions which made it virtually impossible for them to have any meaningful private or family life for the purposes of Article 8".

---

[114] *Botta v Italy* (1998) 26 EHRR 241.
[115] (1998) 26 EHRR 241 at para. 34. However, the ECtHR decided that this case concerned interpersonal relations of such broad and indeterminate scope that there could be no conceivable direct link between the measures the State was urged to take and the applicant's private life.
[116] [2002] EWHC 2282 (Admin).

In the case of *Zehnalova v Czech Republic*[117] the positive obligations on a local authority under Article 8 were again considered. The local authority did not comply with local technical requirements which would have made public buildings and buildings open to the public accessible for people with impaired mobility. In this case Article 8 ECHR was found to entail a positive obligation on the authority to ensure that people with impaired mobility enjoyed adequate access to and use of public buildings but a breach of the article would only be found where there was a special link between the lack of access and the particular needs of the individual claiming a breach in respect of their private life. It would apply when the failure to carry out a positive obligation interfered with the complainant's right to personal development and to establish and maintain relationships with the outside world.[118]

Some other cases have raised essentially environmental issues under Article 8. For example, the duty of State bodies to protect home and private life under Article 8 were violated in the case of *Lopez-Ostra v Spain*[119] where a family were forced to move from their home as a result of smells and nuisance from a waste treatment plant.

The case of *Hatton v UK* in *the* Grand Chamber of the ECtHR had to decide whether in implementing a policy on night flights at Heathrow airport, a fair balance had been struck between the competing interests of the individuals affected by the night noise and the community as a whole. The ECtHR held that the economic value of night flights as part of the economic interest in maintaining a full service to London from distant airports was sufficiently important in the Government decision, and that within its margin of appreciation a fair balance had been struck.[120]

In *Geurra v Italy*[121] the ECtHR held that the direct effect of toxic emissions emanating from a chemical factory, which had resulted in one hundred and fifty families being hospitalised for arsenic poisoning, breached Article 8. In *Moreno-Gomez v Spain*[122] the failure by the State to tackle night-time noise disturbances caused by nightclubs breached the positive obligation to guarantee the applicants right to respect for her home as guaranteed by Article 8. In the case of *Fadeyeva v Russia,*[123] a violation of a Russian woman's rights under Article 8 was found where the government had failed to prevent or adequately regulate the environmental pollution from a steel plant which adversely affected her quality of life and made her more vulnerable to disease. However, the ECtHR pointed out that Article 8 is not violated every time that environmental deterioration occurs. In order to raise an issue under Article 8 the interference must directly affect the applicant's home, family or private life.[124]

---

[117] ECtHR Admissibility Decision 38621/97, 14 May 2002.
[118] In this case the plaintiff did not establish such a link.
[119] (1991) 14 EHRR 319.
[120] (2003) 37 EHRR 28.
[121] (1998) EHRR 357.
[122] (2005) 41 EHRR 40.
[123] (2005) 45 EHRR 10.
[124] *ibid*, para. 68.

The right to receive and impart information on environmental issues is protected by Article 10 ECHR. In *Steel and Morris v UK*[125] (the so-called *MacLibel* case) the ECtHR considered that in a democratic society even small and informal campaign groups, such as London Greenpeace, must be able to carry on their activities effectively.

Article 14 ECHR (Non-Discrimination) and Local Authorities

In *Larkos v Cyprus*[126] a tenant of the state enjoyed less security than he would have had under domestic law had he been a tenant of a private landlord. This engaged both Articles 8 and 14. The Court held that no reasonable and objective justification had been given by the State for not extending these protections to State tenants. In Ireland, local authorities are now using the Rental Accommodation Scheme (RAS), to meet their social housing obligations in line with the Housing (Miscellaneous Provisions) Act 2009, creating a different set of tenancy terms to their other (and current) social housing tenants. Both sets of tenants are subsidised by the State and in similar financial circumstances. Yet, RAS tenants have access to an independent and impartial body to deal with disputes — the Private Residential Tenancies Board, as well as increased security of tenure.[127]

Different treatment by local authorities in relation to same-sex and opposite-sex couples in the area of housing could possibly be in breach of Article 8 read with Article 14.[128] In *Mendoza v Ghaidan*[129] the UK Court of Appeal ruled that a same-sex partner of a deceased statutory tenant was entitled to succeed to a statutory tenancy and to treat him differently than a survivor of a heterosexual couple would be an impermissible discrimination under Article 14.[130] The definition of "private life" will have major implications in relation to family law tenancy agreements.[131]

Article 1, Protocol 1 and Local Authorities

Local authorities are regularly involved in expanding and controlling the value of property through zoning, planning and compulsory purchase.[132] The issues arising under Article 1, Protocol 1 were considered in detail in the Article 26 reference of the Planning and Development Bill 1999.[133] The justification for State interference

---

[125] Application no. 68416/01. Judgment, 15 February 2005.

[126] (1999) 30 EHRR 597.

[127] See Housing (Miscellaneous Provisions) Act 2009, s 25. The same argument could apply to those social housing tenancies provided by Housing Associations which are 100% State capital funding.

[128] See Fergus Ryan, "Sexuality, ideology and the Legal Construction of "Family"; *Fitzpatrick v Sterling Housing Association*", IJFL, 3, pp 2–9.

[129] [2002] EWCA Civ. 1533.

[130] See also *Wandsworth LBC v Michalak* [2002] EWCA Civ. 271.

[131] *Karner v Austria* (2004) 38 EHRR 24; *Dudgeon v UK* (1981) 4 EHRR 149; *Norris v Ireland,* A 142 (1988)

[132] See for example The Land Clauses Consolidation Act 1845; Public Health (Ireland) Act 1878; Housing of the Working Classes Act 1890; Housing Act 1960; Local Government Act 2001, s 21.

[133] *In Re: Article 26: Part V, Planning and Development Bill 1999* [2000] 2 IR 321; [2001] 1 ILRM 81.

with property rights was set out in terms that were resonant with Convention requirements:

> "[I]t must relate to concerns pressing and substantial in a free and democratic society. The means chosen must pass a proportionality test.
>
> (a) be rationally connected to the objective and not be arbitrary, unfair or based on irrational considerations;
> (b) impair the right as little as possible; and
> (c) be such that their effects on rights are proportional to the objective".[134]

The level of compensation for compulsory purchase of land has been a regular source of legal challenge both on procedural grounds and in the assessment of the level of compensation.[135] The ECtHR in its consideration of Article 1, Protocol 1 distinguishes between deprivation of property and control on the use of property.[136] But modern governmental activity often involves only the imposition of restrictions on the free enjoyment of property rights. According to Gray:

> "It simply cannot be the case that all regulatory subtractions from a landholder's user rights necessarily constitute compensable deprivations of "property'...The progress of civilised society would effectively grind to a halt if every minor regulatory act of the State provoked an immediate entitlement to a carefully calculated cash indemnity for the affected landowner."[137]

While there is, in theory, no explicit rule requiring compensation the question of whether or not compensation has been paid will generally be an important factor in the assessment of the proportionality of the interference with the property right in question.[138] There have been no cases in which the exceptional circumstances leading to failure to pay compensation for the interference with property rights have been justified.

In relation to controls on use, however, there is no equivalent presumption in favour of compensation. State action involving control on use does not, as a rule, contain any right to compensation. The ECtHR has held that controls on use which reduced the value of the applicant's freehold property without compensation was permissible,[139] as was the withdrawal of planning permission without compensation.[140] Problems arise when the State introduces regulatory measures

---

[134] [2001] 1 ILRM 81 at 110.

[135] See Butler *op. cit.*, Chps 9 and 10. See also *Murphy v Dublin City Council* [1979] IR 115.

[136] D Anderson, "Compensation for Interference with Property", (1999) *EHRLR* 543. See also *Former King of Greece v Greece* (2001) 33 EHRR 516.

[137] K Gray, "Land Law and Human Rights" in L Tee (ed) (2002) *Land Law, Issues, Debates, Policy* (Willan, Devon, 2002), p 223.

[138] Anderson, *op. cit.* at 549. See also *James v United Kingdom* (1986) 8 EHRR 123.

[139] *James v United Kingdom* (1986) 8 EHRR 123.

[140] *Pine Valley Developments v Ireland* (1991) 14 EHRR 319.

which reduce the value of property without taking it away, or which comprise a taking of land, without actually being acknowledged as a "taking". In *Sporrong and Lonnroth v Sweden*[141] the ECtHR accepted that a regulation on land use may constitute a *de facto* expropriation if it affects the substance of the property that takes away all its meaningful use. But, if the property or land can be used for any purpose, such as farming, then compensation for expropriation may not be payable.[142]

Of course, human rights protections under Article 1, Protocol 1 are not confined to those relating to land. There is a long line of ECtHR cases showing that entitlements to social assistance can amount to a property right engaging Article 1, Protocol 1.[143] Local authorities administering benefits and grants must, in accordance with Section 3 of the ECHR Act, operate in a manner compatible with the Article 1, Protocol 1, and regard such entitlements as "possessions" in certain cases. In the case of *Stretch v UK*[144] the notion of "possessions" included the tenant's interest in the continuation of a tenancy. Once this pecuniary or possessory right is established then any interference with that right must satisfy the requirements of Article 1, Protocol 1, Article 6 ECHR and Article 14 ECHR.

ECHR Act Cases Involving Irish Local Authorities

To date, there have been a small number of cases where local authorities have been found to be in breach of the ECHR Act.

In *Dublin City Council v Laura McGrath,*[145] the local authority sought to evict a tenant as part of the redevelopment of Ballymun. The High Court held that the protection afforded by the ECHR Act must be taken into account in an action for an injunction. In the case of *Dublin City Council v Jeanette Fennell*[146] the local authority had issued a Notice to Quit and obtained an order for possession in the District Court. Ms Fennell lodged an appeal to the Circuit Court on 23rd December 2003, before the ECHR Act came into force. She pointed out that the proceedings were in motion at the time of the Act's coming into force on 30th December 2003. The Supreme Court held, unanimously, that the appeal to the Circuit Court, although consisting of a *de novo* hearing, did not exist in a vacuum.[147] Mr Justice Kearns, speaking for the Court, said:

> "The parties' legal rights and obligations were, in my view, fixed and determined once the wheel was set in motion by the service of a Notice to Quit, an act which triggered the provisions, requirements and consequences of s 62 of the Housing

---

[141] (1982) 5 EHRR 35.

[142] *Pine Valley Developments v Ireland* (1991) 14 EHRR 319.

[143] See, for example: *X v Sweden* (1986) 8 EHRR 252; *Muller v Austria* (1975) 3 DR 25; *Gaygusuz v Austria* (1996) 23 EHRR 364; *Feldbrugge v The Netherlands* (1986) 8 EHRR 425; *Koua Poirrez v France* (2005) 40 EHRR 2 ECHR.

[144] (2004) 38 EHRR 12.

[145] [2004] IEHC 111; [2004] 1 IR 216.

[146] [2005] IESC 33.

[147] See *Outline Submissions made on behalf of the IHRC,* which acted as *amicus curiae* in the case on website: http://www.ihrc.ie/documents.

> Act, 1966. That is the moment when the invocation of legal rights determined the applicable law and the position of the parties".

However, while the substantive issue of the compatibility of the procedures under s 62 of the Housing Act, 1966 was not considered in the judgement, Mr Justice Kearns commented, *obiter,* that:

> "It goes without saying therefore that the position of the tenant of a housing authority compares unfavourably with that of a private law tenant under contract or under the Landlord and Tenant Acts, the Rent Restrictions Acts or a variety of other statutes. It may also be seen that the summary method whereby possession of such dwellings may be recovered, notably in circumstances where the tenant is regarded as having through misbehaviour brought about the termination of his own tenancy and thus forfeited the right to any alternative accommodation, may arguably infringe certain articles of the European Convention on Human Rights, and in particular, Articles 6, 8 and 13 thereof, and also Article 1 of Protocol 1 (Protection of property) of the Convention".

In *McConnell v Dublin City Council and others*[148] the High Court distinguished the statute and statutory framework of the Housing Act 1966 from the (UK) Caravan Sites Act 1968, where similar procedures had been found in breach of the ECHR in *Connors.*[149] In *Gifford and Another v Dublin City Council*[150] the plaintiffs unsuccessfully sought an interlocutory injunction restraining the Council from enforcing a warrant for possession under s 62. The action was taken on the basis that s 62 was incompatible with Articles 6, 8, 13 and 14 ECHR, and that the Council had failed to perform its functions in a manner compatible with the ECHR Act.[151]

In *Leonard v Dublin City Council*[152] the Council had included a condition in a tenancy that if a tenant's son was found in the rented property she would be evicted. He was found in the property and s 62 proceedings were instituted. The applicant contended that the summary procedure of s 62 was incompatible with the ECHR Act. However, the Court held that Article 6 and 8 ECHR were satisfied since judicial review provided an adequate procedural safeguard.

In *O'Donnell v South Dublin County Council*[153] the judgment of Laffoy, J considerably clarified the obligations of local authorities under the ECHR Act. The plaintiffs were disabled children of a Traveller family living in a mobile home at a temporary halting site in Dublin and they sought a wheelchair-accessible caravan with indoor and wheelchair-accessible shower, toilet, sanitary facilities and central heating.

---

148 [2005] IEHC 7.
149 *Connors v UK* [2004] 40 EHRR 189.
150 [2007] IEHC 387.
151 However, in *Byrne v Dublin City Council* [2009] IEHC 122 an interlocutory injunction (with conditions as to the family members who could occupy the property) was granted by Murphy J. This restrained the local authority from implementing the warrant for possession already granted under s 62 of the Housing Act 1966.
152 [2008] IEHC 79.
153 [2007] IEHC 204.

While the High Court did not find a breach of other statutory or constitutional rights, there was a breach of the rights established under the ECHR Act. As noted above, Article 8 gives rise to positive obligations on the part of organs of the State to vindicate a person's right to respect for their private and family life and their home. The local authority contended that Article 8 did not confer any right to be provided with a home or any positive obligation to provide alternative accommodation of an applicant's choosing. The Court considered the UK judgments in *R (Bernard) v Enfield LBC*[154] and *Anufrijeva v Southwark LBC*[155] which involved the provision of services to people with disabilities, and the Strasbourg judgment of *Moldovan v Romania*[156] in relation to the alleged breaches of Articles 3 and 8.

This case was distinguished on the facts from *Doherty v South Dublin County Council*,[157] where Charleton J refused to find a breach of the ECHR Act in circumstances where an elderly Traveller couple in poor health, living in a caravan with only basic electricity, no internal plumbing, toilet or central heating were refused a centrally heated, insulated and plumbed caravan. The elderly couple had refused an offer from the local authority of a two-bed roomed ground floor apartment.

Laffoy J considered that the level of disability and dependency of the children in the *O'Donnell* case, the degree of care and supervision they required, together with the appalling housing conditions and the meagre offer by the local authority distinguished the situation from the *Doherty* case.

While not finding a breach of Article 3, Laffoy, J did find a violation of Article 8, and stated:

> "The question which arises in determining whether there has been a breach of Article 8 is whether practical and effective respect for the private and family life and of the home of each of the plaintiffs requires the defendant to adopt the measure which the plaintiffs contend is necessary to alleviate the overcrowded and potentially unsafe conditions in which the plaintiffs are living."[158]

Thus, even in the absence of a statutory provision, there may still be a breach of an Article 8 right. She went on to state that if there was no relevant statutory protection, in certain circumstances such a lacuna could represent a failure on the part of the State and its organs to function in a manner compatible with Article 8 ECHR.[159]

---

[154] [2002] EWHC 2282 (Admin).
[155] [2004] 1 All ER 833.
[156] *Moldovan v Romania* (No. 2) (2007) 44 EHRR 16.
[157] [2007] IEHC 4.
[158] [2007] IEHC 204 at 41.
[159] *O'Donnell v South Dublin County Council* [2007] IEHC 204 at p 44.

In *Donegan v Dublin City Council*[160], the procedures under s 62 of the Housing Act 1966 were found to be in breach of Article 8. Laffoy J after considering the relevant Strasbourg case law, stated:

> "A statutory regime under which possession of the home of an occupier, whether a licensee or tenant, can be recovered by a public authority which does not embody procedural safeguards whereby the occupier can have the decision which will inevitably result in his eviction from his home reviewed in accordance with Convention recognised fair procedures (as illustrated by the decision in *Tsfayo*), in my view, cannot fulfil the *Connors* test of being fair and affording due respect to the rights protected by Article 8.
>
> Accordingly, in the light of decisions of the ECtHR in Connors and Blecic the procedure provided for in s 62, cannot be regarded as proportionate to the need of the housing authority to manage and regulate its housing stock in accordance with its statutory duties and the principles of good estate management."[161]

The decision, which is clearly in line with *McCann v United Kingdom*,[162] found that the operation of s 62 the Housing Act 1966 in the manner impugned was incompatible with the ECHR. A declaration of incompatibility under s 5 of ECHR Act was made in this case and also in the case of *Dublin City Council v Gallagher*.[163] In the latter case, which again highlighted the incompatibility of the Housing Act 1966 with the ECHR Act, O'Neill J found that the facts were analogous to *Donegan*.[164]

In the *Pullen v Dublin City Council*[165] the possession procedures under s 62 of the 1966 Housing Act were again found to breach Article 8 ECHR, contrary to s 3 of the ECHR Act. The interference was disproportionate as the local authority had available to it an alternative procedure to obtain possession under s 14 of the Conveyancing Act 1881. Had this procedure been utilised it would have provided the necessary safeguards under Article 8 ECHR while meeting the requirements of the local authority. The Court also found that the local authority failed to have regard to the plaintiff's rights under Article 6(1) ECHR in performing its functions as an organ of the State.

In March 2009, in a policy statement on housing, the Irish Human Rights Commission (IHRC) called for law reform based on ECtHR jurisprudence. It stated:

> "... the IHRC recommends that the Government takes steps to remedy the current lack of protection of the rights of local authority tenants under Articles 6, 8 and 14 of the ECHR by amending the existing legislation. Pending the

---

[160] [2008] IEHC 288.
[161] [2008] IEHC 288.
[162] Application no 19009/04. Judgment, 13 May 2008.
[163] [2008] IEHC 354.
[164] [2008] IEHC 288.
[165] [2008] IEHC 379.

> introduction of such legislation, the IHRC recommends that local authorities be advised by Government of their statutory obligations under section 3 of the ECHR Act 2003 and of the alternative legal mechanisms available to them in terms of possession proceedings."[166]

Clearly, the ECHR Act is already impacting on the activities of local authorities, in the area of housing. It remains to be seen how long it will take for the Act to impact on other areas of local authority activity.

Implementation at Policy Level — Effecting a Paradigm Shift

The implementation of the ECHR Act, in the sense of giving life and meaning to the provisions of the ECHR, crucially depends on legal implementation, policies, guidelines and training.[167] But it also requires penetrating the internal world — in the institutional and administrative senses — of local government. Since these human rights norms can appear or be made to appear weaker than the prevailing cultural, political, social and managerialist norms, the ECHR Act will require significant emphasis and promotion to be made effective.

It is arguable that implementation of human rights generally has been retreating within the Irish State over the past ten years, despite the development of new institutions and a burgeoning literature on rights. This failure to advance rights-based approaches to public services may be partly attributable to the perspective of political organisations which, like certain charitable bodies, can view legally based entitlements as a threat to the agency relationship that they have fostered with people requiring their assistance.

At another level, perceptions and caricatures of egotism, elitism and intellectual arrogance in relation to human rights advocacy abound. Of course, patronising approaches by human rights advocates to public sector workers who often deal with hugely stressful demands on scarce resources or who are expected to resolve issues largely outside their control, does not advance the issue and can be counter-productive. Indeed, in the absence of any programmatic approach or training, the exposure by local authority staff to the ECHR Act has been mainly through cases of evictions of tenants. Perceptions may well emerge that the Act is being used to frustrate the professional efforts of local authority officials to manage local authority housing and that evictions for anti-social behaviour cannot be secured without engaging a vast array of due process rights. In this way local authority staff experience the ECHR Act in a negative manner from a narrow and threatening legal base. Of course, local authority tenants are entitled to the protections of the Convention but it may appear that that there is no opportunity within broader local government policy-making for the Convention's protections to be integrated meaningfully except in defending expensive and lengthy court cases. In many cases,

---

[166] See IHRC *Policy Statement on s 62 of the Housing Act 1966 for the Recovery of Possession of a Local Authority Dwelling* — March 2009. Available at: http://www.ihrc.ie/documents/documents.asp?NCID=2&L=1.

[167] See *Human Rights – Improving public service delivery*, (UK Audit Commission Report, 2003), at p 10.

a conservative political and social barrier exists, denying that people have enforceable human rights in their dealings with local authorities.

It would appear that no formal training has been provided for local authority staff in relation to their obligations under the ECHR Act to date. Equally, there seems to be little evidence that the Act has been considered in policy or decision-making at central or local government level almost six years after coming into force. In a clear illustration of the irrelevance of the ECHR Act to developing State policies on local government, the Green Paper published in 2009, *Stronger Local Democracy — Options for Change,*[168] failed to make any reference to the ECHR Act or, indeed, to human rights at all.

This situation can be contrasted with that in Northern Ireland, where the near equivalent UK Human Rights Act 1998 has prompted the development of a mechanism for human rights-proofing of policy and practice of State agencies.[169] A *Human Rights Act Impact Assessment Proforma* has been prepared which allows those preparing policies or proposals to consider whether and how these engage any of the rights in the HRA.[170] The question of how the policy or proposal interferes with or limits the right is then examined. The proposer must then identify who could be affected by the proposed interference or limitation and explain how they could be affected. The assessment then seeks to identify whether there is a law which allows the interference of the rights identified. Even if the interference or limitation in the policy or proposal is in accordance with law there are further conditions to be met such as demonstrating that it is justifiable as "necessary in a democratic society". The *Impact Assessment Proforma* requires that the policy proposer identifies how the proposed interference or limitation is proportionate and whether the measure could be discriminatory in relation to the exercise of Convention rights.

Of course, successful legal challenges with all of their associated costs can result in occasional common law and legislative changes. Many human rights lawyers view successful litigation as a key driver of policy and legal change, but it can equally be argued that the narrow sets of circumstances upon which legal decisions are based neglects more fundamental or broader deficits requiring change. Individual cases do little to change the fundamental inequality, lack of social and economic resources and the lack of power or opportunities which often lie behind these cases, especially in the area of housing.

Human rights-based approaches have been promoted to integrate the language of rights into service delivery policies and practices,[171] but the major questions about

---

[168] Government of Ireland (2009) *Green Paper on Local Government — Stronger Local Democracy Options for Change,* (The Stationery Office, Dublin).
[169] See *Getting in on the Act,* The Equality and Human Rights Unit, OFM/DFM, Northern Ireland. See website: http://www.ofmdfmni.gov.uk/index/equality/human-rights.htm
[170] The pro-forma is available at: http://www.ofmdfmni.gov.uk/humanrightsproforma.doc.
[171] See Amnesty International Irish Section, *Building Ireland's Future: A Human Rights Handbook,* available at: http://www.amnesty.ie/live/irish/article.asp?id=30296&page=00.

control of overall resource allocation in Irish society must also be considered. Of course, the State response the ECHR Act and other rights developments in the future may involve a superficial integration of the language of human rights into local authority and other policy documents, establishing an array of "participation", "consultation" and "monitoring" mechanisms with selected individuals and groups, in a manner akin to the way the State has managed the social inclusion approach.

Judicial review is useful in identifying breaches of the obligations contained in the ECHR Act but its utility is limited by costs, delay and stress on litigants, not to mention reservations as to its ultimate impact in effecting systemic change. Authoritative research on the enforcement of legal obligations on local authorities through judicial review shows that it has minor or negligible impact on policies or procedures.[172] Indeed, a key issue is whether the ECHR Act will lead to any increase in human rights-consciousness, changes in the policies and practices of organs of the State, or just to a more defensive "bullet-proofing" of decisions.[173] The language of human rights can easily be appropriated within existing policies, procedures and recorded decisions without effecting any real paradigm shift.

Conclusion

The ECHR Act has been in force for almost six years, and in many ways is the State's best kept secret. Despite Francesca Klug's assertion that human rights constitute "values for a godless age",[174] the domestication of the European Convention on Human Rights raises major issues of implementation of human rights in Ireland today. The test of success in implementation is whether the human rights standards are adopted as authoritative by local authorities and officials in such manner that their practical actions and decisions are in compliance with the rights and freedoms set forth in the ECHR.[175] In other words, can those human rights norms replace existing norms and understandings within institutions of local government that constitute an obstacle to human rights?

---

[172] Hertogh and Halliday. (eds), *Judicial Review and Bureaucratic Impact* (CUP, Cambridge, 2004); Sunkin, Calvo, Platt and Landman, "Mapping the Use of Judicial Review to Challenge Local Authorities in England and Wales", [2007] 77 *Public Law* 545. See also Sunkin, Calvo and Platt, "Does Judicial Review Influence the Quality of Local Authority Services?" The Public Services Programme. Discussion Paper Series: No. 0801. March 2008. ESRC, available at: http://www.publicservices.ac.uk/wp-content/uploads/dp0801_final.pdf.

[173] This is a practice where State agencies use legal knowledge to immunise their decisions against potential judicial scrutiny. See S Halliday, *Judicial Review and Compliance with Administrative Law*. (Hart Publishing, Oregon, 2004), ch 3. The decision in *O'Keefe v An Bord Pleanala* [1993] 1 IR 39. almost encourages this approach, since including any relevant material as a basis for a decision will satisfy the requirements of judicial review.

[174] See F Klug, *Values for a Godless Age*, (Penguin, London, 2000).

[175] D Galligan, and D Sandler, "Implementing Human Rights" in S Halliday, and P Schmidt, *Human Rights Brought Home; Socio-Legal Perspectives on Human Rights in the National Context*. (Hart, Oxford, 2004), p 29.

To date, the ECHR Act has made little difference to local authorities beyond a few individual housing cases. Implementing human rights within Irish local government raises significant questions about the role, accountability and operational norms of the Irish State at local level. The ECHR Act awards only a limited number of civil and political rights, and as such is limited by the boundaries of legal liberalism. Of course, the diminution and degrading of the status, financial and other support for the public sector, within the current political system, creates enormous difficulties in developing any new approaches. However, the failure to implement even these limited rights effectively clearly demonstrates that the local element of the Irish State cannot promote rights-based empowerment and emancipation. Perhaps the potential of the ECHR Act will only be realised when its rights are successfully integrated into the political process.

Privacy — Confusing Fundamental Values and Social Traditions

Marie McGonagle*

Voluntarily or not we are all public men to some degree.[1]
Exposure of the self to others in varying degrees is a concomitant of life in a civilised country.[2]

Introduction

The word "privacy" is like so many other words in our daily lexicon in so far as we all use it with ease and general understanding but if asked to define it we encounter grave difficulty.[3] We talk about our private life, discuss aspects of it openly or in confidence among family or friends but defend our right to protect it and keep it from the public glare, except when we wish to attract sympathy, attention, gain celebrity or notoriety or some other benefit that we intuitively or calculatedly regard as more valuable in either the short or long term. The "big brother" phenomenon and the cult of celebrity are two facets of modern day life that raise complex issues surrounding the generic right to privacy.[4]

* Lecturer in Law, School of Law, NUI Galway.

[1] Brennan J in *Rosenbloom v Metromedia* 403 US 29, 47 (1971).

[2] Brennan J in *Time, Inc. v Hill* 385 US 374, 388 (1967).

[3] The word "privacy" comes from the Latin verb "privare", meaning "to deprive" (privatum – deprived), and referring originally to being deprived of public office and status. See S Marks and A Clapham, *International Human Rights Lexicon*, (OUP, 2005) p 241; p 259 "Privacy". Much has been written about the difficulties of definition. See, for example, Barendt: "an elusive concept" ("Privacy and freedom of speech" in Kenyon and Richardson, eds, *New Dimensions in Privacy Law*, (CUP, 2006, 11, at 12); Rehnquist, J "defying categorical description" (*Paul v Davis* 424 US 693, 713 (1976)); Irish Law Reform Commission: "Privacy as a concept is notoriously resistant to definition" (Consultation Paper: *Privacy: Surveillance and the Interception of Communications*, 1996, p 1); Working Group on Privacy (Ireland): "notoriously difficult" (Report 2006, para 1.03). The European Court of Human Rights itself acknowledged this in *Peck v UK* (2003) 36 EHRR 719, para 57: "private life is a broad term not susceptible to exhaustive definition"; *Hatton v UK* (2003) 37 EHRR 611, para 10: "Privacy is a heterogeneous prerogative. The specific contours of privacy can be clearly distinguished and perceived only when it is being defended against different kinds of encroachments." See also *Niemietz v Germany*, judgment of 16-12-92, at para 29 and *Pretty v UK*, (2002) 35 EHRR 1, judgment of 29-4-02, para 60. While the Court has not attempted a definition of "privacy" as such, it has defined the other aspects or foci of privacy specified in Article 8.1, namely family life, home and correspondence, in its case law.

[4] As Barendt, *Freedom of Speech*, (2nd ed, OUP, 2005) p 199 puts it: "How to reconcile freedom of speech with personal privacy is now a matter of considerable controversy in all cultures where people are fascinated by the conduct of celebrities." Reality television and the ubiquitous "fame phenomenon" now prevalent in western cultures have expanded the public space and contracted the private space. Rights to publicity (the right not to have one's name, likeness, image or public persona exploited for commercial purposes without one's consent)

Concepts of Privacy

Warren and Brandeis conceived of privacy as the right to be let alone, while Prosser proceeded to identify four torts of privacy.[5] The American courts tended to adopt the idea of a reasonable expectation of privacy in light of existing social practices and social values,[6] whereas European countries fashioned it on the mantle of human dignity.[7] Today, privacy is a right enshrined expressly in international and regional human rights instruments and some national Constitutions.[8] Nonetheless, the right to privacy remains elusive and hard to pin down. For Robert C Post, the American law professor who has written extensively and insightfully about the right to privacy and its social foundations, privacy:

> "[I]s a value so complex, so entangled in competing and contradictory dimensions, so engorged with various and distinct meanings, that I sometimes despair whether it can usefully be addressed at all."[9]

Since the definition proffered by Warren and Brandeis, relying on Judge Cooley, of a right to be let alone, many attempts at definition have emerged. The idea of freedom from "unwarranted" intrusion gained support, signalling that some intrusion may be justifiable and that in today's society some level of intrusion is

---

are now of more interest to many than traditional rights to privacy. They enable a celebrity to control the commercial value of their persona or identity; in that sense they are in the nature of a property right rather than a "personal" right to privacy: see, for example, RC Post, "Rereading Warren and Brandeis: Privacy, Property and Appropriation", 41 Case W. Res. L.Rev. 647 (1990-1), at 666-674, where he speaks of the "commodified personality" and the "value" of the image or name.

[5] "The Right to Privacy", 4 Harv. Law Rev. 193 (1890); Dean Prosser, "Privacy", 45 Calif. L. Rev. 383 (1960). The central thrust of Warren and Brandeis's article, according to RC Post ("Rereading Warren and Brandeis: Privacy, Property and Appropriation", 41 Case W. Res. L. Rev. 647 (1990-1), is "to disentangle privacy from property", although Warren and Brandeis (at 196) were also concerned with decency and propriety. Glancy, "The Invention of the Right to Privacy", 21(1) *Arizona Law Review*,1, at 2 says: "In simplest terms for Warren and Brandeis the right to privacy was the right of each individual to protect his or her psychological integrity by exercising control over information which both reflected and affected that individual's personality." As is apparent from these and other commentaries, some of which are referred to below, Warren and Brandeis's article was a complex work and can be read at a number of levels.

[6] Particularly in the jurisprudence of the Fourth Amendment; for a comparative analysis of the American and European concepts of privacy see Whitman, "The Two Western Cultures of Privacy: Dignity versus Liberty", 113 Yale LJ 1151, 2004; for an analysis of the torts propounded by D Prosser and of the Restatement, see McClurg, "Bringing Privacy Law out of the Closet: A Tort Theory of Liability for Intrusions in Public Places", 73 NCL Rev. 989 (1995).

[7] See, for example, Whitman, above n 6.

[8] It is an unspecified or unenumerated right in the Irish Constitution (Article 40.3.1).

[9] RC Post, "Three Concepts of Privacy", 89 Geo. LJ 2087, 2000-1. See also: Post, "The Social Foundations of Privacy: Community and Self in the Common Law Tort", 77 Cal. L. Rev. 957 (1989) and Post, "Rereading Warren and Brandeis: Privacy, Property and Appropriation", 41 Case W. Res. L.Rev. 647 (1991).

almost inevitable.[10] The idea of "unreasonable" intrusion was also embraced, signifying that in some circumstances intrusion may be reasonable.[11] A Resolution of the Parliamentary Assembly of the Council of Europe conceived privacy as "the right to live one's life with a minimum of interference", reflecting the aim of the ECHR to protect rights to the greatest extent possible.[12]

Reasons given to justify privacy as a fundamental right deserving of protection have tended to focus on the individual and the value or utility to the individual of protecting privacy. In that regard, appeals have been made variously or collectively to broad notions of individuality, dignity, personality, intimacy, autonomy, self-determination and liberty.[13] For the most part the focus has been on zones of privacy, in terms of conduct or relations, and spatially. In the past, once one left the seclusion of one's home or a private place, one's claim to privacy all but disappeared. When that narrow realm of privacy began to be challenged, attempts were made to fix the boundaries, even delineate in measurements the spatial area of one's private space when venturing beyond the confines of the private arena.[14]

Recent reflections on the right have been prompted mainly by concern with technological developments and their capacity to enable governments and private

---

[10] See, for example, in the Irish context, *Kennedy and Arnold v Ireland* [1987] IR 587. See also the ongoing debate about search engines such as Google.

[11] See, for example, in Ireland the Broadcasting Acts 1960-2009 and the Radio and Television Act 1988. A different perspective was taken by Gavison ("Privacy and the Limits of the Law", 89 Yale LJ 421, 428 (1980)), when she focused not on intrusion but on access: "a limitation of others' access to an individual". Access to individuals in the online world is being greatly extended by individuals' own postings and interactions (e.g. blogs and chat-rooms) and by search engines and other organisations compiling (through various technological devices) and disseminating data. Measures taken by governments also in the name of security and combating terrorism, especially post- the attacks of 9/11, are eroding the private space of individuals online.

[12] Resolution 428 (1970).

[13] See generally, Barendt, *Freedom of Speech*, (2nd ed) p 230; Fenwick and Phillipson, *Media Freedom under the Human Rights Act*, (OUP, 2006) ch 13; McGonagle, *Media Law*, (Round Hall, 2003) ch 5; O'Dell, "When Two Tribes go to War: Privacy Interests and Media Speech, in McGonagle, ed., *Law and the Media – The Views of Journalists and Lawyers*, (Round Hall Sweet & Maxwell, Dublin, 1997) p 181. FH Cate, *Privacy in Perspective*, (AEI Press, Washington, 2001) p 3, refers to "a disparity of views on what *privacy* means" and lists autonomy, solitude and intimacy, confidentiality, anonymity, security, freedom from intrusion and control of information about oneself, before going on to consider the underlying concepts; Post, 2000-1, at 2092, argues that "autonomy" refers to the ability of persons to create their own identity and in this way to define themselves. Dignity, by contrast, he argues (quoting Taylor, *Sources of the Self: The Making of Modern Identity*, 1989, 15) refers to "our sense of ourselves as commanding (attitudinal) respect". Identity, on the other hand, according to Post, depends on aspects of the self that are public (such as one's work) and on aspects that are private (such as sexuality) — Post, 2000-1, at 2091. He also instances the conflict between "desiring" a certain public image and a reluctance to disclose private information (*ibid*), and the incompatibility of privacy as dignity and privacy as freedom or liberty (at 2095); *cf.* Whitman, above, n 6.

[14] E.g. the California anti-paparazzi statutes — see, for example, "Privacy, Technology and the California 'Anti-paparazzi statute'" (1999) 112 *Harvard Law Review*, No.6, 1367-1384, and (Note) "Privacy, Photography and the Press", 111 *Harvard Law Review*, 1086.

institutions to amass, store and use personal data for all manner of purposes. This has become known as informational privacy.[15] A further area of concern has been technology's facilitation of greater media intrusion into private life and its enabling of the dissemination of private information by written word, audio or visual means on a global scale. In the latter case, attention has moved from the purely private sphere to consider the *public* dimension and role of privacy. Privacy is no longer restricted in spatial terms, but has extended into the public sphere, both spatially and ideologically. The social value of privacy is now being analysed, as well as its instrumental role in achieving wider societal goals or benefits, and its public value and utility to individuals as participants in society.[16]

The perplexing concept of a right to public privacy has arrived. With it comes recognition of an individual's right to a reasonable expectation of privacy even in respect of certain activities carried out in the public domain. That reasonable expectation of privacy has to be tempered, however, if it is not to encroach on the collective and individual right of others to function freely in public, unburdened by the fear of invading other people's privacy.[17] This is particularly pertinent in the case of the media.

The ECHR

The European Convention on Human Rights protects privacy in Article 8. That article states that everyone is entitled to respect for private and family life, home and correspondence[18]:

1. Everyone has the right to respect for his private and family life, his home and his correspondence.
2. There shall be no interference by a public authority with the exercise of this right except such as is in accordance with the law and is necessary in

[15] See Feldman, "Secrecy, Dignity or Autonomy? Views of Privacy as a Civil Liberty", 47 (2) CLP 42, at 51, referring to "a given sphere of existence" and encompassing four dimensions: space, time, action and information.

[16] See Mead, "It's a Funny Old Game: Privacy, Football and the Public Interest", [2006] EHRLR 5, 541. Mead considers social interaction and includes the creation of reciprocal trust and, citing Feldman ("Privacy-related Rights and their Social Value", in Birks, ed., *Privacy and Loyalty*, Clarendon, Oxford, 1997), "social co-operation" and "mutually dependent ... purposeful co-operative activity" among the social values of privacy (at 546-7). See also in relation to photographs, "Note", 111 Harvard L. Rev. 1087 (1997-8) to the effect that "as a matter of public policy, the societal interest in protecting photographic expression, including unfettered photographic newsgathering, outweighs the interests that would be furthered by the expansion of privacy protections beyond current legal limitations." (at p 1087 and Part V).

[17] See McClurg, *op. cit.*, at 1056. Post (1990-1, at 651-3) further distinguishes between "descriptive" and "normative" privacy, the latter closely linked to social norms.

[18] See also the formulations in UN Declaration of Human Rights, Article 12; ICCPR, Article 17; UNCRC, Article 16; ACHR, Article 11. The EU Charter on Fundamental Rights has followed but updated the wording of Article 8 ECHR by substituting the word "communications" for "correspondence". For the text and an analysis of Article 7 (Respect for private and family life) and Article 8 (Protection of personal data) of the EU Charter, see EU Network of Independent Experts on Fundamental Rights, *Commentary on the Charter of Fundamental Rights of the European Union*, 2006.

a democratic society in the interests of national security, public safety or the economic well-being of the country, for the prevention of disorder or crime, for the protection of health or morals, or for the protection of the rights and freedoms of others.

On one reading of Article 8, it offers protection for a bundle of related rights, all separate but connected to the private sphere of the individual's life in society. On another, it offers protection for a wide right to privacy, the key facets of which are specified.[19] Either way, it is of very broad scope. Each area specified is potentially very wide. Even a cursory glance at the case law of the European Court of Human Rights or at any textbook on the Convention gives an indication of the breadth of Article 8. It has been described as "one of the most open-ended provisions of the Convention".[20] Not only is it very broad, it is also unevenly developed in the case law and in some respects undeveloped or underdeveloped.[21]

---

[19] The word "privacy" itself is not used in the text. The case law of the Court suggests that Article 8 protects a range of interests rather than a single right to privacy. See Van Dijk, Van Hoof *et al.*, *Theory and Practice of the European Convention on Human Rights,* (4th ed., Intersentia, 2006) at p 665: "The Court seems willing to accept that Article 8 is to be understood as containing various guarantees to personal autonomy, personal privacy, personal identity, personal integrity, personal development, personal identification and similar concepts linked to the individual notion of personhood." Article 8, therefore, protects much more than a straightforward "right to privacy". In reality, the Court has interpreted the Article very broadly. Pronouncements in case law under the Irish Constitution vary. For example, Hamilton P in *Kennedy and Arnold v Ireland* [1987] IR 587 at 593 spoke of "the nature of the right to privacy" and identified privacy in one's telephone calls as an aspect of that right; Henchy J, dissenting, in *AG v Norris* [1984] IR 36 viewed privacy as "a complex of rights, varying in nature, purpose and range, each necessarily a facet of the citizen's core of individuality within the constitutional order". However, he then went on to talk about other aspects of the right [singular]— *ibid,* at 71-2.

[20] Jacobs and White, *The European Convention on Human Rights,* (4th ed, Oxford, 2006) p 241. The Court itself has said on occasion, for example in *Gunnarsson v Iceland* (Appn No. 4591/04, decision of 20 October 2005) that the concept of private life is broad and not susceptible to exhaustive definition. The Court has not engaged in any systematic way in a detailed analysis of the text of Article 8, although it did point out in *Gunnarsson* that Article 8 did not expressly guarantee a right to protection of honour and reputation.

[21] *ibid.* "Though there is abundant case law under the article and there has been much development in particular of the notion of private life, there remains much potential for development of the rights protected by Article 8." On the concept of a right to privacy generally, Whitman (at 1154) asks: "If privacy is a universal human need that gives rise to a fundamental human right, why does it take such disconcertingly diverse forms?" The problem is not helped by the use of "intuitionist" arguments, which differ greatly from society to society and have shifted and mutated over time (*ibid*). Whitman instances the European — in contrast to American — protectiveness of many kinds of "privacy" in many realms of life, including consumer data, credit reporting, workplace privacy, discovery in litigation, the dissemination of nude images on the Internet or shielding criminal offenders from public exposure (at 1156). Americans, he says, are just as protective of privacy as their European counterparts but their obsession is with different aspects of privacy (at 1158). In other words, the European and American approaches to privacy represent two different cultures of privacy "which are home to different intuitive sensibilities, and which have produced two significantly different laws of privacy." (at 1160).

In addition, questions surround the nature and scope of the protection, which is either broad and comprehensive or limited and vague, depending on how one interprets the term "respect".[22] Respect afforded to a person by others is closely linked to the concept of dignity, which in turn "depends on intersubjective norms that define the forms of conduct that constitute respect between persons."[23] To equate privacy with dignity, according to Post, is to ground privacy in social norms of respect that we owe each other as members of a common community. So understood, Post argues, privacy presupposes persons who are socially embedded, whose identity and self-worth depend upon the performance of social norms, the violation of which constitutes "intrinsic" injury.[24] The concepts of respect and privacy contained in Article 8 are thus the product of a long history of what Post and others would regard as a levelling-up of social status.[25]

Debate as to whether the protection in Article 8 is passive or active, in the sense of whether it requires positive action on the part of States, has been answered in the affirmative by the Court.[26] States do (or "may") have a duty to take action to ensure respect for privacy (as delimited by Article 8) but the question remains as to whether

---

[22] The term is imprecise but laden with positive moral and ethical values. Clearly, any action or inaction on the part of a State that amounted to (serious) disrespect for an aspect of the Article 8 right(s) would constitute a violation, unless otherwise justified; in some instances also, as recognised by the Court, some form of safeguard or pre-emptive intervention by a State to ensure respect will be required to avoid being in violation; however, that raises questions of prior restraint on freedom of expression, which the Court has said in the context of Article 10 cases, would require particular scrutiny. The key question for current purposes is whether the test of proportionality allows that different levels or forms of intervention will suffice to ensure respect for different facets of the right(s) — see further below.

[23] Post, 2000-1, at 2092.

[24] *ibid*, "If privacy is understood as a form of dignity, there can ultimately be no other measure of privacy than the social norms that actually exist in our civilization." *cf.* Whitman (at 1160-2), who recognises that the European and American sensibilities about privacy grow out of much larger and much older differences over basic values, rooted in much larger and much older differences in social and political traditions. In Europe privacy is largely concerned with shielding individuals against unwanted public exposure and public indignity; therefore the media is a prime target of privacy laws. In the US, Whitman argues, the concern is more with private sovereignty in one's own home and therefore focuses comparatively little on the media.

[25] See Whitman, *op. cit.* at 1165-7: "What we see in continental law today is the result of a centuries-long, slow-maturing revolt against that style of status privilege", which once belonged only to the higher orders in society.

[26] The Court has said in a number of cases (e.g. *Rees*, judgment of 17-10-86; *Powell and Rayner*, judgment of 21-2-90; *Cossey* , judgment of 27-9-90, at para 37, *B v France*, judgment of 25-3-92; *Lopez Ostra*, judgment of 9-12-94) that the term "respect" in Article 8.1 is not clear-cut and that in determining whether a positive obligation exists "regard must be had to the fair balance that has to be struck between the general interests of the community and the interests of the individual" (see also, regarding family life, Van Dijk and Van Hoof, *op. cit.*, pp 739–742). Elsewhere (e.g. *Hatton v UK*, judgment of 7-8-03) the Court has said that where the State has not itself or through its agents interfered with the claimant's rights, its positive obligations consist of taking "reasonable and appropriate measures to secure the applicant's rights" under Article 8.1.

each right — or each aspect of the general right, depending on one's interpretation of the text — requires the same level or degree of positive action. Are some rights / facets of the right more central or fundamental than others; are some merely penumbral or tangential to the central core or zone(s) of privacy? The Court has acknowledged that there are different degrees and the more intimate the aspect of private life being interfered with, the more serious the reasons for interference must be.[27] Conversely, the weightier the public interest issues involved, the more likely the interference with privacy will be tolerated.[28] A public interest defence is therefore an important element of any privacy law.[29]

The Scope of the Article 8 Protection

The case law of the European Court of Human Rights indicates that the Article 8 protection extends to all aspects of private life (whatever that entails, but including sexuality, relationships, transsexualism, immigration, deportations),[30] to family life (issues pertaining to the role and relationships of the adults in a family as partners and as parents; issues relating to children, including custody and access, adoption, inheritance rights, schooling and many others), to the privacy of the home (issues of housing, search and seizure,[31] surveillance, environment) and to correspondence (including prisoners' correspondence, telephone tapping, data protection[32]). There is extensive case law on many of these areas, particularly on family life, which is generally perceived as being at the core of the wider concept of private life.[33] It is also clear that these areas are not static and more and more facets of them will be presented to the Court for recognition.

---

[27] See, for example, *Dudgeon v UK* (1981) 4 EHRR 149, which is cited in the Irish case *Aherne v RTE*, the Leas Cross nursing home case, Clarke, J, High Court, 8 June 2005.

[28] The public interest weighed heavily in *Aherne* (above, n 27), for example, while there was no significant public interest in cases such as *Douglas v Hello!* (No.1 [2001] QB 967; No.2 [2003] EMLR 28; No.3 [2005] 3 WLR 881) in the UK. The issues in the latter case were closer to copyright and related rights than to privacy.

[29] Not least by analogy with defamation law, where both in the jurisprudence of the European Court and in the UK (as a result of the *Reynolds* line of cases, most recently *Jameel v Wall Street Journal* [2006] UKHL 44, HL, 11 October 2006), a defence for reasonable publication has been established. A defence of fair and reasonable publication is also included in the Irish Defamation Act 2009.

[30] See the specific areas set out in Van Dijk and Van Hoof, for example, at pp 666–690. In *Kaftailova v Latvia,* judgment of 22 June 2006, the Court spoke of the personal, social and economic relationships which constitute the private life of any human being.

[31] For example, *Niemetz v Germany* (1993) 16 EHRR 97; *Roemen and Schmidt v Luxembourg,* judgment of 25 February 2003.

[32] Although data protection can also come under the concept of "private life".

[33] This is the area where there is the highest expectation of privacy, particularly when people are in their own homes. Case law in Member States of the Council of Europe also revolves mainly around issues of family life (parental leave, immigration, deportations), transsexualism, telephone tapping (see Blackburn and Polakiewicz (eds), *Fundamental Rights in Europe*, OUP, 2001) and increasingly data protection — see further below. In the United States also the concept of a right to privacy has emerged from and centred on issues involving family, sexuality, reproductive choices. See, for example, the discussion in Belsky, "Privacy: The Rehnquist Court's Unmentionable 'Right'", 36 Tulsa LJ 43 (2000-1).

There have been various attempts by legal analysts to categorise the areas protected, for example under the headings of physical and mental integrity, moral and intellectual freedom, honour and identity, confidential information, professional secrecy.[34] Categorisation of the subject-matter of the case-law is useful, particularly as claims continue to be made for protection under the umbrella of privacy for newer and more diverse forms of interference.[35] At one level, it can help to bring clarity to the existing jurisprudence, and to identify the consistencies and inconsistencies in the Court's treatment of the various areas and issues. At another, it can help determine the *basis* for the protection and the *degree* of protection warranted. At yet another, it can assist with identification of fundamental principles to apply to new situations — for example, to interference with aspects of privacy in the virtual world.

Most of the case law to date revolves around action or inaction on the part of the State or State agencies. In contrast, there is only one case of note to date concerned directly with the intrusive actions of the media in a public place.[36] That case, *Von Hannover v Germany* arose from activities closely associated with the cult of the celebrity, and the concomitant growth of the paparazzi. The conduct of the paparazzi in ruthlessly pursuing celebrities can be categorised variously as

[34] See, for example, the various texts on the ECHR, referred to above, and NA Moreham, "The Right to Respect for Private Life in the European Convention on Human Rights: A Re-examination", [2008] EHRLR, 44, where the author identifies five sub-categories. The Court itself in *Von Hannover* (para 50) speaks of private life including a person's "physical and psychological integrity"; *cf. Pretty,* at para 60, where the Court also referred to "physical and social identity", "personal development" and "the right to establish and develop relationships with other human beings and the outside world". The Court also stated that while no previous case law had established any right to self-determination under Article 8, it considered that the notion of personal autonomy was an important principle underlying its interpretation of the Article 8 guarantees (*ibid*). Since 2004, in *Radio France v France* (Appn no. 53984/00, judgment of 30 March 2004), the Court has considered reputation as an aspect of private life — see further discussion below.

[35] Recent examples in Ireland include a successful claim for invasion of privacy by a family targeted when police disclosed that a sex offender was staying in their home (see "€70,000 for family in ruling against Garda", *The Irish Times,* 18 January 2007) and a successful claim to the right to privacy under the ECHR by a family of travellers, whose only caravan was unfit to accommodate several disabled members of the family (*O'Donnell v South Dublin County Council,* Laffoy J, High Court, 22 May 2007, holding that the rights of the plaintiffs were not "effectively and practically respected").

[36] Other cases where the relationship between freedom of expression and privacy were considered include: *Le Plon v France,* Appn. No. 58148/00, judgment of 18-5-04 — a permanent injunction on distribution of a book, which included details of an undisclosed illness of President Mitterand, was deemed a violation of Article 10; *Tammer v Estonia,* Appn No. 41205/98 judgment of 6 February 2001; *News Verlags v Austria* (Appn no. 31457/96, paras 52 *et seq.,* ECHR 2000-I) and *Krone Verlag v Austria* (Appn no. 34315/96, paras 33 *et seq.,* 26 February 2002). A number of cases since 2004 consider reputation as an aspect of privacy but apart from some discussion of Article 8 in *Pfeifer v Austria* (Appn No. 12556/03, judgment of 15 November 2007) the reputation cases concern themselves mainly with Article 10 principles.

harassment, (aggressive) newsgathering, provision of infotainment or entertainment, or simply gossip-gathering or even gratuitous pursuit of human weakness, and, having migrated from its original home in the US, is becoming increasingly prevalent throughout Europe. As such, *Von Hannover* relates directly to only one aspect of media activity, namely the pursuit by photographers of public personae in public places and the resultant publication of the photographs obtained.[37] The judgment is essentially a first outing on the area by the European Court of Human Rights, and therefore, while significant, it is the Court's first word on the subject and in all probability not its last.[38]

The Scope of the Article 10 Protection

Nonetheless, with the decision in *Von Hannover*[39] a new imperative exists to clarify the relationship between privacy under Article 8 and freedom of expression, particularly of the media, under Article 10. Both are primary rights in the Convention and both are considered fundamental and instrumental. Article 10(1) establishes a right to freedom of expression: "This right shall include freedom to hold opinions and to receive and impart information and ideas without interference by public authority and regardless of frontiers." The scope of the right is thus indicated.

Article 10(2) then sets out the permissible areas of limitation or restriction, including the "protection of the reputation or rights of others". Privacy, as one of the "rights of others" is a compelling interest, a potential limiting factor on freedom of expression provided for in Article 10(2).[40] On the other hand, there is no corresponding right to "privacy" as such in Article 8; instead there is a right to "respect" for certain aspects of one's life, namely one's private and family life, home and correspondence. The word "privacy" is not used in the text of Article 8,

---

[37] There are other aspects of media activity that could raise issues of privacy, for example, the publication of true but private information (an issue raised in *Le Plon v France,* above n 36, or incursions on private property to obtain such information (an issue raised in cases such as *Aherne v RTE,* above n 27, and *Roemen and Schmidt,* above n 31).

[38] As Belsky says (above n 33 at 58): "A saying exists that "hard cases make bad law". In the case of privacy rights, controversial cases make *ad hoc* law".

[39] *Von Hannover v Germany,* Appn No. 59320/00, judgment of 24-6-04, [2004] EMLR 21.

[40] Barendt, for instance, speaks of "privacy rights or interests": "Privacy and freedom of speech" in Kenyon and Richardson, (eds) *New Dimensions in Privacy Law,* (CUP, 2006) p 11, at 14. Larry Alexander argues, however, albeit from an American First Amendment standpoint, that there is no human right to freedom of expression: Alexander, *Is There a Right to Freedom of Expression?,* (CUP, 2005) while Barendt argues (*op. cit.* at 23) that there is no human right to freedom of the press: "press freedom is parasitic to some extent on the underlying free speech *rights* and interests of readers and listeners, and the role which the press and other media play in informing them." [emphasis added].

although it did appear in some earlier drafts of the article.[41] Given the uncertainties and the potential scope of the term "privacy", the decision to drop the word "privacy" and opt instead for a more concrete and indicative wording was perhaps a judicious and farsighted one. Instead of a right to "privacy" as such, in the formulation adopted in Article 8 everyone has the right to "respect" for specified aspects of one's life. One potential limiting factor on that right to "respect", however, is the "rights and freedoms of others" (Article 8, paragraph 2), which would include one's right to freedom of expression.

Two conclusions on the formulation of Articles 8 and 10 suggest themselves: i) that the difference in formulation as between the "right to freedom of expression" and the "right to respect for" elements of private life needs to be explored[42]; and 2) that not only is neither right absolute, there can be no uniform application of either, since in some instances each must yield to the other, becoming a compelling interest or counterweight to the enjoyment of the other. A balancing exercise is therefore inevitable. In some situations freedom of expression will prevail: in others it will be

[41] The point of departure was the guarantee of privacy in Article 12 of the Universal Declaration of Human Rights, adopted on 10 December 1948. Indeed, early drafts of or suggested wording for Article 8 in 1949, contained references to Article 12 UDHR. The preliminary draft prepared by the Committee of Experts at its first meeting in 1950 included the word "privacy". The UK delegation proposed a negative formulation that everyone have a "freedom from governmental interference with his privacy, family, house or correspondence" — thus separating "privacy" from the other areas of family, house and correspondence. The wording eventually adopted was agreed by the Committee of Ministers on 7 August 1950. There was no debate on the wording of Article 8 at the Consultative Assembly and no alteration was proposed. See generally, European Commission of Human Rights, "Preparatory Work on Article 8 of the European Convention on Human Rights", Information Document prepared by the Secretariat of the Commission, 9 August 1956, DH (56) 12, and the full text of the preparatory work available in Council of Europe, *Collected Edition of the "Travaux Préparatoires" Of the European Convention on Human Rights*, (The Hague, Martinus Nijhoff, 1977). Vols i-viii. Document DH (56) 12 also points out that until 1953, although the process was begun in 1949, the ICCPR contained no equivalent of Article 12 UDHR or of Article 8 ECHR. An appendix to DH (56) 12 contains an extract from the Annotation on Draft Covenants prepared by the Secretary-General of the UN in 1955 (Doc. A/2929, pp 145–148), which states that in the discussion of Article 17 ICCPR, the view was expressed (at para 99) that "it would be very difficult to translate the general principles enunciated in Article 12 of the Declaration [UNDHR] into precise legal terms ...". See also para 102.

[42] The more oblique formulation of the right in Article 8, compared to the direct formulation of freedom of expression in Article 10, may be understandable in light of the amorphous nature of the concept of privacy. Would it have been feasible, for instance, to formulate the right to privacy in a similar manner to freedom of expression? Would the wording "Everyone has the right to privacy. This right shall include the freedom to conduct one's private and family life, home and correspondence without interference by public authority and regardless of frontiers" amount to a stronger and broader protection for the right(s) envisaged? If so, what was the barrier to its adoption? (See references to the *Travaux* above at n 41.) Conversely, would the formulation of Article 8 if adopted in relation to freedom of expression in Article 10 result in a weakening of the protection of the latter right?

curtailed in the interests of respect for an aspect or aspects of privacy. The converse is also true: in some instances respect for privacy will prevail; in others it will be curtailed in the interests of freedom of expression and its corollary, the right of the public to know.[43]

The respective weighting or balance to be effected when the media are involved is a particularly intriguing one.[44] The jurisprudence of Article 10 is already well-developed with regard to the media, whereas that of Article 8 with regard to the media is largely undeveloped.[45] Given that imbalance, the decision in *Von Hannover* is significant but its importance liable to be over-stated.

The remainder of the current study will focus primarily, therefore, on the relationship between freedom of expression and privacy with regard to the media. (For ease of reference the word "privacy" will be used.) In assessing that relationship, the jurisprudence of the European Court of Human Rights, particularly the judgment in *Von Hannover*, will provide a useful, though not conclusive, yardstick.

State Obligations under Article 8, (Degree / Extent of the Protection Required)

As indicated above, inaction on the part of the State can amount to a violation of Article 8. That is so even if the intrusion on privacy is the result not of State agencies but of private actors. Indeed, that was a central issue in *Von Hannover*, where the Court said that State obligations "may involve the adoption of measures designed

---

[43] The Court in *Von Hannover* specifically refers to the right of the public to be informed as an essential right in a democratic society in para 64.

[44] Mead, above n 16, believes that the relationship between freedom of expression and privacy is "more textured" and that freedom of expression is in fact "parasitic" on privacy, that it depends on there being privacy to think and reflect before pronouncing or publishing, "to experiment and make mistakes away from prying or critical public gaze" (at 546). Both Mead and Chadwick, "The Value of Privacy", [2006] EHRLR 495, at 497, regard privacy as a precondition to freedom of expression (at 547 and 498, respectively). Barendt (*op. cit.*, 2006 at 18) says that the two rights "must be balanced within the context of the particular facts; otherwise the courts would in effect sacrifice privacy or freedom of speech altogether in order to safeguard the other right.". Warren and Brandeis themselves (*op. cit.* at 215) recognised the need for elasticity to take account of varying circumstances. Phillipson (in Kenyon and Richardson, 2006, at 214, and in previous work) advocates a "dual exercise in proportionality" or "parallel analysis".

[45] See McGonagle, 2003, above n 13, ch 5 and the texts on the ECHR referred to above. The *Radio France* line of cases which mainly concern unsuccessful defamation plaintiffs who claim that the State has failed to accord them respect for their privacy under Article 8, involve a balancing of freedom of expression and reputation, the latter now recognised by the court not just as a potential ground for restricting expression but also as a right in itself under Article 8 as an aspect of privacy.

to secure respect for private life even in the sphere of the relations of individuals between themselves."[46]

Cases can only be taken to Strasbourg against States, however, complaining of an interference with Convention rights by States. Nonetheless, the Court has developed the concept of positive obligations on the State extending to the acts of third parties or private actors.[47] It may be argued, therefore, that the State has an obligation to intervene to provide or to ensure that there exist safeguards against media intrusion on the privacy of the individual, at least where the intrusion is enough to amount to a serious level of disrespect or lack of effective respect for the privacy of the individual. However, that is not to say that the obligation extends in every instance to introducing legislation.[48] The requirement is to provide or ensure that there exist reasonable, appropriate and effective measures, which in some circumstances may involve legislation, whereas, in other situations, administrative or co- or self-regulatory measures may suffice.[49]

---

[46] At para 57, with reference also *mutatis mutandis* to *X and Y v the Netherlands,* judgment of 26 March 1985, Series A no. 91, p 11, para 23; *Stjerna v Finland,* judgment of 25 November 1994, Series A no. 299-B, pp 60–61, para 38; and *Verliere v Switzerland,* (dec.) no. 41953/98, ECHR 2001-VII). In relation to pictures, which were an issue in *Von Hannover,* the Court added that the adoption of measures to protect private life also applies to the protection of a person's picture against abuse by others. In support of this it cited *Schussel v Austria,* (dec.), no. 42409/98, 21 February 2002. Note the language used: "in addition to this primarily negative undertaking, there *may* be positive obligations ... These obligations *may* involve ...". Regarding the intention to include private or non-State actors in the ICCPR, see UN Doc. A/2929, para 100.

[47] At para 57: "The boundary between the State's positive and negative obligations under this provision does not lend itself to precise definition. ... In both contexts regard must be had to the fair balance that has to be struck between the competing interests of the individual and of the community as a whole: and in both contexts the State enjoys a certain margin of appreciation."

[48] See Resolution 1165 (1998) of the Parliamentary Assembly of the Council of Europe on the right to privacy. The Resolution, which was adopted following the death of Princess Diana, recognises that personal privacy can be invaded even in countries with specific legislation to protect it, as indeed was the case in Germany where the Von Hannover complaints arose. The Resolution (Art. 8) refers to what it calls "a one-sided interpretation of the right to freedom of expression" used to claim that readers are entitled to know everything about public figures. It asserts (Art. 11) that freedom of expression and privacy are "neither absolute nor in any hierarchical order, since they are of equal value." It calls on governments to pass legislation, if none already exists, to guarantee the right to privacy and offers guidelines specifically aimed at forms of invasion of privacy by the media (Art. 14).

[49] See also above n 26 re *Hatton*. Rosen (2000-1, at 2137) also argues the need to explore non-legal mechanisms for discouraging privacy invasions by the media, which can redress the dignitary injury to privacy victims. He advocates public censure, which can "have the effect of reintegrating the victims into the community, restoring the chains of demeanor and deference, and therefore healing — rather than compunding — the injuries to dignity and personality." This "can often be achieved with less collateral damage by writers and journalists rather than by lawsuits." (at 2137). In the preparatory work for Article 17 ICCPR, reference was made to the requirement in Article 2 of the draft Covenant for each State party "to take the necessary steps ... to adopt such legislative or other measures as may be necessary to give effect to the rights recognised in this covenant." (Annotation on draft Covenants prepared by the Secretary-General of the UN in 1955 at the request of the General Assembly (Doc. A/2929, para 104).

The requirement is that the rights guaranteed in the Convention must be effective; they must not be mere paper rights but must be capable of being exercised in practice.[50] Thus, any unjustified barrier to their exercise will be suspect and an effective remedy will be required. The Court in *Peck v UK*,[51] a case involving CCTV pictures of an attempted suicide in a public place, which were subsequently published in the media, found there was a lack of effective remedy. The facts of the case did not meet the requirements necessary under English law to bring an action for breach of confidence or for any tort[52]; nor did they come within the remit of the Press Complaints Commission, which might have provided an extra-judicial remedy. In such a situation where safeguards are either inadequate or non-existent, Barendt, in particular, has argued in favour of a privacy law, while other academic authorities and practitioners have argued that the introduction of a privacy law is not mandated by the ECHR.[53] If effectiveness is the requirement, it may well be that a variety of methods is necessitated, which may or may not include legislation or may vary with the particular form of intrusion.[54] Forms of co or self-regulation, or a combination of alternative remedies, may be more effective in some circumstances.[55]

---

[50] See Von Hannover, paras 57 and 71; *Artico v Italy*, judgment of 13 May 1980, Series A no. 37, pp 15–16, para 33. See also Article 19, Memorandum on the Defamation Bill 2006 and the Privacy Bill 2006 of the Republic of Ireland, London, 29 September 2006, p 13, regarding the least restrictive means possible to balance free expression with media regulation.

[51] Decision of 28 January 2003.

[52] See the careful analysis of the later development of the breach of confidence approach in *Campbell v MGN* by Phillipson in Kenyon and Richardson, 2006, above n 3, at 187ff; also Wacks, "Why there will never be an English common law privacy tort", in Kenyon and Richardson, (eds) (2006) above n 3, at pp 162ff; Markesinis *et al.*, "Concerns and Ideas About the Developing English Law of Privacy (And How Knowledge of Foreign Law Might Be of Help)", (2004) 52 Am. J. Comp. L. 133.

[53] See *Privacy and media intrusion*, House of Commons Culture, Media and Sport Committee, 2002-3, HC 458-1, pp 39–43. Barendt argued *inter alia* that it was anomalous that privacy was not protected, that it was artificial to rely on the breach of confidence and other remedies, and that while case law was bound to develop there would be an extended period of uncertainty which itself could chill investigative journalism. He pointed out that legislation had a declaratory quality and that there was value in society declaring that privacy was a fundamental human right (at pp 40–1). Interestingly, early drafts of Article 10 had a reference to "a right of reply or a similar corrective remedy" — see DH (56) 15, p 5. See also the arguments in favour of privacy legislation in the English context in Markesinis *et al.*, 2004, above n 52.

[54] Resolution 1165 (1998) also referred to the new communication technologies which make it possible to store and use personal data, and the importance therefore of adding to the 1970 definition of privacy "the right to control one's own data". That aspect of the right is the subject of legislation in many countries, and indeed is the area that has been most revised and updated in recent years: Data Protection Acts, Information Privacy Acts are common but often have exemptions or qualifications in relation to the media; Freedom of Information Acts, and other legislation with built-in safeguards for private and personal information are also gaining currency.

[55] In the UK, the House of Commons Culture, Media and Sport Committee, for example, urged that Ofcom, the broadcasting regulator, and all the broadcasters should engage with the Press Complaints Commission and press industry to develop ways of tackling the media scrums that gather at the scent of a story, described by Lord Wakeham, then Chairman of the PCC, as "a form of collective harassment" (*op. cit.*, para 39). The Committee also believed the PCC should provide guidance to the press and public on such issues (*ibid*, 62).

An interference with freedom of expression in Article 10 must be "prescribed by law" (Art.10.2). An interference with respect for private life in Article 8, on the other hand, must be "in accordance with the law".[56] "Prescribed by law" has been interpreted by the Court to mean that there must be a law in place to authorise any restriction to be imposed and that law must be sufficiently clear and accessible to enable those affected to decide their conduct accordingly.[57] "In accordance with the law" (particularly with the inclusion of "the" rather than "in accordance with law"), on the other hand suggests compliance with the general law or alternatively that, if there is a law allowing for restrictions, any restriction to be imposed must be in accordance with it. The Court has said that this means that there must be "adequate safeguards" and that national law must offer a minimum degree of protection against arbitrariness.[58] It is submitted, therefore, that with regard to an interference with "respect" for private life, a proportionate measure is what is required, and that may or may not involve specific legislation or common law measures, such as torts or actions for breach of confidence.[59]

---

[56] The UK delegation in 1950 had proposed that no restrictions should be placed on the exercise of the right other than such as were "in accordance with law". At the last examination of the text by a Committee of Legal Experts on 3 November 1950 the word "the" was inserted: "in accordance with the law". See DH (56) 12 at p 9. The Convention was signed the next day.

[57] *Sunday Times v UK* Series A No.30, (1979) 2 EHRR 245. As Van Dijk and Van Hoof (*op. cit.* at 665-6) point out, in order to rely on the elements of privacy included as restrictions on freedom of expression in Article 10, an express legal basis is required. However, despite the indications from the *travaux préparatoires* of the Convention (see generally European Commission of Human Rights, "Preparatory Work on Article 10 of the European Convention on Human Rights", Information Document Prepared by the Secretariate of the Commission, 17 August 1956, DH (56) 15), the Court in *Niemietz v Germany*, (1993) 16 EHRR 97 and *Fayed v UK*, Series A No. 294B, 1994, 18 EHRR 393, for example, appears to include reputation as an element also of Article 8 (Van Dijk and Van Hoof, *op. cit.* at 666). It is submitted that this ties in with the Court's interpretation of Article 8 as embracing a broad concept of personhood but adds to the lack of clarity surrounding the nature of the right to privacy as such and makes it more difficult to define and legislate for. It leads to the conclusion that Article 8 is not concerned with a right to privacy as such but with ensuring respect for certain private interests associated with the physical and psychological well-being of the "person". However, it is submitted that the Court is unhelpfully overstepping the limits inherent in the wording of Article 8 and developing a seemingly unlimited and lopsided concept of personhood which far outstretches the areas of intimacy or seclusion — private and family life, home and correspondence — envisaged in Article 8. While there has to be room to accommodate new experiences and threats to intimacy and seclusion that arise, a clearer, more defined concept of the overall or umbrella right is required.

[58] See, for example, the cases listed in Van Dijk and Van Hoof, *op. cit.*, at 745-7.

[59] It may, for example, be sufficient that a Press Council, whose remit includes dealing with privacy complaints against the press, is simply referred to in statute (as is the case in Ireland in the Defamation Act 2009), or, alternatively, although not referred to in statute, is effective in providing protective measures and "adequate safeguards" as a self-regulatory body; in contrast an over-protective statute could run the risk of being declared disproportionate. As the Court said in the *Kruslin* and *Huvig* cases (judgment of 24-4-90) in relation to telephone-tapping, as tapping represents a serious interference with private life and correspondence, it must be based on a law that is particularly precise and clear, detailed rules are required especially when the technology is continually becoming more sophisticated (at paras 33-4).

Balancing Privacy and Freedom of Expression

The Court engages in a balancing act when two competing rights conflict; the goal is to interfere with the enjoyment of the two rights to the minimum extent necessary.[60] A margin of appreciation is applied, which gives States some leeway as to how they protect rights in practice and where they draw the line or reconcile them in cases of conflict. While a high level of protection may be required to ensure respect for the intimacies of family relationships or health or sexual matters, particularly in the case of individuals who have not courted publicity, the level required in the case of celebrities must be considerably lower. That is not to say that they are not entitled to some level of protection and, indeed, in their case, too, the appropriate level will depend on their functions in society or their iconic status as role-models. Such a distinction was drawn by the Court in *Von Hannover* (discussed further below).

Article 10 ECHR

Respect for privacy, therefore, is protected specifically as a "core" right in Article 8 of the ECHR. Privacy is also, however, one of the "rights of others", which can give rise to a justifiable restriction on freedom of expression as protected by Article 10, provided the basis of the intrusion is, in addition, prescribed by law and necessary in a democratic society. In other words, any intrusion on freedom of expression in support of the privacy of others must correspond to a pressing social need and the measure(s) adopted in support of it must be proportionate to the legitimate aim, i.e. to protect the privacy of others.

While *Von Hannover* was a case taken under Article 8 to test the parameters of the guarantee of privacy as applied to the media, a more interesting question would arise if a case were taken by the media themselves in similar circumstances under Article 10, claiming that a restriction on their activities imposed in the interests of privacy amounted to a breach of their freedom of expression. In such a scenario, privacy, a primary right under Article 8, would effectively become a compelling interest to be weighed in the balance with freedom of expression in Article 10. The restriction which had been imposed would most likely be prescribed by law, in support of a legitimate aim and the key question, therefore, would be whether it was necessary in a democratic society, in that it corresponded to a pressing social need. Cases taken under Article 10 to date, involving restrictions on the media in the interests of aspects of privacy, such as *Le Plon v France* (book disclosing President Mitterand's undisclosed illness while President),[61] *News Verlags v Austria* (pictures and comments on a person accused of sending letter bombs),[62] *Krone Verlag v Austria*

[60] Resolution 428 (1970) on mass communication media and human rights defined the right to privacy as "the right to live one's life with a minimum of interference". Likewise, freedom of expression as protected by Article 10 is the norm and the restrictions on it the exception. Therefore, the balancing process must endeavour to give maximum effect to both rights or, in negative terms, to restrict each to the minimum extent possible.

[61] Appn No. 58148/00, judgment of 18 May 2004.

[62] Appn No. 31457/96, judgment of 11 April 2000 (final).

(reference to a politician's three salaries),[63] each resulted in a finding of a violation of Article 10. In other words, freedom of expression prevailed in the particular circumstances.[64]

As evident from the formulation of Article 8 (whether, as indicated above, it is conceived of as a broad-ranging sole right or as a bundle of related rights) privacy is not a single interest but rather a cluster of interests: family matters, issues of sexuality, the seclusion of the home, and so forth.[65] It is not immediately clear whether the cluster is static in the sense that all the components are there and are unchanging but have to be recognised or discovered over time, or whether the cluster is variable or not static in that the components of the cluster migrate to it and from it as societal standards and needs change in response to stimuli or challenges. In either case, the discovery rate or the responses to stimuli may vary from country to country, culture to culture, age to age. A uniform cluster of privacy interests may eventually emerge in a globalised world but that day has not yet arrived. As the European Court of Human Rights has observed in cases raising issues of public morals, there is no uniform European consensus on morality.[66] The same could be said of privacy.

As a result, the Court allows States a wider margin of appreciation in relation to restrictions imposed on freedom of expression in the interests of public morals than it does in other areas, particularly political speech. By analogy, one would expect that the margin of appreciation in respect of aspects of privacy would also be wide. However, public morals only have the status of a compelling interest acting as a potential limiting factor on freedom of expression. Public morality is not a primary right in itself in the way that privacy is under Article 8. Indeed, aspects of public morals may arise within the rubric of privacy in Article 8, although privacy and public morals should in theory and in practice be separate issues. For example, publication of a nude photograph of an individual may, depending on the circumstances, be both an invasion of the individual's privacy and contrary to the prevailing concept of public morals; or it may be an invasion of the individual's privacy and considered in bad taste but not necessarily contrary to public morals. Where it is contrary to public morals regarding decency, it is likely also to amount

---

[63] Appn No. 34315/96, judgment of 26 February 2002; see in particular paras 29, 36, 37. See also *Verlagsgruppe News GMBH v Austria (No.2)*, Appn No. 10520/02, judgment of 14 December 2006 (photograph of a business magnate under investigation for large scale tax evasion).

[64] See, however, *Tammer v Estonia*, Appn No. 41205/98 judgment of 6 February 2001, where no violation of Article 10 was found. The case involved aspects of the private life of a former politician but the conviction in the national courts had been for the insult caused by the form of attack rather than the actual details of private and family life of which the applicant had herself written in her autobiography.

[65] This is recognised also in Ireland in the Report of the Working Group on Privacy, above, n 3, at p 11: "what is often termed a right to privacy entails in fact not a single, but a number of (sometimes disparate) entitlements".

[66] E.g. *Otto-Preminger v Austria* Series A No. 295-A, (1995) 19 EHRR 34; *Wingrove v UK* Appn No. 17419/90, (1997) 24 EHRR 1. Neither is there any uniform consensus on privacy, although a harmonised one may be emerging in the wake of the combined effect of *Von Hannover*, EU Data Protection legislation and other recent developments relating to aspects of individual privacy.

to disrespect or lack of effective respect (for privacy) and therefore come within Article 8. Nonetheless, the margin of appreciation allowed to States in relation to privacy appears to be narrower than that afforded in the realm of public morals. The Court in *Von Hannover*, for instance, referred to "a certain margin of appreciation" which States enjoy in effecting "a fair balance" between the competing interests of the individual and of the community as a whole.[67] The categorisation of the margin as "a certain" margin rather than as a broad or wide one as is afforded to public morals would seem to reflect the difference in status between the two as a right (privacy) and an interest (public morals).

Another conundrum is the size or extent of the cluster of privacy interests in Article 8, whether it is fixed or fluid. In claiming that a particular act or omission is an invasion of privacy, the claimant brings to bear a pre-conceived sense of a sphere of seclusion in life that is being threatened or diminished in some way or one that is deserving, in the claimant's view, of extension beyond the commonly conceived limits.[68] Despite the difficulties of definition and delineation, the sense of "I know it when I see it" which most people possess is strong. However, privacy is often the label used not only to signify an interference with an individual's right to intimacy, personality, autonomy or physical and psychological integrity but also to denounce occurrences that others perceive to be an affront to them or an embarrassment rather than a lack of respect or mark of disrespect, and which have more to do with others' concepts of taste and decency than with any objective sense of privacy interests.[69]

Von Hannover v Germany

Many of the foregoing issues arose in *Von Hannover v Germany*. The case, which involved Princess Caroline and which was decided in Strasbourg in June 2004, received a disproportionate amount of attention, mainly because it was the first decision of the Court on an issue that has been gathering momentum since the focus on the paparazzi following the death of Princess Diana in 1997.[70]

---

[67] Para 57, citing *Keegan v Ireland* (judgment of 26 May 1994, Series A no.290, p 19, para 49) and *Botta v Italy* (judgment of 24 February 1998, *Reports of Judgments and Decisions* 1998-I, p 422, para 32).

[68] Schauer, "Internet Privacy and the Public-Private Distinction", 38 *Jurimetrics* 555, 560-1 (1998).

[69] For example, an analysis of Irish newspaper records of complaints categorised by complainants as invasions of privacy revealed that most concerned matters of taste and decency and very few concerned the privacy interests set out in Article 8 ECHR – see Boyle and McGonagle, *Media Accountability – the Readers' Representative in Irish Newspapers* Dublin, NNI, 1995, pp 27–8. See also Richardson and Hitchens, "Celebrity privacy and benefits of simple history" in Kenyon and Richardson, 2006 at 251, where they question the language of "privacy" and consider whether it has become a mask for protection of other interests not really to do with privacy at all; also Phillipson, *ibid*, at 203-4 regarding the use of the words "private" and "public" by the European Court of Human Rights.

[70] That event led to changes in the Code of the Press Complaints Commission in the UK, for example, and was also the catalyst for the adoption by the Parliamentary Assembly's Resolution on the right to privacy in 1998 (Resolution 1165 of 1998).

It is tempting to view the decision as a policy-oriented one rather than a legally mandated outcome; one that is the result of abhorrence of the tabloidisation of the media, the cult of the celebrity and the excesses of the paparazzi, as well as apprehension about the potential of new communications technologies to erode aspects of privacy.[71] It is also possible, of course, that it is more attributable to the influence of the Continental European concept of privacy linked to honour and dignity.[72]

The consideration of the legal issues in the judgment of the Court is relatively short.[73] Indeed, the area of privacy raised was relatively narrow: the taking of photographs of a public figure in non-secluded public places.[74] The facts of the situation of the applicant and her ten-year battle with the paparazzi were set out. The stronger protection she enjoyed under French law was being systematically circumvented by photographs being taken in France, where her consent would have been required for publication, and then being sold and published in Germany.[75] In

---

[71] The Court said (at para 70) that "increased vigilance in protecting private life is necessary to contend with new communications technologies which make it possible to store and reproduce personal data .... This also applies to the systematic taking of specific photos and their dissemination to a broad section of the public."

[72] For instance, the German Basic Law Article 5(2) recognises honour, usually associated with reputation, as an aspect of the constitutional rights to dignity and personality in Article 2. In the US, see Bloustein, "Privacy as an Aspect of Human Dignity: An Answer to Dean Prosser", 39 NYUL Rev. 962, 970-71 (1964).

[73] Paras 43-81, made up of the submissions (paras 44-6), the domestic courts' position (paras 54-5), consideration of the general principles (paras 56-60), their application to the case (paras 61-75) and the conclusion (paras 76-81). In some respects, the observations of the German courts are more interesting, for example the views of the Constitutional Court (included in para 25 of the *Von Hannover* judgment of the European Court) that the function of the press in forming public opinion "does not exclude entertainment from the functional guarantee under the Basic Law. The formation of opinions and entertainment are not opposites. Entertainment also plays a role in the formation of opinions. It can sometimes even stimulate or influence the formation of opinions more than purely factual information." The Constitutional Court went on to say: "Personalisation is an important journalistic means of attracting attention. Very often it is this which first arouses interest in a problem and stimulates a desire for factual information. ... Additionally, celebrities embody certain moral values and lifestyles. Many people base their choice of lifestyle on their example. They become points of crystallisation for adoption or rejection and act as examples or counter-examples. This is what explains the public interest in the various ups and downs occurring in their lives." The German Constitutional Court also recognised the increased importance given today to illustrated information, the significance of the role-model function of celebrities and the negative impact that a "selective" portrayal of them would have in depriving the public of "certain necessary judgmental possibilities in respect of figures of socio-political life". One cannot help but feel that the German Constitutional Court had its finger on the public pulse more firmly than the European Court had. German law of privacy had a very nuanced approach to privacy and some of the photographs of Princess Caroline did amount to invasion of privacy under that law. However, the European Court took a different approach, modelled on French law.

[74] Although in seeking a corner of a restaurant in which to hold hands with her boyfriend, Princess Caroline was deemed to be seeking seclusion. It must be remembered also that not all of the photos complained of were in issue as the German courts had already ruled on some of them.

[75] Para 44 of the judgment.

considering the applicability of Article 8 ECHR, the Court first reiterated that the concept of private life in that article extends to aspects of personal identity, such as name and picture, and also to a person's physical and psychological integrity. The purpose of Article 8, the Court said, is primarily to ensure development, without outside interference, of the personality of each individual in his relations with other human beings. "There is therefore a zone of interaction of a person with others, even in a public context, which may fall within the scope of 'private life'".[76]

The focus has switched, therefore, to a zone of interactivity, rather than the previous idea of a zone of intimacy and to a zone of interactivity in public, rather than in private. However, this new zone of interactivity is not unlimited: it is a zone of interactivity "even" in a public context, which "may" fall within the scope of "private life", as the term is used in Article 8.[77] Use of the word "even" suggests that the application of privacy principles in a public context is to be the exception, while use of the word "may" makes it even more tentative. As in previous cases, the Court referred to a "legitimate expectation" of protection and respect for private life.[78] It also referred, without comment, to earlier cases in which the Commission had regard to photographs and considered whether they related to private or public matters and whether the material thus obtained was envisaged for a limited use or was likely to be made available to the general public.[79]

In applying the general principles to the facts of the *Von Hannover* case, the Court observed that the applicant complained not of an action by the State but of the "lack of adequate State protection of her private life and her image".[80] Although the object

---

[76] Para 50, with reference to *P.G. and J.H. v UK* (Appn No. 44787/98, para 56, ECHR 2001-IX, and *Peck v UK* (Appn No. 44647/98, para 57, ECHR 2003-I); *Botta v Italy*, Appn No 21439/93, judgment of 24-2-98, (1998)26 EHRR 241, para 32: the common thread is the aim of ensuring "the development, without outside interference, of the personality of each individual in his relations with other human beings". Thus stated, the concept is very broad indeed. See the criticisms expressed by S Marks and A Clapham, *International Human Rights Lexicon,* (OUP, 2005) at 268, with regard to addressing privacy in terms of the protection of private life from unjustified interference. The authors take the view that this approach masks the unequal and violent character of private life experienced by many, perpetuating instead a romanticised conception of family. Rights *within* the private sphere also need to be protected.

[77] See *Peck v UK,* at para 57 and Phillipson, in Kenyon and Richardson, 2006, above n 3, at 203.

[78] Para 51, with reference to *Halford v UK* (25 June 1997, *Reports* 1997-III, p 1016, para 45).

[79] Para 52, with reference to *Friedl v Austria* (judgment of 31 January 1995, Series A no. 305-B, opinion of the Commission, p 21, paras 49-52), *P.G. and J.H. v UK* (above n 76) and *Peck v UK* (above n 3).

[80] Para 56. The Court also said that the obligations on the State apply to protection of a person's "picture" against abuse by others (at para 57); see also para 50: "The Court reiterates that the concept of private life extends to aspects relating to personal identity, such as a person's name ... or a person's picture (see *Schussel v Austria* (dec.), no. 42409/98, 21 February 2002)." It is not altogether clear whether this refers to a person's face, image or, more comprehensively, one's profile. In any event, the Court has now embraced reputation in the concept of personal identity: in *Pfeifer v Austria,* Appn No. 12556/03, judgment of 15 November 2007, the Court said a person's reputation 'forms part of his or her personal identity and psychological integrity and therefore also falls within the scope of his or her "private life"' (at para 35).

of Article 8 is essentially that of protecting the individual against arbitrary interference by public authorities, it does not merely compel the State to abstain from such interference; in addition to this primarily negative undertaking, there "may", according to the Court, be positive obligations inherent in an "effective" respect for private or family life.[81] The Court then goes on to say that these obligations "may" involve the adoption of "measures" designed to "secure" respect for private life.[82] A "fair balance" has to be struck between the competing interests of the individual and "of the community as a whole".[83]

In particular, protection of private life has to be balanced against the freedom of expression guaranteed by Article 10. In considering freedom of expression the Court reiterated its usual litany of observations about freedom of expression, including that it constitutes one of the essential foundations of a democratic society and that the press plays an essential role in a democratic society.[84] However, it went on effectively to distinguish the publication of photographs, at least where they do not concern the dissemination of ideas or contribute to public debate, as perceived by the Court.[85] There is little consideration in the judgment of the intrinsic nature or value of photographs as such or of the fact that the visual is now an integral and very effective part of news presentation.[86] The concern of the Court was not with the medium but with the subject or content.

---

[81] Para 57. See above, n 26: "reasonable and appropriate measures" (*Hatton v UK*); also that States are required to "minimise, as far as possible, the interference ... by trying to find alternative solutions and by generally seeking to achieve their aims in the least onerous way as regards human rights" (*Lopez Ostra* — re environmental issues).

[82] Para 57. Taken cumulatively, the language appears rather tentative and does not add up to a strong argument that positive obligations always exist or that legislation is mandated. Indeed, the Court does say that the "boundary between the State's positive and negative obligations ... does not lend itself to precise definition." (para 57). Accordingly, a margin of appreciation applies.

[83] The broad interests of the community as a whole are set out in Article 8, paragraph 2.

[84] Para 58.

[85] To suggest that photographs of celebrities in whatever guise do not contribute to public debate is questionable in today's society, when a spat or rude or racist remarks on a "Big Brother" television show can lead to reaction on a global scale and make the front pages of every newspaper, even the most conservative broadsheets (e.g. *Big Brother*, Channel 4, January 2007, newspapers of 21-1-07). The test of public debate is logical and clear-cut in respect of political speech. It is less so in the case of artistic expression, for example the contribution of film and video to public debate. At a theoretical level, the European Commission of Human Rights and the Court itself recognised the value of "ideas" and "art" in *Muller v Switzerland* (Series A No. 133 (1991) 13 EHRR 212) but have not engaged in a debate themselves as to the notions of worthiness and gratuitousness which are implicit, or in some instances explicit, in their judgments and decisions in cases such as *Otto Preminger v Austria* (film) and *Wingrove v UK* (video) — above, n 66.

[86] See the comments at para 59. The integral role played by photographs applies not only in the case of those supplied by photographers who are media employees or by paparazzi but also by "citizen journalists" armed only with a mobile phone camera, who capture events as they happen, as in the case of the London bombings in July 2005, for example. Apart from the relevance of photographs to the dissemination of ideas and contribution to public debate, there might have been more attention paid to the aspects of photographs that intensify the

Photographs, the Court said, are an area where the protection of the rights and reputation of others (limiting factors on freedom of expression set out in Article 10, paragraph 2) take on "particular importance". The photographs in the present case, according to the Court, were "images containing very personal or even intimate "information" about an individual. However, what the very personal or intimate nature of the photographs was or could be said to be is puzzling, given that they were mainly of her shopping or engaging in leisure activities.[87] The German courts had already found that some other photographs were in breach of privacy under the German Basic Law and had found a violation of her privacy with regard to those, so the case before the European Court of Human Rights was confined to the least intimate photographs complained of by Princess Caroline. There is more weight in the Court's observation, therefore, that photographs taken in a climate of "continual harassment" induce in the person concerned a very strong sense of intrusion into their private life or even of persecution.[88]

In its earlier case law in which it had had to balance the protection of private life and freedom of expression, the Court had always stressed the contribution made by

---

extent of invasion of privacy (although see below, text accompanying n 102, regarding a further remark made by the Court). McClurg (above n 6, at 1041-4) instances three important ways in which photographs can heighten the invasion of privacy: a photograph makes a permanent record, so that the "victim loses control over an aspect of her self"; because of this permanent record, information may be revealed that would not be noticed by transitory observation with the naked eye; again, because of the permanent record of a scene, the photograph has the "potential to multiply the impact of the original invasion through wide dissemination"; moreover, a photograph "permits dissemination of an image not just to a larger audience, but to different audiences than the subject intended." McClurg, writing in 1995, was responding to an observation of D Prosser that equated observation by the naked eye with photography. Had he been writing today, McClurg would no doubt have added reference to the effects of the Internet and of digital technology, including digital manipulation of photographs. To his observations on the permanence and dissemination enabled by videotaping and the use of camcorders, he would have had to factor in the even greater capabilities of mobile phone and Internet technology.

[87] It is unclear what the "intimate" information could be, since the photos were mainly of the subject shopping, dining in a restaurant, horse-riding, skiing on holidays and such like, all accompanied by "innocuous" titles, apart from one which bore the caption "The kiss. Or: they are not hiding anymore" (para 61) and one showing her tripping and falling (para 17). The photos of the Princess and her children had already been deemed in breach of privacy by the German Constitutional Court. See the useful examples distinguishing between private and non-private activities given by Phillipson in Kenyon and Richardson, 2006, at p 205. See also the account of the situation regarding photographs in public places in other jurisdictions in Yan Mei Ning, "Media Photography in Hong Kong streets: The impact of proposed privacy torts", (2006) 11 *Media and Arts law Review* 161.

[88] See, for example, the sociologist R Merton's definition of privacy as "freedom from observability" and his argument that privacy is necessary because without it "the pressure to live up to the details of all (and often conflicting) social norms would become literally unbearable": Merton, *Social Theory and Social Structure,* 429, (1968), cited in Rosen, "The Purposes of Privacy: A Response", 89 Geo. LJ 2117, 2000-1, at 2124. Rosen says that uncertainty about pervasive surveillance makes the development of the subjective self impossible and is an intrinsic injury against the autonomous self (*ibid*).

photographs or articles in the press to a debate of general interest.[89] In *Von Hannover* it reiterated this principle and stated that this was the "decisive factor" in balancing protection of private life against freedom of expression.[90] It also made a further distinction between facts contributing to public debate that relate to politicians in the exercise of their functions and details of the private life of an individual, like Princess Caroline, who does not exercise official functions. This distinction it refers to as "fundamental". However, the effect of this distinction is to relegate the Princess Carolines of this world to the status of an ordinary private citizen and ignore their function, unofficial though it may be, as icons and role models in society.[91] It also ignores the relationship that many such people have with the media, and their use and manipulation of the media for their own public relations purposes and to maintain their celebrity lifestyle.

The ruling may benefit such people in the conduct of their ordinary lives but it also reduces the media to public relations organs, who can only carry such photographs as the celebrities themselves authorise or declare to relate to their official functions, even when in the public sphere. Although the judgment does not go so far as to require it, it does raise the spectre of consent as a prerequisite for the taking of any photographs in public places in which individuals, groups or crowds are captured. Not only would that put celebrities (and non-celebrities) in control and be more akin to publicity and image rights than privacy, literally construed, it would also

[89] In this regard it listed *Tammer v Estonia* (Appn No. 41205/98, paras 59-63, ECHR 2001-I), *News Verlags v Austria* (Appn no. 31457/96, paras 52 et seq., ECHR 2000-I) and *Krone Verlag v Austria* (Appn no. 34315/96, paras 33 *et seq.*, 26 February 2002). In *Tammer* the Court found that the conviction of a journalist for insulting remarks about the private life of a former political advisor was not a violation of Article 10. The remarks — the case did not concern photographs — were degrading to her honour and dignity and were not justified by matters of public concern or a matter of general importance. In *News Verlags* the Court found that a ban on the publication of photographs of a person charged in connection with letter bomb offences was disproportionate, that it went further than was necessary to protect the accused person against defamation, invasion of privacy or violations of the presumption of innocence. In *Krone Verlag* it held with regard to the publication of a picture and information about a politician drawing down three salaries that, as the matter was a news item of major public concern and did not disclose any details of private life, there was a violation of Article 10. As pointed out above, the Court has taken a similar line in relation to "artistic speech", for example films and videos, considering whether they contribute to public debate.

[90] Para 76. It said it was clear in the circumstances of the *Von Hannover* case that the photos made no such contribution to a debate of general interest and that the public did not have a "legitimate interest" in knowing where the applicant is and how she behaves generally in her private life. Besides, even if a public interest did exist, and indeed the commercial interest of the magazines concerned, in the instant case it would have to yield to the applicant's right to effective protection of her private life (para 77).

[91] The Court referred to Princess Caroline as a "private" individual, who was of interest to the public and press "based solely on her membership of a reigning family" (para 72). Whitman, in a reference to Princess Caroline, states (*op. cit.* at 1169): "The conception of privacy as control of one's image rests, at base, on the idea that one ought to be able to keep one's name and picture out of the newspapers. This is obviously a conception that matters primarily to members of "society" as the term is used in the phrase "society pages"." On that view, the decision of the European Court of Human Rights marks a "society" conception of privacy.

hamper legitimate newsgathering.[92] It would also be largely impractical given the prevalence of camera mobile phones, which have proven so useful on occasion to record events as they happened and before media photographers could get to the scene.[93]

To say, as the Court does, that such pictures as those of Princess Caroline do not contribute to imparting information and ideas on matters of public interest is to ignore the unofficial role and the social value of the role such people play and thereby to take a narrow view of "ideas" and the "public interest".[94] It is also to take a very narrow view of the scope of freedom of expression, but the Court argues that a narrower view of freedom of expression is called for in these circumstances.[95]

Such a pronouncement is worrying. It restricts freedom of expression to a very limited informational role, one that applies to information regarded essentially as weighty and worthy in the political sphere rather than the social sphere.[96] Such an approach was not new on the part of the Court, as it has taken a similar view in the area of artistic expression.[97] However, it was new for the Court to explicitly state that a narrower view of freedom of expression is called for.

---

[92] A technological device such as pixillation would become commonplace and take from the reality that faces can bring to any news story. An implied consent not to be singled out might allow for general crowd scenes but the immediacy of the individual focus would be lost. A defence of incidental intrusion would be of little consolation to the media. A strong and wide-ranging public interest defence would be necessary.

[93] E.g. the London bombings, July 2005.

[94] Para 63. The Court took the view that the pictures had the "sole purpose" of satisfying the "curiosity of a particular readership" (para 65). To criticise the Court's stance is not to say that readers are entitled to know everything about public figures, as referred to in Article 8 of Resolution 1165 (1998) of the Parliamentary Assembly of the Council of Europe. Instead, it is to argue that the consequences of such a stance are that such public figures will be able to control the image and portrayal of them that appears in the media. In another sense it may cool the ardour of certain sections of the media for indulging in perpetuating the cult of the celebrity, which might have beneficial consequences but more likely will be replaced by another form of content playing to the public's interest in lifestyle and voyeurism.

[95] Para 66. In so saying it relies on *Prisma Presse v France* (dec.), nos 66910/01 and 71612/01, 1 July 2003. To say that the pictures do not amount to a watchdog role on authority on the part of the press is more palatable than to say that they do not impart information or ideas.

[96] There could be many psychological and social benefits for members of the public, especially in increasingly secular western societies, to see that successful or famous people promote their health and well-being by engaging in sport or to see that they are human and can fall or stumble like the rest of us. Such pictures could contribute much more to the public interest in tackling obesity levels or adopting positive lifestyles than photographs of the same people officially shaking hands or taking a photo-call at some official event.

[97] See, for example, cases like *Muller v Switzerland, Otto Preminger v Austria* (above n 85). See also a number of the cases against Turkey (available at www.echr.coe.int) and *Lindon Otchakovsky-Laurens and July v France* (Appn Nos 21279/02 and 36448/02, judgment of 5 September 2007), where the Court considered artistic expression in relation to a novel based around real events and entitled *Jean-Marie le Pen on Trial.*

Whether the content or subject-matter of the photographs should be a factor in the assessment of whether or not there has been a violation of privacy is another pertinent question. While embarrassment (tripping on the pavement) or the desire to be left alone (when shopping or engaging in sport) may be an element of any right to privacy, it is not the central concept. On the other hand, as pointed out above, particularly offensive photographs will probably amount to disrespect for the privacy of the individual concerned.[98]

Protection of private life, the Court says, extends beyond the private family circle and also "includes a social dimension".[99] However, the social dimension the Court has in mind is the social dimension of an individual's life, not the social value to the public of having role-models or icons. It would be easy for the Court to use its sense of the "social dimension" of private life to draw the line: pictures of a celebrity merely socialising with family or friends would be off line, whereas *formal* occasions, public appearances or performance of official duties would be fair game. Such an approach would, it is submitted, strike a more equitable balance and clarify the zone of "legitimate expectation". It would give celebrities a considerable measure of control over their public image and persona, and at the same time preserve to a reasonable extent the right of the media to cover their public activities.[100] However, as the German courts pointed out, if this were to happen, it would favour a "selective" presentation "that would deprive the public of certain

---

[98] See, for example, the Restatement (Second) of Torts in the US, s 652D regarding dissemination of private matter that would be "highly offensive to a reasonable person" and which is not of "legitimate" public interest. However, it appears the offensiveness refers to the fact of dissemination rather than content — see McClurg, p 1073. An example of the application of an offensive dissemination case in Ireland is *Sinnott v Carlow Nationalist*, involving the publication in a newspaper of a photograph of a GAA player whose football shorts had fallen down during a match. The case resulted in a Circuit Court award of €6,500 to the player who had claimed damages for breach of privacy, intentional infliction of emotional harm and negligence. An appeal to the High Court failed. Budd J held that there had been a negligent intrusion on the player's right to privacy and increased damages to €11,000. (see *The Irish Times*, 27 January 2007, 17 February 2007).

[99] Para 69. It goes on to say that "spatial isolation although apposite in theory, is in reality too vague and difficult for the person concerned to determine in advance." (para 75); *cf.* Mead, above n 16. Private space as now understood has both a locational (physical) and psychological dimension and is no longer therefore confined to the private family circle in the way that Dean Prosser and others would have confined it (see Prosser, *loc. cit,* at 391-92: that it was not an invasion to take photographs of people in public places). However, the arguments for expanding private privacy to encompass "public privacy" have been mounting in recent years (see, for example, McClurg, "Bringing Privacy Law out of the Closet: A Tort Theory of Liability for Intrusions in Public Places", 73 NCL. Rev. 989, at 995, 1025 *et seq*. (1995)).

[100] That said, the experience of the strong French law of privacy, which does not appear to have a major deterrent effect — see, for example, the large number of privacy actions taken there by celebrities and public figures — and the existence of other channels such as the Internet to by-pass laws and regulations suggests that the problem would simply move to other countries and other media or communications delivery systems.

judgmental possibilities in respect of figures of socio-political life, having regard to the function of role model of such figures and the influence they exert."[101] If a strong public interest defence were built in to such a delimited scope of public engagement, however, it would protect freedom of expression and allow the media to step outside the mark where there was a strong public interest for doing so.

Taking the issue a step further and identifying an additional concern, the Court refers to the need for increased vigilance to contend with new communications technologies, which make it possible to store and reproduce personal data.[102] The photographs and information about Princess Caroline could be stored, collated, even manipulated, and reproduced in the future. That argument would carry some weight if the photographs were offensive or deeply intrusive on the intimacies of her life. They were not and their future use (unless offensively manipulated, which could form a separate cause of action) would at most cause the same kind of embarrassment that we all feel when we see photographs of ourselves taken at an earlier point in our lives.[103] The Court in *Von Hannover* would have been much better to confine its judgment to the harassment aspects of the case.[104]

Commentaries on the decision in *Von Hannover* have taken the view that the Court has in fact rejected the German law of privacy in favour of French law. If that is so, and it is not intended to analyse the judgment in those terms in the present article,[105] the Court has chosen a path which provides extensive protection for celebrities of various hues, and a right of control of their public image that allows them to require consent, which once given in one set of circumstances or sphere can be withdrawn or re-demanded in yet another. The scope that the French law of privacy gives them to manipulate and control the media is far-reaching. For all that, its deterrent effect

---

[101] An extract from the judgment of the German Federal Constitutional Court of 15 December 1999 is included in para 25 of the *Von Hannover* judgment.

[102] Citing Resolution 1165 (1998) of the Parliamentary Assembly of the Council of Europe on the right to privacy, *Amann v Switzerland* [GC], no. 27798/95, paras 65-67, ECHR 2000-II; *Rotaru v Romania* [GC], no. 28341/95, paras 43-44, ECHR 2000-V; *PG and JH v UK*, no.44787/98, ECHR 2001-IX, and *Peck v UK*, no. 44647/98, ECHR 2003-I.

[103] A good example is an Irish case, where a woman, a private citizen, whose face when she was a nine year old child had been used on holiday brochures, lost her claim to privacy: *Murray v Falcon Holidays* (Circuit Court, 6 May 2005, reported in *The Irish Times*, 7 May 2005). The photograph taken in a swimming pool in Greece was "a happy holiday picture" and the plaintiff could not succeed either under the law of tort, or breach of confidence, constitutional rights or breach of contract, the judge said.

[104] A detailed examination of the other issues arising in relation to electronic communications, storage and reproduction, while increasingly important, is outside the scope of the present article.

[105] See, however, Phillipson in Kenyon and Richardson, 2006, at 212, where he argues that an absolutist reading of *Von Hannover* would have the effect of requiring all Council of Europe States to "move to something like the French model of privacy", whereas a more nuanced reading would be more realistic. See also the discussion of the origins and development of both French and German law of privacy in Whitman, *op. cit.*, at 1171-1195. Whitman points out that Warren and Brandeis were familiar with both and attempted to import them into the common law (at 1204-8).

on certain elements of the media appears negligible, and breach of privacy cases in France appear to occur as frequently as defamation cases in Ireland, which is very telling.

The danger, of course, in such a judgment emanating from the European Court of Human Rights, especially one based on rather feeble argument, is that it will become the bench-mark for courts in all the member states of the Council of Europe which subscribe to the Convention and hence to the jurisprudence of the Court. By contrast with the Strasbourg judgment, the judgment of the German Federal Constitutional Court of 15 December 1999 is much better contextualised (by reference to the free development of the personality), more realistic in its understanding of the role that celebrities (as role-models) and entertainment play in the formation of opinions in modern society and more clearly and convincingly argued. Besides, the German courts had already differentiated between the photographs and ruled against some of them. Those that were the subject of the Strasbourg hearing were, therefore, the least intrusive.

The bottom line may well be that the Strasbourg Court was trying to tackle more than it could handle and was not paying enough heed to the realities of the communications and entertainment world today. While a means of curbing the harassment aspects of paparazzi activities could extend benefits to celebrities and reach all media including the Internet, the limitations imposed on content based on a strict interpretation of what is private will not. Such is the nature of technology that rules and regulations, even law, can and will be bypassed or circumvented. That is not to say that law and courts should simply give up the fight but rather that they should take cognisance of the realities of the modern world.

However, judgments of the Court since *Von Hannover* under both Articles 10 and 8 have suggested that the Court is intent on (re-)drawing the balance between freedom of expression (Article 10) and respect for privacy (Article 8), recovering the ground perhaps between protection of the collective democracy and the individual. Its activism in this regard can be seen in the manner in which it has established that the scope of private life in Article 8 encompasses or extends to reputation. Having "observed" in passing in *Radio France v France*[106] that "the right to protection of one's reputation is of course one of the rights guaranteed by Article 8 of the Convention, as one element of the right to respect for private life", it went on in *Chauvy v France*[107] to strengthen that observation to "souligne." The biggest step, however, was taken in a case decided by the Grand Chamber in 2007, *Lindon v France*.[108]

---

[106] Appn no. 53984/00, judgment of 30 March 2004, followed in *Chauvy v France* (Appn No. 64915/01, judgment of 29 June 2004).

[107] In *Abeberry v France* Appn no. 58729/00, 21 September 2004, while in *Gunnarsson v Iceland* (Appn No. 4591/04, decision of 20 October 2005) the judges were not convinced and in *White v Sweden* (Appn No. 42435/02, judgment of 19 September 2006) they again stated that reputation was a right under Article 8 without elaborating on it. It should be noted that these were all decisions of Sections of the Court.

[108] Appn Nos 21279/02 and 36448/02, judgment of 5 September 2007.

Lindon v France involved a novel entitled *Jean-Marie le Pen on Trial* and based on real events. In relation to reputation, the Court observed that "the reputation of a politician, even a controversial one, must benefit from the protection afforded by the Convention."[109] However, it was in the concurring opinion of Judge Loucaides that an explanation for the inclusion of reputation under Article 8 was to be found. In his view, freedom of expression had on occasion been over-protected as compared with interference with "the right to reputation". The former had been upheld as "a value of primary importance" which "in many cases could deprive deserving plaintiffs of an appropriate remedy for the protection of their dignity."[110]

By the end of 2007 in *Pfeifer v Austria*[111] the Court was able to state that it had already been accepted in the Convention organs' case-law that a person's right to his or her reputation was encompassed by Article 8 as being part of the right to respect for private life. The Court then, for the first time, made some attempt to explain why that was so. A person's reputation, the Court said, "forms part of his or her personal identity and psychological integrity and therefore also falls within the scope of his or her 'private life'". In a recent case decided in October 2008, *Petrina v Romania,*[112] the Court held unanimously that there had been a breach of Article 8 when a politician, who had been unsuccessful in defamation proceedings against a satirical weekly, complained that his right to respect for his honour and his good name had been violated.

Conclusion

There can be no doubt but that the right to respect for privacy in Article 8 is expanding in ways that would not have been foreseen even a decade ago. Each culture, even each generation has, of course, its own distinct concept of privacy[113]; therefore it is not static or finite. As there is no uniform sense of privacy among European States, States could expect to be entitled to meet their obligations to ensure respect for private life in a variety of ways by adopting measures appropriate to the particular harm to be avoided. There is nothing in the case law of the Court to date to suggest that legislation is always mandated or that an effective Press Council or Complaints Commission route, for example, would not suffice at least in relation to some forms of invasion of privacy or in a climate where invasion of privacy was not wholesale or endemic.[114]

---

[109] At para 57.

[110] He went on to say in what appears to be a reproach to the Court in respect of its earlier case-law: "This approach cannot be in line with the correct interpretation of the Convention. The right to reputation should always have been considered as safeguarded by Article 8 of the Convention, as part and parcel of the right to respect for one's private life."

[111] Appn No. 12556/03, judgment of 15 November 2007.

[112] Appn No. 780601/01, judgment of 14 October 2008.

[113] Barendt, 'Privacy and the Press', *Yearbook of Media and Entertainment Law,* (OUP, Oxford, 1995) 23, at 33, says this "cultural and temporal relativism" should not be exaggerated. He points to a core of privacy recognised in all western European societies in all recent generations and instances the publication without consent of personal diaries and letters, photographs of a couple love-making or a woman giving birth (at 34).

[114] See, for example, *Stoll v Switzerland* (Appn No. 69698/01, Grand Chamber judgment of 10 December 2007), where the views of the Press Council were considered.

However, there can be no doubt but that privacy is coming of age, that a shift is taking place in the European Court of Human Rights, a refashioning of the contours and content of the right, as well as its relationship with freedom of expression. Unfortunately, much of the debate on that shift is taking place largely in the context of protecting celebrities, politicians and other public figures from the press rather than in more core areas that impact on the more vulnerable in society whose human rights, including privacy, need respect and protection in many aspects of life far removed from the spotlight of fame or notoriety.

Privacy is not and should not be solely or primarily about celebrities. Celebrities cultivate and live off their celebrity status. Media coverage, usually planned and contracted for or orchestrated through agents or public relations companies or specialists, is their life-blood. In a question particularly pertinent in the case of celebrities, Robert C Posts asks whether people care more about their privacy or about their image.[115] He also points out that there is an "internal contradiction in the position of a plaintiff who alienates and objectifies her image and simultaneously claims that it is integral to her very identity".[116] A case can be made for separating out image rights (often called publicity rights) from privacy rights. Image rights, since they relate to the public image and celebrity status of an individual(s) as a commodity can be readily accommodated by other areas of law such as the law of copyright, trademarks and patents.

However, in modern-day society celebrity is a much-prized and much sought-after status. Celebrities thus become icons and role-models and coverage of celebrities, trivial or not, sells newspapers and increases ratings figures — hence the opportunity for the paparazzi. However distasteful constant pursuit and intrusiveness by the paparazzi may be to celebrities themselves and to large sections of the public, the truth is that nowadays in a globalised economic and cultural environment, celebrities are more important to significant numbers of the population than are politicians and other societal leaders. It is easy to deny or downplay the significance of this phenomenon but to do so is to marginalise those who are already disengaged from political life or the traditional serious side of life. Besides, while a tort and offence of harassment can address the persistence and intrusive aspects of the pursuit of celebrity by the paparazzi (and thus cut off or reduce the iconic flow of information to the tabloid reader), unless carefully circumscribed it could also interfere with genuine newsgathering and

---

[115] RC Post, 2000-1, at 2091. Whitman, at 1170, says that at best continental privacy law "is not a form of protection for universal human 'personhood', but a means of regulating the relations between celebrities and the rest of us".

[116] 1990-1, at 677. Post concludes (1990-1, at 680) that the "legacy of Warren and Brandeis contains both insight and warning. The insight is that the law is a powerful instrument for fashioning the forms of our social life. The warning is that we must take care that the forms of life the law creates are those we desire to inhabit".

investigative journalism (and thus cut off or reduce the flow of serious information to the broadsheet reader).[117]

Yet, two core principles which have entered and informed the debate about celebrities have the capacity to address the wider implications of privacy in the non-celebrity sphere also. These are the concept of "reasonable expectation" of privacy and the concept of the "public interest". Neither is new but both need to be reconsidered and redefined. The test applied by the European Court of Human Rights regarding the (lack of) capacity of a publication of private facts to contribute to a debate in a democratic society may need to be widened or reassessed to encompass consideration of the new public debate that centres on celebrity culture.

The concept and scope of public debate is changing in part as the result of major developments like globalisation, prompted by numerous factors, including technology, which has resulted in a proliferation of news and information sources, interactive and self-selection audiovisual services, and an end to the one single major source that dominated public debate for much of the twentieth century. In Ireland's case, the days of RTÉ or the "Indo" (*Irish Independent*), or indeed the *Irish Press* in its heyday determining the news agenda for the whole population for the day are long since gone. As the recent Presidential election in the United States has shown, the Internet is now a greater player in galvanising and influencing large sections of the population than the traditional media. Indeed, today's generation of young people have effectively eschewed privacy in favour of public disclosure on social networking sites such as Bebo, Facebook and MySpace. Besides, a significant part of the content of many of the now endless sources of news and information is entertainment. The protection of artistic (or entertainment) speech has become as important in modern society as political speech. To judge artistic speech by the same standards as political speech in terms of contribution to a public debate of weighty import, as the European Court of Human Rights

[117] See, McGonagle, "A tort of privacy?" 1(4) *Quarterly Review of Tort Law*, Winter 2006, 1. The tort of nuisance only protects when the impact is in relation to the use and enjoyment of one's property; the tort of trespass in all its forms is likewise limited; the courts have been reluctant to develop the tort of intentional infliction of emotional suffering to meet privacy concerns, e.g. *Thomas v Independent Newspapers* (*The Irish Times*, 26 July 1988), although the last-mentioned was one of the grounds that founded a successful action in *Sinnott v Carlow Nationalist* (above, n 98, Circuit Court award of €6,500 in 2006 to a GAA player as the result of a photograph, upheld on appeal to the High Court on the grounds of negligent intrusion on the right to privacy, see *The Irish Times* 17 February 2007). RC Post (2000-1, at 2091) offers an interesting observation also in relation to breach of confidence and the injury that results, which, he says, is more in the way of an "injury of betrayal" than a breach of privacy, although the information disclosed may include private facts. Post speaks of the connections between privacy and the "independent harm of violation", which derives from the rupture of significant normative expectations (at 2092): "privacy inheres in social norms that define the forms of respect that we owe to each other. These norms are socialized into the identities of persons. Infringements of these norms are experienced as intrinsically harmful, because they are violative of the self." By intrinsically harmful he means that harm is caused regardless of contingent consequences, like public misrepresentations.

continues to do, is no longer feasible or acceptable. To conceive of a "legitimate" public interest and a "narrow" freedom of expression, as the Court has done in recent cases, especially *Von Hannover* and the reputation as privacy cases outlined above,[118] is an exercise in standard-setting designed to exclude not just the extremes of popular culture but to ignore the reality of post or neo-democratic society. It does not take account of the contractual and managed relationship between celebrities (and indeed politicians) and the media; in fact, it facilitates public relations and spin-doctoring by placing much of the non-public-relations managed areas of celebrities' (and politicians') lives off-limits; it facilitates artificially constructed "good news" journalism.

That said, it is the business of law to set standards and not merely to react to changes or developments in society. It is important in the case of both celebrities and politicians that they be encouraged to enter public life and give the fruits of their creativity or leadership qualities to the public; therefore there has to be some protection of privacy so as not to discourage them.[119] Equally, protection for privacy must pertain to, be readily accessible to and effective in the case of non-public figures — and designed with them in mind just as much as their famous or better-known counterparts.

Laws have traditionally focused on injury or harm, direct or indirect, rather than audience or reader choices.[120] In an increasingly digital and interactive world, audience access to, control and use of media are greater and more significant than before.[121] The degree of harm to privacy occasioned by one of many audiovisual services may therefore be lessened in some respects. However, the need for control of personal data in the light of extensive business and social use of the Internet and faced with data surveillance and data retention by governments in the fight against terrorism, is a key factor emerging for any future regulatory regime.

A common thread between substantive, relational and informational privacy, is the desire to exert control: controlling one's own development as an individual, in one's

---

118 While it is beyond the scope of the present article to discuss other aspects of these "reputation as privacy" cases, some of them portray serious departures from previous jurisprudence on freedom of expression — see, for example, the dissenting opinions of four of the judges in *Lindon v France.*

119 This was one of the arguments made by Judge Loucaides in his concurring opinion in *Lindon v France* (above) in support of reputation as a right in itself under Article 8.

120 See Alexander, *op. cit.*, pp 56–7 regarding different types of content regulations and effects on audiences.

121 In such a world where control is dispersed and public debate is no longer centrally informed, the traditional focus is somewhat misplaced. On the other hand, the sheer capacity of the Internet, of blogging, googling and virtual existence in an unlimited virtual sphere throws up new challenges to privacy and calls for new measures to be devised to afford the necessary protections.

relations with others and in the flow and use of one's personal information.[122] With control comes independence. For those with little or no political or monetary power, no ready access to media or other influence in society, that becomes critical.

On the media side, some heart-searching needs to take place also. The media scrums and frenzy, the incessant chases and stalking by the paparazzi, the mushrooming of reality television, the failure to distinguish between public relations/spin doctoring and honest news reporting, all need to be challenged and reassessed. As long as newspapers and television channels are willing to pay for pictures and footage, the paparazzi or their equivalent will continue to thrive. Press Councils and Ombudsmen could provide the forum for newspapers to arrive voluntarily at an agreed policy on the use, if any, of paparazzi originated photographs, whether in their printed or Internet editions.[123] Broadcasting Complaints Commissions can fulfil a similar role in relation to broadcast pictures, and industry or sector players in the mobile phone and Internet spheres must also meet these challenges.

Even if the paparazzi were to disappear overnight, however, the problem would not be solved. The ubiquitous presence of CCTV, mobile phones equipped with ever-improving camera facilities, Internet access and many other technological capabilities, means that the professional paparazzi are being joined by citizen cameramen and women. Reality and citizen journalism can offer a new and important level of coverage of events as they unfold before staff reporters, stringers or freelances can get to the scene. However, the blurring of reality with either public relations or entertainment can have serious side effects.[124] Media literacy, with its emphasis on educating the public to the inner workings of media, particularly new media, can help to address some of the ill-judgment that Warren and Brandeis decried and can help to forge a new understanding of and relationship with the world of celebrity and entertainment.

---

[122] See, for example, Lord Hoffman in *Campbell v MGN*, [2004] 2 WLR 1232, HL, at paras 50-1; also Warren and Brandeis's argument (*op. cit.* at 198, 206) that the right of determining to what extent a person's thoughts, sentiments and emotions shall be communicated to others is so important that a person ought legally to retain control over them, as indeed, they argued, authors and artists could under the law of copyright (at 198); further analysed by Gavison, "Privacy and the Limits of the Law", 89 Yale LJ 421 (1980) and Post, 1990-1, at 651, 654. See also Rosen, "The Purposes of Privacy: A Response", 89 Geo. LJ 2117 (2000-1) at 2120, privacy as the ability to exercise control over personal information, which is the information over which one reasonably expects to exercise control.

[123] Irish newspapers have generally not taken pictures from paparazzi but, in any event, the new Press Council and Press Ombudsman which came into being in September 2007 will operate on the basis of a Code which contains provisions regarding privacy.

[124] The Australian Law Reform Commission conducted a national phone-in in June 2006, which demonstrated that telemarketing and information privacy were the main community concerns. With CCTV, mini-cams, etc., people felt that little they do is private any more. The Press Council in its preliminary submission to the ALRC (8 August 2006) stated: "While potential intrusion onto the privacy of private individuals by the media is not as pervasive as other forms of privacy invasion, the rare examples of it fuel a perception that the media are contributing to this sense of a loss of privacy".

That said, the right to privacy as currently conceived is a shapeless, overflowing entity that is expanding out of control in unprecedented directions. It needs to be unpacked and very carefully repackaged in a more manageable way on the basis of clear principles. Much of the peripheral content needs to be taken out, re-sorted and either discarded or placed in other appropriate packages, distinct from the essentials, for appropriate labelling and redress. Harassment, personality rights, breach of confidence, issues of taste and decency, injury to feelings, and so forth need to be detached and treated separately. Only then can privacy become a meaningful and practical vehicle for the protection of key aspects of life. Only then will it be in a position to develop in a coherent, cohesive and consistent way and only then will its fluidity, so essential to keep pace with developments in society and culture, be manageable and doctrinally secure. Without such rationalisation, to quote Alexander, "[a]t most, courts could prevent the notions of privacy and offense from becoming so capacious that practically all expression could be deemed violative of privacy or offensive."[125] The European Court of Human Rights in its next outings needs to reconsider and refine the unprecedented and ill thought-out step it took in *Von Hannover* and subsequently in expanding privacy to encompass a right to reputation without providing proper reasoning.

Note: Since this article was written, the European Court of Human Rights has addressed some of the issues raised above. *Karako v Hungary*[126] concerned unsuccessful proceedings for libel of a politician. The politician complained that the Austrian authorities had failed to protect his rights, including his right to reputation, under Article 8. The Court took the opportunity to address the "purported" conflict between Articles 8 and 10, which it said "is one of appearance only".[127] It also emphasised the importance of a "prudent approach to the State's positive obligations to protect private life in general", and the "need to recognise the diversity of possible methods to secure its respect". The "nature of the State's obligations depends on the aspect of private life concerned" and the "choice of measures designed to ensure compliance with that obligation falls within the Contracting State's margin of appreciation", the Court said, but "as a minimum requirement...an effective legal system must be in place and operating".[128]

Perhaps most importantly, the Court goes on to address the issue of cases taken under Article 8 which involve freedom of expression: the protection granted by the State in such cases "should be understood as one taking into consideration its obligations under Article 10 of the Convention."[129] Interestingly, given the observations and criticisms in the article above, the Court endeavours to clarify the

---

[125] *op.cit.* at 190. For further discussion of some of the issues raised above, see also McGonagle, "Defamation Law in Europe — a rapprochement between *Reynolds* and the ECHR", (2009) 14 MALR 166; and Barendt, "Balancing Freedom of Expression and Privacy: The Jurisprudence of the Strasbourg Court", [2009] 1 *Journal of Media Law* 49.

[126] Appn No. 39311/05, judgment of 28 April 2009.

[127] At para 17.

[128] At para 19.

[129] At para 20. It is interesting to note that the Court in this paragraph refers also to the drafters of the Convention in relation to Article 10.

approach and scope of Von Hannover, drawing a distinction between "personal integrity" in Von Hannover and "reputation". It also tries to explain away some of its subsequent case law, claiming that reputation had only been deemed to be an independent right "sporadically", as in Petrina (above) and "mostly" — but as illustrated above, not always by any means — "when the factual allegations were of such a seriously offensive nature that their publication had an inevitable direct effect on the applicant's private life.[130]

Nonetheless, the tide, it seems, may be turning back in the right direction.

[130] At paras 21-23.

Children's Rights in Ireland: Legacy Issues and Future Prospects

Professor Pat Dolan*

Introduction

The Irish State's interest in and requirement to uphold the rights of children as specified in the UN Convention on the Rights of the Child (UNCRC) should not be seen as a phenomenon of novel provenance. The need for an active children's rights agenda has been identified in numerous policy reports over the years up to and including the report of the All-Party Oireachtas Committee on the Constitution regarding an amendment to the Irish Constitution to explicitly provide for children's rights.[1] Despite notable problems within the Irish child care system, both for universal populations and children with specific needs, this deficit has been counter-balanced by investment and some improvement in terms of meeting the needs of children, particularly in the last decade. In its most recent international review on child welfare standards, the UNICEF review group found Irish child care policies and services in mid-table position among the twenty-four countries surveyed.[2] Whether one views this as a positive or a negative result, overall, it remains the case that many children still suffer poverty, neglect and are at risk of abuse. Constitutionally, and in practice, their rights are not always explicitly protected or upheld.

This article explores the children's rights landscape in Ireland as a case study taking legislative, policy and practice implementation perspectives with some particular focus on issues relating to children within the justice system. Following a brief description of children's rights within a model of social justice, the current context in which child welfare occurs is considered both for children as a universal population and for those with more serious social needs. In order to understand this current context, a retrospective view is outlined so as to inform the ongoing journey to achieve optimal rights for Irish children. Finally, based on past and current learning, a future agenda is proposed within a set of illustrated practical frameworks aimed at the judiciary and social service managers as key interlocutors

---

* Holder of the UNESCO Chair in Children, Youth and Civic Engagement and Director of the Child and Family Support Centre, NUI Galway. The author wishes to thank Ms. Sinead McCoole, Historian and Curator of the Jackie Clarke Museum, Ballina, Co, Mayo for her assistance in completing the research for this article.

[1] Government of Ireland Joint Committee of the Oireachtas on the *Constitutional Amendment on Children: Proposed Amendment to Article 42 (A) of the Constitution*, (Stationery Office, Dublin 2006).

[2] J Bradshaw, P Hoelscher and D Richardson (2007), "Comparing Child Well-Being in OECD Countries: Concepts and Methods", *Innocenti Working Paper* No. 2006-03 (UNICEF Innocenti Research Centre, Florence).

in the realisation (or not) of children's rights. Rather than seeing these messages as representing a form of "diktat" they are intended more as guidance for all those stakeholders with an interest in the human rights of children.

Children's Rights as a Principle of Social Justice

The UNCRC is the most obvious starting point for describing and understanding children's rights in Ireland particularly as an explicit statement of intent on the part of the Irish state. The UNCRC was adopted by the General Assembly of the United Nations in 1989.[3] Its fifty-four articles describe the protection and promotion of children's development and participation in society. The articles combine a set of human rights, civil and political rights and the child's right to participate in decisions that affect them.

Whereas these rights speak for themselves, one needs to consider factors that can be associated with their actualisation for any child, particularly given that children need to be assured of ongoing support from adults including their parents. Axel Honneth[4] frames rights for all people, including young and old, within a "Social Justice Theory" model which implies an innate set of human rights that incorporates the key principle of "recognition" of any person" Where children experience such recognition in ample amounts and of good quality not just from their parents, extended family peers and community memberships but at a wider societal level, it could be argued that they are living within an "active rights rich" environment. Recognition by the adult community of young people implies a belief in the bonds that children hold with other people even where they demonstrate difficulties and/or experience distress. These three forms of recognition are now briefly described.

(1) Primary Relationships of Positive Regard

Honneth[5] indicates that positive regard, (which includes respect and, within some relationships, love) is a key part of reciprocal recognition between people. In effect, for children this means that their emotional needs are satisfied through relationships forged out of love, respect and understanding. From such relationships many children grow healthily over time and this may be viewed by them and others as an automatic right that can be taken for granted. Conversely, where such recognition and respect is not present — for example, as a result of acts of child abuse — this lack of rights can result in devastating results for a child in terms of sadness and distress.

(2) Legal Relations Involving Rights

Honneth's second principle indicates that when respect is given personal rights are being acknowledged. In many societies, structurally, children's rights have been

[3] United Nations Convention on the Rights of the Child, Resolution No.s 44/25 Ratified by the Assembly on 20 November 1989 (United Nations Press Office).

[4] A Honneth, *The Struggle for Recognition: The Moral Grammar of Social Conflicts,* (Polity Press, Cambridge, 1995).

[5] A Honneth and N Fraser, *Redistribution or Recognition? A Political-Philosophical Exchange,* (Verso, London, 2003).

historically coded and been formalised through legal processes. This suggests formally endowing children as active citizens with civil, political and social welfare entitlements which are recognised by society as a given. Conversely, where no legal rights are present or are weak or are denied for children, their resultant experiences will include social injustices such as, for example, sectarianism, racial prejudice and material inequities.

(3) Community of Value and Solidarity

Within this principle Honneth suggests that a person's self-esteem rises when they achieve culturally defined goals and subsequently have their accomplishments recognised. For children to grow in a socially constructive, positive environment or community, being valued positively by themselves and others, is important not just as a personal right but also in relation to how they behave,[6] are resilient to risk,[7] and engage with wider society.[8] Where this principle is upheld a child can foster "felt concern" for others and their values which is a central function of positive civic engagement.[9] Conversely, for a child where such a sense of "community" is not present, they may see themselves as devalued and thus value others less, in terms of their sense of dignity.

At its most basic, it could be argued that one of the main benefits of a strong rights culture for children is that it realises a young person's "right to his or her rights". However, apart from seeing this as an assumed given, Honneth's three social justice principles coupled with the UNCRC can enable a young person to have and maintain relationships of positive regard formally structured via a legal recognition of rights embedded in a community that contains reciprocal value.

A Current Perspective

Despite Ireland's ratification of the UNCRC the question remains — how, in practice, are children (as a universal population) respected within Irish society and, more specifically, how are troubled and troublesome children respected? The National Children's Strategy, *Our Children Their Lives*,[10] remains the key Irish policy document that aims to support and underpin the UNCRC. It advocates:

> "Supporting children to focus on their particular interest and responsibility while, at the same time, recognising the multidimensional aspect of children's lives"
> *(Government of Ireland, 2000,* p 24)

---

[6] M Herbert, "Children in Control: Helping Parents to Restore the Balance", In J Canavan, P Dolan and J Pinkerton (Eds.) *Family Support: Direction From Diversity*, (Jessica Kingsley, London, 2000) Ch4, pp 79–102.

[7] M Rutter, H Giller, and A Hagel. *Antisocial Behaviour by Young People*, (Cambridge University Press, Cambridge, 1998).

[8] O Gill, and G Jack. *Child and Family in Context: Developing Ecological Practice in Disadvantaged Communities*, (Russell House, Lyme Regis, 2007).

[9] D Watson, *Managing Civic and Community Engagement. Managing Universities and Colleges: Guides to Good Practice*, (Open University Press, UK, 2007).

[10] Government of Ireland, *National Children's Strategy: Our Children Their Lives*, (Stationery Office, Dublin, 2000).

This child-positive aspiration and intent, portrayed as a lynchpin within the strategy, is particularly relevant given the recent mid-table showing for Ireland in relation to its capacity to uphold the rights of children, resulting from a study of 24 countries by the United Nations.[11] While one could argue that this result suggests a mediocre showing in terms of how children are valued and cared for in Irish society it is important to note that it is an overall improvement on an earlier audit of child welfare in Ireland done by the UN in 2003. Whether it's a case of the cup being half-full or half-empty it calls for a more probing consideration of the status of children's rights in Ireland.

Leaving aside the more "macro" consideration of the absence of an explicit constitutional guarantee of children's rights there is a much more "mundane" level of denial of children's rights. Take the following three simple but clear examples:

- How often are children bypassed in queues in shops or restaurants while adults are served ahead of them?
- How often are adolescents who buy a coffee in a restaurant asked by management or serving staff to make a further purchase or move on, while adults can take hours over one coffee to work on their laptops?
- Would adults allow the use of piercing sound alarms in busy shopping centre's (that only they can hear) to ensure they don't loiter?

Similarly, teenagers who innocently linger and converse with peers on street corners are often labeled as "causing trouble" while adults who behave similarly are seen as "active community participants" increasing local social capital. These scenarios are not unique to Ireland.[12] To some they may seem trivial but for many young people they are perceived as real demonstrations of how their rights are overlooked or deemed unimportant by adults in wider civic society. If older people received the same treatment on a wide scale phone-in radio programmes would be awash with angered adult listeners and newspaper editors would be busy choosing between which complainant letters they should publish.

At a far more serious level, for children who suffer abuse or neglect or those suffering the acrimony of their separating parents, how child-friendly is the law and court system?[13] What further abuse do children suffer in giving evidence in courtrooms which are not conducive or sensitive to the needs of children.[14] Coulter, in her pioneering research on the family courts, has questioned how family-friendly it is from the perspective of participants in family law proceedings.[15] This raises questions about the extent to which children are respected within the processes and

---

[11] J Bradshaw, P Hoelscher and D Richardson "Comparing Child Well-Being in OECD Countries: Concepts and Methods". *Innocenti Working Paper* No. 2006-03 (UNICEF Innocenti Research Centre, Florence, 2007).

[12] I Davies and M Evans, *Encouraging Active Citizenship Educational Review, Vol. 54, No. 1, 2002.*

[13] G Shannon, *Family Law Society of Ireland Manual* (Oxford, November, 2007).

[14] L Colligan and H Buckley, "Community based professional responses to child sexual abuse" *Irish Journal of Family Law*, 4, 2–7 2004.

[15] C Coulter *Family Law in Practice: A Study of Cases in the Circuit Court* (Clarus Press, Dublin, 2009).

procedures of the Irish legal system. This lack of regard for basic rights is also evident in other areas of service provision. For example, until recently the placing of children in adult psychiatric hospitals or adult prison systems had still been practiced by professionals[16] despite the obvious risks to children's rights.

Massad Hoghughi[17] suggests that children who are orphaned, neglected or living in general deprivation are sometimes termed "sad", whereas children with severe mental health difficulties or chronic depression are termed "mad". Troubled and troublesome young people, who attract so much attention in the media and within the court system and are out of the control of family, school and community, are often seen as *"bad"*. This population is most frequently given attention by legal and social work professionals, partly because they cause most harm to adults in communities and account for most service funding from helping agencies.[18] In summary from a rights perspective, given the status of a child being of limited capacity up to the age of 18 years, we need to remember that, despite behaviour or deprivation, he or she is often sad, sometimes mad, but not bad and should not be dealt with on the latter basis. This rights principle is advocated with full knowledge of the severe difficulties in trying to work with young people who are out of control and sometimes violent.[19]

However the Irish case should not be seen as totally negative. In fact, Ireland is well equipped in terms of robust child policy. In addition to the National Children's Strategy[20] there is also solid child protection policy[21] as well as a Commission on the Family[22] and the more recent *Youth Justice Review.*[23] There remains a need for more or new policies in the area of child welfare and its implementation to alleviate some of the negative scenarios discussed above. In particular, the *Agenda for Children Services Policy Handbook*[24] offers hope if its intent for on-the-ground service delivery for children with joined-up thinking and a multi-disciplinary approach to a "family support agenda"[25] by all relevant professionals comes to fruition.

---

[16] Barnardos' submission to the Joint Committee on the Constitutional Amendment on Children: Proposed Amendment to Article 42 (A) of the Constitution, January, 2008.

[17] M Hoghughi. "Troubled and Troublesome: Perspectives on Adolescent" Hurt in B Tizard and V Verma (Eds.) *Vulnerability and Resilience in Human Development: A Festchrift for Ann and Alan Clarke* (Jessica Kingsley, UK, 1999) Chapter 13.

[18] K Lalor, F Ryan, M Seymour and C Hamilton, *Young People and Crime, Research, Policy and Practice,* (Conference Proceedings Report Centre For Social and Educational Research, Dublin Institute of Technology Publ., Dublin, 2007).

[19] The author worked with Adolescents in Residential Care, Mental Health Services and Community Based Youth Work Programmes for over 20 years.

[20] National Children's Strategy Our Children Their Lives, *ibid*.

[21] Government of Ireland, *Children First Guidelines,* Gov of Ireland, 2000.

[22] Government of Ireland, *Strengthening Families for Life, Commission on the Family Report* (Stationery Office Dublin, 1998).

[23] Government of Ireland, *Report on TheYouth Justice Review,* Department of Justice Equality and Law Reform (Stationery Office, Dublin, 2006).

[24] Government of Ireland *Agenda for Children Services: A Policy Handbook* (Stationery Office, Dublin, 2007).

[25] See further: J Canavan, P Dolan and J Pinkerton (Eds) *Family Support: Direction from Diversity* (Jessica Kingsley Publishers, London, 2000).

Similarly, the actual situation in relation to Irish childcare services is not all bad and, in fact, recent reasonable steadiness in the number of young people in the residential care system, more community-based prevention services[26] and the establishment of the Office of the Minister for Children and Youth Affairs at the Department of Health and Children are positive initiatives. Furthermore, the establishment of the Children Act Advisory Board to implement the Children Act 2001[27] is important evidence of an explicit national commitment to children including those who present as out of control. At a more universal level an active office of Ombudsman for Children[28] has helped to ensure respect for the general Irish child population. Taken together, these initiatives represent a positive pro-child policy culture in Ireland that certainly was not there as recently as ten years ago.

At a universal level, in terms of the civic engagement of young people and evidence of their being given "a voice" in society, a developing body of positive practices hold promise[29]. For instance, youth participation programmes like the Foroige Active Citizenship Model[30] and, more nationally, the children's parliament ("Dail Na nOg") evidence movement in a positive direction. However, it remains to be seen if these groupings have "real voice" and policy impact. In recent debates about children's evidence procedures in rape cases and in respect of the Irish performance under the UN Convention on the Rights of the Child it could be argued that these groupings were not consulted fully or quickly enough as equal stakeholder experts.

A Past Perspective — Women Who Pioneered Children's Rights

It would be wrong to assume that children's rights or the children's rights movement in Ireland have no history antecedents. Prior to the formation of the Irish state there is evidence that, however tentatively, children's rights were pioneered by women such as Countess Markievicz, Maud Gonne, Dr Kathleen Lynn, Sinéad de Valera (nee Flanagan) and others.[31] It is noteworthy that they did this over one hundred years ago at a time when child death was far more common in Ireland. At that time many children were living in abject poverty, most notably in Dublin City,[32] which, in the early 1900s, contained some of the worst slums in Europe.[33] These

[26] K McKeown, *Springboard Promoting Family Well-being thorough Family Support Services*, Final Evaluation Report of Springboard January 2000 to May 2001 (A Springboard Publication, Dept. of Health and Children, Stationery Office Dublin, 2001).
[27] Children Act 2001.
[28] Ms Emily Logan the Irish Ombudsman for Children was appointed Chair of European Network of Ombudsmen for Children in September 2008.
[29] E Fahmy "Social Capital and Civic Action: A Study of Youth in the United Kingdom," *Young* 14(2): 101–118., 2006
[30] Foroige Active Citizenship Programme, Foróige Publication 2008 — (Foróige is an Irish National Youth Work Organisation).
[31] A M Haverty, *Constance Markievicz: Irish Revolutionary* (Pandora Publ, 1988).
[32] P Dolan and S McCoole "Time for us to deliver on children's rights" Opinion, *The Irish Times* Wed, 10 October 2006.
[33] J Robins, *The Lost Children*.

women advocated for children when the concept of a child having rights and being seen as "individual" was unheard of. According to Ó h'Ógartaigh,[34] women political activists in the early years of the twentieth century saw themselves as working towards an improvement of society for Irishmen, Irishwomen *and* Irish children. McCoole concurs with this view and found that. at that time, by taking a "rights perspective" they saw the importance of children as a future generation. They had a holistic approach to educate the young while also caring for their health and alleviating their hunger.[35] Specifically, this manifested itself in a number of ways. By creating of *Inghinidhe na hEireann* (the Daughters of Ireland) in 1900, the importance of educating children in the Irish language, dance, songs and ancient Irish history, as a given right, was emphasised. Free classes for children took place in the poorest areas of Dublin. This was also seen as a way of forestalling recruitment to the British Army. Later, many of these children became members of *Na Fianna* a political youth scout movement, co-founded by Countess Markievicz.[36]

Inghinidhe na hEireann began as a group of women headed by Maud Gonne who organised an event "just for children". A picnic for "loyalist" children had taken place during the visit of Queen Victoria in 1900 and nationalists decided to hold an alternative picnic called the "Patriotic Children's Treat" to reward children who had not cheered for Queen Victoria. This committee successfully brought 30,000 children to "Clonturk Park" (*sic* Croke Park, Dublin) without incident. Notwithstanding the overtly political nature of this event, one could argue that these women were ahead of their time in organising a mass gathering of children (probably for the first time) and recognising them as important citizens or rights-holders.[37] Apart from its political purpose this event was also an act of civic engagement with and for children.

Similarly, there is evidence that adolescent girls in their mid-teens were both civic and political activists for both a nationalist Ireland and for social justice. At least one of these, Eilis Dolan (an aunt of the author) is known to have been arrested and imprisoned where, with others, she utilised the collective "autograph book" to give testament to her view and value for Ireland.[38]

For many women Irish independence was idealised as bringing about a new state with a new social order in which children's rights would be upheld while attempting to redress inequality and poverty. By 1910 the members of *Inghinidhe na hEireann* had expanded their activities to providing food for school children through setting up and running school canteens in the poorest sections of Dublin.

---

[34] M Ó hÓgartaigh, *Kathleen Lynn: Patriot, Irishwomen, Doctor* (Irish Academic Press, 2006).
[35] S McCoole, *No Ordinary Women: Irish Female Activists in the Revolutionary Years* (O'Brien Press, Dublin, 2004).
[36] M Ó hÓgartaigh *ibid.*
[37] S McCoole, *ibid.*
[38] In McCoole (above n 35) there is a copy of a coloured portrait of "Róisín Dubh" and accompanying inscription "We will stand by Róisín Dubh and the Irish Republic forever" (p 137) by Eilís Dolan (aunt of the author) at the time aged 16 years and an inmate in North Dublin Union.

Maud Gonne wrote that children in schools were being provided with "food for the mind" but that the authorities were ignoring the need for "food for the body."[39] By 1914 this initiative was taken over by Dublin Corporation and today it is continued by Dublin City Council.

The same women were behind some of the greatest improvements in the welfare of children in Dublin during this time. St Ultan's, the first infant hospital in Ireland, was founded by members of *Inghinidhe na hEireann*, Dr Kathleen Lynn and Madeliene French Mullen in 1919.[40] Witnessing the rising infant death rate from the 1918 flu epidemic as well as from diseases brought back from the First World War, these women set about combating the problem by establishing a hospital for the treatment of infants and young children. One contemporary is reported as saying: "If they were men I would say they are mad —but they are women so they may succeed".[41]

At the outset only women staffed the hospital. The hospital pioneered new advancements in medicine — such as the use of the BCG vaccination — over ten years before it was in general use in Ireland. In 1934 Dr Maria Montessori, the first female medical doctor to qualify in Italy, visited St Ultans and a Montessori ward was established at the hospital.[42] Thus, between 1900 and 1934 a group of women political activists took an active interest in children's rights and mobilised services to meet their health and educational needs.

This is not to suggest that women were the only people motivated to support and protect the rights of children. There were notable philanthropists (mostly men) that engaged in altruistic initiatives for children in Ireland. For example, pioneers like Victor Bewley (Bewley's Café) and Thomas John Barnardo (Barnardo's Fur Shop) in the early twentieth century established a range of social services and children's homes.[43] Their goodwill reflected similar initiatives in England at the time such as the Joseph Rowntree Foundation's establishment of "The Village Project".[44] These men recognised a duty to help children who were poor and they and others did so at a time when there was essentially no state aid for families in the form of a welfare state. Similar to the kindness shown by women political activists, early philanthropists saw the need to act in tangible ways to support deprived and depraved children. While the current major development programme funded by Chuck Feeney's Atlantic Philanthropies Ireland[45] is a major boost to child welfare services it does build on a history of business-funded community support for children.

[39] Dolan and McCoole, *ibid.*
[40] Ó hÓgartaigh, *ibid.*
[41] S McCoole, *ibid.*
[42] O hOgartaigh, *ibid.*
[43] J Robins, *ibid.*
[44] *The Joseph Rowntree Inheritance 1904 – 2004*, Joseph Rowntree Foundation Foundation 2004.
[45] C O'Clery *The Billionaire Who Wasn't: How Chuck Feeney Secretly Made and Gave Away a Fortune* (PublicAffairs 2007).

It could be could be argued that, despite genuineness and good intent on the part of the Irish state in terms of the development of legislation to protect and support children, change has been driven by tragic events in the lives of families and outcries from concerned individuals. Unfortunately one finds it hard to retrospectively name any Irish or international children's policy that was borne from proactive planning rather than from state embarrassment and/or a "child harm" crisis. It may be that this is the harsh reality of how policy operates. If so, it could be argued that it behoves all stakeholders to understand and work within this somewhat sporadic framework for the betterment of children. To illustrate this two "turning point events" are now described. Both acted as "lynchpins" in the development of Irish child care services

The Kennedy Report (1970) — Changes in the Treatment of Children in Care in Ireland

Up to the 1960s services for children in care in Ireland were relatively unmonitored, lacked policy underpinnings and were essentially "void" in terms of standards and provision. However, it should not be assumed that Irish child care was policy-less. In fact, both the Curtis Report[46] and the Tuairim Report[47] highlighted the need for coherent policy and proper services for children in the care of the state. Sr Stanislaus Kennedy argues that the Tuarim Report "represented the first time child care in this country was put under the spotlight"[48] earlier Monsignor Flanagan,[49] on a month long visit to Ireland in the Summer of 1946 expressed strong concern regarding the lack of Irish child care policy, the plight of young people in the care system and the horrific conditions they suffered.[50] However in a real way it was not until the Kennedy Report in 1970[51] that real improvements occurred. In her pioneering report advocating for the rights of children Judge Eileen Kennedy recommended major changes in service provision by religious communities, social workers and others. In effect her report provided for the first time in Ireland a tangible direction for child welfare. It recommended that:

> "The whole aim of the child care system should be geared towards the prevention of family breakdown and the problems consequent on it. The committal or admission of children to residential care should be considered only where there is no satisfactory alternative".

[46] Curtis Report, *ibid*.
[47] Government of Ireland, *Tuairim Report* (Stationery Office, Dublin, 1966).
[48] Sr S Kennedy Care Report, (1995, p vii).
[49] Monsignor Edward Flanagan was founder of the Boystown Programme a residential based child care centre for disadvantaged children, now titled Boys and Girlstown based in Nebraska USA.
[50] M Raftery and E O'Sullivan, *Suffer the Little Children; The Inside Story of Ireland's Industrial Schools* (Continuum International Publishing Co, UK, 2001).
[51] Government of Ireland, *The Reformatory and Industrial Schools Systems Report (The Kennedy Report)* (Stationery Office, Dublin, 1970).

The changes in policy and practice that ensued post-publication of the Kennedy Report proved to be its strongest legacy.[52] These changes included:

- The establishment of regional Health Boards with social workers being given specific responsibility for supporting families and the placement of children in care;
- The development of foster care as the preferred care placement choice for children (where possible and practicable) leading to a massive drop in the number of children in residential care;
- The movement from large institutional orphanage care settings to small more familial types of group homes;
- The commencement of children in care being sent to local schools and their better engagement in local school activities;
- The move from co-called Reformatory Schools to Special Schools with improved quality of care including therapeutic work with children; and
- A process for the professionalisation of workers including the development of training courses.

By today's standards some of these changes may seem minor but, relative to the time, it is clear that the Kennedy Report was a watershed in child welfare development in Ireland.[53] What is more important in relation to Kennedy is not that it was established as part of a political agenda but, rather, was an initiative taken at the time by a small group of policy advocates for children, most notably Judge Eileen Kennedy herself. *CARE*, an organisation that advocated for children and was founded in the aftermath of the Kennedy Report, suggested that children should be managed singularly by government. It took the view in the late-1970s that having three government departments dealing with children's rights and needs was too complicated and unhelpful. Today, it is possible to identify seven government departments participating in the same set of functions. Despite the best intentions and the establishment of one co-ordinating structure for children and young people, the plethora of government departments with responsibility for children remains complex and confusing.

Subsequent to and partially as a result of the Kennedy Report the establishment of the Task Force Committee for Child Care Services and its subsequent two reports[54/55] led to a variety of changes to legislation which updated the Children Act 1908.[56] In particular, the passing by the Oireachtas of the Child Care Act 1991[57] provided for better care and protection of children and a recognition of the need to support families experiencing adversity and poverty. Although formally on the statute book since 1991 it was the occurrence of two later tragic events that enabled its actual implementation.

---

[52] M Raftery and E O' Sullivan *ibid.*

[53] J Robins *ibid.*

[54] Government of Ireland, *Task Force on Child Care Services,* Interim Report to the Minister For Health (Stationery Office, Dublin, 1975).

[55] Government of Ireland, *Task Force on Child Care Services,* Final Report to the Minister For Health (Stationery Office, Dublin, 1975).

[56] Children Act 1908.

[57] Child Care Act 1991.

Firstly, following a much publicised case of incest in Co. Kilkenny, the subsequent *Kilkenny Incest Report* by Mrs. Justice Catherine McGuinness and colleagues, published in 1993,[58] amplified a hitherto taboo subject of public discourse in Ireland. Even for child care professionals the disclosure of a girl's sexual abuse by her father was of major importance. It is noteworthy that the then existing Child Abuse Guidelines of 1987[59] — a key document for social workers and others — did not define or describe the term sexual abuse. Importantly, the *Kilkenny Incest Report* gave life to the concept of protection of children, as a right, via the implementation of the Child Care Act 1991. It led to a massive investment (relative to previous expenditure) by the state in the development of services for children in Ireland, including the development of community-based prevention programmes for families in need. Following the Kilkenny incest case the horrific death of a neglected and abused teenage girl, Kelly Fitzgerald, and the publication of a subsequent inquiry report in 1996[60] reinforced the need to fully implement the Child Care Act 1991.

Looking Ahead — "Practical Frameworks" for Helping to Ensure Children's Rights are put into Practice

Given this past interest in children's rights and the current interest in child advocacy a set of recommended basic but practical frameworks as enhancing a model "rights in practice" is now outlined. These frameworks are orientated towards both the judiciary with an interest in child welfare and the wider set of helping social services professionals. More specifically it comes with the current implementation agenda for children services as set out in the Policy Handbook for Children[61] in mind.

Practical Framework One — What Legislators, Service Providers and Campaigners for Children can do Together

Issues pertaining to the rights and needs of children need to remain paramount to concerns of parents but both can counter-balance one another. Using social network support theory as a foundation, it is possible to take a coherent view of children in families in a way that is applicable across such a context. This perspective facilitates the ultimate goal of attaining the rights of children and young people through meeting their needs within their families. This can be modeled within a set of levels of support as demonstrated in Figure 1.1 (below).[62] The emphasis on levels of support contained within the cupped model is consistent with the social support and wider family support literature.[63] Beyond the nuclear family, there are extended

---

[58] C McGuinness, *The Report of the Kilkenny Incest Investigation* (Government Publications. Stationery Office Dublin, 1993).

[59] Department of Health *Child Abuse Guidelines* (Stationery Office Dublin, 1987).

[60] Government of Ireland, *"Kelly a Child is Dead"*, Report of Inquiry into the Death of Kelly Fitzgerald (Stationery Office, Dublin, 1996).

[61] Government of Ireland, 2007.

[62] Adapted from Government of Ireland, *Agenda for Children Services: A Policy Handbook for Services* (Stationery Office, Dublin, 2007).

[63] See, for example, P Dolan, J Canavan and J Pinkerton, (eds) *Family Support as Reflective Practice* (Jessica Kingsley Publishers, London, 2006).

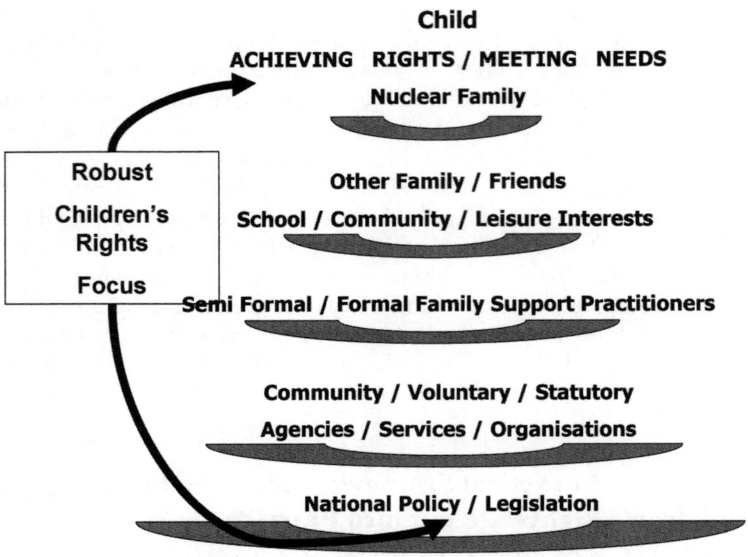

Figure 1.1 A Cupped Model for achieving children's rights and meeting needs

family and friends, then the school and community which in turn are supported by wider organisational networks and, finally, national policy and legislation. A robust focus on children's rights at both ends of the cupped model enhances the prospect of a child having his/her rights met all the way from legislation and social policy through to support from family via services and professionals.

Practical Framework Two: Factors That Lead to Better Outcomes for Children — For Consideration by those who Interview Children in Court or those who Enact or Deliver Legislation

Overall, what we want most for children are a range of capacities which include their ability to be resilient and to cope,[64] to exist in a state of perceived happiness and safety, and the possibility of living in a loving family. This is not dissimilar to what we want for ourselves as adults. A key ingredient in all of this is the concept of social support provision. Such social supports are typically sourced through families[65] and include the following:

- **Concrete Support** which relates to practical acts of assistance between people (e.g. child-minding a sister's young baby while she goes shopping).

[64] R Gilligan, *Promoting Resilience: A Resource Guide on Working with Children in the Care System* (British Agencies of Adoption and Fostering, London, 2001).

[65] CE Cutrona, "Social Support Principles for Strengthening Families: Messages form America", in J Canavan, P Dolan and J Pinkerton (Eds.), *Family Support: Direction From Diversity* (Jessica Kingsley Publ., London, 2000) Ch5, pp 103–122.

It has been noted that too often a family's need for basic practical help is either missed or underestimated by professionals[66];

- **Emotional Support** comprises acts of empathy, listening, and generally "being there" for someone when needed. There is a need to be discrete in how one offers emotional support, but it has particularly strong currency in that, even if offered as an alternative to other types of need, it is generally perceived as helpful[67];
- **Advice Support** can be more complicated and is often sought within families for its comfort and reassurance rather than for the actual nature of the advice itself[68]. For example, in dealing with a family member with an illness, such as cancer, it has been well established that other family members often seek advice which reassures them that they are doing their best for the sick person[69]; and
- **Esteem Support** centres on how one person rates and informs another in terms of personal worth. For families, it is the foundation stone of their personal support system.[70]

The following "quality" factors of social support are also important:

- **Closeness** Within family and other contacts, a person is more likely to access support from those that he/she sees as responsive and those with whom there is a shared sense of closeness. For example, research in Ireland[71] and the US[72] shows that this is particularly the case in respect of teen parents.
- **Reciprocity** involves acts whereby help is exchanged between people, ensuring that a person does not feel beholden to another. Very often within families this occurs automatically and its value lies in the comfort of knowing that the exchange of support is ready-made and available if and when it is needed.
- **Durability** relates to the contact rates and length of time people are known to each other. Ideally, reliable members are those who are known for a long period, are nearby to offer help and, typically, are not intrusive.[73]

---

[66] P Dolan and S Holt "What Families Want in Family Support: An Irish Case Study" *Child Care in Practice*, Volume 8 No. 4 (October) pp 239–250, 2002.
[67] CE Cutrona, *Social Support in Couples, - Marriage as a Resource in Times of Stress*, Sage Series on Close Relationships (Sage Publications, London, 1996).
[68] J Cotterell, *Social Networks and Social Influences in Adolescence* (Routledge, London, 1996).
[69] P Aymanns, H Sigrun and T Klaur, "Family Support and Coping with Cancer: some Determinants and Adaptives Correlates" *British Journal of Social Psychology*, pp 107–124, 1995,
[70] J Cotterell, *ibid*.
[71] S Riordan, *Final Evaluation Report of the Teen Parents Support Initiative*, Dublin Institute of Technology for the Department of Health and Children (Stationery Office, Dublin, 2002).
[72] CE Cutrona and V Cole Optimizing Support in the Natural Network in S Cohen, LG Underwood and BH Gottlieb (Eds.) *Social Support Measurement and Intervention: A Guide for Health and Social Scientists* (Oxford University Press, Oxford, 2000) Ch9, pp 278–308.
[73] EM Tracy and JK Whittaker, *The Social Network Map: Assessing Social Support in Clinical Practice Families in Society, Journal of Contemporary Human Servic*es, Oct 1990, pp 461–470.

If the aim of a rights-based agenda for children means anything it should include the aspiration of ensuring children's support needs are met by family, school and community. Sadly, we know that where children's needs are consistently unmet or where they are at risk of most harm they have least protective support, particularly from family. Ultimately, this is played out in a court environment for many children which is not always a child-friendly setting. Cutrona[74] has developed a model to counteract this which, though aimed at professionals such as social workers and childcare workers, has resonance for those working within the legal system. It has been developed by others[75] and illustrated graphically in figure 1.2 (below) and operates on the simple principle that the support offered to children, young people and their families matches their specific needs.

Practical Framework Three: Reflective "Test" Messages for the Judiciary and Related Professionals

Thirdly, it is known that how professionals intervene with children and families is equally important as the support they offer. This applies to legal professionals as much as to social or health care workers. Apart from an ongoing need for training for all concerned, a set of "ten practice principles" were recently developed for the Irish Government for child welfare professionals as part of the *Policy Handbook for Children*.[76] Six of these principles may have strong relevance to the judiciary and, perhaps less directly, for others in the legal profession. Two preliminary core and self-reflective questions arise in considering each of these principles:

1. Do I hold these principles as fundamental and central to my work with and for children within the Irish court system?
2 If yes to each one, how do I uphold each principle in my work?

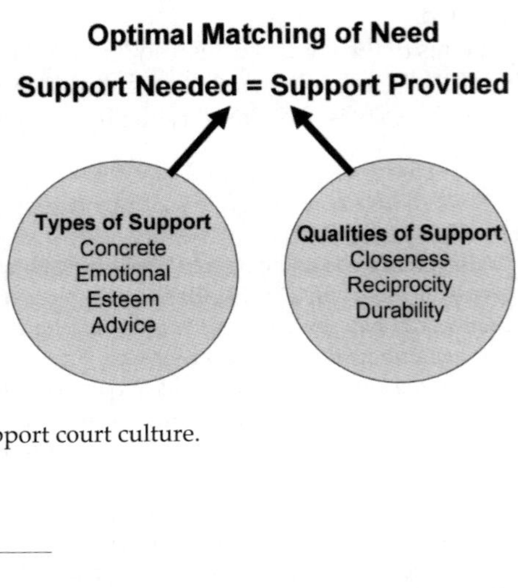

Figure 1.2 A family support court culture.

[74] Cutrona 2000, *ibid*.
[75] P Dolan, "Assessment, Intervention and Self Appraisal Tools for Family Support" in P Dolan, J Pinkerton and J Canavan (Eds) *Family Support as Reflective Practice* (Jessica Kingsley Publications, UK, 2006) Ch13 pp 196 – 213.
[76] Government Publications, *ibid*.

Recommended — Six Practice Principles[77] for Guidance Purposes for the Judiciary

- Working in partnership is an integral part of family support. Partnership includes children, families, professionals and communities;
- Family Support interventions are needs-led and strive for the minimum intervention required;
- Family support requires a clear focus on the wishes, feelings, safety and well-being of children;
- Family support services reflect a strengths-based perspective which is mindful of resilience as a characteristic of many children and families lives;
- Family support promotes the view that effective interventions are those that strengthen informal support networks;
- Family support is accessible and flexible in respect of location, timing, setting and changing needs and can incorporate both child protection and out-of-home care.

Conclusion

In this article, Irish children's rights have been considered from a theoretical and practical basis of social justice and in the context of the UN Convention on the Rights of the Child. Issues in relation to the realisation of children's rights in current Irish policy and practice contexts have been explored in relation to universal populations and those young people who experience adversity. This has also been contextualised by consideration of past pioneers of children's rights in Ireland and key landmark events of a tragic nature which enabled the implementation of vital child protection and welfare legislation. It has been emphasised that Ireland is now "policy-rich but implementation-poor" in relation to children but with a view to this changing for the better. This has afforded an opportunity to explore some specific and practical considerations for legal and child welfare professionals on the way forward as small steps to put child rights into practice. Overall, such ongoing invigoration of the rights of children through collective action by the state services (including the legal profession), civic society and children's own voices is vital to realising their rights and, thus, helping to activate a "must happen" pathway to better outcomes for all children including those who are troubled and troublesome.

[77] Government Publications, *ibid.*

Part II

Case Notes

Feature Case Note

The Islamic Headscarf Dilemma: *Leyla Şahin v Turkey*

Dr Tarlach McGonagle*

Introduction

The "Islamic headscarf debate" is spreading rapidly throughout Europe. Increasingly, questions relating to the regulation of religious clothing — particularly the Islamic headscarf — are gaining prominence on the agendas of policy — and law-makers alike. A considerable variety of regulatory and other approaches to relevant issues can be discerned across European States and any semblance of consistency of approach has thus far proved elusive.[1] Much more troubling than the absence of a common approach, however, is the fact that the divisiveness of the debate is showing little sign of subsiding. Against this background, any case on relevant questions coming before international adjudicative bodies, such as the European Court of Human Rights, will necessarily draw close public scrutiny. The case, *Leyla Şahin v Turkey*[2] — ultimately heard by the Grand Chamber of the Court — provided an excellent opportunity to engage with crucial issues. In the heel of the hunt, though, the Court balked at the opportunity, opting instead to once again bury its head expeditiously in the sand of the margin of appreciation doctrine.

* Lecturer at the Institute for Information Law (IViR), Law Faculty, University of Amsterdam.

[1] For overviews and commentary, see: (generally) Emmannuelle Bribosia & Isabelle Rorive, "Le voile à l'école: une Europe divisée", *Revue trimestrielle des droits de l'homme*, 2004, pp 951–983; (France, Germany and the Netherlands) Aernout Nieuwenhuis, "State and Religion, Schools and Scarves, An Analysis of the Margin of Appreciation as Used in the Case of *Leyla Sahin v Turkey*, Decision of 29 June 2004, Application Number 44774/98.", 1 *European Constitutional Law Review* (No. 3, 2005), pp 495–510; (France and the United States) T Jeremy Gunn, "Religious Freedom and Laïcité: A Comparison of the United States and France", 2004 BYUL Rev. 419; (France) C Laborde, "Secular Philosophy and Muslim Headscarves in Schools", 13 *The Journal of Political Philosophy* (No. 3, 2005), pp 305–329; (Germany) C Langenfeld & Sarah Mohsen, "Germany: The teacher head scarf case", 3 Int'l. J. Con. Law, (No. 1, 2005): pp 86–94, O Gerstenberg, "Germany: Freedom of conscience in public schools", 3 Int'l. J. Con. Law, (No. 1, 2005): pp 94–106, M Mahlmann, "Religious Tolerance, Pluralist Society and the Neutrality of the State: The Federal Constitutional Court's Decision in the *Headscarf* Case", 4 *German Law Journal* (No. 11, 2003), pp 1099–1116; (United Kingdom) G Davies, "Banning the Jilbab: Reflections on Restricting Religious Clothing in the Light of the Court of Appeal in *SB v Denbigh High School*. Decision of 2 March 2005", 1 *European Constitutional Law Review* (No. 3, 2005), pp 511–530, A Scolnicov, "A dedicate follower of (religious) fashion?", 64 *The Cambridge Law Journal* (No. 3, 2005), pp 527–529.

[2] Judgment of the European Court of Human Rights (Grand Chamber) of 10 November 2005, Application No. 44774/98.

This article will provide a *résumé* of: the facts of the case; the judgment of the Grand Chamber, and the dissenting opinion of Judge Tulkens. Finally, a critical analysis of the case will be mounted.

Factual Backdrop

As noted by the Court, the applicant "comes from a traditional family of practising Muslims and considers it her religious duty to wear the Islamic headscarf".[3] During the fifth year of her medical studies at the Faculty of Medicine at Bursa University, she enrolled at the Cerrahpaşa Faculty of Medicine at Istanbul University. Some months afterwards, the Vice-Chancellor of the University of Istanbul issued a circular which provided, *inter alia*, that "students whose 'heads are covered' (who wear the Islamic headscarf) and students (including overseas students) with beards must not be admitted to lectures, courses or tutorials".[4] Subsequently, the applicant, who continued to wear the headscarf, was therefore denied admission to sit a written examination; refused permission to enrol for a particular course, and denied admission to another written examination.[5]

The applicant applied to the Istanbul Administrative Court for an order setting aside the Vice-Chancellor's circular. The Court dismissed her application, finding: (i) that the Vice-Chancellor, as the executive organ of the university, did have the power to regulate students' dress for the purpose of maintaining order, and (ii) that the exercise of such powers had to be — and in the instant case was — in conformity with relevant legislation and the settled case-law of the Constitutional Court and Supreme Administrative Court. The applicant subsequently appealed this judgment on points of law, but her appeal was dismissed by the Supreme Administrative Court.

The university instituted disciplinary proceedings against the applicant, firstly for her failure to comply with the regulations on dress, and later on account of her participation in a collective protest against those regulations. The proceedings resulted in her suspension from the university for one semester. Her application to the Istanbul Administrative Court to overturn the decision to suspend her was dismissed by the Court "on the ground that in the light of the material in the case file and the settled case-law on the subject, the impugned measure could not be regarded as illegal".[6] The applicant again appealed the Court's judgment on points of law.

The entry into force of a new law granted the applicant and similarly affected students an amnesty, scrapping previously imposed penalties and resultant adverse consequences. The Supreme Administrative Court found that the entry into force of that new law made it unnecessary to examine the merits of the applicant's appeal that had been pending before it. In the meantime, however, the applicant had

[3] *ibid*, para 14.
[4] *ibid*, para 16.
[5] *ibid*, para 17.
[6] *ibid*, para 25.

abandoned her studies in Turkey, opting instead to continue her university education in Vienna University, where she had since enrolled.

Judgment of the European Court of Human Rights

After setting out relevant domestic law and practice,[7] the European Court of Human Rights proceeded to explore the historical specificities of religion, religious dress and the principle of secularism in Turkey.[8] It traced relevant legislative history[9] by way of background to its consideration of the regulations at Istanbul University, which were of central importance in the instant case.[10] Significant attention was also paid to the law and practice governing the wearing of the Islamic headscarf in educational environments in various European States.[11] The level of detail provided is instructive. It is clear that a wide variety of (regulatory) approaches are in place throughout Europe. Consideration is also given to relevant Council of Europe texts on higher education.[12]

In essence, when it considered the case initially, the Fourth Section of the Court found that:

> "the Istanbul University regulations restricting the right to wear the Islamic headscarf and the measures taken thereunder had interfered with the applicant's right to manifest her religion. It went on to find that the interference was prescribed by law and pursued one of the legitimate aims set out in the second paragraph of Article 9 of the Convention. It was justified in principle and proportionate to the aims pursued and could therefore be regarded as having been 'necessary in a democratic society'" (see paragraphs 66 to 116 of the Chamber judgment).[13]

Under Article 43, ECHR, the applicant requested that the case be referred to the Grand Chamber of the Court. Her request was acceded to and she contested the grounds on which the Fourth Section of the Court had found that there had been no violation of her rights under Article 9, ECHR.

The Grand Chamber endorsed the Chamber's finding that there had been an interference with the applicant's right to manifest her religion, citing the Chamber judgment as follows:

> "The applicant said that, by wearing the headscarf, she was obeying a religious precept and thereby manifesting her desire to comply strictly with the duties imposed by the Islamic faith. Accordingly, her decision to wear the headscarf

---

7 *ibid*, para 29.
8 *ibid*, paras 30-35.
9 *ibid*, paras 36-41.
10 *ibid*, paras 42-51.
11 *ibid*, paras 55-65.
12 *ibid*, paras 66-69.
13 *ibid*, para 71. See further: *Leyla Şahin v Turkey*, Judgment of the European Court of Human Rights (Fourth Section) of 29 June 2004.

may be regarded as motivated or inspired by a religion or belief and, without deciding whether such decisions are in every case taken to fulfil a religious duty, the Court proceeds on the assumption that the regulations in issue, which placed restrictions of place and manner on the right to wear the Islamic headscarf in universities, constituted an interference with the applicant's right to manifest her religion."[14]

The Grand Chamber was also satisfied that the impugned measures were "prescribed by law"[15] and noted that the "legitimate aims of protecting the rights and freedoms of others and of protecting public order" were "not in issue" between the parties.[16] The crucial matter for assessment by the Grand Chamber was therefore the necessity of the impugned interference in a democratic society. To that end, the Court began with a restatement of its general principles.

Freedom of thought, conscience and religion is one of the cornerstones of the kind of "democratic society" envisaged by the ECHR and a prerequisite for pluralism. While it is a vital aspect of the identity of believers and their worldview, it is also of value to non-believers as well. The freedom entails the right to hold religious beliefs and to practise a religion (or not).[17] As well as being primarily a matter of individual conscience, the freedom also includes the right to manifest one's religion (as spelt out by Article 9(2), ECHR, through worship, teaching, practice and observance), "alone and in private, or in community with others, in public and within the circle of those whose faith one shares". Not "every act motivated or inspired by religion or belief" is protected under Article 9[18]: the coexistence of several religions in democratic society may require restrictions to be imposed on freedom to manifest one's religion or belief in order to reconcile the interests of the various groups and ensure that everyone's beliefs are respected. This follows from Articles 1 and 9(2), ECHR.[19]

States ought to be neutral and impartial in the matter of religions, and that duty "is incompatible with any power on the State's part to assess the legitimacy of religious beliefs or the ways in which those beliefs are expressed".[20] States are also required to ensure mutual tolerance between opposing groups — thus, "not to remove the cause of tension by eliminating pluralism".[21] Although individual interests must on occasion be subordinated to those of a group, democratic society requires the equitable balancing of majority and minority interests.[22]

In matters concerning the relationship between the State and religions, special importance must be given to "the role of the national decision-making body",

[14] *ibid*, para 78; Judgment of 29 June 2004, para 71.
[15] *ibid*, paras 84-98.
[16] *ibid*, para 99.
[17] *ibid*, para 104.
[18] *ibid*, para 105.
[19] *ibid*, para 106.
[20] *ibid*, para 107.
[21] *ibid*.
[22] *ibid*, para 108.

especially in respect of the regulation of the wearing of religious symbols in educational institutions. There is neither uniformity of approach by national authorities concerning such matters, nor any uniform European conception of the significance of religion in society. Thus, "the meaning or impact of the public expression of a religious belief will differ according to time and context" and "[r]ules in this sphere will consequently vary from one country to another according to national traditions and the requirements imposed by the need to protect the rights and freedoms of others and to maintain public order". As such, States enjoy a certain margin of appreciation for regulation of this domain.[23] As always, that margin of appreciation is subject to European-level supervision "embracing both the law and the decisions applying it". "In delimiting the extent of the margin of appreciation in the present case the Court must have regard to what is at stake, namely the need to protect the rights and freedoms of others, to preserve public order and to secure civil peace and true religious pluralism, which is vital to the survival of a democratic society".[24]

Directly relevant jurisprudence was also recalled. The Court noted that in the earlier cases of *Karaduman v Turkey* and *Dahlab v Switzerland* (both discussed in greater detail *infra*):

> "the Convention institutions found that in a democratic society the State was entitled to place restrictions on the wearing of the Islamic headscarf if it was incompatible with the pursued aim of protecting the rights and freedoms of others, public order and public safety. In the *Karaduman* case, measures taken in universities to prevent certain fundamentalist religious movements from exerting pressure on students who did not practise their religion or who belonged to another religion were found to be justified under Article 9 § 2 of the Convention. Consequently, it is established that institutions of higher education may regulate the manifestation of the rites and symbols of a religion by imposing restrictions as to the place and manner of such manifestation with the aim of ensuring peaceful co-existence between students of various faiths and thus protecting public order and the beliefs of others (see, among other authorities, *Refah Partisi and Others*, cited above, § 95). In the *Dahlab* case, which concerned the teacher of a class of small children, the Court stressed among other matters the "powerful external symbol" which her wearing a headscarf represented and questioned whether it might have some kind of proselytising effect, seeing that it appeared to be imposed on women by a religious precept that was hard to reconcile with the principle of gender equality. It also noted that wearing the Islamic headscarf could not easily be reconciled with the message of tolerance, respect for others and, above all, equality and non-discrimination that all teachers in a democratic society should convey to their pupils."[25]

When it applied the foregoing principles to the facts of the case at hand, the Grand Chamber closely followed the reasoning of the Fourth Section of the Court in its

---

[23] *ibid*, para 109.
[24] *ibid*, para 110.
[25] *ibid*, para 111.

earlier judgment in the *Sahin* case. It affirmed, for instance, the pronouncement in the *Refah Partisi* case, that "An attitude which fails to respect [the principle of secularism] will not necessarily be accepted as being covered by the freedom to manifest one's religion and will not enjoy the protection of Article 9".[26] The Grand Chamber acknowledged the importance of gender equality in the Turkish constitutional system, as the Fourth Section had done earlier, and then went on to approvingly cite the following passages from the Fourth Section's judgment:

> "... In addition, like the Constitutional Court..., the Court considers that, when examining the question of the Islamic headscarf in the Turkish context, there must be borne in mind the impact which wearing such a symbol, which is presented or perceived as a compulsory religious duty, may have on those who choose not to wear it. As has already been noted (see *Karaduman*, decision cited above; and *Refah Partisi and Others*, cited above, § 95), the issues at stake include the protection of the "rights and freedoms of others" and the "maintenance of public order" in a country in which the majority of the population, while professing a strong attachment to the rights of women and a secular way of life, adhere to the Islamic faith. Imposing limitations on freedom in this sphere may, therefore, be regarded as meeting a pressing social need by seeking to achieve those two legitimate aims, especially since, as the Turkish courts stated..., this religious symbol has taken on political significance in Turkey in recent years.
>
> ... The Court does not lose sight of the fact that there are extremist political movements in Turkey which seek to impose on society as a whole their religious symbols and conception of a society founded on religious precepts... It has previously said that each Contracting State may, in accordance with the Convention provisions, take a stance against such political movements, based on its historical experience (*Refah Partisi and Others*, cited above, § 124). The regulations concerned have to be viewed in that context and constitute a measure intended to achieve the legitimate aims referred to above and thereby to preserve pluralism in the university."[27]

Against that background, the Grand Chamber found the principle of secularism to be "the paramount consideration underlying the ban on the wearing of religious symbols in universities".[28] After considering the circumstances of the case, it stated that "Article 9 does not always guarantee the right to behave in a manner governed by a religious belief [...] and does not confer on people who do so the right to disregard rules that have proved to be justified".[29] It held, by 16 votes to one, that no violation of Article 9 had taken place.

Although the mainstay of the applicant's case was the claim that her rights under Article 9 had been breached, she also invoked her rights under Articles 8, 10 and 14,

---

[26] *ibid*, para 114; *Refah Partisi* case, *op. cit.*, para 93.
[27] (Citation abridged by author) *ibid*, para 115.
[28] *ibid*, para 116.
[29] *ibid*, para 121.

ECHR, and Article 2 of Protocol 1 to the ECHR (hereinafter "P1-2")). The claims based on Articles 8, 10 and 14 were quickly and unanimously rejected by the Grand Chamber, but the claim based on P1-2 was subjected to lengthier scrutiny before also being denied (again by 16 votes to one). The applicant's claim implicated the first sentence of P1-2: "No person shall be denied the right to education". As a preliminary matter, the Court established that "any institutions of higher education existing at a given time come within the scope of the first sentence of Article 2 of Protocol No. 1, since the right of access to such institutions is an inherent part of the right set out in that provision". However, the Court was at pains to point out that this finding should not be construed as creating any new obligations for States Parties.[30]

According to the relevant general principles of the Court, rehearsed here by the Grand Chamber, P1-2 guarantees everyone a right of access to educational institutions existing at a given time.[31] That right applies equally to pupils in State and independent schools.[32] In order for the right to be effective, it also extends to considerations such as the official recognition of studies completed.[33] The right is, however, subject to certain limitations and the Court noted that "the regulation of educational institutions may vary in time and in place, *inter alia,* according to the needs and resources of the community and the distinctive features of different levels of education".[34] A certain margin of appreciation is therefore granted to States in this regard. Any measures interfering with the right must be foreseeable for those concerned, pursue a legitimate aim and there should be reasonable proportionality between the means employed and the identified aim.[35] P1-2 should be read consistently with the ECHR, especially Articles 8, 9 and 10 of the latter.[36] Finally, the Court re-affirmed that "[t]he right to education does not in principle exclude recourse to disciplinary measures, including suspension or expulsion from an educational institution in order to ensure compliance with its internal rules".[37] This is premised on the assumption that the imposition of disciplinary measures are an integral part of the school's broader educational purpose and process ("including the development and moulding of the character and mental powers of its pupils").[38]

When applying these general principles to the facts of the instant case, the Court stressed that such an analysis "cannot in this instance be divorced from the conclusion reached by the Court with respect to Article 9".[39] It noted that the "obvious purpose of the restriction was to preserve the secular character of educational institutions".[40] The Court insisted on its finding of proportionality in

[30] *ibid,* para 141.
[31] *ibid,* para 152.
[32] *ibid,* para 153.
[33] *ibid,* para 152.
[34] *ibid,* para 154.
[35] *ibid.*
[36] *ibid,* para 155.
[37] *ibid,* para 156.
[38] *ibid,* para 156.
[39] *ibid,* para 157.
[40] *ibid,* para 158.

respect of its analysis of Article 9 earlier in the judgment, before underscoring a number of factors. It considered, first of all, that the impugned measures "manifestly did not hinder the students in performing the duties imposed by the habitual forms of religious observance".[41] It found that the relevant decision-making process implementing the regulations did adequately weigh up the various interests at stake, and that it contained the necessary safeguards for the protection of students' interests (e.g. conformity with legislation and judicial review). It also considered that the "university authorities judiciously sought a means whereby they could avoid having to turn away students wearing the headscarf and at the same time honour their obligation to protect the rights of others and the interests of the education system".[42] The Court also deemed the consequences of continued contravention of the impugned measures to be foreseeable to the applicant.[43] Drawing on the foregoing observations, the Court found that the first sentence of P1-2 had not been breached.[44]

Dissenting Opinion

In her dissenting opinion, Judge Tulkens began by subscribing to the "general principles" reiterated in the Grand Chamber's judgment.[45] She pointed out that the role of the Court in cases concerning conflicts between religious communities is to seek to reconcile universality and diversity, and not to "express an opinion on any religious model whatsoever".[46] Her objections to the manner in which the majority of the Court applied the margin of appreciation doctrine in the *Sahin* case were twofold. First, she argued that the considerations of comparative approaches do not point towards a lack of relevant consensus at the European level as none of the approaches surveyed extended to university education (where students are less amenable to pressure). Second, she opined that there was little evidence of the requisite level of European supervision accompanying the margin of appreciation in the instant case.[47] She felt that the majority relied exclusively on reasons invoked by the Turkish authorities and courts by way of justification of the ban on wearing the headscarf. She also felt that the majority put forward in general and abstract terms the two main arguments of secularism and equality. While endorsing those principles, she objected to the manner in which they were interpreted in the instant case.[48]

Judge Tulkens insisted that alongside secularism, "Religious freedom is, however, also a founding principle of democratic societies".[49] She continued, trenchantly:

> "Accordingly, the fact that the Grand Chamber recognised the force of the principle of secularism did not release it from its obligation to establish that the

[41] *ibid,* para 159.
[42] *ibid.*
[43] *ibid,* para 160.
[44] *ibid,* paras 161-162.
[45] Dissenting opinion of Judge Tulkens, *ibid,* para 1.
[46] Dissenting opinion of Judge Tulkens, *ibid,* para 2.
[47] Dissenting opinion of Judge Tulkens, *ibid,* para 3.
[48] Dissenting opinion of Judge Tulkens, *ibid,* para 4.
[49] Dissenting opinion of Judge Tulkens, *ibid,* para 5.

> ban on wearing the Islamic headscarf to which the applicant was subject was necessary to secure compliance with that principle and, therefore, met a "pressing social need". Only indisputable facts and reasons whose legitimacy is beyond doubt – not mere worries or fears – are capable of satisfying that requirement and justifying interference with a right guaranteed by the Convention. Moreover, where there has been interference with a fundamental right, the Court's case-law clearly establishes that mere affirmations do not suffice: they must be supported by concrete examples [...]."[50]

She then pointed up some inconsistencies in the relevant case-law of the Court. According to her, the Court "has been very protective (perhaps over-protective) of religious sentiment" in cases like *Otto-Preminger-Institut v Austria*[51] and *Wingrove v United Kingdom*,[52] "it has shown itself less willing to intervene in cases concerning religious practices (*Cha'are Shalom Ve Tsedek v France*, judgment of 27 June 2000; *Dahlab v Switzerland*, decision of 15 February 2001), which only appear to receive a subsidiary form of protection (see paragraph 105 of the judgment)".[53] She also underscored the fact that the symbolic importance of the headscarf (or other external symbols of religious practice) "may vary greatly according to the faith concerned".[54]

Her critical scrutiny then turned to the majority's consideration that wearing the headscarf contravenes the principle of secularism and stated that this amounts to taking a "position on an issue that has been the subject of much debate, namely the signification of wearing the headscarf and its relationship with the principle of secularism".[55] In her view, this generalised assessment overlooks the applicant's (undisputed) submission that she had no intention of calling the principle of secularism into question. Similarly, it overlooks the absence of evidence that the applicant's "attitude, conduct or acts" had actually contravened the principle. Furthermore, the *Dahlab* case was relied upon in the majority opinion, rather than distinguished. In that case, the applicant was a teacher, not a student like Leyla Şahin, and the role-model aspect of the teacher was accordingly emphasised by the Court. Judge Tulkens reasoned that "While the principle of secularism requires education to be provided without any manifestation of religion and while it has to be compulsory for teachers and all public servants, as they have voluntarily taken up posts in a neutral environment, the position of pupils and students" appears different.[56]

The dissenting opinion then adverts to the need to avoid equating the wearing of the headscarf with fundamentalism, especially in the absence of any suggestion that

[50] Dissenting opinion of Judge Tulkens, *ibid*, para 5.

[51] Judgment of the European Court of Human Rights of 20 September 1994, Series A, no. 295-A.

[52] Judgment of the European Court of Human Rights of 25 November 1996, Reports of Judgments and Decisions, 1996-V.

[53] Dissenting opinion of Judge Tulkens, *Leyla Şahin v Turkey*, *op. cit.*, para 6.

[54] Dissenting opinion of Judge Tulkens, *ibid*, para 6.

[55] Dissenting opinion of Judge Tulkens, *ibid*, para 7.

[56] Dissenting opinion of Judge Tulkens, *ibid*, para 7.

the applicant herself held fundamentalist views. Judge Tulkens added that "it is vital to distinguish between those who wear the headscarf and "extremists" who seek to impose the headscarf as they do other religious symbols".[57] Finally, in this connection, "[t]he applicant's personal interest in exercising the right to freedom of religion and to manifest her religion by an external symbol cannot be wholly absorbed by the public interest in fighting extremism".[58]

Having dispensed with the principle of secularism, Judge Tulkens then turned her attention to the principle of equality, pointing out that the implied linkage between the ban on the headscarf and equality between men and women is never rendered explicit by the Court. She further ventured that wearing the headscarf can have various significations, and referred to such a finding by the German Constitutional Court in 2003 in support of her view.[59] She criticised the Grand Chamber's reliance on what is for her "the most questionable part of the reasoning in [the *Dahlab*] decision, namely that wearing the headscarf represents a "powerful external symbol", which "appeared to be imposed on women by a religious precept that was hard to reconcile with the principle of gender equality" and that the practice could not easily be "reconciled with the message of tolerance, respect for others and, above all, equality and non-discrimination that all teachers in a democratic society should convey to their pupils" (see paragraph 111 of the judgment, *in fine*)".[60] She reasoned that:

> "It is not the Court's role to make an appraisal of this type – in this instance a unilateral and negative one – of a religion or religious practice, just as it is not its role to determine in a general and abstract way the signification of wearing the headscarf or to impose its viewpoint on the applicant. The applicant, a young adult university student, said – and there is nothing to suggest that she was not telling the truth – that she wore the headscarf of her own free will. In this connection, I fail to see how the principle of sexual equality can justify prohibiting a woman from following a practice which, in the absence of proof to the contrary, she must be taken to have freely adopted. Equality and non-discrimination are subjective rights which must remain under the control of those who are entitled to benefit from them. [...]".[61]

Her final argument in this connection is that if the wearing of the headscarf really was contrary to the principle of gender equality, the State would be under a positive obligation to prohibit it in all places, both in public and in private.[62]

Judge Tulkens also disagreed with the majority opinion that no violation had taken place of the applicant's right to religion. She agreed with the Grand Chamber that

---

57 Dissenting opinion of Judge Tulkens, *ibid*, para 10.
58 Dissenting opinion of Judge Tulkens, *ibid*, para 10.
59 Dissenting opinion of Judge Tulkens, *ibid*, para 11.
60 Dissenting opinion of Judge Tulkens, *ibid*, para 12.
61 Dissenting opinion of Judge Tulkens, *ibid*, para 12.
62 Dissenting opinion of Judge Tulkens, *ibid*, para 12.

P1-2 is applicable to higher and university education.[63] Where she differed from the majority was again in the assessment of the relevance and sufficiency of the reasons adduced for the interference with the applicant's right to education.[64] Unlike the majority, Judge Tulkens argued that "no attempt was made to try measures that would have had a less drastic effect on the applicant's right to education in the instant case".[65] She added that the Grand Chamber: "does not weigh up the competing interests, namely, on the one hand, the damage sustained by the applicant — who not only was deprived of any possibility of completing her studies in Turkey because of her religious convictions but also maintained that it was unlikely that she would be able to return to her country to practise her profession owing to the difficulties that existed there in obtaining recognition for foreign diplomas — and, on the other, the benefit to be gained by Turkish society from prohibiting the applicant from wearing the headscarf on the university premises".[66] This, she suggested, could lead to risks of exclusion from educational and employment sectors, as well as societal radicalisation and intolerance.[67]

Critical Analysis

This commentary will begin with an overview of the most relevant case-law of the European Court of Human Rights before proceeding to roundly endorse Judge Tulkens' criticisms of the majority opinion in the *Şahin* case. It will then consider a recent attempt by the United Nations Human Rights Committee to deal with issues strikingly similar to those raised in *Şahin*. Finally, some apposite concluding remarks will be offered. The commentary will, in general, lean more heavily towards the right to manifest one's religious beliefs than the right to education.

Overview of Relevant ECHR Case-Law

Article 9, ECHR, should be cited as a matter of course. It reads as follows:

1. Everyone has the right to freedom of thought, conscience and religion; this right includes freedom to change his religion or belief and freedom, either alone or in community with others and in public or private, to manifest his religion or belief, in worship, teaching, practice and observance.

2. Freedom to manifest one's religion or beliefs shall be subject only to such limitations as are prescribed by law and are necessary in a democratic society in the interests of public safety, for the protection of public order, health or morals, or for the protection of the rights and freedoms of others.

It is clear from the wording of the Article that the essence of the right is the protection it affords the *forum internum* or "sphere of personal beliefs and religious

[63] Dissenting opinion of Judge Tulkens, *ibid,* para 14.
[64] Dissenting opinion of Judge Tulkens, *ibid,* paras 15 *et seq.*
[65] Dissenting opinion of Judge Tulkens, *ibid,* para 17.
[66] Dissenting opinion of Judge Tulkens, *ibid,* para 17.
[67] Dissenting opinion of Judge Tulkens, *ibid,* para 19.

creeds".[68] Whereas the *forum internum* may be considered to be inviolable,[69] the outward expression or "manifestation" of such beliefs and creeds is not.[70] Protection only extends to acts that are "intimately linked" to such beliefs and creeds, but any permissible restrictions must be in accordance with the criteria specified in Article 9(2). It has consistently been held by the judicial organs of the ECHR that Article 9 "does not protect every act motivated or inspired by a religion or belief".[71] The exercise of determining whether certain acts are or are not motivated by religious convictions has often proven difficult.[72] Borderline cases abound.

However, some acts, while closely linked to religion or belief, have consistently been found by the European Court of Human Rights to be beyond the pale of Article 9 protection. A pertinent example is "an expression that is, in regard to objects of veneration, gratuitously offensive to others and profanatory".[73] Another example is "improper proselytism, such as the offering of material or social advantage or the application of improper pressure with a view to gaining new members for a Church".[74] The Court has taken a particularly dim view of improper proselytism in the context of clear hierarchical structures.[75] Furthermore, engagement in particular types of employment (e.g. defence forces,[76] public education sector,[77] etc.) may imply certain restrictions on the freedom to manifest one's belief. Invariably, when assessing the necessity of an interference with the right to manifest one's religion, the Court will consider the effect of the impugned measure.[78] When a measure is only of limited effect, for example in terms of its duration or its application to a specified, confined area,[79] it will have a better chance of avoiding censure.

---

[68] *VRU v the Netherlands*, Decision of inadmissibility of the European Commission of Human Rights of , Appn. No. 11308/84; *Van den Dungen v the Netherlands*, Decision of inadmissibility of the European Commission of Human Rights of 22 February 1995, Appn. No. 22838/93.

[69] See further, P van Dijk and GJH van Hoof, *Theory and Practice of the European Convention on Human Rights* (3rd Edition, Kluwer Law International, The Hague, 1998), pp 541–542.

[70] A variety of possible forms of manifestation are countenanced in this regard: "worship, teaching, practice and observance".

[71] *Kalac v Turkey*, Judgment of the European Court of Human Rights of 23 June 1997, para 27; the term "influenced" is used instead of "inspired" in *Arrowsmith v The United Kingdom*, Report of the European Commission of Human Rights of 12 October 1978, Appn. No. 7050/75.

[72] See, by way of illustration, relevant considerations in *Arrowsmith v the United Kingdom*, Report of the European Commission of Human Rights of 12 October 1978, Appn. No. 7050/75.

[73] *Wingrove v the United Kingdom*, *op. cit.*, para 52.

[74] *Larissis & Others v Greece*, Judgment of the European Court of Human Rights of 24 February 1998, para 45, following *Kokkinakis v Greece*, *op. cit.*, para 48.

[75] *Larissis & Others v Greece*, *op. cit.*, para 51.

[76] *Kalac v Turkey*, Judgment of the European Court of Human Rights of 23 June 1997, para 28; *Engel & Others v the Netherlands*, Judgment of the European Court of Human Rights of 8 June 1976, Series A, No. 22, para 57.

[77] *Dahlab v Switzerland*, *infra*; *X. v the United Kingdom*, Decision of inadmissibility of the European Commission of Human Rights of 12 March 1981, DR 22, p 27, Appn. No. 8160/78; *Glasenapp v Germany*, Judgment of the European Court of Human Rights of 28 August 1986, Series A, No. 104; *Kosiek v Germany*, Judgment of the European Court of Human Rights of 28 August 1986, Series A, No. 105; *Vogt v Germany*, Judgment of the European Court of Human Rights of 26 September 1995, Series A, No. 323.

[78] *Chaare Shalom Ve Tsedek v France*, *op. cit.*, para 87.

[79] *Van den Dungen v The Netherlands*, *op. cit.*

A current source of friction in a number of European States is the extent to which the manifestation of religious beliefs can be compatible with the secular or non-denominational ethos of the education sector. Such points of friction often concern the wearing — out of tenaciously-held religious convictions — of particular items of clothing, artefacts or insignia. In their relevant case-law, the European Court and Commission of Human Rights have paid particular attention to the impact of such symbols on relevant third parties.

In *Karaduman v Turkey*,[80] the applicant student challenged her university's refusal to issue her with a degree certificate because she had submitted an identity photo in which she was wearing an Islamic headscarf. The university authorities (and subsequently the Turkish courts) were of the view that the photo contravened university regulations prohibiting the wearing of headscarves in the name of preserving the republican/secular nature of the university. The European Commission of Human Rights found that there had not been an interference with the applicant's freedom of religion, as protected by Article 9, ECHR. In reaching its conclusion, the Commission was swayed by two main arguments in addition to the objectives of the university dress regulations.

First, it considered that "by choosing to pursue her higher education in a secular university a student submits to those university rules, which may take the freedom of students to manifest their religion subject to restrictions as to place and manner intended to ensure harmonious coexistence between students of different beliefs".[81] The second argument was an extension of the first: "[e]specially in countries where the great majority of the population owe allegiance to one particular religion, manifestation of the observances and symbols of that religion, without restriction as to place and manner, may constitute pressure on students who do not practise that religion or those who adhere to another religion".[82] More specifically, the Commission seemed to follow the observations of the Turkish Constitutional Court, *viz*. that "the act of wearing a Muslim headscarf in Turkish universities may constitute a challenge towards those who do not wear one".[83]

The case of *Dahlab v Switzerland* focused on the prohibition of a primary-school teacher in a State school from wearing an Islamic head-scarf while carrying out her professional activities. The impressionability of the pupils weighed heavily on the Court in its finding that the interference with the applicant's freedom of religion was justified as "necessary in a democratic society".[84] The Court described the wearing of the headscarf as "a powerful external symbol" and expressed concern about its potential proselytising effect on young children. It also followed the Swiss Federal Court by querying the compatibility of wearing the headscarf with the

---

[80] Decision of inadmissibility of the European Commission of Human Rights of 3 May 1993, Appn. No. 16278/90, DR 74, p 93.

[81] *ibid*, p 108.

[82] *ibid*.

[83] *ibid*.

[84] The Court had regard "above all, to the tender age of the children for whom the applicant was responsible as a representative of the State": p 13 of the judgment.

principle of gender equality. This reasoning prompted the Court to state that it "appears difficult to reconcile the wearing of an Islamic headscarf with the message of tolerance, respect for others and, above all, equality and non-discrimination that all teachers in a democratic society must convey to their pupils".[85]

In its assessment of restrictions on the right to freedom of religion, the Court has not always adhered to the same evidentiary standards. In some cases, it insisted — correctly, it is submitted here — that a general reference to the creation of tension (arising from divided religious communities, or the existence of more than one religious leader) was not sufficient to warrant State interference. Such a reference would necessarily have to be bolstered by an allusion to specific "disturbances that had actually been or could have been caused" by relevant circumstances.[86] By way of contrast, the Court has shown itself elsewhere in its jurisprudence to be very impressionable as regards vague fears of tension or unrest arising from religious disaccord.[87] In those cases, it did not hold out for compelling evidence of the likelihood that the stated fears of the respondent governments would indeed materialise in practice.

The Şahin Case: Some Cautionary Tales

The European Court of Human Rights would do well to regard Judge Tulken's dissent in the *Şahin* case as a serious shot across its bows. Her criticisms of the reasoning applied by the majority in that judgment are well-calibrated and have a real urgency about them. While I — by and large — subscribe to those criticisms, there is little point in re-itemising them at this juncture. Instead, a number of general criticisms will be distilled from her specific criticisms, and fortified with further analysis.

First, the real nub of the case — the individual right of Leyla Şahin to manifest her religious beliefs by wearing the Islamic headscarf in a university setting — was largely sidelined by abstract assertions of various principles, such as secularism and equality.

Secularism

In the absence of any evidence that the applicant — either in her intentions or actual conduct — sought to dispute or otherwise undermine the principle of secularism that is so cherished in the Turkish Constitutional system, it was disingenuous of

---

[85] *ibid.*

[86] *Serif v Greece*, Judgment of the European Court of Human Rights (Second Section) of 14 December 1999, Reports of Judgments and Decisions 1999-IX, para 53; *Agga v Greece (No. 2)*, Judgment of the European Court of Human Rights (First Section) of 17 October 2002, para 60.

[87] *Murphy v Ireland*, Judgment of the European Court of Human Rights (Third Section) of 10 July 2003, Reports of Judgments and Decisions 2003-IX; *Refah Partisi v Turkey, op. cit.* See further: (i) concerning the *Murphy* case, Tarlach McGonagle, "Commercial expression — the usefulness of an imperfect notion?" in Eoin O'Dell, Ed., *Freedom of Expression* (Ashgate Publishing Ltd., England, 2006); (ii) concerning the *Refah Partisi* case, Kevin Boyle, "Human Rights, Religion and Democracy: The Refah Party Case", 1 *Essex Human Rights Review* (No. 1, 2004), pp 1–16.

the European Court to accept the primacy of that principle as a legitimate ground for upholding the impugned interference with Leyla Şahin's right to manifest her religious beliefs by sartorial means. Properly conceived, secularism should be perfectly reconcilable with the principle of (vibrant) religious pluralism. As Kevin Boyle has argued: "if pluralism is a defining value of democratic societies, as suggested by the European Court, then there must be "pluralism of ideologies", to include spiritual as well as secular traditions".[88] As alluded to in Judge Tulken's dissenting opinion, the preservation of a secularist ethos in the education sector can legitimately be achieved by imposing certain regulations on State employees in that sector; whether the extension of relevant regulations to the beneficiaries of education is permissible is a much more contentious question. Secularism has a very specific and sensitive history in Turkey,[89] but such contextual particularities do not mean that the European scrutiny so essential to the margin of appreciation doctrine should be waived. Indeed, precisely because of the Turkish experience of secularism as an imposed ideology since the foundation of the State, the margin of appreciation doctrine should not be allowed to cordon off the principle from careful scrutiny.

Gender Equality

Recurrent references in the majority opinion to the upholding of gender equality similarly fail to convince. Such assertions are premised on the presumption that the Islamic headscarf is symbolically and instrumentally repressive of women's rights and that the decision to wear the headscarf is (to some extent) coerced rather than a matter of individual choice. Certainly, this is one prevalent interpretation of the symbolism of the headscarf, but it is by no means the only one. The decision to wear the headscarf can also be entirely of an individual woman's own volition, and moreover, wearing it can have emancipatory consequences for her, by facilitating her involvement in a range of public and professional activities. Symbolism and signification, therefore, are highly subjective notions and are best determined in concrete situations — not in sweeping generalisations such as those indulged in by the majority of the Grand Chamber. Moreover, as Judge Tulkens insisted, it is not even the task of the European Court of Human Rights to pronounce on the signification of religious symbols.

In its superficial and disjointed handling of concerns for gender equality, the Court overlooked the potentially far-reaching exclusionary impact of a ban on wearing the headscarf in educational environment.[90] A very "prudential calculus" is

[88] K Boyle, "Human Rights, Religion and Democracy: The Refah Partisi Case", *op. cit.*, p 16. See further: R Künneman, "A Coherent Approach to Human Rights", 17 *Human Rights Quarterly* (No. 2, 1995), pp 323–342, at 340.

[89] See further, K Boyle, "Human Rights, Religion and Democracy: The Refah Partisi Case", *op. cit.*, pp 14 *et seq.*

[90] See further: D Christopher Decker, "Case Comment: Leyla Sahin v Turkey", EHRLR 2004, 6, 672-678, at p 678; T Lindholm, "The Strasbourg Court Dealing with Turkey and the Human Right to Freedom of Religion or Belief: A Critical Assessment in the Light of Recent Case Law (*Leyla Sahin v Turkey*, 29 June 2004)", n.d., available at: http://www.strasbourgconference.org (visited on 29 May 2006) p 13 of document.

involved here, and in any case one that contemplates the likely longer-term implications of such a prohibition.[91] Jacob T Levy has the measure of this calculus when he asks:

> "Would a ban mostly have the effect of getting Muslim girls in public school to leave their scarves behind, or would it mostly have the effect of keeping them out of the public schools, perhaps encouraging the growth of private schools in which they gain less exposure to a world outside their own community?"[92]

Such trends can ultimately make the realisation of societal goals, such as integration and the promotion of inter-group understanding and tolerance, significantly more difficult.

The Court also put store by the argument that permitting the headscarf to be worn could pressurise others into also wearing the headscarf, but against their will. However, given that no evidence was adduced of any examples of such pressure, such a fear can only be regarded as theoretical. Furthermore, as suggested by Judge Tulkens, university students generally exhibit a heightened capacity to resist such peer pressure, unlike their younger school-going counterparts. Both of the foregoing arguments bring the necessity of the impugned measures even further into question. In any event, the argument itself diverts attention away from the motivation and conduct of the wearer of the headscarf to those around her. As Gareth Davies has pointed out in respect of a different (but not entirely dissimilar) case, shifting the focus to how certain conduct is interpreted by third parties "comes dangerously close to allowing individuals to be judged by the prejudices of others",[93] a practice which he regards as being "entirely at odds with both reason and the law".[94]

Public Order

As with the "pressure on others" argument, the justification of the impugned measures on the grounds of maintaining public order also rings hollow.[95] Again, no evidence of the applicant causing any disruption to public order was submitted to the Court. What did weigh heavily on the Court's reasoning, though, was the politicisation of the headscarf by extremist political movements in Turkey. In the absence of any evidence (or even assertion) before the Court that the applicant had any connection with, or inclination towards, Islamic fundamentalism or other forms of political extremism, the Court's reliance on this justification is misplaced. It could be taken as implicitly tarring the applicant and religious fundamentalists with the same brush, thereby fuelling suggestions that the Court's approach was founded on

---

[91] JT Levy, *The Multiculturalism of Fear* (Oxford University Press, New York, 2000), p 61.
[92] *ibid.*
[93] G Davies, "Banning the Jilbab", *op. cit.*, p 520.
[94] *ibid,* p 522.
[95] See further, T Lindholm, "The Strasbourg Court Dealing with Turkey and the Human Right to Freedom of Religion or Belief", *op. cit.*, pp 11–12 of document.

fear and distrust of unfamiliar cultures,[96] or the "Threatening Other", as Tore Lindholm has put it.[97] It could also be seen as another example of the Court's apparent inability to see Islam other than as a monolithic religion. The reality, of course, is that Islam comprises many different strands, just like other major religions. Finally, in this connection, the *Refah Partisi* case raised very serious questions about the Court's approach to the tenets and practices of Islam,[98] and it is to be regretted that the Court in *Şahin* has opted to reiterate some of its more troublesome findings in the *Refah Partisi* case.[99]

The UN Human Rights Committee's Approach: Another Lesson in Methodological Shortcomings

The foregoing section dealt with the protection of the right to manifest one's religion, as vouchsafed by Article 9, ECHR. On a more global canvas, the protection of the right to freedom of thought, conscience and religion is guaranteed by Article 18 of both the Universal Declaration of Human Rights[100] and the International Covenant on Civil and Political Rights (ICCPR). A lesser level of protection is asserted by the — deceptively more detailed — UN Declaration on the Elimination of All Forms of Intolerance and of Discrimination Based on Religion or Belief.[101] Article 18, ICCPR, elaborates on the right provided for in the corresponding provision of the Universal Declaration of Human Rights, as follows:

1. Everyone shall have the right to freedom of thought, conscience and religion. This right shall include freedom to have or to adopt a religion or belief of his choice, and freedom, either individually or in community with others and in public or private, to manifest his religion or belief in worship, observance, practice and teaching.
2. No one shall be subject to coercion which would impair his freedom to have or to adopt a religion or belief of his choice.

---

[96] For further exploration of the theoretical and practical implications of such a fear-grounded policy, see: JT Levy, *The Multiculturalism of Fear*, *op. cit.*, pp 33 *et seq*.

[97] T Lindholm, "Comments on the Case of Leyla Sahin v. Turkey: Political and Public Morality Aspects", n.d., available at: http://www.strasbourgconference.org (visited on 29 May 2006), p 3 of document.

[98] For example, K Boyle has suggested that "The Refah case can be read to suggest that peaceful advocacy of the tenets of Islam is unprotected under the European Convention" (footnote omitted): K Boyle, "Human Rights, Religion and Democracy: The Refah Party Case", *op. cit.*, p 12.

[99] A full exploration of the problematic aspects of the Refah Partisi case is beyond the scope of this note, but see generally, K Boyle, "Human Rights, Religion and Democracy: The Refah Party Case", *op. cit.*, and B Olbourne, "Refah Partisi (The Welfare Party) v Turkey´, EHRLR 2003, 4, 437-444.

[100] It reads: "Everyone has the right to freedom of thought, conscience and religion; this right includes freedom to change his religion or belief, and freedom, either alone or in community with others and in public or private, to manifest his religion or belief in teaching, practice, worship and observance."

[101] Proclaimed by United Nations General Assembly resolution 36/55 of 25 November 1981. For commentary, see, for example: Natan Lerner, "The Nature and Minimum Standards of Freedom of Religion and Belief", 2000 BYUL Rev. 905.

3. Freedom to manifest one's religion or beliefs may be subject only to such limitations as are prescribed by law and are necessary to protect public safety, order, health, or morals or the fundamental rights and freedoms of others.
4. The States Parties to the present Covenant undertake to have respect for the liberty of parents and, when applicable, legal guardians to ensure the religious and moral education of their children in conformity with their own convictions.

As with Article 9, ECHR, the ICCPR also explicitly sets out the right to manifest one's "religion or belief in worship, observance, practice and teaching" (Article 18(1)). Freedom to exercise that right may only be abridged when the requirements of Article 18(3) are strictly complied with. Moreover, pursuant to Article 4(2), ICCPR, the right to freedom of thought, conscience and religion is non-derogable — even in times of public emergency. This is a categorical affirmation of the fundamental nature of the right.

The United Nations Human Rights Committee has also considered and pronounced on issues relating to the regulation of religious attire (or, to be more specific, the Islamic headscarf), but not in a dispositive manner. In *Hudoyberganova v Uzbekistan*,[102] the author of the Communication claimed that (as summarised by the Human Rights Committee) "her right to freedom of thought, conscience and religion was violated as she was excluded from University because she refused to remove the headscarf that she wore in accordance with her beliefs".[103] As such, the material facts of the case were very similar to those in the *Şahin* case. The following passage captures the essence of the Human Rights Committee's examination of the merits of the case:

> "The Committee considers that the freedom to manifest one's religion encompasses the right to wear clothes or attire in public which is in conformity with the individual's faith or religion. Furthermore, it considers that to prevent a person from wearing religious clothing in public or private may constitute a violation of article 18, paragraph 2, which prohibits any coercion that would impair the individual's freedom to have or adopt a religion. As reflected in the Committee's General Comment No. 22 (para.5),[104] policies or practices that have the same intention or effect as direct coercion, such as those restricting access to education, are inconsistent with article 18, paragraph 2. It recalls, however, that the freedom to manifest one's religion or beliefs is not absolute and may be subject to limitations, which are prescribed by law and are necessary to protect public safety, order, health, or morals, or the fundamental rights and freedoms of others (article 18, paragraph 3, of the Covenant). In the present case, the author's exclusion took place on 15 March 1998, and was based on the provisions of the Institute's new regulations. The Committee notes that the State party has not invoked any specific ground for which the restriction imposed on the author

[102] *Raihon Hudoyberganova v Uzbekistan*, Communication No. 931/2000, 18 January 2005.
[103] *ibid*, para 6.2.
[104] Author's footnote: General Comment No. 22: The right to freedom of thought, conscience and religion (Art. 18), adopted by the UN Human Rights Committee at its 48th session on 30 July 1993.

> would in its view be necessary in the meaning of article 18, paragraph 3. Instead, the State party has sought to justify the expulsion of the author from University because of her refusal to comply with the ban. Neither the author nor the State party have specified what precise kind of attire the author wore and which was referred to as "hijab" by both parties. In the particular circumstances of the present case, and without either prejudging the right of a State party to limit expressions of religion and belief in the context of article 18 of the Covenant and duly taking into account the specifics of the context, or prejudging the right of academic institutions to adopt specific regulations relating to their own functioning, the Committee is led to conclude, in the absence of any justification provided by the State party, that there has been a violation of article 18, paragraph 2."[105]

It was submitted *supra* that the Human Rights Committee's consideration of the underlying issues in this case was not "dispositive". That assessment is based on the inadequate factual and also contextual detail which informed the Committee's findings. From the information before the Committee, it was not readily apparent precisely what kind of clothing the author was wearing (neither the author nor the State offered any specification in this regard). This is a crucial factual element for any examination of whether the particular circumstances of the case could constitute a breach of the author's rights under Article 18, ICCPR. Moreover, as pointed out in the individual (dissenting) opinion of Committee Member Mr Hipólito Solari-Yrigoyen, "the exclusion of the author, according to her own statements, arose from more complex causes, and not only the religious clothing she wore or her demand to cover her face within the Institute".

Absent adequate factual detail, Committee Member Sir Nigel Rodley offers apposite qualification of the Committee's findings in his individual opinion. Although in general agreement with the Committee, he explicitly dissociates himself from its assertion "duly taking into account the specifics of the context". He explains:

> "The Committee is right in the implication that, in cases involving such "clawback" clauses as those contained in articles 12, 18, 19, 21 and 22, it is necessary to take into account the context in which the restrictions contemplated by those clauses are applied. Unfortunately, in this case, the State party did not explain on what basis it was seeking to justify the restriction imposed on the author. Accordingly, the Committee was not in a position to take any context into account. To assert that it has done so, when it did not have the information on the basis of which it might have done so, enhances neither the quality nor the authority of its reasoning."

The third individual opinion in this case — that of Committee Member Ms Ruth Wedgwood — also picks up on the factual ambiguities of the case. For her, the failure to specify whether the author was prevented from wearing a *hijab* or head scarf "covering the hair and neck" or a garment covering the face (as prohibited by

---

105 *Raihon Hudoyberganova v Uzbekistan, op. cit.*, para 6.2.

Institute regulations) is of pivotal importance. Such specification could have a determinative impact on the evaluation of the circumstances in which the alleged violation of the author's rights took place. Emphasising some very pragmatic considerations, she argues: "a state may be allowed to restrict forms of dress that directly interfere with effective pedagogy, and the covering of a student's face would present a different set of facts".

It is interesting to note — by way of aside — that pragmatic considerations such as these have shaped the relevant approaches of the competent authorities in a number of States.[106] In the Netherlands, for example, the Equal Treatment Commission (CGB) "does not easily consider the importance of communication in an employment relation to be an objective justification for indirect discrimination on the grounds of religion". It has, however, carved out an exception to this rule that recognises "the importance of good communication in the context of learning processes/education". For example, in a recent opinion, it held that:

> "good communication in an educational setting, in combination with the importance of identification and future occupational participation, constituted an objective justification for the indirect discrimination practised by the school in that it prohibited wearing a niqaab (CGB 20 March, opinion 2003-40)."[107]

Conclusion

The headscarf debate is proving polemical and divisive at national and international levels alike. There is considerable divergence across States in terms of approaches and attitudes and the reality of such divergence is unlikely to disappear in the near future. Similarly, the contestation of various approaches adopted by States is likely to continue before international bodies. The initial attempts by the European Court of Human Rights and the United Nations Human Rights Committee to deal with relevant matters in a decisive and convincing manner have been found wanting.

In the *Şahin* case, the Court showed rather unquestioning deference to arguments of principle advanced by the Turkish authorities and to specific contextual factors obtaining in Turkey, despite their often tenuous relevance to the facts of the instant case. Considerations of secularism and political extremism in Turkey are prime examples of this. As a result, the Court will find it difficult to refute claims that it has — not for the first time in respect of cases against Turkey — succumbed to "the insidious temptation to resort to a "variable geometry" of human rights which pays undue deference to national or regional 'sensitivities'".[108] Another highly problematic aspect of the *Şahin* judgment is the lack of refinement in its

[106] As documented in *Leyla Şahin v Turkey*, Grand Chamber Judgment, *op. cit.*, paras 63 & 64.
[107] "Advisory opinion of the Dutch Equal Treatment Commission on Employment, religion and equal treatment", 12 August 2004, Doc. CGB advisory opinion/2004/06, p 9. See also, *Leyla Şahin v. Turkey*, Grand Chamber Judgment, *op. cit.*, para 64.
[108] Lord Lester of Herne Hill, QC, "The European Convention on Human Rights in the New Architecture of Europe: General Report", 38 *Yearbook of the European Convention on Human Rights* (1995), pp 223–236, at 226-227.

consideration of matters relating to Islam. In sum, it is regrettable that in this case, the Court would appear to have ascribed its own subjective significations to the Islamic headscarf (as a religious symbol) and imputed motivations to the applicant that were not supported by the evidence before the Court. It is imperative for the credibility of the Court that this emergent doctrinal blight be prevented from spreading to other stalks of the Court's jurisprudence.[109]

It can only be hoped that the emergent jurisprudence of the European Court of Human Rights can be sensibly and sensitively consolidated, as its exposure to, and experience with, relevant issues increases. The impact of the Court's standard-setting role in this regard is far-reaching, as evidenced, *inter alia*, by references to the *Şahin* case by the United Nations Human Rights Committee. This makes the Court's responsibility all the greater.

[109] See further, T Lindholm, "The Strasbourg Court Dealing with Turkey and the Human Right to Freedom of Religion or Belief", *op. cit.*, pp 17–18 of document.

Recognition of Canadian Same-Sex Marriage: *Zappone and Gilligan v Revenue Commissioners and Others*[*]

Brian Tobin[**]

Background and Facts

The plaintiffs, Katherine Zappone and Ann-Louise Gilligan, Irish citizens, were married in Canada in 2003, following the opening up of the institution of marriage to same-sex couples in that jurisdiction. Upon their return to Ireland they wrote to the Revenue Commissioners with a view to claiming the tax benefits bestowed on married couples. The Revenue Commissioners responded by stating that although Irish tax legislation does not define husband or wife, the Oxford English Dictionary defines "husband" as a married man and "wife" as a married woman and, therefore, the plaintiffs' claim was disallowed.

The plaintiffs then sought and were granted leave to apply for judicial review of the Revenue Commissioners' decision not to recognise their Canadian marriage and provide them with married couples' tax benefits. The plaintiffs claimed that the Revenue Commissioners' decision violated their right to equality before the law under Article 40.1 and their right to marry under Article 41 of the Irish Constitution, as well as their right to marry under Article 12 of the European Convention on Human Rights. The case was decided by Dunne J in the High Court on 14 December 2006.

The Decision

The Constitution of Ireland, Article 41.3.1

Dunne J noted that, although marriage is not defined in Article 41.3.1 of the Constitution,[1] "the traditional understanding of marriage" as "understood by the framers of the Constitution" is the oft-cited common law definition of marriage, as stated by Lord Penzance in *Hyde v Hyde, i.e.* "the voluntary union of one man and one woman, to the exclusion of all others".[2] Such definition, she observed, has been reiterated in a number of domestic cases. In fact one of these decisions, *DT v CT*[3] "was given as recently as 2003".[4] Upon consideration of this body of case law Dunne J felt that it could not be said that the concept of marriage as between two persons

[*] [2008] 2 IR 417

[**] Adjunct Lecturer, School of Law, University of Dublin, Trinity College.

[1] Article 41.3.1 provides: "The State pledges itself to guard with special care the institution of Marriage, on which the Family is founded, and to protect it against attack."

[2] (1866) LR 1 P and D 130, at p 133 (Lord Penzance).

[3] [2003] 1 ILRM 321.

[4] *Zappone and Gilligan v Revenue Commissioners and Others* [2008] 2 IR 417, at 504.

of the opposite sex "is some kind of fossilised understanding of marriage".[5] Thus, the learned judge refused to redefine marriage under Article 41.3.1 of the Constitution so as to include two persons of the same sex and "to mean something which it has never done to date".[6]

Dunne J quoted from the judgment of Walsh J in *McGee v Attorney General,* where it was stated that "[n]o interpretation of the Constitution is intended to be final for all time. It is given in the light of prevailing ideas and concepts".[7] However, she found that, because marriage under the Constitution "has always been understood as being opposite sex marriage", there was no basis for the interpretation of prevailing ideas and concepts. She adopted the historical test of constitutional interpretation used by the Supreme Court in *Sinnott v Minister for Education*[8] and held that the notion of marriage must be defined in the light of practice in 1937 (i.e. heterosexual marriage or marriage between persons of the opposite sex) and that issues such as capacity must be understood in the light of present law (i.e. the Civil Registration Act 2004, which expressly precludes same-sex marriage).

The judge rejected the plaintiffs' argument that the right to marry under the Constitution should be considered to have changed so as to embrace same-sex marriage by reason of the existence of a changing societal consensus. She pointed out that "the consensus around the world does not support a widespread move towards same-sex marriage" and noted the emergence of same-sex marriage in but six jurisdictions globally, namely Canada, Massachusetts, South Africa, Spain, Belgium and the Netherlands. On this basis she held that it was difficult to see this "limited support for the concept of same-sex marriage…as a consensus, changing or otherwise".

The Civil Registration Act 2004, Section 2(2)(e)

Dunne J noted that "as recently as 2004, s 2(2)(e) of the Civil Registration Act was enacted" which reiterates the common law exclusion of same-sex couples from marriage in the following terms: "For the purposes of this Act there is an impediment to a marriage if…both parties are of the same sex". The learned judge believed that the statute was "of itself…an expression of the prevailing view as to the basis for capacity to marry."[9]

Equality before the Law

Dunne J simply stated "that if there is in fact any form of discriminatory distinction between same-sex couples and opposite-sex couples by reason of the exclusion of same-sex couples from the right to marry, then Article 41 in its clear terms as to guarding provides the necessary justification."[10]

---

[5] *ibid.*
[6] *ibid,* at p 505.
[7] *McGee v Attorney General* [1974] IR 284, at p 319 (Walsh J).
[8] [2001] 2 IR 545.
[9] *Zappone and Gilligan v Revenue Commissioners and Others,* (n 4), at p 506.
[10] *ibid,* at p 507.

Article 12 ECHR

> "Men and women of marriageable age have the right to marry and to found a family, according to the national laws governing the exercise of this right."

In considering Article 12 of the European Convention on Human Rights Dunne J relied heavily on the judgment of Potter P in the English High Court (Family Division) case of *Wilkinson and Kitzinger v Attorney General*[11] because she found it "compelling" since it "set out clearly the position in relation to the right of marriage as identified by the European Court of Human Rights" in *Goodwin v United Kingdom.*[12] In *Wilkinson and Kitzinger* Potter P noted that in *Goodwin* — a case taken by a post-operative transsexual — the European Court of Human Rights found "that gender can be determined by criteria other than simply biological factors" and hence "limiting the ambit of Article 12 to marriage between persons of the opposite biological sex was too restrictive". He held that the court took no more than an incremental step in *Goodwin* by broadening the scope of Article 12 to recognise "the phenomenon of *re-assigned gender* whereby the applicant became eligible to marry, *as a woman,* a man of her choice".[13] This conclusion was endorsed by Dunne J.

The Margin of Appreciation

Potter P pointed out that although there has been a general move towards the legal recognition of same-sex relationships across Europe in recent years only "Netherlands, Belgium and Spain have passed laws providing for same-sex marriage." Therefore he asserted that the issue of regulating or recognising same-sex marriage was one clearly falling within the margin of appreciation granted to the Contracting States by the European Court of Human Rights because the phenomenon:

> "...cannot be said to be an area where there is a Europe-wide consensus on the subject, by reason or reference to which the Convention should be treated as having evolved and expanded its scope to encompass same-sex relationships within the concept of marriage."[14]

Having analysed the judgment in *Wilkinson and Kitzinger,* Dunne J asserted that she could see no reason for reaching an alternative conclusion as to the application of a broad margin of appreciation.[15]

Analysis

"Constitutional Families"

In *Zappone and Gilligan* Dunne J utilised the "definitional argument" to dismiss the plaintiffs' claim for the recognition of same-sex marriage under Article 41.3.1 of the

---

[11] [2007] 1 FLR 295.
[12] *Goodwin v United Kingdom* (App no. 28957/95) (2002) 35 EHRR 18.
[13] [2007] 1 FLR 295, at para 61.
[14] *ibid,* at para 62
[15] *Zappone and Gilligan v Revenue Commissioners and Others,* (n 4), at p 510.

Irish Constitution. This is not so much an argument as a bald assertion that because marriage has always been a union between two parties of the opposite sex then that is what it must remain. Walsh and Ryan have observed that:

> "[a]lthough this conclusion may well be in keeping with conventional social and political understandings of marriage...the proposition that marriage is exclusively a heterosexual union is presented...as self-evident, as a conclusion that requires no precedential support or logical reasoning."[16]

The definitional argument is "an appeal solely and exclusively to history"[17] which, by its unrelenting reliance on incontrovertible historical fact and its preference for a form over substance approach to relationships, is based on a "lazy, unthinking perception of the essence of marriage".[18]

It would appear that procreation is not an essential element of marriage under Irish law. In *Murray v Ireland,* Costello J held that: "[t]he words used in Article 41 to describe the 'Family' are...apt to describe both a married couple with children and a married couple without children...."[19] Furthermore, in *Zappone and Gilligan* it was not even suggested by counsel acting on behalf of the State that the justification for the exclusion of same-sex couples from marriage was their inability to procreate. So one might ask just what is regarded as the essence of marriage under Irish law? In *Murray v Ireland* Costello J spoke of the notion "of partnership...which establishes...a unique and very special life-long relationship..." to which each party is committed.[20] Thus, it is at least arguable that Irish law would appear to recognise that "it is the exclusive and permanent commitment of the marriage partners to one another, not the begetting of children, that is the *sine qua non* of civil marriage".[21]

Given that the substantive content of same-sex unions can be virtually identical to that of their opposite-sex counterparts it is submitted that both types of relationship are equally as capable of satisfying this "essence" of civil marriage for the purposes of Irish law.[22] Indeed in *Zappone and Gilligan*, Dunne J pointed out that it "is clear that [the parties] have a long-lasting loving relationship of mutual commitment"[23] and it is submitted that this observation could apply to many of the 2,090 cohabiting same-sex couples living in Ireland.[24]

In light of the foregoing, one might question why the gender of parties to a committed relationship should continue to determine their capacity to enter into a

---

[16] J Walsh and F Ryan, *The Rights of de facto Couples,* (IHRC, Dublin 2006), at p 91.
[17] *Zappone and Gilligan v Revenue Commissioners and Others,* (n 4), at 497.
[18] F Ryan, "Marriage at the Boundaries of Gender: The "Transsexual Dilemma" Resolved"? (2004) 1 IJFL 15, at 22, n 11.
[19] [1985] IR 537.
[20] *ibid,* at p 536.
[21] *Goodridge v Dept. of Public Health* (2003) 798 NE2d 941, at p 961 (Marshall CJ).
[22] See *Ghaidan v Godin-Mendoza* [2004] 2 AC 557 at p 607 (Baroness Hale).
[23] *Zappone and Gilligan v Revenue Commissioners and Others,* (n 4), at p 501.
[24] Census 2006, *Principal Demographic Results: Commentary* (CSO, Dublin, 2007).

marriage contract in this jurisdiction and consequently form a family unit for the purposes of Article 41?

Statutory Provision

However disappointing that a broader functional view of the notion of marriage which would have met the "needs, capacities and circumstances"[25] of same-sex partners was not adopted by the High Court in *Zappone and Gilligan*, this was perhaps unsurprising given the express prohibition on same-sex marriage contained in s 2(2)(e) of the Civil Registration Act 2004. In the last decade the Irish courts have displayed a fairly consistent deference to the legislature where controversial constitutionally protected rights are at issue.[26] Indeed, Dunne J felt quite emphatically that the 2004 Act was "*of itself*"" an indication of what marriage is and how it should be defined in Ireland and went on to assert that "*ultimately, it is for the legislature to determine the extent*" of the legal recognition to be accorded to same-sex unions.[27]

There is cause for concern here because Dunne J appears to be granting the Oireachtas primacy in this contentious matter. The Oireachtas has recently chosen registered civil partnership as the appropriate model of relationship recognition for same-sex couples by the publication of the Heads of Bill to legislate for Civil Partnership.[28] Thus when the appeal of the *Zappone and Gilligan* case reaches the Supreme Court it might simply display the same legislative deference as the High Court and refuse to broaden Article 41.3.1 of the Constitution so as to encompass gay marriage because in any event there is civil partnership legislation on the way which will in practice grant same-sex couples rights largely akin to marriage though simply under a different nomenclature.

The Equality Dimension

Oran Doyle observes that constitutional case law in Ireland illustrates that:

> "[E]quality-derogating classifications that are not justified by reference to a difference between the persons distinguished might nonetheless be legitimate where they support…another constitutional value." [29]

In *Zappone and Gilligan* Dunne J appears to have adopted this restrictive approach, holding that the common law and statutory exclusions of homosexual persons from

---

[25] *Halpern and Ors v AG of Canada* 2002 CanLII 42749 (ON S.C.D.C.), para. 202 (LaForme J).

[26] See for example: *Sinnott v Minister for Education* [2001] 2 IR 545; *TD v Minister for Education* [2001] 4 IR 259. See generally Foley, "Diceyan Ghosts: Deference, Rights, Policy and Spatial Distinctions" (2006) 13 (1) DULJ 77.

[27] *Zappone and Gilligan v Revenue Commissioners and Others*, (n 4), at p 513.

[28] See M Hennessy and C O'Brien, "Bill to Grant Legal Protection to Same-Sex Couples", *The Irish Times*, (Dublin, 25 June, 2008) at p 3.

[29] O Doyle, *Constitutional Equality Law*, (Thomson Round Hall, Dublin, 2004) at p 99.

the institution of marriage, which are *prima facie* discriminatory measures, are nonetheless justifiable because:

> "[I]f there is in fact any form of discriminatory distinction between same-sex couples and opposite-sex couples by reason of the exclusion of same-sex couples from the right to marry, then Article 41 in its clear terms as to guarding provides the necessary justification."[30]

The judge failed to have regard to the potential of Art. 40.1 in this area. Hence the Irish courts, by "deeming rational classifications which serve other constitutional values"[31] and thereby treating the equality guarantee contained in Article 40.1 as surplusage are able to dispose of an equality-based argument in favour of the recognition of same-sex marriage with ease.

It is submitted that the constitutional equality guarantee contained in Article 40.1 might not fetter the recognition of a right to gay marriage in this jurisdiction if liberally construed by the Supreme Court in the appeal from the High Court decision in this case. The first sentence would surely aid a dignity-based argument for gay marriage since "[a]ll citizens" are entitled to equality before the law by virtue of their being "human persons". The "dignity and freedom of the individual" referred to in the Preamble to the Constitution and Denham J's acknowledgment of an unenumerated constitutional right to dignity in *Re a Ward of Court (No.2)*[32]could be used to reinforce this argument.

Furthermore, the second sentence of the Article allowing for "due regard to differences of capacity, physical and moral, and of social function" might not be invoked against same-sex couples because it may not be pertinent for the courts to do so for the following reasons. Since Irish law would, as aforementioned, seem to regard the life-long loving commitment of the parties and not procreation as being fundamental to a marital union,[33] it may be unfeasible for the courts to deny same-sex couples access to the institution of marriage on the basis of either their differing physical capacity or their social function. For the purposes of Irish law it would appear to be irrelevant that such couples are physically incapable of having children and because they possess "normative familial characteristics"[34] such as "mutual interdependence, sharing of lives, caring and love, commitment and support",[35] it is strongly arguable that they can perform the social function of marriage, i.e. the promotion of domestic and, ultimately, social stability.

In addition, the courts might be unlikely to rule out a right to same-sex marriage on equality grounds due to homosexual couples' difference of moral capacity, because

---

[30] *Zappone and Gilligan v Revenue Commissioners and Others,* (n 4), at 507.
[31] O Doyle, (n 29) at p 99.
[32] [1996] 2 IR 79, at p 163.
[33] See above.
[34] L Glennon, "Fitzpatrick v Sterling Housing Association Ltd – An Endorsement of the Functional Family?", (2000) 14 IJLPF 226, at p 236.
[35] *ibid.*

in the *Zappone and Gilligan* case counsel for the State did not choose to argue that marriage should be restricted to heterosexual couples for "moral reasons".[36] This indicates that in an Ireland where homosexuality has been legalised for some fifteen years now, the State is unwilling to take a moral stand on the issue, and the courts might be just as reluctant. While all of this seems promising, Wintemute nonetheless opines that:

> "[i]t seems unlikely that the Supreme Court of Ireland would interpret the equality provision (Article 40.1) as requiring equal access to legal marriage for same-sex couples. This is for the simple reason that, *to date, no appellate court in Europe has been willing to interpret a national constitutional provision as requiring equal access,* and the Supreme Court will probably not choose to be the first."[37]

The European Convention on Human Rights

It is submitted that in *Zappone and Gilligan* Dunne J is correct in approving Potter P's analysis in *Wilkinson v Kitzinger* of the European Court of Human Rights decision in the *Goodwin* case. After all that case was concerned with a post-operative transsexual's right to marry and not that of a same-sex couple and so, for now, a difference in gender is still essential in order for the parties to exercise their right to marry under Article 12 of the Convention. Nonetheless, later in her judgment Dunne J went on to endorse Potter P's assertion that:

> "If marriage is by longstanding definition and acceptance a formal relationship between a man and a woman primarily (though not exclusively) with the aim of producing and rearing children...and if that is the institution contemplated and safeguarded by Article 12 then to accord a same sex relationship the title and status of marriage would be to fly in the face of the Convention as well as to fail to recognise physical reality."[38]

Such continued adherence to a Judeo-Christian notion of marriage under Article 12 is clearly unsupportable in the aftermath of *Goodwin* where, contrary to its earlier case law, a unanimous European Court of Human Rights made it clear that the right to marry is now divorced from a couple's ability to found or raise a family by stating that:

> "Article 12 secures the fundamental right of a man and woman to marry and to found a family. The second aspect is not however a condition of the first and the inability of any couple to conceive or parent a child cannot be regarded as *per se* removing their right to enjoy the first limb of this provision."[39]

---

[36] *Zappone and Gilligan v Revenue Commissioners and Others,* (n 4), at p 450.
[37] Wintemute, "Marriage or 'Civil Partnership' for Same-Sex Couples: Will Ireland Lead or Follow the United Kingdom?", in Doyle and Binchy (eds.), *Committed Relationships and the Law,* (Four Courts Press, Dublin, 2007), at pp 100-101. Emphasis added.
[38] *Wilkinson v. Kitzinger* [2007] 1 FLR 295, at para. [120].
[39] *Goodwin v United Kingdom* (n 12), at para 98.

In light of this statement it would appear that what Potter P refers to and Dunne J sanctions as "marriage" is no longer the exact "institution contemplated and safeguarded by Article 12". The Irish courts may one day have to reconsider their traditional approach to marriage because the European Court of Human Rights' change of attitude in *Goodwin* would appear to lean in favour of the eventual recognition of gay marriage under Article 12.

Firstly, as seen, the Court held that the right to marry is not reliant on the ability of "any couple to conceive *or* parent a child".[40] This is significant not only because the Court uses a gender-neutral construction by referring to a "couple" rather than a man and a woman, but also because the court's reasoning, while applicable to a post-operative transsexual and his/her partner who cannot "conceive" a child, could equally apply to same-sex partners who cannot in various Contracting States legally adopt and consequently "parent" a child but who may, under the *Goodwin* test, enjoy the right to marry.[41]

Secondly, the Court notes that a corresponding provision guaranteeing the right to marry, — Article 9 of the Charter of Fundamental Rights of the European Union, — departs "no doubt deliberately" from the wording of Article 12 of the ECHR in removing the reference to men and women.[42] It is even more intriguing that the court's vibrant reinterpretation of Article 12 in *Goodwin* brings it very much in line with Article 9, which states that "the right to marry *and* the right to found a family shall be guaranteed in accordance with the national laws governing the exercise of these rights".[43] As we can see, the rights to marry and to found a family are separate and distinct rights under Article 9, as under Article 12 post-*Goodwin*. The Court could, in the future, make Article 12 further akin to Article 9 by stating that, although the former provision's language is gender-specific, it "does not explicitly state that men and women may only marry *each other*".[44]

As Wintemute points out "much of the language in [*Goodwin*] leaves the door open to acknowledge same-sex marriage *at some point in the future*".[45] The author is most likely correct, same-sex marriage may eventually be recognised under Article 12 but perhaps not in the near future because of the impact of the margin of appreciation doctrine and the varying practice of Member States.

It is clear that there is no visible agreement amongst the Contracting States in relation to the controversial issue of same-sex marriage. Therefore Dunne J's statement in *Zappone and Gilligan* that "[c]learly, there is a wide margin of

---

[40] *Goodwin v United Kingdom,* (n 12), at para 98. Emphasis added.

[41] In Ireland for example, unmarried couples, whether heterosexual or homosexual, have never been allowed to adopt children. See the Adoption Act 1991, s 10.

[42] *Goodwin v United Kingdom,* (n 12), at para 100.

[43] Article 9, EU Charter of Fundamental Rights. Emphasis added.

[44] J Walsh and F Ryan, (n 16), at p 56.

[45] Wintemute, *'The Massachusetts Same-Sex Marriage Case: Could Decisions from Canada, Europe, and South Africa Help the SJC?'* (2004) 38 (3) New Eng L Rev 505 at p 510.

appreciation given to Contracting States in [the area of same-sex marriage]..."[46] is unassailable and the recognition of same-sex marriage under Article 12 would, for the time being, seem to flounder because of the application of this test.

Conclusion

As a result of the High Court's decision in *Zappone and Gilligan* the right to marry under the Constitution of Ireland is confined exclusively to heterosexual couples even though procreation is not a prerequisite to its exercise. Homosexual persons' inherent capacity as human beings to establish intimate committed relationships, which because of their substance are as worthy of being recognised as civil marriages as heterosexual unions, is being eschewed in favour of a formalistic concept of marriage notwithstanding the existence of a constitutional equality guarantee.

The right to marry under the European Convention on Human Rights would appear to be moving towards the eventual recognition of gay marriage. In the landmark case of *Goodwin* the European Court of Human Rights expressly rejected procreation as a prerequisite for marriage and veered away from the necessity of biological sexual dimorphism in the context of the right to marry under Article 12. Yet by agreeing with Potter P's outmoded understanding of marriage in *Wilkinson v Kitzinger*, Dunne J in *Zappone and Gilligan* limits the significance of *Goodwin* for the future interpretation of marriage under the European Convention on Human Rights as applied in Irish domestic law. Even allowing for the current impediments imposed by the application of a broad margin of appreciation this is regrettable.

However, the socio-legal recognition of gay marriage would appear to be slowly gaining impetus with Norway becoming the fourth Council of Europe Member State to open up civil marriage to same-sex couples with effect from 1 January 2009.[47] Thus it is not beyond the realm of possibility that in a future case appealing for a right to same-sex marriage under the Convention, the European Court of Human Rights might finally be willing to hold that the framers' reference to "men and women" in Article 12 was descriptive of an assumed reality in 1950 rather than prescriptive of a normative structure for all time. Indeed, in the South African same-sex marriage case of *Minister of Home Affairs v Fourie*, Sachs J so held in relation to Article 16 of the Universal Declaration on Human Rights of 1948, which is virtually identical to Article 12 of the European Convention on Human Rights because he felt that "as ideas of justice and equity evolve, so do concepts of rights take on new texture and meaning".[48]

---

[46] *Zappone and Gilligan v Revenue Commissioners and Others*, (n 4), at p 512.

[47] On 11 June 2008 the Norwegian Parliament approved a Bill providing for same-sex marriage. Since then the Bill has been granted Royal assent by the King and it became law on 1 January 2009.

[48] *Minister of Home Affairs and Another v Fourie and Another* (2006) 3 BCLR 355 (C.C.), at paras 100 and 102 (Sachs J). Article 16 (1) of the Universal Declaration on Human Rights provides that "men and women of full age, without any limitation due to race, nationality or religion, have the right to marry and to found a family. They are entitled to equal rights as to marriage, during marriage and at its dissolution".

Jurisdictional Issues: *Bosphorus Airways v Ireland*[*]

Professor Rick Lawson[**]

Background of the Case

The *Bosphorus* case originated from a case against Ireland but the issues raised by it are a matter of great interest to all EU Member States and, indeed, to many other countries. Even if some questions remained unanswered in this case, it was already obvious in 2005 that the judgment of the European Court of Human Rights would be the leading authority on the relationship between the ECHR and international organisations. Subsequent case-law has confirmed that this is indeed the case.

What is at issue in *Bosphorus* is the extent to which States may be held responsible for alleged breaches of human rights when implementing EC law. At first sight this might appear to be a very technical issue but quite the opposite is true. Currently, not a single international organisation is a signatory to any human rights treaty. This may raise very real questions in practice: what if a UN or NATO peace keeping operation is said to have violated the ICCPR or the Geneva Conventions on international humanitarian law? Are the organisations bound by these standards? Could States be held liable for the conduct of international organisations of which they are members? In daily practice these questions are raised most often in connection with the European Community / Union not, of course, because it violates human rights on a systematic basis but, rather, because far-reaching powers have been transferred to it.

The essence of the matter at hand is not very complicated. A number of States which are parties to a human rights treaty, establish an international organisation and transfer certain powers to it. Next it appears, or it is alleged, that the organisation does not comply with the standards to which its founding fathers have committed themselves. The organisation itself is not bound by these standards, so it cannot be challenged. Could a court hold the Member States accountable? A strong argument in favour of a positive reply is that one secures compliance with fundamental rights by not allowing a vacuum to exist. A powerful counter-argument is that "Member State responsibility" essentially negates the separate identity of the international organisation, as well as the fact that Member States sometimes have limited control over that organisation's conduct. The latter argument loses some of its strength if a specific Member State is very closely involved in the alleged violation, for instance by executing a decision of the international organisation. In the latter case the alleged violation is committed by State agents, acting not on their own initiative

[*] Bosphorus Hava Yolari Turism Ve Ticaret A.S. ("Bosphorus Airways" v Ireland) Judgment of 30 June 2005 (Appl. No. 45036/98)

[**] Prof.dr. RA Lawson, *Europa Instituut*, Faculty of Law, University of Leiden, The Netherlands.

but on behalf of the organisation. This might make it easier to accept the attribution of liability to the particular State in question. But it does not make life easier for the domestic courts: they might be "sandwiched" between Luxembourg and Strasbourg, if one European Court tells them to follow a certain approach and the other tells them *not* to.

The position of the European Court of Human Rights in Strasbourg on this issue had been unclear. Most cases that raised the issue of potential "Member State responsibility" for the conduct of EC institutions were rejected by the European Commission of Human Rights (while it existed pre-Protocol 11), which meant that they never made it to the Court of Human Rights. The leading case was *M. & Co v Germany*.[1] Basically the Commission found that fundamental rights enjoyed an "equivalent protection" in the Community legal order and concluded from this that it was not competent to entertain complaints involving the European Communities.

Only one case resulted in a Court judgment: *Matthews v UK* (1999). In this case the Court seemed to take a somewhat more assertive stance than the Commission, as it underlined that the rights and freedoms of the ECHR must continue to be secured if States transfer powers to international organisations: "Member States' responsibility continues even after such a transfer".[2] That approach is of course beneficial to the effectiveness of the Convention, but the fact pattern of *Matthews* was very specific. It was not a routine case about implementation of EC law. It was unclear, therefore, if *Matthews* could be generalised. The *Grand Chamber* judgment in *Bosphorus* did offer the clarity that had, up to then, been missing.

Facts of the Case

The dispute in *Bosphorus* was about a Boeing 737 aircraft which a small Turkish charter company had leased from Yugoslav Airlines JAT in 1992. When the aircraft was in Ireland for maintenance, in 1993, it was seized under EC Regulation 990/93 which implemented the UN sanctions against the Federal Republic of Yugoslavia (Serbia and Montenegro). Bosphorus challenged the retention of the aircraft. During the proceedings, the Irish Supreme Court referred a preliminary question to the European Court of Justice (ECJ) on whether the aircraft was covered by the relevant Regulation. The answer was in the affirmative: the ECJ considered that the general interest outweighed the individual rights of Bosphorus.[3] Subsequently, the Supreme Court had little choice but to apply the decision of the ECJ and reject Bosphorus's appeal. The aircraft was the only one ever seized under the relevant EC and UN regulations.

Bosphorus then brought a complaint to the European Court of Human Rights under Article 1 of Protocol No. 1 ECHR (protection of property), arguing that it had to

---

[1] *M. & Co. v Germany — FRG* ECommHR, 9 February 1990, (Appl. No. 13258/87, *Yearbook ECHR*, vol. 33 (1993), p 46).

[2] *Matthews v UK* ECtHR, 18 February 1999 (*Reports 1999*, p 251), para 32.

[3] *Bosphorus v Minister for Transport, Energy and Communications and others* [1996] *ECR* I-3953 ECJ, judgment of 30 July 1996, Case C-84/95.

bear an excessive burden resulting from the manner in which the Irish State applied the sanctions regime and that it suffered significant financial loss. Four years later, in September 2001, the Strasbourg Court held a hearing on the admissibility and merits of the application, following which the case was declared admissible. More than two years later the Chamber relinquished jurisdiction in favour of the Grand Chamber. In May 2004 the President of the Court gave the EU Commission leave to intervene as a third party and, in September 2004, the Court decided to devote a *second* hearing to the case. Judgment was delivered at the very end of June 2005. The length of the procedure suggests that the case was considered highly sensitive.

Judgment of the European Court of Human Rights

The Court of Human Rights unanimously rejected the complaint brought by Bosphorus. At first sight that does not seem to be very spectacular, but this result was only reached after a lengthy analysis which contained many new and interesting elements. The judgment also contains a very extensive description of the European Community legal order, addressing concepts such as the supremacy of Community Law, the system of legal remedies and the position of fundamental rights. Parenthetically it is noted that the description is limited to the "first pillar" of the EU: the Court mentions in passing (in para 72) that this judgment only concerns Community law.

The first substantive question to be answered related to the legal qualification of the impoundment of the aircraft. Was it an act of Ireland? Was it done by the Communities through "local authorities" who happened to be Irish? The Court, rightly in my view, took a matter-of-fact approach. On the one hand it observed that the aircraft was seized by the Irish authorities on Irish territory following a decision by the competent Irish Minister for Transport. In such circumstances Bosphorus Airways fell within the "jurisdiction" of the Irish State. On the other hand the Court accepted that the seizure was not the result of an exercise of discretion by the Irish authorities, either under EC or Irish law, but amounted to compliance by the Irish State with its strict legal obligations flowing from EC law and, in particular, EC Regulation 990/93. The Court observed that, once adopted, this regulation was "generally applicable" and "binding in its entirety" (under Article 189, now Article 249, of the EC Treaty), so that it applied to all Member States, none of whom could lawfully depart from any of its provisions. The Court also agreed that the Irish Supreme Court had no real discretion to exercise either before or after its preliminary reference to the ECJ.

Against this background the Court addressed the alleged violation of property rights. It accepted that the impoundment had interfered with Bosphorus Airways' property rights. The crucial question was whether this interference could be justified. It is at this stage that the Court tackled the heart of the matter: how to balance the imperative of effective human rights protection with the requirements of international cooperation and integration? The answer is given in the following paragraphs:

> "151. The question is therefore whether, and if so to what extent, that important general interest of compliance with EC obligations can justify the impugned interference by the State with the applicant's property rights.

152. The Convention does not, on the one hand, prohibit Contracting Parties from transferring sovereign power to an international (including a supranational) organisation in order to pursue co-operation in certain fields of activity (the *M. & Co.* decision, at p 144 and *Matthews* at § 32, both cited above). Moreover, even as the holder of such transferred sovereign power, that organisation is not itself held responsible under the Convention for proceedings before, or decisions of, its organs as long as it is not a Contracting Party (...).
153. On the other hand, it has also been accepted that a Contracting Party is responsible under Article 1 of the Convention for all acts and omissions of its organs regardless of whether the act or omission in question was a consequence of domestic law or of the necessity to comply with international legal obligations. Article 1 makes no distinction as to the type of rule or measure concerned and does not exclude any part of a Contracting Party's "jurisdiction" from scrutiny under the Convention (...).
154. In reconciling both these positions and thereby establishing the extent to which State action can be justified by its compliance with obligations flowing from its membership of an international organisation to which it has transferred part of its sovereignty, the Court has recognised that absolving Contracting States completely from their Convention responsibility in the areas covered by such a transfer would be incompatible with the purpose and object of the Convention: the guarantees of the Convention could be limited or excluded at will thereby depriving it of its peremptory character and undermining the practical and effective nature of its safeguards (...). The State is considered to retain Convention liability in respect of treaty commitments subsequent to the entry into force of the Convention (...).
155. In the Court's view, State action taken in compliance with such legal obligations is justified as long as the relevant organisation is considered to protect fundamental rights, as regards both the substantive guarantees offered and the mechanisms controlling their observance, in a manner which can be considered at least equivalent to that for which the Convention provides (see the above-cited *M. & Co.* decision, at p 145, an approach with which the parties and the European Commission agreed). By "equivalent" the Court means "comparable": any requirement that the organisation's protection be "identical" could run counter to the interest of international co-operation pursued (paragraph 150 above). However, any such finding of equivalence could not be final and would be susceptible to review in the light of any relevant change in fundamental rights' protection.
156. If such equivalent protection is considered to be provided by the organisation, the presumption will be that a State has not departed from the requirements of the Convention when it does no more than implement legal obligations flowing from its membership of the organisation.
However, any such presumption can be rebutted if, in the circumstances of a particular case, it is considered that the protection of Convention rights was manifestly deficient. In such cases, the interest of international co-operation would be outweighed by the Convention's role as a "constitutional instrument of European public order" in the field of human rights (...).
157. It remains the case that a State would be fully responsible under the Convention for all acts falling outside its strict international legal obligations. [...]
158. Since the impugned act constituted solely compliance by Ireland with its legal obligations flowing from membership of the EC (...), the Court will now

examine whether a presumption arises that Ireland complied with its Convention requirements in fulfilling such obligations and whether any such presumption has been rebutted in the circumstances of the present case."

The Court then proceeded to analyse the protection of fundamental rights by EC law, both from a substantive perspective (which rights are protected by Community law?) and from a procedural point of view (which remedies are available to the individual complaining of rights violations?). It concluded that the Community protection could indeed have been considered to be, and to have been at the relevant time, "equivalent" to that of the Convention system. Consequently, a presumption arose that Ireland did not depart from the requirements of the Convention when it implemented legal obligations flowing from its membership of the EC.

Such a presumption could be rebutted, as we have seen (above) in para 156, if it was considered that the protection of Convention rights was manifestly deficient. However, it considered it clear that in this case there was no dysfunction in the mechanisms of control of the observance of Convention rights. In the Court's view, therefore, it could not be said that the protection of Bosphorus Airways' Convention rights was manifestly deficient. It followed that the presumption of Convention compliance had not been rebutted and that the impoundment of the aircraft did not give rise to a violation of Article 1 of Protocol No. 1.

Comments

Before addressing a number of more or less specific detailed issues, I think I should clarify my basic position on this case. To my mind the Court has managed to develop a sound approach, provided that it is indeed prepared to engage in a critical analysis of the level of human rights protection offered by international organisations. The *Bosphorus* test will lose its credibility if the Court, for instance for diplomatic reasons, is too easily prepared to give its "seal of approval" to an organisation. I will return to this later on. First it should be pointed out that the *Bosphorus* case was not exactly welcomed in all quarters.

On the one hand, there are human rights lawyers who regard the *Bosphorus* judgment with suspicion: why grant special privileges to international organisations? The fact that human rights *tend* to be respected in the laws and practices of a country does certainly not entail that the European Court will only deal with complaints against that country if there is "manifest deficiency". So why be so generous to the EC which, moreover, did not have a constitutional bill of rights?

On the other hand, *Bosphorus* was received with some hostility in Brussels as well, albeit for different reasons. Why didn't the Court decide the case on the basis of the fact that the sanctions on Yugoslavia were imposed by the UN Security Council? The EC was only implementing these sanctions. On the basis of Article 103 of the UN Charter, the measures adopted by the Security Council would have precedence over the ECHR. Instead of rejecting the case in this ground, the argument goes, Strasbourg deliberately chose to ignore the UN dimension of the case. From this perspective, *Bosphorus* could be seen as an open invitation to individuals to apply to the Court and argue that in their case there was a "manifest deficiency".

Without denying the force behind these arguments, I think that they are both one-sided and overlook the reality that the Strasbourg Court had to balance opposing interests. A presumption seems unavoidable since it would not be realistic to expect domestic courts to review each and every EC decision prior to allowing its implementation. On the other hand there is a certain tendency in Brussels, as Luxembourg Prime Minister Juncker noted, to perceive the Council of Europe and the ECHR in an instrumental way.[4] The EU must learn that it is subjected to external review and it would seem that the Strasbourg Court is not too harsh a teacher.

My overall appreciation for the *Bosphorus* test is also prompted by the improvements made to the old *M & Co.* case-law. Whereas the Commission in *M. & Co.* created the impression that a *carte blanche* had been given to the Communities for once and for all, *Bosphorus* makes it clear that this assessment is always of a temporary nature (para 155).

Secondly, in *M. & Co.* the Commission declared itself incompetent to hear claims, whereas the Court in *Bosphorus* reviews the Irish conduct, the Community law dimension coming in when possible justifications for the interference are reviewed. The latter approach is preferable, if only because it would be difficult for Strasbourg, from a logical point of view, to examine if Community law still offers "equivalent protection" if the Court were unable to even take cognisance of fresh complaints.

Thirdly, the newly introduced presumption (para 156) allows for a remedy in case something really went wrong in the EC legal order. Again this represents an improvement when compared to *M. & Co.*

Having said this, a number of questions have been left open. In at least four ways the Court's judgment is limited.

Firstly, as was noted (above) the case only concerns Community Law. We do not know how the Court will address cases that involve the Second and Third Pillars of the European Union. Since the level of judicial protection in both pillars is considerably lower than under Community Law proper, one cannot take for granted that *Bosphorus* will apply to issues of police and justice cooperation. In this area *Matthews* remains the leading authority until further notice. States that did not use the opt-in facility of Article 35 EU, and therefore did not empower the ECJ to deliver preliminary rulings in Third Pillar matters, may find themselves in an awkward position before the Strasbourg Court.

Secondly, each Member State continues to be fully responsible under the Convention "for all acts falling outside its strict international legal obligations" (para 157). This is certainly a justified position: States must be able to be held liable for the exercise of the discretion that their authorities have. Yet one may expect a lot of litigation on the exact scope of the notion "strict legal obligations"; at any rate it will necessarily involve the interpretation of EC law by the Strasbourg Court.

---

[4] JC Juncker, *Council of Europe-European Union: a sole ambition for the European continent* (Strasbourg, 11 April 2006), at www.coe.int.

A third limitation of *Bosphorus* is that the case is about national implementation measures, and not about alleged violations of human rights by the international organisation itself. Here one could think of the official employed by the European Commission who is dismissed after having published a critical book.[5] The *Senator Lines*[6] case offers another example: a company complained that it did not have effective access to court in order to challenge the imposition of a high fine. Without discussing the merits of that complaint the Strasbourg Court dismissed the case when the fine was annulled. How will the Court address this kind of case once it gets to the merits? It is conceivable that a *Bosphorus* type of approach will be followed: the Community offers an "equivalent protection "of rights; hence the member States cannot be held collectively responsible for alleged violations of the Community institutions; but an exception may always be made if in a specific case the protection of Convention rights was manifestly deficient. This category of case will disappear, by the way, once the EC/EU accedes to the ECHR.

Fourthly, and lastly, it is important to underline that *Bosphorus* did not seek to deal with the implementation of sanctions imposed by the UN Security Council on the basis of Chapter VII of the UN Charter.

Another question which is left unanswered in the judgment is when a "manifest deficiency" (para 156) occurs. In his *concurring opinion* Judge Ress gives a number of examples:

> "The protection was manifestly deficient when there has, in procedural terms, been no adequate review in the particular case such as: when the ECJ lacks competence (as in the case of *Segi and Gestoras Pro-Amnistía and Others v. Austria, Belgium, Denmark, Finland, France, Germany, Greece, Ireland, Italy, Luxembourg, the Netherlands, Portugal, Spain, Sweden and the United Kingdom* ((dec.), nos. 6422/02 and 9916/02, ECHR 2002-V); when the ECJ has been too restrictive in its interpretation of individual access to it; or indeed where there has been an obvious misinterpretation or misapplication by the ECJ of the guarantees of the Convention right. Even if the level of protection must only be "comparable" and not "identical", the *result* of the protection of the Convention rights should be the same."

Judge Ress concludes that the protection of the Convention right would be "manifestly deficient" if, in deciding the key question in a case, the ECJ were to depart from the interpretation or the application of the Convention or the Protocols that had already been the subject of well-established ECHR case-law.

A nice academic question is how many individual cases of manifest deficiencies it takes before an organisation loses its "equivalent protection" hallmark.

Let us now turn to the application of the new test to the European Community. The way in which the Court, in paras 159-166, seeks to establish that the Community

[5] See the case of *Connolly* (ECJ, 6 March 2001, C-274/99 P).
[6] *Senator Lines GmbH v 15 EU Member States* (Appl. No. 56672/00) ECtHR, 10 March 2004.

offers an "equivalent protection", is not very convincing. It is remarkable that the Strasbourg Court is willing to take into account the EU Charter of Fundamental Rights: at the time that *Bosphorus* was decided the ECJ itself had not been willing to take that step.[7] It is all the more intriguing to read how the Court describes the Charter as "not fully binding". Then what is it?[8]

A more serious matter is that the Strasbourg Court is very cursory in its review of Luxembourg human rights case-law. A number of very general references are made to treaty provisions, but at no stage does the Strasbourg Court review how high the actual level of protection before the ECJ is. It is one thing to note that the EU Treaty now refers to fundamental rights, or that the ECJ recognises the right to property, but it is an entirely different matter how this right is balanced in practice against the general interest. The European Court of Human Rights does not make any visible attempt to find this out.

Of course one could argue that it would be a bit silly for the Strasbourg Court to check in hindsight if the ECJ had paid sufficient weight to property rights in all sorts of cases *other than Bosphorus*. However, if that would indeed appear to be the problem it does raise questions about the actual usefulness of the *equivalent protection* test.

It is similarly disconcerting that the Court of Human Rights does not really address the limited access of individuals to the ECJ under Article 230 EC. Admissibility requirements have been interpreted strictly since the famous *Plaumann* case of 1963. Every now and then the discussion about the acceptability of the present state of affairs flares up again. In 2002 Advocate General Jacobs, citing Articles 6 and 13 ECHR, argued for wider access to court. The Court of First Instance adopted the same position in the case of *Jégo-Quéré*. The ECJ disagreed, however, and remained faithful to the traditional view.[9]

In *Bosphorus* there is only a very soft reference to this episode: "It is true that access of individuals to the ECJ under these provisions is limited" (para 162.) In essence, AG Jacobs and the Court of First Instance are left in the cold, since *Bosphorus* suggests that they are unnecessarily rigid in applying Articles 6 and 13 ECHR or, at least, more rigid than the Strasbourg Court itself.

---

[7] It was only one year later, in 2006, that the ECJ was willing to refer to the Charter: *Parliament v Council (Family Reunification Directive)*, ECJ, case C-540/03 § 38.

[8] How relevant is a bill of rights that is "not fully binding" if we take into account earlier case-law: "it should be noted that the requirements of Article 13, and of the other provisions of the Convention, take the form of a guarantee and not of a mere statement of intent or a practical arrangement. That is one of the consequences of the rule of law, one of the fundamental principles of a democratic society, which is inherent in all the Articles of the Convention" (*Čonka v Belgium* (Appl. no. 51564/99), ECtHR, 5 February 2002, para 83).

[9] See the Opinion of AG Jacobs (21 March 2002) in *Unión de Pequeños Agricultores v Council*, C-50/00 P, *ECR*. 2002, p I-6677, esp. para 39 ff.; CFI, 3 May 2002, *Jégo-Quéré v Commission*, T-177/01, *ECR*. 2002, p II-2365, para 41 ff.; ECJ 25 July 2002, *UPA*, C-50/00 P, *ECR* 2002, p I-66, para 36 ff..

The key question is whether individual access under Article 230 is so limited that the "*equivalent protection* seal of approval" should be withdrawn. A related question is whether *Bosphorus* was the best case in which to decide that point, since it was immaterial: Bosphorus had full access to the Irish courts and, through the preliminary rulings procedure, to the ECJ. At the same time, the European Court of Human Rights in *Bosphorus* did not refrain from making general statements about the quality of the Community legal order which makes it difficult to ignore this issue.

It is at this point that seven judges express doubts in two concurring opinions. But even they do not go so far as stating that the EC does not offer an "equivalent protection" of fundamental rights. Perhaps the safest thing to say is that this issue is left undecided for the time being.

A last cause for disappointment relates to the last leg of the judgment, where the Court reviews if in the instant case the protection of Convention rights was manifestly deficient. Apparently quite a lot must happen before we may speak of "a dysfunction of the mechanisms of control": Bosphorus Airways had to litigate for twelve years to get its plane back!

Perhaps this very marginal review was also prompted by the fact that *Bosphorus* was about property rights. In that connection a very low level of protection is offered in Strasbourg anyway. Indeed the Court announced in para 149 that it would leave "a wide margin of appreciation" to the domestic authorities in such matters.

More than four years have passed since the *Bosphorus* judgment was delivered. In hindsight it turned out that it was indeed a leading judgment, and it has been relied upon in several cases involving the implementation of Community law.[10] In the case of *Boivin*, which involved a labour dispute between the international organisation *Eurocontrol* and a staff member, the Court observed that it had not been established that the protection of fundamental rights generally afforded by *Eurocontrol* was not "equivalent", within the meaning given to that term in the *Bosphorus* judgment, to that of the Convention system.[11]

The most recent, and most spectacular application of the doctrine occurred in a Dutch case decided in January 2009.[12] The case concerned the fact that, during a preliminary rulings procedure before the ECJ, one of the parties was not allowed to submit a response to the Opinion of the Advocate General before the ECJ gave judgment. Since the applicants believed that this amounted to a breach of their right to adversarial proceedings, as protected by Article 6 ECHR, and since the referring

---

[10] See *Coopérative des Agriculteurs de la Mayenne v France* (Appl. no. 16931/04) ECtHR, 10 October 2006.

[11] *Boivin v 34 Contracting States* (Appl. no. 73250/01) ECtHR, 9 September 2008.

[12] *Cooperatieve Producentenorganisatie van de Nederlandse Kokkelvisserij U.A v Netherlands* (Appl. no. 13645/05) ECtHR, 20 January 2009.

Dutch court applied the ECJ's preliminary ruling, a complaint was brought against the Netherlands before the European Court of Human Rights. In its admissibility decision the Court referred extensively to *Bosphorus* and accepted that the *Bosphorus* presumption applies not only to actions taken by a Member State in order to implement a Community measure, but also to the procedures followed *within* such an international organisation itself and, in particular, to the procedures of the ECJ. In the instant case the Court decided, by a majority, that it had not been shown that the protection afforded to the applicant was 'manifestly deficient': parties may *request* the Court leave to respond to the AG's opinion; the referring national court could have lodged a further request for a preliminary ruling to the ECJ; and the ECJ's ruling did leave a certain degree of discretion to the referring court.

The overall conclusion may therefore be two-fold. Firstly the Court introduced a new test for cases involving international organisations. The test as such is quite attractive but the way in which it was applied, both in *Bosphorus* and thereafter, is not convincing in all respects.

Secondly the domestic authorities managed to escape from a Luxembourg / Strasbourg sandwich — but Bosphorus remained right in the middle. In the short-term the *Bosphorus* judgment must have caused a sigh of relief in Brussels and Dublin, but is it really so desirable in the longer term? There is no need to remind an Irish audience that public support for the EU is sometimes quite low. Will Brussels be able to regain the citizens' confidence once it transpires that Strasbourg will only step in if the Community institutions have really gone way too far?

An Ode to Contextualisation: *İ.A. v Turkey*

Dr Tarlach McGonagle*

Introduction

The central feature of *İ.A. v Turkey*[1] — a conviction arising out of "an abusive attack on the Prophet of Islam" — could hardly be more topical and one could legitimately have expected the European Court of Human Rights to have provided instructive guidance on the interplay of relevant principles in the case. This was not to be, however. The Second Section of the Court held that there had been no violation of Article 10 ECHR, but the judgment was split (by four votes to three)[2] and the joint dissenting opinion was unusually forthright in its suggestion that "the time has perhaps come to 'revisit'" the case-law on which the instant case was based. Nevertheless, the case was not referred to the Grand Chamber under Article 43 ECHR[3] and, as a result, we have been left none the wiser as to the workings of the murky doctrinal interface between the rights to freedom of expression and religion.

Facts

The applicant was the owner and managing director of a publishing company which published a novel, *Yasak Tümceler* ("The forbidden phrases"), in 1993. As noted by the European Court of Human Rights, the book "conveyed the author's views on philosophical and theological issues in a novelistic style".[4] Two thousand copies of the book were printed in a single print-run. In 1994, the Istanbul public prosecutor charged the applicant with blasphemy against "God, the Religion, the Prophet and the Holy Book" under Article 175 §§ 3 and 4 of the Criminal Code for having published the novel. The public prosecutor's indictment was based on a

* Lecturer at the Institute for Information Law (IViR), Law Faculty, University of Amsterdam.

[1] Judgment of the European Court of Human Rights (Second Section) of 13 September 2005.

[2] Judges Baka, Turmen, Ugrekhelidze and Mularoni subscribed to the majority opinion, whereas Judges Costa (Section President), Cabral Barreto and Jungwiert issued a joint dissenting opinion.

[3] Article 43 ("Referral to the Grand Chamber") reads as follows:

> "1. Within a period of three months from the date of the judgment of the Chamber, any party to the case may, in exceptional cases, request that the case be referred to the Grand Chamber. 2. A panel of five judges of the Grand Chamber shall accept the request if the case raises a serious question affecting the interpretation or application of the Convention or the protocols thereto, or a serious issue of general importance. 3. If the panel accepts the request, the Grand Chamber shall decide the case by means of a judgment."

[4] *İ.A. v Turkey*, *op. cit.*, para 5.

specially requested expert report, drawn up by a professor in the Faculty of Theology at Marmara University. In a submission to the Istanbul Court of First Instance, the applicant contested the expert report and requested a second opinion, arguing that as a novel, the book should have been analysed by literary experts, while also questioning the impartiality of the author of the report.

Subsequently, a second report was drafted by three other professors, but its accuracy was also contested by the applicant, who argued that it was a copy of the first report. He further argued that the novel was neither blasphemous nor insulting in the sense of Article 175 § 3 of the Criminal Code and that it merely expressed the philosophical views of the author. Ultimately, his arguments failed to prevail in the Court of First Instance and he was sentenced to two years' imprisonment and a fine. The aforementioned second report and the following excerpt from the impugned book would appear to have weighed on the Court's reasoning:

> "Look at the triangle of fear, inequality and inconsistency in the Koran; it reminds me of an earthworm. God says that all the words are those of his messenger. Some of these words, moreover, were inspired in a surge of exultation, in Aisha's arms. ... God's messenger broke his fast through sexual intercourse, after dinner and before prayer. Muhammad did not forbid sexual relations with a dead person or a live animal."[5]

The Court of First Instance commuted the applicant's prison sentence to a fine, which in effect meant that he was ordered to pay a total sum of approximately 16 USD. He appealed against his conviction in the Court of Cassation, but it upheld the judgment of the Court of First Instance.

Judgment of the European Court of Human Rights

The European Court of Human Rights followed its customary approach to cases involving the right to freedom of expression. It dispensed with the first questions in its standard enquiry expeditiously, noting that both parties accepted that the applicant's conviction did amount to an interference with his right to freedom of expression under Article 10(1) and that the interference was prescribed by law and pursued legitimate aims under Article 10(2), i.e., the prevention of disorder and the protection of morals and the rights of others. The case therefore turned on whether the interference was "necessary in a democratic society".[6]

The Court, as is its wont, re-emphasised the central importance of freedom of expression in democratic society and recalled that, subject to Article 10(2), "it is applicable not only to "information" or "ideas" that are favourably received or regarded as inoffensive or as a matter of indifference, but also to those that offend, shock or disturb".[7] The exercise of the right, however, comes with concomitant

---

[5] *ibid*, para 13.
[6] *ibid*, para 22.
[7] *ibid*, para 23.

duties and responsibilities, including — in the context of religious beliefs — "a duty to avoid expressions that are gratuitously offensive to others and profane". In consequence, "as a matter of principle it may be considered necessary to punish improper attacks on objects of religious veneration".[8]

In the absence of any "uniform European conception of the requirements of the protection of the rights of others in relation to attacks on their religious convictions", Member States are afforded a wide margin of appreciation when addressing "matters liable to offend intimate personal convictions within the sphere of morals or religion".[9] Although it may be legitimate for a State to adopt measures aimed at repressing certain activities, including the dissemination of information and ideas, when such activities are judged to be incompatible with Article 9 ECHR, the European Court of Human Rights is the final arbiter of whether or not such measures are consistent with the Convention. In that capacity, the Court assesses whether, in the circumstances of a particular case, the interference in question corresponds to a "pressing social need" and is "proportionate to the legitimate aim pursued".[10] The Court also recalled that in the spirit of pluralism, tolerance and broadmindedness that is constitutive of democratic society, members of religious groups "cannot reasonably expect to be exempt from all criticism": "They must tolerate and accept the denial by others of their religious beliefs and even the propagation by others of doctrines hostile to their faith".[11]

After setting out the foregoing principles (as well as certain details of its own *modus operandi*), the Court then proceeded to apply them to the circumstances of the case at hand. It did so in just one paragraph:

> "However, the present case concerns not only comments that offend or shock, or a 'provocative' opinion, but also an abusive attack on the Prophet of Islam. Notwithstanding the fact that there is a certain tolerance of criticism of religious doctrine within Turkish society, which is deeply attached to the principle of secularity, believers may legitimately feel themselves to be the object of unwarranted and offensive attacks through the following passages: 'Some of these words were, moreover, inspired in a surge of exultation, in Aisha's arms. ... God's messenger broke his fast through sexual intercourse, after dinner and before prayer. Muhammad did not forbid sexual intercourse with a dead person or a live animal.'"[12]

It then found that the measures interfering with the applicant's freedom of expression aimed to offer protection against offensive attacks on matters regarded as sacred by Muslims and as such, corresponded to a "pressing social need".[13] It

[8] *ibid*, para 24.
[9] *ibid*, para 25.
[10] *ibid*, para 26.
[11] *ibid*, para 28.
[12] *ibid*, para 29.
[13] *ibid*, para 30.

affirmed that the Turkish authorities had not overstepped their margin of appreciation and that the stated reasons for the impugned restrictions were "relevant and sufficient".[14] As regards the proportionality question, the Court referred to the fact that copies of the book had not been seized and also to the "insignificant" nature of the fine imposed.[15]

Joint Dissenting Opinion

The joint dissenting opinion of Judges Costa, Cabral Barreto and Jungwiert is rather forceful, particularly in its candid criticism of the doctrinal precedents on which the instant judgment relies so heavily (see further *infra*). Their dissent raises a number of highly pertinent concerns about the Court's application of key general principles gleaned from its jurisprudence to the specific facts of the instant case.

The joint dissenting opinion begins by cautioning against being *blasé* about the Court's seminal pronouncement in *Handyside* (cited, *infra*), or using it in a merely sloganistic way.[16] It emphasises the "limited practical impact on society of the author's statements"[17] and points out that the likelihood that unorthodox religious views would "offend or shock the faith of the majority of the population" is an insufficient reason "in a democratic society to impose sanctions on the publisher of a book".[18] It readily acknowledges that the attacks on Muhammad contained in the passage from the book quoted *supra* "may cause deep offence to devout Muslims, whose convictions are eminently deserving of respect." In the same vein, it also refers to the "sacred" status of the Prophet in Islam.[19] Nonetheless, it rejects the idea that an entire book be condemned and its publisher criminally sanctioned on the basis of isolated passages in the book. It particularly rues the institution of criminal proceedings by the public prosecutor — and not by an offended member of the public — in the present case.[20] The dissenting judges also took issue with the perceived proportionality of the sanctions imposed on the applicant. They insist that any criminal conviction gives rise to a chilling effect and leads to increased incidence of self-censorship.[21]

The joint dissenting opinion also advances three main critiques of the *Otto-Preminger*[22] and *Wingrove*[23] cases, on which the present case draws extensively. First,

---

[14] *ibid*, para 31.
[15] *ibid*, para 32.
[16] Joint dissenting opinion, *ibid*, para 1.
[17] Joint dissenting opinion, *ibid*, para 2.
[18] Joint dissenting opinion, *ibid*, para 3.
[19] Joint dissenting opinion, *ibid*, para 4.
[20] Joint dissenting opinion, *ibid*, para 5.
[21] Joint dissenting opinion, *ibid*, para 6.
[22] *Otto-Preminger-Institut v Austria*, Judgment of the European Court of Human Rights of 20 September 1994, Series A, no 295-A.
[23] *Wingrove v United Kingdom*, Judgment of the European Court of Human Rights of 25 November 1996, Reports of Judgments and Decisions, 1996-V.

there is the crucial difference between the impact that is likely to be achieved by a novel (in the instant case) and a film (in *Otto-Preminger*) and a short experimental video (in *Wingrove*). Second, it points out that in both cases, the Court occasioned a *volte-face* from the decisions of the Commission[24] and that the final Court judgments were themselves divided.[25] Finally, the real thunder-clap of the dissenting opinion bursts open: "the time has perhaps come to 'revisit' this case-law, which in our view seems to place too much emphasis on conformism or uniformity of thought and to reflect an overcautious and timid conception of freedom of the press."[26]

Commentary

Broadly speaking, apart from one — potentially significant — discrepancy, there is little amiss with the Court's normative principles concerning permissible limits to freedom of expression when the exercise of the right interferes with the religious beliefs and convictions of others (summarised *supra*). Where the Court's approach misfires, and has repeatedly misfired in the past, is in its application of those principles to specific factual situations.

Relevant Case-Law

The critical discharge of the joint dissenting opinion in the *İ.A.* case was aimed specifically at the cases of *Otto-Preminger-Institut v. Austria* and *Wingrove v United Kingdom*. In *Otto-Preminger*, the applicant association (a private film-house) claimed (ultimately unsuccessfully) that its rights under Article 10, ECHR, had been violated by the seizure and forfeiture of a film (*Das Liebeskonzil*) it had planned to screen. The domestic Austrian courts found the characterisations of God, Jesus and Mary in the film to come within the definition of the criminal offence of disparaging religious precepts. Before it could actually be shown, the film was seized by the relevant national authorities in the context of criminal proceedings against the manager of the applicant association concerning the film. At issue in the *Wingrove* case was the rejection by the British Board of Film Classification of an application for a classification certificate for the applicant's film, *Visions of Ecstasy*. The film, a short experimental video work, portrayed Saint Teresa engaging in acts of an overtly sexual nature, including with the body of the crucified Christ.[27]

Other relevant cases that were not explicitly targeted by the dissenting judges in *İ.A.*, but which will be referred to in passing *infra*, include: *Gay News Ltd. & Lemon*

[24] For example, in the *Otto-Preminger* case, the Commission voted by nine votes to five that there had been a violation of Article 10 as regards the seizure of the film, and by 13 votes to one that there had been a violation of Article 10 as regards the forfeiture of the film. The Opinion of the Commission is appended to the Judgment of the Court, *op. cit*.

[25] In *Otto-Preminger*, the Court held by six votes to three that there had been no violation of Article 10 in respect of either the seizure of the film or its forfeiture. In *Wingrove*, the Court held by seven votes to two that no breach of Article 10 had taken place.

[26] Joint dissenting opinion, *ibid*, para 8.

[27] Paras 9, 61.

v United Kingdom,[28] *Müller & Others v Switzerland,*[29] *Choudhury v United Kingdom,*[30] *Murphy v Ireland*[31] and *Giniewski v France.*[32]

Rough Coherence of Principles

Pluralism and tolerance are among the most powerful of the ECHR's animating principles. Time and again, the Court has averred in its case-law on freedom of religion that [societal] pluralism has been hard-won over the ages and that it is indissociable with democratic life. In the same vein, the Court has consistently held in its case-law on freedom of expression that pluralism, along with its kindred concepts of tolerance and broadmindedness, constitutes one of the essential hallmarks of democratic society. Pluralism entails diversity and divergence, which

[28] *X. Ltd. & Y. v United Kingdom,* Application No. 8710/79, Decision of inadmissibility of the European Commission of Human Rights of 7 May 1982, 28 DR 77 (November 1982). The case involved a conviction for blasphemy arising out of the publication of a poem, "The Love that Dares to Speak its Name" by Prof. James Kirkup, in a magazine called *Gay News*. According to the headnote of the House of Lords' decision in the case, the poem "purported to describe in explicit detail acts of sodomy and fellatio with the body of Christ immediately after his death and ascribed to Him during His lifetime promiscuous homosexual practices with the Apostles and other men." — cited in *ibid,* para 1.

[29] *Müller & Others v Switzerland,* Judgment of the European Court of Human Rights of 24 May 1988, Series A, No. 133. In this case, the applicant artists were convicted and their paintings confiscated on the grounds that the latter were obscene; the Court found that the measure served the legitimate aim of protecting public morals and held that Article 10 had not been violated.

[30] *Choudhury v United Kingdom,* Decision of inadmissibility of the European Commission of Human Rights of 5 March 1991, Application No 17439/90. The applicant "sought to have criminal proceedings brought against the author and publisher of "Satanic Verses" in order to vindicate his claim that the book amounted to a scurrilous attack on, inter alia, his religion" — *ibid,* para 1.

[31] Judgment of the European Court of Human Rights (Third Section) of 10 July 2003. In this case, the applicant (a pastor affiliated to the Irish Faith Centre — "a bible based Christian ministry in Dublin" *ibid,* para 7) argued unsuccessfully that the refusal to broadcast an advertisement for the Irish Faith Centre, pursuant to a legislative prohibition on the broadcasting of religious advertising in Ireland, violated his rights under Articles 9 and 10, ECHR. Although the case was not *prima facie* about offence to the religious beliefs of others, the issue was considered in the Court's judgment.

[32] *Giniewski v France,* Judgment of the European Court of Human Rights (Second Section) of 31 January 2006. This case involved the conviction of a journalist (however, he was acquitted on appeal, but ordered to pay nominal damages and to foot the bill for the publication of the appellate decision in one national newspaper) for defamation in respect of an article he had written criticising a Papal Encyclical and exploring possible links between a particular doctrine and the origins of the Holocaust. The European Court of Human Rights found that the applicant's right to freedom of expression had been violated because his article did not set out to attack religious beliefs, but to contribute to an ongoing debate on topics of interest to the general public.

in turn can often involve a certain amount of contention and even antagonism.[33] This is all part of the democratic experiment;[34] the cut and thrust of debate that is free, robust and uninhibited.[35] Thus, as famously stated in the *Handyside* case, information and ideas which "offend, shock or disturb the State or any sector of the population" must be allowed to circulate in order to safeguard the "pluralism, tolerance and broadmindedness" that underpin "democratic society".[36] In principle, this vigorous conception of freedom of expression applies to all matters of general public interest, including religious beliefs and affairs.[37]

But the concepts of pluralism and tolerance, as developed by the European Court of Human Rights, are clearly contiguous. Indeed, we could perhaps — without any sleight of hand — merge the concepts into one and speak more meaningfully about pluralistic tolerance,[38] a notion that implies a certain degree of reciprocal respect between the different constituent groups of any democratic society. Pluralistic tolerance can be well served by robust protection for freedom of expression, for example, when offensive expression advances discussions on matters of public interest. As posited by Robert Post: "Outrageous speech calls community identity into question, practically as well as cognitively, and thus it has unique power to focus attention, dislocate old assumptions, and shock its audience into the recognition of unfamiliar forms of life".[39] However, the operative definition of "outrageous speech" is crucial here and would have to be qualified. In any case, if the right to freedom of expression is to be interpreted consistently with the notion of pluralistic tolerance, the protection of the rights of others must be borne in mind.

In this respect, Article 10(2) refers explicitly to the "duties and responsibilities" on which the exercise of the right to freedom of expression is contingent, and also the

---

33 *Kokkinakis v Greece,* Judgment of the European Court of Human Rights of 19 April 1993, para 33; *Metropolitan Church of Bessarabia and Others v Moldova,* Judgment of the European Court of Human Rights of 13 December 2001, para 123; *Hasan & Chaush v Bulgaria,* Judgment of the European Court of Human Rights of 26 October 2000, para 78; *Serif v Greece,* Judgment of the European Court of Human Rights of 14 December 1999, para 49; *Agga v Greece,* Judgment of the European Court of Human Rights of 17 October 2002, paras 53, 56; *Manoussakis v Greece,* Judgment of the European Court of Human Rights of 29 August 1996, para 44; *Supreme Holy Council of the Muslim Community v Bulgaria,* Judgment of the European Court of Human Rights of 16 December 2004, para 93.

34 Paraphrasal of Holmes, J, dissenting, in *Abrams v US,* 250 US 616 (1919), at p 630, when he described both the US Constitutional enterprise and life itself as being experimental.

35 Paraphrasal of the United States Supreme Court in *New York Times Co. v Sullivan,* 376 U.S. 254 (1964).

36 *Handyside v the United Kingdom,* Judgment of the European Court of Human Rights of 7 December 1976, Series A, No 24, para 49.

37 However, a crucial caveat to this general proposition will be entered *infra.*

38 J Raz sometimes uses the term "pluralist toleration", which seems to have essentially the same meaning: J Raz, "Free Expression and Personal Identification", 11 *Oxford Journal of Legal Studies* (No 3, 1991), pp 303–324, at 322.

39 RC Post, *Constitutional Domains: Democracy, Community, Management* (Harvard University Press, Cambridge, Massachusetts, 1995), p 139.

legitimacy of restricting the exercise of the right in order to protect the rights of others. As regards the application of these considerations to religious beliefs and affairs, the Court recognises the need to protect the deepest feelings and convictions of "others" from substantial or serious offence.[40] Similarly, it considers that the "respect for the religious feelings of believers as guaranteed in Article 9 [...] can legitimately be thought to have been violated by provocative portrayals of objects of religious veneration; and such portrayals can be regarded as malicious violation of the spirit of tolerance [...]".[41] This is because the beliefs in question are qualitatively different to other types of beliefs. One commentator has explained that qualitative difference by observing that "The recognition of what is 'sacred' involves an affirmation of what is believed to be of ultimate value in experience, and of what is of deepest concern in life".[42] That is the transformative factor that legitimates the special consideration for earnestly and deeply held religious beliefs.

Having said that, it is imperative that the exceptional regard in which religious beliefs can be held not be used as a convenient excuse for stifling debate on matters of interest to the public.[43] Again, to cite David Edwards: "The determination of spiritual value is a matter of persuasion, of exposition, and (perhaps) argument, and in any such process there must be the possibility of contradiction, condemnation and offence".[44]

Niggling Definitional Discrepancy

In the *Otto-Preminger-Institut* case, the European Court of Human Rights held that "in the context of religious opinions and beliefs", the duties and responsibilities which accompany the right to freedom of expression, may legitimately include:

> "an obligation to avoid as far as possible expressions that are gratuitously offensive to others and thus an infringement of their rights, and which therefore do not contribute to any form of public debate capable of furthering progress in human affairs."[45]

Whether by accident or design, the reformulation of this principle in *Wingrove v United Kingdom* and in *Murphy v Ireland* differs from its original articulation in *Otto-Preminger*. This is not a problem in itself; indeed, many principles are reworked and refined by the Court in the course of subsequent applications. In this case, however, some unexplained shifts of definitional emphasis appear to have been introduced. Instead of referring to expressions that are gratuitously offensive to others *and* an infringement of their rights *and* worthless from the perspective of public debate, the Court uses the more terse, alternative formula, "gratuitously offensive to others

[40] *Wingrove v United Kingdom, op. cit.*, para 58.
[41] *Otto-Preminger-Institut v Austria, op. cit.*, para 47.
[42] David Edwards, "Toleration and the English blasphemy law", in J Horton and S Mendus, Eds., *Aspects of Toleration* (Methuen & Co, London & New York, 1985), pp 75–98, at 84.
[43] See, in this respect, *Giniewski v France, op. cit.*, paras 50 & 51.
[44] *ibid*, p 82.
[45] *op. cit.*, para 49; *Giniewski v France, op. cit.*, para 43.

and profanatory".[46] No explanation is offered as to why the cumulative elements of the infringement of rights of others and the absence of any contribution to public debate were dropped. Nor is any attempt made to tease out the definitional scope of the notion of profanity, although it could be deduced from *Wingrove* that the "degree of profanation" would have to be "high" and the extent of insult to religious feelings "significant".[47] As a result of this inconsistent use of phraseology in the Court's approach to offensiveness in the context of religious opinions and beliefs, it is not possible to state with much confidence or precision what the official barometer actually is.

Misfiring of the Court

Frederick Schauer has claimed that in previous and ongoing efforts to elucidate the scope of the right to freedom of expression, "there has been too much distillation and not enough dissection".[48] The *İ.A.* case illustrates Schauer's point perfectly. It will be recalled that the essence of the Court's judgment in the case is a distillation of the main principles from its relevant case-law. The Court's application of those principles to the facts of the case is limited to one paragraph. In other words, what is missing is the dissection of key principles through their application to a set of specific factual circumstances.

I have argued elsewhere[49] that when the Court applies its normative principles to specific factual circumstances, it should systematically examine whether sufficient weighting has been given to factors such as: the intent of the speaker; "contextual variables",[50] and the demonstrably harmful impact of the impugned expression. The intent or motivation of the speaker is important as it can have significant bearing on how expression that is offensive to religious convictions is evaluated. There is a world of difference between misguided or thoughtless expression and that which is deliberately calculated to be offensive or which is fuelled by some kind of *animus*. Therefore, proof of an element of *scienter* (i.e., knowledge that the expression will or is likely to cause offence) should be required in order for liability to attach in civil proceedings,[51] and proof of *mens rea* in criminal proceedings.[52] Contextual variables could include the nature and impact of the medium used to

[46] *Wingrove v United Kingdom, op. cit.*, para 52. The formulation, "gratuitously offensive to others and profane", was used in *Murphy v Ireland, op. cit.*, para 65.
[47] *Wingrove v United Kingdom, op. cit.*, para 60.
[48] F Schauer, *Free Speech: A Philosophical Enquiry* (Cambridge University Press, New York 1982), p 85.
[49] T McGonagle, *Minority Rights and Freedom of Expression: A Dynamic Interface* (Ph.D. thesis, University of Amsterdam, 2008).
[50] M Rosenfeld, "Hate Speech in Constitutional Jurisprudence: A Comparative Analysis", 24 Cardozo L. Rev. 1523 (2003), at 1565.
[51] By analogy, the *scienter* element is quite a common feature of (campus) hate speech codes: see further, R Delgado & J Stefancic, *Understanding Words That Wound* (Westview Press, USA, 2004), p 115.
[52] It should however be noted in passing that the European Commission of Human Rights found the strict liability nature of the crime of blasphemous libel unobjectionable in the facts of *Gay News Ltd. & Lemon v United Kingdom, op. cit.*, para 12.

convey the expression; audience-related considerations; socio-political factors; the nature and severity of the sanction imposed, etc. The requirement of "demonstrably harmful impact" is a safeguard measure that insists on the establishment of a clear causal link between the impugned expression and the alleged resultant harm to others (e.g. gratuitous offence to their religious convictions).

Limited Impact of Publication

The joint dissenting opinion in *İ.A.* emphasises the likely impact of the publication. It had a limited,[53] once-off print-run, and the evidence before the Court did not indicate how many people actually read the book. The dissenting judges deduce from the fact that the book was not reprinted that the number of actual readers was small. Thus, one of the frequently-invoked rationales for regulating or restricting expression, *viz.* the impact/influence argument, offers a rather weak justification for interfering with the applicant's right to freedom of expression in the circumstances of the present case. Furthermore, as pointed out by the same section of the Court just a few months before it returned its *İ.A.* judgment, the novel as a medium is "a form of artistic expression that appeals to a relatively narrow public compared to, for example, the mass media".[54] By counterpoising a novel with the "mass media",[55] the Court seeks (albeit with clumsy wording) to distinguish between different media on the basis of their circulation, and by extension, their potential reach and impact. The specificity of a particular medium and its potential impact on the public are rightly considered by the Court to be relevant contextualising factors in many cases.[56] For instance, as the Court has repeatedly pointed out, "the audiovisual media have often a much more immediate and powerful effect than the print media".[57]

For present purposes, it should additionally be noted that there can be no suggestion of a captive audience here, and that members of the public would have had to buy the book in order to be confronted with its content. However, arguments such as these have not had a particularly happy history before the adjudicative organs of the ECHR, or at least not in the context of offence to religious beliefs. They do not, for instance, correspond to the approach taken by the European Commission of Human Rights in the *Gay News Ltd. & Lemon v United Kingdom*.[58] In that case, the

[53] Note that para 5 of the Court's judgment refers to a print-run of 2,000 copies, whereas para 2 of the joint dissenting opinion refers to 2,500. The correct figure would appear to be 2,000 copies, as the original French-language versions of the judgment and joint dissenting opinion both refer to 2,000 copies.
[54] *Alinak v Turkey*, Judgment of the European Court of Human Rights (Second Section) of 29 March 2005, para 41.
[55] One could, for instance, argue that a novel could be included in a definition of "mass media"; it is submitted here that the Court actually intended to distinguish between novels on the one hand, and newspapers and broadcasting on the other.
[56] *Murphy v Ireland, op. cit.*, para 69.
[57] *Jersild v Denmark*, Judgment of the European Court of Human Rights of 23 September 1994, Series A, no. 298, para 31; *Murphy v Ireland, op. cit.*, para 69; *Radio France v. France*, Judgment of the European Court of Human Rights of 30 March 2004, para 39, and (for very similar wording) *Purcell v Ireland*, Decision of inadmissibility of the European Commission of Human Rights of 16 April 1991, Application No 15404/89.
[58] *op. cit.*

Commission observed that "The issue of the applicants' journal containing the incriminated poem was on sale to the general public, *it happened to get known in some way or other* to the private prosecutor who was so deeply offended that she decided to take proceedings against the publication of this poem [...]".[59]

Although the case of *Müller v Switzerland* involved (sexual) morals rather than offence to religious convictions, it offers a useful analogy on the question of the public's exposure to potentially offensive material. In that case, a crucial consideration for the Court was that the impugned paintings were:

> "painted on the spot — in accordance with the aims of the exhibition, which was meant to be spontaneous — and the general public had free access to them, as the organisers had not imposed any admission charge or any age-limit. Indeed, the paintings were displayed in an exhibition which was unrestrictedly open to — and sought to attract — the public at large."[60]

Another — little-known — case, *S. v Switzerland*,[61] also concerning the display of obscene material to the general public, is analogously useful as well. The European Commission of Human Rights concluded from the facts of the case that "There was no danger of adults being confronted with the film against or without their intention to see it" and that it was undisputed "that minors had no access to the film" either.[62] The Commission continued by stating that "since no adult was confronted unintentionally or against his will with the film [...] there must be particularly compelling reasons justifying the interference at issue".[63]

In its *Otto-Preminger* judgment, the Court observed that access to the (proposed) screening of the film was subject to an admission fee and an age-limit. As "the film was widely advertised", "[t]here was sufficient public knowledge of the subject-matter and basic contents of the film to give a clear indication of its nature". The Court then offers a baffling *non sequitur*: "for these reasons, the proposed screening of the film must be considered to have been an expression sufficiently 'public' to cause offence".[64] This finding goes against the grain of the relevant reasoning relied upon in *Müller, supra*. The dissenting judges reached a very different conclusion, *viz.* that the advance publicity material issued by the applicant cinema: (i) aimed to warn the public about the critical way in which the film dealt with the Roman Catholic religion, and (ii) actually "did so sufficiently clearly to enable the

[59] (Emphasis added), *ibid*, para 12. The poem in question was: "The Love that Dares to Speak its Name", written by Prof J Kirkup. It appeared in a magazine called *Gay News*. According to the head-note of the House of Lords' decision in the case, the poem "purported to describe in explicit detail acts of sodomy and fellatio with the body of Christ immediately after his death and ascribed to Him during His lifetime promiscuous homosexual practices with the Apostles and other men." — cited in *ibid*, para 1.
[60] *op. cit.*, para 36.
[61] *S. v Switzerland*, Report of the European Commission of Human Rights of 14 January 1993, Application No. 17116/90, para 62.
[62] *ibid*, para 62.
[63] *ibid*, para 65.
[64] *op. cit.*, para 54.

religiously sensitive to make an informed decision to stay away". These conclusions prompted two further conclusions of note by the dissenting judges: (i) there was "little likelihood" of "anyone being confronted with objectionable material unwittingly", and (ii) the applicant association had acted "responsibly in such a way as to limit, as far as it could reasonably have been expected to, the possible harmful effects of showing the film".[65] It is submitted here that the dissenting opinion is more convincing than the majority opinion on this particular point.

In the *Wingrove* case, the European Commission had placed considerable store by the probability that a short experimental video work would have a very limited reach and impact. The Delegate of the Commission submitted to the Court that "The risk that any Christian would unwittingly view the video was therefore substantially reduced and so was the need to impose restrictions on its distribution".[66] The possibility of further restricting distribution of the video to licensed sex shops was mooted and it was also pointed out that the boxes containing the video cassettes would have included a description of its content.[67] The Court, however, responded by pointing out that once available, videos can be "copied, lent, rented, sold and viewed in different homes, thereby easily escaping any form of control by the authorities".[68] Thus, it found the consideration of the UK authorities that the film "could have reached a public to whom it would have caused offence" to be "not unreasonable" in the circumstances of the case.[69]

Specificity of Genre

A novel should ordinarily be "entitled to be judged by the criteria relevant to that genre including a considerable freedom of imaginative exploration".[70] The applicant argued in domestic proceedings that the impugned novel should have been analysed by literary specialists. This argument does not appear to have been pursued by the applicant before the European Court, which limited itself to acknowledging that the author's views were conveyed in a "novelistic style", without probing the matter any further. The joint dissenting opinion, likewise, failed to adequately pick up on the argument. In its case-law, the Court has consistently held that Article 10 "protects not only the substance of the ideas and information expressed, but also the form in which they are conveyed".[71] It is submitted here that in order to adequately protect the substance of ideas and

[65] *ibid*, Joint dissenting opinion of Judges Palm, Pekkanen and Makarczyk, para 9.
[66] *ibid*, para 62.
[67] *ibid*.
[68] *ibid*, para 63.
[69] *ibid*.
[70] B Parekh, *Rethinking Multiculturalism: Cultural Diversity and Political Theory* (Second Edition) (Palgrave Macmillan, New York, 2006), p 320. Parekh's supporting example relates specifically to Salman Rushdie's novel, *The Satanic Verses*, but it is nevertheless illustrative of a broader range of possibilities: he points out that "The offensive passages occur within the dream of a demented man, and hence not in the same category as unambiguous expressions of abuse and ridicule by the author", *ibid*.
[71] See, amongst other authorities, *De Haes & Gijsels v Belgium*, Judgment of the European Court of Human Rights of 24 February 1997, Reports of Judgments and Decisions 1997-I, para 48.

information expressed in a novel, the Court ought to give due consideration to stylistic and other specificities that are relevant to the genre. Indeed, this is the thrust of one of its main lines of reasoning in the aforementioned *Alinak* case.[72]

By selecting the passages in the book that were deemed to be the most offensive, isolating them and examining them out of context, the conclusion that they were unacceptably abusive was a foregone one. The same conclusion might very well have been reached if the passages had been examined in their original context (as intended by the author), but the conclusion would have been all the stronger for having been subjected to such an embedded analysis. As it stands, without the benefit of any insights that might have been generated by such an analysis, the Court's conclusion may be intuitively correct from a moral perspective, but it lacks methodological rigour.

Proportionality of Sanctions

The Court has frequently observed that "the nature and severity of the penalty imposed are factors to be taken into account when assessing the proportionality of the interference",[73] especially when the penalty in question risks creating a chilling effect on discussion of matters of public interest.

In the present case, the Court takes cognisance, first of all, of the fact that the domestic authorities did not seize the book. Puzzlingly, this seems tantamount to praising the Turkish authorities merely for abstaining from a course of action that is generally regarded as anathema to freedom of expression. As a measure effectively constituting prior restraint, the seizure of the impugned novel would rightly have been regarded as a very far-reaching infringement of the applicant's freedom of expression. However, in the stream of case-law currently under discussion, prior restraint has encountered considerably less resistance than in other types of Article 10 cases. In *Otto-Preminger*, neither the seizure nor the forfeiture of the film was found to amount to a violation of Article 10. However, the dissenting judges in that case did warn that "There is a danger that if applied to protect the perceived interests of a powerful group in society, such prior restraint could be detrimental to that tolerance on which pluralist democracy depends".[74] In *Wingrove*, the ban on the video was total, a fact which prompted the Court to acknowledge that the prior restraint involved in the case called for "special scrutiny".[75] In the heel of the hunt, the measure of "special scrutiny" required was arguably not forthcoming, as the Court professed its satisfaction at the "high threshold of profanation embodied in the definition of the offence of blasphemy under English

---

[72] *op. cit.*, paras 41-45.

[73] *Sürek v Turkey (No. 1)*, Judgment of the European Court of Human Rights of 8 July 1999, Reports of Judgments and Decisions, 1999-IV, para 64.

[74] *op. cit.*, Joint dissenting opinion, para 4.

[75] *ibid*, para 58, following its earlier findings in *Observer & Guardian v United Kingdom*, Judgment of the European Court of Human Rights of 26 November 1991, Series A, no 216, para 60. See also in this connection the dissenting opinions of Judges De Meyer and Lohmus in the *Wingrove* case.

law" and ceded a wide margin of appreciation to the national authorities in the matter.[76]

Secondly, the Court also takes cognisance of the [monetary] insignificance of the fine imposed. The joint dissenting opinion concedes that the fact that the prison sentence was commuted into a modest fine is significant, but the fears of the dissenting judges have not been completely allayed: "Freedom of the press relates to matters of principle, and any criminal conviction has what is known as a 'chilling effect' liable to discourage publishers from producing books that are not strictly conformist or 'politically (or religiously) correct'".[77]

Generally speaking, the Court's approach to the dissuasive impact of a criminal sanction tends to vary according to the circumstances of the case.[78] The least that could be said about the Court's handling of the issue in the present case is that it should have been less perfunctory.

Conclusion

It is most unlikely that the Court will formally take the bold step of severing its own doctrinal chain, as it was urged to do by the dissenting judges in the *İ.A.* case. But perhaps such a radical step, with all the political and face-losing consequences it would likely entail, is not entirely necessary in order to reshape relevant case-law in its future judgments. To the extent that the principle of *stare decisis* "creates a chain of cases, in which each decision is an interpretation of immediately prior decisions", it offers the flexibility of distinguishing between the application of relevant principles in previous and new sets of circumstances.[79] As has been argued throughout this note, the relevant principles are — by and large — sound; it is the application of those principles that has been a source of disappointment. As the principles are not objectionable, there is no pressing need to repudiate them; rather, the focus should be on ensuring that whenever the Court applies relevant principles in the future, it does so in a way that distinguishes unsatisfactory precedents set by the mis application of principles in its earlier case-law. The recent case of *Giniewski* provides useful relevant examples of how this can be done: it distinguishes, *inter alia*, certain contextualising elements of the *Otto-Preminger* and *İ.A.* cases, from the circumstances with which it was faced.[80] A recurrent problem in the relevant case-law of the Court is the inadequate attention it has tended to give to contextualising factors when assessing whether impugned practices measure up to its principles. Contextualising factors can often have a relativising (or occasionally, even a transformative) impact on the interpretation of the bare facts of a case, and the Court

---

[76] *ibid*, para 61.

[77] Joint dissenting opinion, *İ.A. v Turkey* , *op. cit*., para 6.

[78] Contrast, for example, *Sürek v Turkey (No. 1)*, *op. cit.*, paras 63 and 64 and *Chauvy & Others v France*, Judgment of the European Court of Human Rights (Second Section) of 29 June 2004, para 78, with *Jersild v Denmark*, *op. cit*., para 35 and *Giniewski v France*, *op. cit*., para 55.

[79] R Post, "Theories of Constitutional Interpretation", in R Post, Ed., *Law and the Order of Culture* (California, University of California Press, 1991), pp 13–41, at 20.

[80] *op. cit.*, para 52.

should pay increased attention to the importance of contextualising factors in the future.

The foregoing section details specific examples of contextualising factors that have been under-explored in the relevant case-law of the Court. Finally — to round off the foregoing critical dissection with further critical distillation — another lingering problem with *Otto-Preminger* and its jurisprudential progeny must be addressed, or at least flagged for more thorough discussion at a later stage. The problem concerns the lax and seemingly unquestioning manner in which the Court has tended to apply the margin of appreciation doctrine in relevant cases.

It cannot be gainsaid that religious affairs have an immense inherent capacity for contentiousness. It is also generally true that States authorities are in the best position to take the measure of local religious sensitivities (but whether they can be trusted to do so fairly and objectively is another matter entirely). Nevertheless, the margin of appreciation doctrine must not be allowed to become a smoke screen behind which States and the European Court can hide, instead of facing up to complex, divisive issues. In all of the cases analysed *in detail* in this note, the Court has readily endorsed States authorities' justifications of measures restricting the right to freedom of expression. Those justifications have often included the preservation of religious peace and harmony and the avoidance of societal divisions — even when those goals do not seem to be particularly threatened by the impugned expression.[81] The outcome, in each case, has been in favour of majoritarian or orthodox or conventional religious beliefs. Quite simply, as David Richards has pointed out, "the measure of constitutional protection for conscientiously dissenting speech could not be the dominant orthodoxy that it challenged, for that would trivialize the protection of free speech to whatever massaged the prejudices of dominant majorities."[82] Greater critical engagement with the particular circumstances of individual cases is required in order to ensure that the Court's judgments in this area are realistic and convincing.

Context may not be everything (although an old platitude of literary criticism tells us otherwise), but if the European Court of Human Rights continues to ignore the importance of contextualising factors in its jurisprudence, it will surely do so at its peril.

---

[81] For example, it seems both implausible and incongruous that the broadcasting of an informative, inoffensive advertisement for a particular minority religious group would lead to "unrest" in contemporary Ireland. That argument, however, factored into the Court's reasoning in the *Murphy* case: see: *Murphy v Ireland, op. cit.*, paras 73 *et seq.*

[82] DAJ Richards, *Free Speech and the Politics of Identity* (Oxford University Press, Inc., New York, 1999), p 197.

Dublin City Council v Fennell: A Stay of Execution for Section 62 of the Housing Act 1966

Siobhan Phelan*

In May 2005, the Supreme Court gave judgement in the case of *Dublin City Council v Fennell*.[1] The case has a two-fold significance: it was the first real engagement by the Supreme Court with the implications of the European Convention on Human Rights Act 2003 in this jurisdiction and it was also the first time that the Irish Human Rights Commission exercised its power to seek to be joined as *amicus curiae* in a case.

The case came before the Supreme Court by way of consultative case stated from the Circuit Court pursuant to s 16 of the Courts of Justice Act 1947. It arose in the context of an appeal to the Circuit Court from a decision of the District Court pursuant to s 62 of the Housing Act 1966. Section 62 of the Housing Act 1966 provides for a summary procedure whereby a local housing authority can seek to recover possession of a local authority tenancy. Given that this procedure withstood constitutional challenge in the case of *O'Rourke v Kelly*[2] and more recently in the case of *McConnell v Dublin City Council & Ors.*[3] (which was appealed but dismissed without a determination of the substantive issue), the *Fennell* case was nicely poised to demonstrate the potential impact of the ECHR Act 2003 in domestic proceedings involving the exercise of public powers.

The Circuit Court was mindful of the fact, however, that in *Fennell* a warrant for possession was issued by the District Court before the commencement of the Act on the 31 December 2003 and, accordingly, an issue arose as to whether the ECHR Act could be applied in proceedings pending before the Circuit Court or whether arguments based on that Act should fail by reason of non-retrospectivity. Accordingly, the central and rather narrow but significant issue for the Supreme Court was whether the 2003 Act had application to proceedings issued prior to the commencement of the Act. It was only in the event that this question was answered in the affirmative that the Court would then have been required to consider the implications of the Act for proceedings issued pursuant to s 62 of the Housing Act, 1966.

The 1966 Act and Jurisprudence in Relation to Section 62

In its judgment, the Supreme Court set out the statutory position of the housing authority and rehearsed the relevant case law. The Court identified the provision

---

* Barrister-at-Law.

[1] [2005] IESC 33.

[2] [1983] IR 58.

[3] Unreported judgement of Smyth J, delivered on 18 January 2005.

of housing for those of limited means, or those who through disability are unable to provide accommodation for themselves as the primary function and duty placed by statute on housing authorities. As part of the machinery to enable housing authorities to carry out its functions, they have been given the means to recover possession of dwellings provided under the Housing Acts through a special procedure for summary re-possession set out in s 62 of the Housing Act 1966, as amended by s 13 of the Housing Act 1970.

In summary, s 62 provides a simplified method whereby a housing authority can recover possession of a dwelling the subject matter of a tenancy. There is no requirement for cause to be shown before the housing authority can recover possession of a dwelling, nor is there any provision in the legislation for the sort of hearing before a court which normally arises on the termination of a private letting agreement. Once certain minimal formal proofs are in order (i.e. that the Notice to Quit has been duly served and that the tenant has failed to deliver up possession), neither the District Judge nor the Circuit Judge on appeal has any discretion in relation to the eviction but must issue the warrant without inquiring into other matters such as, *inter alia,* the reason for the eviction, the impact on the family of the eviction, whether any other steps could be taken to address the concerns of the housing authority short of eviction or whether eviction was necessary having regard to changed behaviour since the service of a Notice to Quit.

In reviewing the jurisprudence in the area, the Supreme Court considered in particular the judgements in the *State (O'Rourke) v Kelly* and *Dublin Corporation v Hamilton.*[4] In *O'Rourke,* the constitutionality of s 62 of the Housing Act, 1966, was challenged on the ground that it constituted an unwarranted interference in the judicial domain in that it imposed on the District Judge a mandatory obligation to issue the warrant thereby depriving the District Judge of any real judicial discretion. This case did not consider whether there was a failure to vindicate the personal and family rights of the tenant and the precedent value of the case is limited for this reason.[5] *O'Rourke* is not binding authority for the proposition that section 62 is constitutionally safe in that arguments under Articles 40, 41 and 43 of the Irish Constitution 1937 were never canvassed nor addressed by the courts in that case.

The *Hamilton case* did not involve a constitutional challenge to s 62 but rather posited an interpretation of s 62 which was in line with the requirements of constitutional justice. In the *Hamilton case,* counsel on behalf of the tenant had

---

[4] [1999] 2 IR 486.

[5] See for example, the decision of the Supreme Court in *Laurentiu v Minister for Justice* [1999] 4 IR 26 where the Supreme Court held that part of s 5 of the Aliens Act, 1935 was unconstitutional even though its validity had previously been upheld on different grounds. The Supreme Court upheld the decision of the High Court to the effect that it was not bound by the earlier Supreme Court authority so far as the statute was had been challenged on different grounds. See further in this regard the comments of Gerard Hogan in "Some thoughts on the Relationship between the ECHR Act 2003 and the Constitution in the light of *Dublin City Council v. Fenne*ll and *Carmody v Minister for Justice, Equality and Law Reform*", a paper delivered to a Continuing Professional Development Conference on the 3 December 2005.

advanced the argument that the word "duly" which appears in s 62(3) brings into play not just formal proofs but the entire question of whether the plaintiff is carrying out its statutory obligations of housing towards the defendant both in a substantive sense and in the sense of affording the defendant fair procedures, which might well connote a hearing on the merits in certain circumstances. In making this argument, Counsel for the defendant in that case relied on the general tendency of the courts to ensure that statutory obligations be fairly and constitutionally complied with. Thus it was suggested that a tenant is entitled to know the reason for the plaintiff's desire to recover possession and that a District Judge should concern himself with whether the housing authority in ejecting the defendant was then in breach of its own housing obligations towards the defendant, so that if there was a breach of that obligation, particularly in the context of no provision of reasonable alternative accommodation, the application for the warrant could not be said to be "duly" made. The Supreme Court in *Fennell* set out in full the views of Geoghegan J in *Hamilton* rejecting these arguments wherein he stated:

> "... it would seem to me to be both reasonable and constitutional that there be available to a housing authority a rapid method of recovering possession of any one dwelling provided by it without having to give reasons for so doing. The local authority has to consider its overall management of housing and it owes an obligation to all the persons in need of housing as well as to any one individual. In that context, it is and ought to be entitled to plan its arrangements for providing housing and furthermore there may be very good reasons why confidentiality should be maintained in relation to any particular decision to recover possession of a dwelling provided by the housing authority even though the person, the subject matter of the warrant, may then become a person in need of housing. In that case obviously the obligation will then be on the housing authority to provide alternative accommodation as best it can. I also, of course, agree with counsel for the defendant that a housing authority must carry out its obligations in a proper manner and must not abuse its powers or discretion but if it does so, it would be subject to the remedy of judicial review. It is not a matter for the District Judge to consider in a hearing under s 62 of the Act of 1966. It has been argued that judicial review is a cumbersome and expensive procedure and that the ordinary person in need of housing might not even know of its existence but I do not think that that is any reason for importing into s 62 requirements which were never intended to be there".[6]

In reaching his conclusion in the *Hamilton case*, Geoghegan J determined that it would be:

> "inconsistent with the purpose of the section to interpret it in any other way than that formal proofs that the matters set out in this section alone are required and that the District Judge is not entitled to inquire into anything else. If there are wider complaints, there is another forum for dealing with them."[7]

[6] At pp 493-4.
[7] At p 494.

The Decision of the Supreme Court in *Fennell*

The thrust of the case presented on behalf of Ms Fennell in the Supreme Court was that the *relevant decision* and the *substance* of this case were to be found in the prospective decision of the Dublin Circuit Court and the removal of the appellant from her dwelling pursuant to an Order of the Circuit Court as this is the decision which would deprive the appellant of her "home" and, that being so, no true retrospectivity issue arose in the proceedings. The Irish Human Rights Commission further argued in its *amicus* intervention that s 2(2) of the ECHR Act 2003 built retrospectivity into the Act by requiring that existing legislation also be subjected to the obligation imposed on a court by s 2(1) to interpret laws in a manner that was compatible with the Convention in so far as is possible and subject to any other rule of interpretation.

The Supreme Court disagreed, however, concluding that where the proceedings were not merely pending but had proceeded to final determination in one court and a Notice of Appeal had been lodged to another court prior to the coming into operation of the new statute, the parties' legal rights and obligations were fixed and determined once the wheel was set in motion by the service of a Notice to Quit, an act which triggered the provisions, requirements and consequences of s 2 of the Housing Act, 1966. The Supreme Court ruled that this is the moment when the invocation of legal rights determined the applicable law and the position of the parties. The Supreme Court was persuaded by the arguments of Dublin City Council to the effect that the Circuit Court proceedings, although consisting of a *de novo* hearing where points not raised in the court below could still be now argued, did not exist in a vacuum. They existed only because there had already been a determination of legal rights and obligations by reference to defined legal criteria in the court below —in this case, the District Court. The Supreme Court considered that the Circuit Court was performing an appellate function only and, no more than the District Court, it had no other function than to determine whether the statutory requirements of proof under s 62 were complied with and, if so, to confirm the warrant of the District Court. It was the view of the Supreme Court that it would be a bizarre outcome if the first hearing was conducted by one set of legal rules and the appeal hearing by another.

The Court concluded that the concept of fairness, properly understood, would be severely compromised if the statute was retroactive as a housing authority which had *bona fide* exercised its statutory powers to manage its housing stock by reference to certain and defined criteria could thereby find its management policy for the letting of dwellings turned upside down and rendered inoperative. The Supreme Court held that the ECHR Act had no retrospective effect, in part at least because such a construction of that Act would not have been consistent with Article 15.5.1 of the Constitution.

Interestingly, subsequent jurisprudence from the English Court of Appeal suggests that the English courts could be persuaded of a different outcome were this same question of the application of the Convention to pending proceedings before the Courts (notwithstanding that the events which triggered the proceedings predated the Act giving force of law to the Convention) to come before them. This is evidenced by the decision of the Court of Appeal in

Commissioner of Police v Hurst.[8] The UK Court of Appeal confirmed that s 3 of the UK Human Rights Act 1998 (the equivalent but not identical provision to s 2 of the Irish ECHR Act 2003) is of wide application and capable of having retrospective effect even where there would be no retrospective effect under s 6 and s 7 (namely, those sections of the 1998 Act which provide for a cause of action and a remedy for breach of Convention rights). The Court ruled that the application of s 3 of the Human Rights Act 1998 is completely different to a claim under s 6 as s 3 requires the court to have regard to international obligations in reading and giving effect to legislation. Those international obligations pre-date the Human Rights Act 1998 and are not affected in any way by the terms of that Act. The Court recognised a distinction between rights created by the Human Rights Act 1998 and rights pre-existing in international law to conclude that the date of implementation of the Human Rights Act could not be dispositive in determining whether the obligations of the State in international law are potentially available to be taken into account in interpreting legislation that bears on those obligations.

Epilogue

Although the Irish courts, prior to *Fennell,* consistently rejected constitutional challenges to s 62, Kearns J, in delivering judgment for the Supreme Court in that case, acknowledged that the summary method whereby possession of such dwellings may be recovered, notably in circumstances where the tenant is regarded as having through misbehaviour brought about the termination of his own tenancy and thus forfeited the right to any alternative accommodation, may infringe certain articles of the European Convention on Human Rights, and in particular, Articles 6, 8 and 13 thereof, and also Article 1 of Protocol 1 (Protection of Property) of the Convention. Despite this clear suggestion from the Court that section 62 may fall foul of the requirements of the Convention, the Supreme Court in *Fennell* does not acknowledge the fact that the constitutionality of the section has yet to be finally established and no reference whatsoever is made to the requirements of the Constitution which provide for broadly equivalent protections to those identified by Kearns J under the Convention, namely the protections provided under Articles 40, 41 and 43 of the Constitution.

Eventually the High Court granted declarations of incompatibility under Section 5 of the ECHR Act in two subsequent cases involving s 62 — *Donegan v Dublin City Council*[9] and *Gallagher v Dublin City Council.*[10] Notably, in *Gallagher,* the learned trial judge identified clear analogies between the right to constitutional fair procedures and procedural rights protected under Articles 6 and 8 of the Convention before granting a declaration of incompatibility. The issue in *Gallagher* came before the

[8] [2005] EWCA Civ. 890 (judgment of the Court handed down on the 21 July 2005, over two months after the Supreme Court decision in *Dublin City Council v Fennell* where reliance was placed on the decision of the House of Lords in *In Re McKerr* [2004] 1 WLR 807 which case has since been distinguished in the *Hurst* case.

[9] [2008] IEHC 288. The declaration of incompatibility was in respect of Art 8 ECHR.

[10] (2008) Unreported, High Court, 11 November 2008. The declaration of incompatibility was in respect of Art 6 ECHR.

Court by way of consultative case stated and the learned trial judge did not address whether an alternative remedy under the Constitution could be availed of by the tenant. In a further challenge to the exercise of a power to seek summary eviction under s 62, damages were awarded pursuant to s 3 of the ECHR Act in *Pullen v Dublin City Council.*[11]

It is understood that these three cases are under appeal to the Supreme Court and the Irish Human Rights Commission, which intervened as *amicus curiae* in the *Pullen* case, has called on the Government to amend s 62 to take account of the findings in these cases.

[11][2009] IEHC 452. Ms Justice Irvine found that the local authority had not acted compatibly with Arts 8 and 6(1) ECHR. She found that there was an alternative legal mechanism open to the local authority under s 14 of the Conveyancing Acts 1881 by which it could seek to evict the plaintiffs while giving them a full opportunity to challenge the reasons for eviction in a court hearing.

Torture and Diplomatic Assurances: *Agiza v Sweden*[*]

Siobhán Cummiskey[**]

Background of the Case

This case concerns the prohibition on *non-refoulement* and the use of diplomatic assurances. The prohibition on torture has risen to the level of a peremptory norm of international law and the principle of non-refoulement is thought to share in this characterisation. The former UN Special Rapporteur on Torture has confirmed the *jus cogens* character of *non-refoulement* in stating in a Report to the General Assembly in 2004 that it is: "an inherent part of the overall and absolute nature of the prohibition on torture". Moreover, the Committee Against Torture itself, in the case of *Tapia Paez v Sweden*,[1] stated that the test of Article 3 (*non-refoulement*) is absolute and that the activities of the person concerned cannot be a material consideration.

The question is then raised as to whether diplomatic assurances will suffice to guard against the breach of this right and, moreover, whether states have discharged their obligation to protect against torture under the principle of *non-refoulement* in their use of such assurances. The current UN Special Rapporteur on Torture, Manfred Nowak, has been categorical in his rejection of such assurances as an adequate form of protection since its use became widespread in late 2005: "diplomatic assurances are unreliable and ineffective in the protection against torture and ill-treatment and such assurances are sought usually from States where the practice of torture is systematic".[2]

The European Court of Human Rights has addressed the issue of State Parties' reliance on diplomatic assurances as a safeguard against violations of States' obligations under Article 3 (prohibition against torture) of the European Convention on Human Rights. In *Chahal v United Kingdom*[3], the court ruled that the return to India of a Sikh activist would violate the obligations of the UK under Article 3, despite the fact that the State had secured diplomatic assurances from the Indian government that Chahal would not suffer mistreatment stating that:

> "Although the Court does not doubt the good faith of the Indian Government in providing the assurances mentioned above, it would appear that, despite the

[*] (Decision of the Committee Against Torture) Judgment of 20 May 2005 (Appl. No. 233/2003).

[**] LL.B., LL.M., Attorney-at-Law, Solicitor with the Irish Traveller Movement Independent Law Centre.

[1] Communication No.39/1996, 28 April 1997.

[2] GA/SHC/3830 Sixtieth General Assembly Third Committee 24 and 25 Meetings (AM and PM).

[3] 1996 [ECHR] 54.

> efforts of that Government, the NHRC and the Indian courts to bring about reform, the violation of human rights by certain members of the security forces in Punjab and elsewhere in India is a recalcitrant and enduring problem. ... Against this background, the Court is not persuaded that the above assurances would provide Mr. Chahal with an adequate guarantee of safety."[4]

The *Chahal* ruling is widely cited as an authoritative restatement by the court of the absolute nature of the prohibition against torture under the European Convention on Human Rights. Moreover, it establishes that diplomatic assurances are an inadequate guarantee where torture is "endemic," or a "recalcitrant and enduring problem" that results, in some cases, in fatalities.

By way of contrast, in the case of *Aylor-Davis v France*,[5] the European Court of Human Rights held that guarantees from the receiving country, the United States, were found to eliminate the risk of the applicant being sentenced to death. However, the use of diplomatic assurances in this context is more amenable to review and carries an internal safeguard: the death penalty could only be imposed if it was actually sought by the State prosecutor.

The decision of the Grand Chamber of the European Court on Human Rights, on 4 February 2005, in the case of *Mamatkulov v Turkey*[6] is also instructive. This case concerned the applicants' extradition in March 1999 to Uzbekistan under a bilateral treaty with Turkey. The assurances stated that Uzbekistan was a party to the Convention Against Torture and in the assurance the State reaffirmed its obligation to comply with the requirements of the provisions of the Convention "as regards both Turkey and the international community as a whole". Officials from the Turkish embassy visited the applicants in their respective places of detention. They did not complain about their prison conditions. Turkey also invoked medical certificates drawn up by military doctors in the prisons and the applicants were reportedly in good health. The European Court assessed the existence of the risk primarily with reference to those facts that were known or ought to have been known to the State party at the time of the extradition. Information coming to light subsequent to the extradition potentially being of value in confirming or refuting the appreciation that had been made by the State party of the well-foundedness or otherwise of a complainant's fears. The Court concluded that it had to assess Turkey's responsibility under Article 3 by reference to the situation that obtained on the date of the applicants' extradition. On the facts and against the background of the assurances obtained by Turkey and the medical reports from the doctors in the Uzbek prisons in which the applicants were held, the Court found that it was not able to conclude that substantial grounds existed at the relevant date for believing that the applicants faced a real risk of treatment proscribed by Article 3 of the European Convention.

---

[4] Paragraph 105.

[5] App. no. 22742/93 of 20 January 1994.

[6] [2005] ECHR 64.

The use of diplomatic assurances in respect of *non-refoulement* has become widespread in recent years. The irony of its use is apparent in the fact that a State party must be aware of the risk of torture and as a result seek to obtain a guarantee that the human rights of those expelled would be respected. Such assurances are typically vague in nature and reliant on the good faith of the State in question. Considering the focus human rights place on the individual, it is contradictory in the extreme to use State-to-State diplomacy as a means of ensuring these rights.

Facts of the Case

The applicant, Mr Ahmed Hussein Mustafa Kamil Agiza, was detained in Egypt at the time of submission of the complaint. Ahmed Agiza and Mohammed al-Zari (Al-Zari has lodged an application with the European Court of Human Rights), both Egyptian nationals, sought asylum in Sweden in 2000. Their asylum applications were rejected, despite acknowledgement by the Swedish authorities that both men had a well-founded fear of persecution. In the days before their expulsion, Sweden secured diplomatic assurances from the Egyptian government that the men would not be subjected to torture or ill-treatment upon return, and that they would not be sentenced to death. Assurances were also given that the men would be afforded fair trials in Egypt, including a re-trial for Agiza, who had been tried and convicted *in absentia* by an Egyptian military court in April 1999. The Swedish government arranged access to monitor the trials and to visit the men in prison. However, these arrangements were not included in the assurance.

Agiza claimed that his removal by Sweden to Egypt on 18 December 2001 violated Article 3 of the Convention Against Torture.[7] The issues raised by the applicant were the removal of the applicant from Sweden by the government without review and *non-refoulement* under Article 3. The latter complaint led to the consideration by the Committee of the status of diplomatic assurances in cases of *non-refoulement*.

In 1982, the complainant was arrested on account of his family connection to his cousin, who had been arrested for suspected involvement in the assassination of the former Egyptian President, Anwar Sadat. Before his release in March 1983, he was allegedly subjected to torture. In 1998, the complainant was tried in Egypt for terrorist activity directed against the State before a "Superior Court Martial" *in absentia*, along with over one hundred other accused. He was found guilty of belonging to a terrorist group and was sentenced, without possibility of appeal, to twenty-five years' imprisonment. In 2000, concerned that improving relations between Egypt and Iran would result in his being returned to Egypt, the complainant and his family bought air tickets, under Saudi Arabian identities, to Canada. The applicant and his family claimed asylum during a transit stop in Stockholm, Sweden, on 23 September 2000.

[7] Article 3: 1. No State Party shall expel, return ("refouler") or extradite a person to another State where there are substantial grounds for believing that he would be in danger of being subjected to torture. 2. For the purpose of determining whether there are such grounds, the competent authorities shall take into account all relevant considerations including, where applicable, the existence in the State concerned of a consistent pattern of gross, flagrant or mass violations of human rights.

On 30 October 2001, the Security Police advised the Migration Board that the complainant held a leading position in an organisation guilty of terrorist acts and was responsible for the activities of the organisation (in a statement, the complainant denied belonging to the organisation referred to in the Security Police statement, arguing that one of the designated organisations was not a political organisation but an Arab-language publication). The Migration Board thus forwarded the complainant's case, on 12 November 2001, to the Government for a strength of the decision under chapter 7, s 11(2)(2), of the Aliens Act.[8]

The Swedish government concluded it was "both possible and meaningful" to obtain guarantees or diplomatic assurances in respect of the treatment of the applicant and his family in accordance with international law upon return to Egypt. On 13 December 2002, the requisite guarantees were provided. On 18 December 2001, the Government rejected the asylum applications of the complainant and of his wife, the applicant was immediately removed and his wife went into hiding. The reasons for these decisions were omitted from the text of the decision of the Committee Against Torture at the State Party's request and with the agreement of the Committee. The applicant's attorney was issued with a removal order the day after the applicant was expelled from Sweden.

Upon his return to Egypt, the applicant was imprisoned in Masra Torah prison in Cairo. The issue of torture is in dispute in this case. The applicant's parents stated that he appeared to have been beaten and he allegedly told his mother of several incidences of torture both aboard the US airplane that returned him to Egypt and in the Cairo prison. The Swedish Ambassador and other diplomats visited the complainant on a number of occasions to ensure his welfare and they stated in several reports that his health was good and that they never saw any signs of torture.

Judgment of the Committee Against Torture

The Committee found the State Party to be in breach of Articles 3 and 22 of the Convention. Among the issues before the Committee was whether removal of the complainant to Egypt violated the State party's obligation under Article 3 of the Convention (*non-refoulement*). The Committee acknowledged that measures taken to fight terrorism deriving from binding Security Council Resolutions are both legitimate and important. Their execution, however, must be carried out with full respect to the applicable rules of international law, including the provisions of the Convention, the right to freedom from torture being absolute. According to the Committee, the test for substantial grounds for the belief that a person may be subjected to torture upon their return "must be decided in the light of the information that was known, or ought to have been known, to the State party's

[8] In the Board's view, on the information before it, the complainant could be considered entitled to claim refugee status; however, the Security Police's assessment, which the Board saw no reason to question, pointed in a different direction. The balancing of the complainant's possible need for protection against the Security Police's assessment, thus had to be made by the Government.

authorities *at the time* of the removal. Subsequent events are relevant to the assessment of the State party's knowledge, actual or constructive, at the time of removal."[9] Therefore the relevant time of assessment of the state party's notice of a risk of torture is the day of extradition. This reasoning is in line with that of the European Court of Human Rights on this issue.

The Committee must also evaluate whether there were substantial grounds for believing that the complainant would be "personally in danger of being subjected to torture upon return".[10] The existence of a consistent pattern of gross, flagrant or mass violations of human rights in a country does not as such constitute a sufficient ground for determining that a particular person was in danger neither does its absence mean the applicant is not in danger. The Committee considered at the outset that it was known, or should have been known, to the Swedish authorities at the time of the complainant's removal that Egypt resorted to consistent and widespread use of torture against detainees, and that the risk of such treatment was particularly high in the case of detainees held for political and security reasons. The State party was also aware of the interest in the complainant by the intelligence services of two other States: according to the facts submitted by the State party to the Committee, the first foreign State (the United States), offered through its intelligence service an aircraft to transport the complainant to the second State, Egypt, where to the State party's knowledge, he had been sentenced *in absentia* and was wanted for alleged involvement in terrorist activities. In the Committee's view, the natural conclusion from these combined elements is that the complainant was at a real risk of torture in Egypt in the event of expulsion.

With regard to the diplomatic assurance, the Committee affirmed: "the procurement of diplomatic assurances, which, moreover, provided no mechanism for their enforcement, did not suffice to protect against this manifest risk [of torture]".[11] Further, the Committee stated that the breach by Egypt of the element of the assurances relating to guarantee of a fair trial, goes to the weight that can be attached to the assurances as a whole.[12] The Committee in adopting this reasoning was following the approach of the European Court of Human Rights in *Mamatkulov et al. v Turkey.*[13] The actions of the receiving State after removal is indicative of the weight that may be attached to the veracity of the removing State's assessment of the risk of torture. The Separate Opinion of Committee Member Mr Alexander Yakovlev was dissenting, in part. Yakovlev states that the former Special Rapporteur of the Commission on Human Rights on Torture accepted in his 2002 report to the Commission that the use of such assurances in certain circumstances, urging States to procure "an unequivocal guarantee ... that the persons concerned will not be subjected to torture or any other forms of ill-treatment upon return".

[9] Paragraph 13.2 (Emphasis added).
[10] Paragraph 13.3.
[11] Paragraph 13.4.
[12] Paragraph 13.5.
[13] [2005] ECHR 64.

Yakovlev simply states that "[t]his, which is precisely what the State party did, is now faulted by the Committee".[14]

The Committee also undertook a procedural assessment of the case. The exercise of the right of complaint under Article 22 of the Convention must be meaningful rather than illusory, according to the Committee. In the present case, the Committee observed that the complainant was arrested and removed by the State party immediately upon the Government's decision of expulsion being taken. In fact, the formal notice of decision was only served upon the complainant's counsel the following day. As a result, it was impossible for the complainant to consider the possibility of invoking Article 22 and bringing a complaint forward to the Committee. It follows that the State party committed a breach of its obligations under Article 22 of the Convention by neither disclosing to the Committee relevant information, nor presenting its concerns to the Committee for an appropriate procedural decision prior to expulsion.

Comments

Diplomatic assurances are very useful tools in the domain of international relations and have been used consistently as a courtesy between States. However, they are inadequate and unsafe in the context of *non-refoulement* for four main reasons.

Firstly, diplomatic assurances are by nature vague and couched in non-confrontational and "friendly" terms. This is out of line with human rights law, which imposes obligations on States in clear and certain terms with mechanisms for complaint and redress. It is therefore difficult to reconcile diplomatic assurances with the obligations of States under international human rights law in this context. Moreover, without certainty of terms, it is often difficult if not impossible to state with confidence that an assurance has been breached.

Secondly, these assurances are difficult to monitor. It is rare that such assurances incorporate a follow-up procedure to ensure enforcement. In fact, diplomatic assurances by their very nature imply that no such procedure is necessary. Furthermore, even if a breach could be proven, such assurances lack the character of a legal instrument and are inherently unenforceable as a result.

Thirdly, owing to their diplomatic nature, there is also an issue of transparency. Many States refuse to disclose the details of a diplomatic assurance by reason of a long-standing international practice of confidentiality relating to assurances. This re-establishes the inappropriate nature of diplomatic assurances in relation to the right to freedom from torture, in that it fails to follow one of the basic tenets of human rights: accountability.

Fourthly, there is an irony in seeking such assurances in the context of torture in that it seems to justify the evil it seeks to prevent. In relying on their assurance not to

[14] Para 1 of the text of a separate opinion, dissenting in part, by Committee member Mr Alexander Yakovlev, appended to the decision.

torture one person, the State essentially accepts that State's use of torture against others. Not alone this, but it acknowledges the widespread use of torture and accepts its use against those who fall outside of the assurance. This in itself undermines the universal nature of human rights and is contrary to the norms espoused in the Convention Against Torture and Other Cruel, Inhuman or Degrading Treatment or Punishment.

For counsel for the applicant, the key issue was not whether a guarantee was given by a government official, but rather whether it can be implemented and, if so, how. Counsel indicated that the guarantee in question was obtained at short notice, vague in its terms and provided no details on how the guarantees would be given effect with respect to the complainant; nor did the Swedish authorities request any such information. The arrangement for monitoring was considered ineffective, with particular reference to the fact that the first visit took place over a month after the complainant's removal. According to counsel, this appeared to be an ad hoc reaction rather than part of a properly conceived monitoring plan. Counsel observed that the standard routines in such cases applied by organisations such as the International Committee of the Red Cross had not been met and submitted that if the Committee were to accept guarantees such as those offered in the present case as sufficient protection against torture:

> "At least in circumstances where there was a limited will and capability on the part of the removing state appropriately to monitor the consequences, the results could readily be wide scope for authorities of the receiving state to engage in and conceal torture and ill-treatment."[15]

The Partly Dissenting judgment of Yakovlev adduces cogent arguments with regard to the statements of the former Special Rapporteur of the Commission on Human Rights, Mr Van Boven. Mr Van Boven accepted in his 2002 report to the Commission on Human Rights the use of such assurances in certain circumstances, urging States to procure "an unequivocal guarantee ... that the persons concerned will not be subjected to torture or any other forms of ill-treatment upon return". The weakness of such a dissent is that it neglects to see the jurisprudence of the Committee as ever-evolving in line with international standards. Furthermore, the current Special Rapporteuron torture and other cruel, inhuman or degrading treatment or punishment, Professor Manfred Nowak has implicitly over-ruled this opinion.

In conclusion, the Committee appears to adopt a test to determine whether the State has substantial grounds for believing a person may be subjected to torture upon return (Article 3). This test consists of actual and constructive notice "at the time of removal", with subsequent events in this assessment of notice being "relevant" only. With regard to diplomatic assurances, the Committee confirmed that the use of diplomatic assurances did not suffice to protect against the risk of torture. However, the Committee stopped short of saying that the procurement of such an assurance itself constituted constructive notice of the risk of torture at the time of removal, a statement that has the potential to turn this contradictory practice on its head.

---

[15] Paragraph 5.4.

Damages for Defamation: *Independent News and Media and Independent Newspapers Ireland Limited v Ireland*

Senator Alex White*

The passing of the Defamation Act 2009 has raised once again for public debate the balance which ought to be struck between the constitutional rights to freedom of expression, and the right to one's good name. A number of significant and arguably long overdue reforms are introduced by the Act, including the introduction of a defence of "fair and reasonable publication on a matter of public importance". It also introduces new remedies for defamation, including declaratory orders by the High Court, and correction orders, whereby a court may direct a defendant to publish a correction of a defamatory statement. These new sanctions seem likely to shift the focus away from damages as the sole remedy hitherto available to an aggrieved individual, in the context of defamation.

While much of the debate on these issues has been confined to lawyers, academics and the media, the level of damages in defamation actions is one aspect which has attracted wider public interest and debate. The media, as may be expected, have agitated for some form of control over the size of compensation awards, claiming that high awards lead to a chilling effect on true freedom of expression. Nevertheless there has been a marked reluctance on the part of politicians to address this issue, at least until now.

The level of compensation awards in defamation actions, and specifically the question of whether juries ought to be given guidance as to the level of such awards, has exercised the European Court of Human Rights (ECtHR) on more than one occasion in recent years. The case of *Independent News and Media and Independent Newspapers Ireland Limited v Ireland*[1] arose from a successful action brought by Proinsias de Rossa against the applicants, who are the publishers of the *Sunday Independent* and other titles in Ireland. The issue which arose for consideration by the ECtHR was whether there was a breach by Ireland of Article 10 of the European Convention on Human Rights in view of the unusually high award of damages in the case (IR£300,00), and the absence, as claimed by the applicants, of "adequate safeguards" against disproportionate awards in Irish law.

The Supreme Court, by a majority, upheld the High Court jury's award in *de Rossa v Independent Newspapers*.[2] Many commentators thought that this judgment would

---

* Barrister-at-Law.

[1] Application no. 55120/00; judgment 16 June 2005.

[2] [1999] 4 IR 432.

not survive scrutiny by the ECtHR, especially in the light of that court's judgment in *Tolstoy Miloslavsky v United Kingdom.*[3] However, in the event the applicants' claim was rejected. Indeed, the judgment in *Independent News* is clear authority for the proposition that where a contracting State has in place adequate safeguards against disproportionate awards (as the ECtHR found was the case in Ireland), there is no breach of Article 10 of the European Convention on Human Rights, which provides *inter alia* as follows:

> "1. Everyone has the right to freedom of expression. This right shall include freedom to hold opinions and to receive and impart information and ideas without interference by public authority...
>
> 2. The exercise of these freedoms, since it carries with it duties and responsibilities, may be subject to such formalities, conditions, restrictions or penalties as are prescribed by law and are necessary in a democratic society..."

de Rossa v Independent Newspapers (High Court)

Proinsias de Rossa, now a Member of the European Parliament was, at the time of the publication of the newspaper article concerned, a TD and leader of the political party, *Democratic Left*. In its summation of the facts and circumstances of the case, the ECtHR referred to the December 1992 *Sunday Independent* article entitled, "Throwing good money at jobs is dishonest", which contained a reference to a recently discovered letter dating from September 1986 addressed to the Central Committee of the Communist Party of the Soviet Union, and co-signed by Mr de Rossa. The court noted that this letter:

> "...referred to 'special activities' that had previously met shortfalls in the funding of the Worker's Party, a political party of which Mr de Rossa had been leader. At the time of publication, Mr de Rossa was leader of another political party (the Democratic Left), he was a member of parliament and he was engaged in post-election negotiations about his party's participation in government".

The article went on to characterise the "special activities" as criminal in nature, and as including "armed robberies and forgery of currency". It continued:

> "The people engaged in this business occupied that twilight world where the line blurs between those who are common criminals and others of that ilk who would claim to be engaged in criminal activity.
>
> This world is inhabited by myriad groups, some dealing in drugs, prostitution, protection rackets, crimes of which the weakest members of society are invariably the victims...

---

[3] [1995] 20 EHRR 442.

> There is no doubt that elements of Proinsias de Rossa's Workers Party were involved in "special activities". What remains unproven is whether de Rossa knew about the source of his party's funds. There is evidence that.....that de Rossa was aware of what was going on...
>
> Proinsias de Rossa's political friends in the Soviet Union were no better than gangsters. The Communists ran labour camps. They were anti-Semitic".

After two re-trials of the action in the High Court, the trial judge directed the jury as follows on the question of damages:

> "...damages are meant to compensate a person for a wrong...The only remedy available to a person who says he has been wronged in a newspaper is damages. Damages are meant to put a person, in so far as money can do it, in the position that he or she would have been if the wrong had not taken place. That is the enterprise you are engaged in, in relation to damages."

The trial judge continued by quoting with approval a judgment of Henchy J in *Barrett v Independent Newspapers Ltd*[4] as follows:

> "It is the duty of the Judge to direct the Jury that the damages must be confined to such money as would fairly and reasonably compensate the Plaintiff for his injured feelings, and for any diminution in his standing among right-thinking people as a result of the words complained of...among the relevant considerations proper to be taken into account are the nature of the libel, the standing of the Plaintiff, the extent of the publication, the conduct of the Defendant at all stages of the case, and any other matter which bears on the extent of the damages".

The ECtHR noted that the jury found the impugned words implied that Mr de Rossa had been involved in or tolerated serious crime and that he personally supported anti-semitism and violent communist oppression. The jury went on to assess damages at IR£300,000. The Defendant appealed to the Supreme Court.

de Rossa v Independent Newspapers (Supreme Court)

The case made on appeal was that whereas the Defendant accepted that the jury had been directed on damages in accordance with the law, the trial judge had been therefore obliged to confine his directions to a statement of general principles and to eschew any specific guidance on the appropriate level of general damages. The fact that neither counsel nor the trial judge could suggest any figures to the jury was, it was claimed, inconsistent with the provisions of the Constitution and of the ECHR.

It was contended that specific guidelines ought to be given to the jury in such cases, including a reference to the purchasing power of any award made, and to the

---

[4] [1986] IR 13.

income which the award could produce. It was further argued that reference should be made to what the trial judge and counsel considered to the appropriate level of damages, and also to the level of awards in personal injuries and other libel cases. In addition, it was argued that the common law and the Constitution required the appellate court to subject jury awards in defamation actions to stricter scrutiny so that (in the ECtHR's summary of the case made) "the test which had been outlined by Mr Justice Henchy in the above-cited *Barrett* case was no longer sufficient".

In this regard, the appellants in the Supreme Court relied on *Rantzen v M.G.N. Ltd*[5] and on the ECtHR judgment in *Tolstoy Miloslavsky*. They argued that the proper test was that outlined in *Rantzen*, namely, whether "a reasonable jury [could] have thought that this award was necessary to compensate the plaintiff and to re-establish his reputation".

The majority in the Supreme Court disagreed.

Chief Justice Hamilton pointed to the fact that the assessment of damages in libel cases was "peculiarly the province of the jury". He also recalled the words of former Chief Justice Finlay in *Barrett* that the assessment by a jury of damages for defamation had a "very unusual and emphatic sanctity" so that the appellate courts had been extremely slow to interfere with such assessments.

Hamilton CJ went on to outline the relevant domestic law, concluding that there was no conflict between the common law and constitutional principles on the one hand and Article 10 ECHR on the other. The effect of Article 10 had been stated in the *Tolstoy Miloslavsky* judgement as requiring that "an award of damages for defamation must bear a reasonable relationship of proportionality to the injury to reputation suffered". The Chief Justice continued by referring to the right to freedom of expression at Article 40.6.1 of the Irish Constitution, and the requirement at Article 40.3.1 and 40.3.2 for the State to vindicate the good name of every citizen, stating:

> "The law must consequently reflect a due balancing of the constitutional right to freedom of expression and the constitutional protection of every citizen's good name (*Hynes-O'Sullivan v O'Driscoll* [1998] IR 436). This introduces the concept of proportionality which is recognised in our constitutional jurisprudence."

Accordingly, it would appear that in the view of the majority of the Supreme Court, Irish law already provided for proportionality in the matter of assessment of damages. In particular, the Supreme Court emphasised that the appellate courts could and can intervene in order to set aside a "disproportionately high" award. The court was not persuaded to adopt the approach favoured in *Rantzen* (and developed further in *John v M.G.N. Ltd*[6]) whereby a jury would have various comparator and other figures suggested to them. If this were to occur, the jury

[5] [1993] 4 All ER 975.
[6] [1996] 2 All ER 35.

would be "buried in figures", and the giving of such figures, even in guideline form, would constitute an unjustifiable invasion of the domain of the jury. The court was not prepared to change the approach previously taken.

On the question of appellate reviews of jury awards in defamation actions, the Chief Justice summarised the position as follows:

> "…an appellate court should only set aside … an award made by a jury in a defamation action if the award is one which no reasonable jury would have made in the circumstances of the case and is so unreasonable as to be disproportionate to the injury sustained."

This *Rantzen* test ("could a reasonable jury have thought that this award was necessary to compensate the plaintiff and to re-establish his reputation") was expressly rejected by the Supreme Court in this context as constituting a departure from the principles which hitherto had been applied in Irish law. Such a test would remove the "very unusual and emphatic sanctity" attaching to juries in this context.

Applying the correct test, the Supreme Court went on to consider whether the damages awarded to Mr de Rossa were excessive and disproportionate to any damage done to him. In relation to the gravity of the libel, the Chief Justice observed that it was hard to imagine a more serious libel given the nature of the allegations, the profession in which Mr de Rossa was engaged and the fact that he was involved in negotiations concerning his possible participation in government. The plaintiff had given evidence in the High Court regarding the hurt and humiliation caused to him by the newspaper article concerned and this evidence had been accepted by the jury. As to the extent of publication, this was very wide as conceded by all parties. As to the conduct of the defendant newspaper, the Chief Justice noted that no apology had been forthcoming at any stage, and Mr de Rossa had been forced to endure three trials in order to secure vindication of his reputation. The Chief Justice stated:

> "The jury found that the words complained of by the Respondent meant that the Respondent was involved in or tolerated serious crime and personally supported anti-Semitism and violent Communist oppression. If these allegations were true, the Respondent was guilty of conduct, which was not only likely to bring him into disrepute with right-minded people but was such as to render him unsuitable for public office. No more serious allegations could be made against a politician such as the Respondent herein. Having regard to the serious nature of the said libel, its potential effect on the career of the Respondent, and the other considerations as outlined herein, it would appear to me that the jury would have been justified in going to the top of the bracket and awarding as damages the largest sum that could fairly be regarded as compensation.
>
> Bearing in mind that a fundamental principle of the law of compensatory damages is that the award must always be reasonable and fair and bear a due correspondence with the injury suffered and not be disproportionate thereto, I am not satisfied that the award made by the jury in this case went beyond what a reasonable jury applying the law to all the relevant considerations could reasonably have awarded and is not disproportionate to the injury suffered by the Respondent."

Mrs Justice Denham, in a dissenting judgment, was of the view that further guidelines should be given to jurors, including with regard to previous libel awards made or affirmed by the Supreme Court, prior awards in personal injuries cases, the purchasing power of an award and the income it might produce, together with guidance on the level of award deemed appropriate. She thought that the award in *de Rossa* was too high and ought to be reduced to IR£150,000.

Proportionality: Principle in Tolstoy Miloslavsky

In embarking on its assessment in *Independent News* the European Court of Human Rights made extensive reference to the principles elucidated in its earlier judgment in *Tolstoy Miloslavsky*, stating that: "The Court considers that the Tolstoy Miloslavsky judgment must be its point of departure in examining this case". In that case the ECtHR had been asked to consider *inter alia* whether an award of £1.5m was disproportionate to the legitimate aim of protecting the rights of the defamed individual in that UK case. (Lord Aldington had successfully sued Count Tolstoy Miloslavsky in relation to a pamphlet written by the Count in which allegations were made concerning Lord Aldington's activities during the Second World War). The court noted that the award was three times the size of any previous award and that at the material time the national law allowed great latitude to the jury. The court also noted that the test applied by the Court of Appeal in considering whether an award should be set aside was whether "it was so unreasonable that it could not have been made by sensible people and must have been arrived at capriciously, unconscionably or irrationally."

The Court continued:

> "In a more recent case, *Rantzen v [M.G.N.]*, the Court of Appeal itself observed that to grant an almost limitless discretion to a jury failed to provide a satisfactory measurement for deciding what was "necessary in a democratic society" for the purpose of Article 10 of the Convention. It noted that the common law — if properly understood – required the courts to subject large awards of damages to a more searching scrutiny than had been customary.
>
> As to what guidance the judge should give to the jury, the Court of Appeal stated that.... the jury should be invited to consider the purchasing power of any ward which they might make and to ensure that any award they made was proportionate to the damage which the plaintiff had suffered and was a sum which it was necessary to award him to provide adequate compensation and to re-establish his reputation... .
>
> The Court cannot but endorse the above observations by the Court of Appeals to the effect that the scope of judicial control, at the trial and on appeal, at the time of the applicant's case did not offer adequate and effective safeguards against a disproportionately large award."

The Court went on to set out "the essential question" to be answered in this case as:

> "...whether, having regard to the size of the present award, there were adequate and effective domestic safeguards, at first instance and on appeal, against

> disproportionate awards which assured a reasonable relationship of proportionality between the award and the injury to reputation".

It did not accept an argument advanced by the Irish government to the effect that it was only when a damages award was found to be disproportionate that a review of the safeguards became necessary. Rather, the Court considered that a general finding that an award of damages is "unusual" was sufficient to prompt a review by the court of the adequacy and effectiveness of the relevant domestic safeguards against disproportionate awards.

Proportionality in Practice in Irish Case Law

An extensive review of the relevant law and practice in Ireland was conducted by the European Court, including the amounts of defamation awards in a number of leading cases and, crucially, the principles followed by the Irish appellate courts when called upon to consider such awards.

For example, the court noted that in *Barrett* the Supreme Court had set aside an award of IR£65,000 as "disproportionately high". In *McDonagh v News Group Newspapers Limited*[7] whereas the Supreme Court had declined to set aside the award, it had observed that the award "though undoubtedly high and at the top end of the permissible range, [was] not beyond that in the sense that it is so incorrect in principle that having regard to the general approach of an appellate court to damages assessed by a jury for defamation it should be set aside".[8]

In *Dawson*, the Supreme Court set aside the award of damages, O'Flaherty J stating: "I have reached the clear conclusion that the award is so excessive as to call for the intervention of this Court. It is wholly disproportionate to any injury suffered by the plaintiffs." And O'Flaherty J commented:

> "…unjustifiably large awards, as well as the costs attendant on long trials, deals a blow to the freedom of expression entitlement that is enshrined in the Constitution".

In *O'Brien v M.G.N. Ltd*[9] the Supreme Court refused to reconsider its earlier judgment in *de Rossa* but nevertheless set aside the jury award in *O'Brien*, the Chief Justice applying the general proportionality principle outlined by Henchy J in *Barrett*.

In *Hill v the Cork Examiner Publications Limited*[10] the jury award was not set aside. Mr Justice Murphy observed as follows:

> "Whilst other jurisdictions have accepted the concept of [such] guidelines that concept has been rejected in this jurisdiction. Apart from any other consideration there would appear to be insuperable difficulties for any judge to assemble the appropriate body of information on which to base such guidelines."

---

[7] Unreported, Supreme Court, 23 November 1992.
[8] Per Chief Justice Finlay.
[9] Unreported, Supreme Court, 25 October 2000.
[10] Unreported, Supreme Court, 14 November 2001.

Assessment and Conclusions of the ECtHR

While the court did not favour the "direct mathematical comparison" advanced by the Irish government in its attempt to distinguish *Independent Newspapers* from *Tolstoy Miloslavsky* nevertheless the court noted that Irish case law:

> "...indicates that the award against the first applicant was not as unusual as that at issue in *Tolstoy Miloslavsky*: in that case the award was three times the size of the highest libel award previously made in England and it had not yet been matched when this Court examined that case."

The court proceeded then to consider the effect of the absence of any requirement that Irish juries be given directions or guidance as to the size of their awards. The applicants contended that the absence of such guidelines amounted to an infringement of Article 10 ECHR. Significantly, the court considered this question against the background of the following observations:

> "The main purpose of the Convention is to lay down certain international standards to be observed by States but that this does not mean that absolute uniformity is required. A State remains free to choose the measures which it considers best adapted to address domestically the Convention matter at issue...Accordingly, while in *Tolstoy Miloslavsky* the Court endorsed the developments in English law towards giving further guidance in the *Rantzen* and *St John* cases...this does not mean that it considered the *Rantzen* route as the only means of safeguarding respondents against disproportionate awards. The important question is whether, having regard to the entire proceedings, the protection against disproportionate awards sufficed."

The Court noted that there were a number of points of distinction between the impugned jury direction in *Tolstoy Miloslavsky* and that in the present case. In particular, it noted that in *de Rossa* the trial judge had given the jury two concrete indications, not provided in the *Tolstoy Miloslavsky* case, as to the level of any damages to be awarded. The judge (in *de Rossa*) had provided an example of a relatively minor defamatory comment to allow the jury to assess the relative seriousness of the defamatory article concerned. He had then followed up with a clear direction to the jury that, if it was to award damages, they would have to be substantial. In the light of this, the ECtHR considered that:

> "...the trial judge's directions in the present case can be considered to have given somewhat more specific guidance to the jury that those examined in the *Tolstoy Miloslavsky* case."

The Court then proceeded to examine the Supreme Court judgment and in particular the rationale applied by that court in considering whether to set aside a jury award on appeal.

The applicants contended that this test was no stricter than the appellate review test in *Tolstoy Miloslavsky* (i.e. whether the award was "so unreasonable that it could not have been made by sensible people and must have been arrived at capriciously, unconscionably or irrationally"), and which was found to be inadequate. However, the court rejected this contention, and held that the appellate review was one of the main points of distinction between the two cases:

> "...the nature of the Supreme Court's review was more robust that that at issue in the *Tolstoy Miloslavsky* judgment because of the requirement in Irish domestic law that jury awards in libel cases be proportionate...It was the absence of this proportionality requirement in English law which meant that the libel award in the *Tolstoy Miloslavsky* case was considered to be 'particularly open to question'"...
>
> That this requirement of proportionality distinguished the appellate review at issue in the present and *Tolstoy Miloslavsky* cases is evident from the actual review conducted by the Supreme Court in the present case".

The ECtHR noted that the Supreme Court had taken a number of relevant factors into account including the gravity of the libel, the effect on Mr de Rossa who was a party leader involved at the material time in negotiations to form a coalition government, the extent of publication of the libel, the conduct of the newspaper and the necessity for the plaintiff to endure three long and difficult trials. In the words of the court: "Having assessed these factors, it [the Supreme Court] concluded that the jury would have been justified in going to the top of the bracket and awarding as damages the largest sum that could fairly be regarded as compensation".

Clearly satisfied that the Supreme Court's review of the award was sufficiently robust as to meet the objectives of the Convention, notwithstanding the absence of jury guidelines, the European Court concluded that there had been no violation of Article 10 and the applicants' claim failed.

Discussion

A significant element of the Court's decision was its readiness to distinguish this case from the earlier judgment in *Tolstoy Miloslavsky*. The award in the latter case was £1.5m, five times larger than the award in *de Rossa*, which itself was acknowledged throughout the various stages of the case as an unusually high award. Of more importance, however, was the Court's conclusion that the threshold for appellate intervention in *Tolstoy Miloslavsky* was so high as to fail to provide for a requirement of proportionality. This was contrasted with the approach of the Irish Supreme Court, which commended itself to the ECtHR as ensuring (or at least striving for) the proportionality which the court identified as being necessary in order to meet the objectives of the Convention.

Nevertheless, it will have been disappointing to many observers (and not just to the media owners) that the court was not prepared to take a somewhat more interventionist approach, in the sense of querying the sheer size of the award in *de Rossa* in the context of freedom of expression, and the laudable objectives set out in Article 10 of the Convention. In his dissenting opinion in *Independent News*, Judge Cabral Barreto was of the view that the amount of damages in *de Rossa* was so high that the "reasonable relationship between the interference and the legitimate aim pursued was not observed."

It would appear that the question of jury guidelines in this jurisdiction has been disposed of as a result of the judgment in *Independent News*. Certainly it is clear that there is no *requirement* under the Convention that such guidelines be introduced. It will be recalled that Mrs Justice Denham, in her dissenting judgment in *de Rossa*, felt that guidelines on levels of damages given by a judge "would aid the administration of justice". The Report of the Legal Advisory Group on Defamation (cited in *Independent News*) proposed that the parties to the proceedings should be able to make submissions to the court and address the jury concerning damages. The Group also proposed that a statutory provision should be introduced which would require the judge in the High Court proceedings to give directions to the jury. The Report continued:

> "Such a provision should be general in nature but would, in an appropriate case, allow a judge to refer to the purchasing power of the likely award, the income it might produce, the scale of awards in previous defamation cases and the appropriate level of damages in all the circumstances of the case"

Section 29 of the Defamation Act 2009 deals with the issue of damages, providing at s 29(1) as follows:

> "The parties in a defamation action may make submissions to the court in relation to the matter of damages."

Section 29(2) provides as follows:

> "In a defamation action brought in the High Court, the judge shall give directions to the jury in relation to the matter of damages"

A range of factors are set out at s 29(4) to which the court is to have regard in assessing damages. The Act does not provide for guidelines and given the relative detail of the matters set out at s 29(4), against the background of the Supreme Court judgment in *de Rossa*, it is arguable that the Oireachtas has expressly excluded any such guidelines.

One final observation arises from the dissenting judgment of Judge Barreto wherein he remarked:

> "As to the limits of acceptable criticism, they are wider with regard to a politicianacting in his public capacity than in relation to a private individual.
>
> A politician inevitably and knowingly lays himself open to close scrutiny of his every word and deed by both journalists and the public at large, and he must display a greater degree of tolerance, especially when he himself makes public statements that are susceptible of criticism.
>
> Above all, I would emphasise that the present case clearly involved a political debate on matters of general interest, an area in which restrictions on the freedom of expression should be interpreted narrowly."

The Defamation Act 2009 introduces into Irish defamation law a defence of "fair and reasonable publication on a matter of public importance". This is a welcome departure in Irish law, though it remains unclear as to how the defence might operate in practice, especially in the light of the considerable number of qualifications set out in s 24 of the Act. The trend in many jurisdictions has been to allow for some form of "public figure" defence, and whereas it may be argued that the Sunday Independent article concerning Mr de Rossa would not have passed the rather rigorous test set out in s 24 of the Act, the introduction of such a defence is surely not before its time.

Issue Estoppel in Criminal Proceedings: *Lynch v Judge Caroll Moran and the DPP**

Emer Meeneghan**

Background

This case concerned the role of issue estoppel in criminal proceedings. During the course of the applicant's trial for manslaughter before the Circuit Criminal Court in Limerick, the defence sought rulings in *voir dire* hearings in respect of the admissibility of evidence of an identification parade and identification evidence to be given by a particular witness.

The trial judge, the first named respondent, ruled against the applicant on these issues and held that the evidence was admissible. After several days of trial, however, the jury failed to reach a verdict and evidence was discharged. When the matter was re-listed, the first named respondent ruled that the issues in the forthcoming retrial that had already been decided by him in the prior trial would not be required to be re-litigated by reason of issue estoppel.

The applicant sought judicial review of the decision, arguing that the ruling was a breach of the applicants' rights under Article 38.1 of the Constitution and Article 6 ECHR — in particular a breach of the "equality of arms" principles — and of Article 13 ECHR.

In the High Court, Murphy, J relied on the case of *The People (DPP) v Keith O'Callaghan,*[1] where it was held that issue estoppel as between one criminal trial and another should be regarded as available in Ireland so that an individual, discrete issue might be regarded as finally and validly determined by a court, even though the court's verdict on the general issue might be set aside on an appeal. He refused the application for judicial review.

The matter came before the Supreme Court by way of appeal from the High Court where the Supreme Court held, allowing the appeal and quashing the decision of the Circuit Court Judge, that issue estoppel has no role in Irish criminal proceedings.

Submissions

The argument on behalf of the applicant in the Supreme Court was two-fold. Firstly, that *res judicata* only arises where there is a final judgment. If a mistrial occurs the

* [2006] IESC 31.

** Barrister-at-Law.

[1] *The People (DPP) v Keith O'Callaghan* [2001] 1 IR 584.

case has collapsed and all of the matters are to be retried *de novo*. Secondly, that if the decision in *People (DPP) v Keith O'Callaghan* was correct, then it only operates for the benefit of an accused and not in favour of the prosecution.

On behalf of the respondents, it was argued that *People (DPP) v Keith O'Callaghan* was correct, and that if issue estoppel was available to the defence it must also be available to the prosecution. If however, it was held that *People (DPP) v Keith O'Callaghan* was incorrect, then issue estoppel should not be available to either party and there should be no unreciprocated advantage to an accused person arising from rulings made in a first trial.

Position in Ireland

In *The People (DPP) v Keith O'Callaghan*, the accused was charged with causing damage by fire contrary to the Criminal Damage Act 1991. During his trial the judge ruled in favour of the defendant that certain evidence was inadmissible, namely the statement of a witness who was the occupant of the house that had been damaged by the fire that the accused had arrived at her house late at night and wanted her to go out with him. The trial judge had held that the evidence was irrelevant and excluded it on that basis. The trial collapsed and a retrial was ordered. Although the same evidence was challenged during the retrial, it was admitted by the second judge who held that it was relevant and admissible as part of the *res gestae* and the applicant was convicted. When the matter came before the Court of Criminal Appeal, the issue was whether the finding of the first trial judge that the evidence was inadmissible precluded its admission at the second trial. The Court of Criminal Appeal held that the second judge was estopped from holding the evidence to be relevant, the applicant's conviction was quashed and a further retrial ordered. The Court did, however, point out that while the retrial was to proceed on the basis that the evidence in question was inadmissible, a turn in the evidence may render previously irrelevant evidence relevant.

The decision in *O'Callaghan* in favour of issue estoppel was reached after consideration of the decisions *Kelly v Ireland*[2] and *Breathnach v Ireland*[3], which cases are authority for the proposition that the determination of an issue in criminal proceedings can give rise to an issue estoppel in later civil proceedings. The plaintiffs in both cases had been charged in connection with the Sallins Mail Train Robbery. Each had made an application to have an incriminating statement excluded from consideration on the grounds that they had been signed as a result of assaults by members of An Garda Síochána. The Special Criminal Court, which tried the matter, refused the applications stating that they were satisfied that the statements were not made as a result of any assaults by members of An Garda Síochána. Mr Breathnach appealed to the Court of Criminal Appeal and his conviction was quashed on the basis that the trial court had not been entitled to be satisfied that the statement was voluntarily made. However, the Court of Criminal Appeal did not interfere with the decision of the trial court that the allegations of assault were untrue. Thus, when Mr Breathnach later took civil proceedings for assault and battery, he was found to be

---

[2] *Kelly v Ireland* [1986] ILRM 318.

[3] *Breathnach v Ireland* [1989] IR 489.

estopped from relying on the alleged assault as a result of the decision of the trial court. Similarly, Mr Kelly — who had, in the meantime, received a presidential pardon - subsequently sued for assault and battery and was estopped from relying on the alleged assault. It is noteworthy that neither of these cases specifically dealt with issue estoppel between criminal proceedings.

The court also had regard to the decision of *People (DPP) v Quilligan*,[4] where doubt had been expressed as to the availability of issue estoppel in cases other than where a final verdict has been reached or decisions which were reviewable on appeal, and also to the decision in *Corporation of Dublin v Flynn*.[5] In the latter case, issue estoppel had been fully considered by the Supreme Court. Here an individual was prosecuted for the continuing offence of failing to comply with a planning notice. The Corporation were unable to prove the making or service of an enforcement notice and sought to argue that, because in the earlier prosecution it had been proven that the notice had been served on Mr Flynn and was valid, those issues should stand determined conclusively as a matter of *res judicata*. Henchy, J rejected the argument on the basis that it would be contrary to principle to permit the prosecution to prove certain issues by giving evidence that they had been determined against the accused in an earlier prosecution. In holding that there could be no issue estoppel, he attached importance to the unitary nature of the criminal process and the undesirability of a criminal trial being fettered or complicated by rulings made in previous trials. While Henchy J stated, *obiter*, that if issue estoppel was available at all, it was only available to the accused, this did not decide the issue of whether issue estoppel was in fact available to an accused.

Thus, in the case under discussion, *Lynch*,[6] when the Supreme Court were faced with deciding the correctness or otherwise of the decision in *O'Callaghan* they acknowledged that the question of whether issue estoppel was available between criminal proceedings had not yet been clearly established in Irish law. *Kelly* and *Breathnach* did not deal with issue estoppel between criminal proceedings, the Court of Criminal Appeal in *Quilligan* showed a reluctance to accept issue estoppel other than in respect of final decisions, and while *Corporation of Dublin v Flynn* established that issue estoppel was not available to the prosecution, it did not decide if it was available to the defence. In those circumstances, while the Supreme Court acknowledged the purpose and value of issue estoppel as outlined in *O'Callaghan*, it nevertheless identified a reluctance on the part of the Irish courts (as set out above) and courts in other jurisdictions to apply issue estoppel to criminal proceedings.

Other Jurisdictions

England

The position in England with regard to issue estoppel was clarified in *R v Humphrys*[7] when it was stated that issue estoppel has not and has never had a place in English criminal law. In *Humphrys*, the applicant was acquitted of driving while

[4] *People (DPP) v Quilligan* [1993] 2 IR 305.
[5] *Corporation of Dublin v Flynn* [1980] IR 357.
[6] *Enda Lynch v His Honour Judge Caroll Moran and Director of Public Prosecutions* [2006] IESC 31.
[7] *R v Humphreys* [1977] AC 1.

disqualified. In a later charge of perjury based on an allegation that he had lied during the first trial, the defendant argued that the prosecution could not introduce evidence of a police officer that he had been driving when he was disqualified as that issue had been finally decided. The House of Lords rejected this argument, distinguishing issue estoppel from the principles of *autrefois acquit* and *autrefois convict*. It was pointed out that while the latter two concepts were grounded on the universal maxim of the common law of England, that no man is to be brought into jeopardy of his life more than once for the same offence, in the present case, the defendant was not at the second trial being tried for a crime in respect of which he had previously been acquitted or convicted. The offence of perjury is not the same or substantially the same as the offence of which he had been acquitted.

In reaching this decision the House of Lords also pointed out other reasons why issue estoppel should not and does not have a role to play in criminal proceedings. Firstly, that it was inappropriate in criminal proceedings as there are no pleadings identifying how issues were decided. Also, since juries give general verdicts of "guilty" or "not guilty" it would often be difficult, if not impossible to do more than guess how they had decided any issue capable of identification. Also, even in the rare cases in which the issues could be identified, estoppel would be artificial and unfair. For example, where the jury decides an issue in the defendant's favour, because they are in doubt as to whether the contrary had been proved, it would be artificial and unjust if the issue should thereafter be irrevocably decided in his favour. For those reasons, the English House of Lords held that issue estoppel, was an "unnecessary importation" that could "lead to absurd and unjust results".

Australia

In Australia, a majority of the High Court of Australia held in *Rogers v The Queen*,[8] that the doctrine of issue estoppel, as it had been developed in civil proceedings, was not applicable to criminal proceedings. Two factors were identified as operating strongly against the application of issue estoppel. The first was the absence of any appeal on the particular issue governed by issue estoppel. Though the *voir dire* is, in a sense, autonomous it is nevertheless totally dependant upon the main trial for its appeal process.

The second objection was that the requirement of mutuality would run contrary to the basic notion that the accused is entitled to the presumption of innocence until the jury are satisfied of his guilt beyond reasonable doubt. It would be contrary to the fundamental principles of the criminal law that the members of a jury should be obliged by the decision of another tribunal to bring in a verdict against an accused person, without themselves being satisfied that issues which the accused wished to contest had been proved against him.

Canada

The absence of an appeal from a specific issue was also a factor in dissuading the Supreme Court of Canada in *Duhamel v The Queen*[9] from extending the doctrine of

[8] *Rogers v The Queen* [1994] 181 CLR 251.
[9] *Duhamel v The Queen* [1085] 14 DLR (4th) 92.

res judicata to include issue estoppel. It was held that, in the absence of the availability of an autonomous appeal of findings as to the admissibility of confessions, there was no clear advantage to the administration of justice in extending the doctrine of *res judicata*. The question of applying the doctrine of issue estoppel to a finding made on a *voir dire* arose. Lamer J pointed out that although the *voir dire* is in a sense autonomous it is totally dependent upon the main trial for its appeal process. Thus, where a statement is wrongly excluded and the accused is convicted, the benefit of the doctrine of *res judicata* would then be founded on an error of law beyond the reach of redress.

The Decision in *Lynch*

The Supreme Court in *Lynch* held that issue estoppel has no place in criminal proceedings. In the situation where a criminal trial collapses the effect of the application of issue estoppel would be that an accused would lose a clear right of appeal in respect of what might be a critical part of their case. The Court held that this would violate Article 34 of the Irish Constitution as well as Article 2(1) of Protocol No 7 of the European Convention on Human Rights — which Article guarantees the right to have a conviction and / or sentence reviewed in accordance with the law — and might also be impermissible having regard to Article 6 ECHR which provides for a trial in due course of law.

Also, having regard to the concept of "equality of arms" as developed by the European Court of Human Rights, the Court held that if issue estoppel cannot operate in favour of the prosecution, it should not operate in favour of the defence by way of unreciprocated advantage.

Comment

The effect of the decision in *Lynch v Moran*,[10] is that it is now an established principle of Irish law that issue estoppel does not apply in the context of two sets of criminal proceedings save in the context of *autrefois acquit* or *autrefois convict*.[11] Although the decision overturns the decision of the Court of Criminal Appeal in *O'Callaghan* - which decision has been described as "unexpected and courageous"[12] — this can be viewed as a positive development in light of difficulties which that decision raised. In particular, the decision left unanswered the question of whether issue estoppel between two sets of criminal proceedings should be available to the prosecution as well as to the defence. *Lynch v Moran* makes it clear that, even if the doctrine of issue estoppel were available in criminal proceedings, it would operate in favour of neither the prosecution nor the defence. Moreover, the judgment in *O'Callaghan* did not give any guidance as to how to reconcile the decision that issue estoppel was available between criminal proceedings, with the idea that the criminal process is

---

[10] *Enda Lynch v His Honour Judge Caroll Moran and Director of Public Prosecutions* [2006] IESC 31.

[11] Following the decision in *Lynch v Moran*, the Court of Criminal Appeal rejected an appeal from a conviction in the Special Criminal Court on grounds raised in the context of issue estoppel. *The People (DPP) v Matthews*, Unreported, Court of Criminal Appeal , 14 July 2006.

[12] PA McDermott, *Evidence and Procedure Update*, (2001) 11 (3) ICLJ 27.

a discrete process that should not be concerned with the outcome of other proceedings. This is no longer an issue. For this alone, the decision is invaluable.

However, it is still not entirely clear what the position is with regard to criminal proceedings that are followed by civil proceedings. While the existence of a criminal acquittal or conviction will not bar subsequent civil proceedings, it appears from the judgments in *Kelly*[13] and in *Breathnach*[14] that a court in the latter proceedings will be estopped from deciding issues that were decided in the criminal set of proceedings:

> "In the rare case where a clearly identifiable issue has been raised in the course of a criminal trial and has been decided against a party to those proceedings by means of a judgment explaining how the issue has been decided, I would be prepared to hold that such a decision may give rise to issue estoppel in later civil proceedings in which that party is also involved"[15]

The first decision in the United Kingdom in which it was sought to challenge in a civil action a final decision of a court in the criminal jurisdiction was the case of *Hunter v Chief Constable of the West Midlands & Others*.[16] The appellant and others had been arrested following bomb explosions in Birmingham. They made statements to the police regarding their parts in planting the bombs. At the trial the admission into evidence of their statements was objected to on the grounds that they had been induced by violence and threats by the police. The six men were nevertheless convicted. Leave to appeal was refused. The men then issued civil proceedings claiming damages against the police for injuries caused by the assaults — which were the same allegations as had been made during the criminal trial — and sought to introduce evidence in this regard.

The House of Lords, on appeal, looked at two suggested tests that would justify the introduction of such evidence. Firstly, that the new evidence must be such "as entirely changes the aspect of the case"[17] and, secondly, where the new evidence "would probably have an important influence on the result of the case though it need not be decisive".[18] In circumstances where the fresh evidence sought to be relied on was available at trial or could have been obtained at that stage, it was held by the House of Lords that the proper method of attacking the decision that the appellant had not been assaulted was to make it a ground of appeal against his conviction. In circumstances where the plaintiff had not sought to do this, but had instead launched a collateral attack on the conviction in civil proceedings, it was held that the former more rigorous test was required. While avoiding the use of the phrase "issue estoppel", stating that it would be best if that term were restricted to estoppel that may arise in civil actions between the same parties, the House of Lords

---

[13] *ibid*, n 2.
[14] *ibid*, n 3.
[15] *ibid*, n 2 at 318.
[16] *Hunter v Chief Constable of the West Midlands & Others* [1982] AC 529. This case is more popularly known as the case of "The Birmingham Six".
[17] *Phosphate Sewage Co. Ltd. v Molleson* (1879) 4 App.Cas. 801, 814.
[18] *Ladd v Marshall* [1954] 1 WLR 1489.

refused to re-examine the decision that the appellant had not been assaulted, referring to complications such as the differing onus of proof in criminal and civil proceedings. It concluded that where a final decision had been made by a criminal court of competent jurisdiction the use of a civil action to initiate a collateral attack on that decision was an abuse of process of the court.[19]

The question of criminal proceedings followed by civil proceedings came before the European Court of Human Rights a number of times in 2003. In the case of *O v Norway*[20] the applicant had been charged with sexual offences against his daughter. He was acquitted and lodged a claim for compensation which was rejected. On appeal, the Supreme Court held that his acquittal was not sufficient to entitle the applicant to compensation, that it had not been shown on the balance of probabilities that he had not committed the offence. The applicant applied to the European Court of Human Rights arguing that the compensation proceedings were sufficiently linked to the criminal proceedings so as to bring him within the remit of Article 6(2) ECHR. The Court held there had been a violation of Article 6(2). It was not satisfied that the refusal to award compensation did not call into doubt the correctness of the applicant's acquittal and held that this was incompatible with the presumption of innocence enshrined in that provision of the Convention.

Civil proceedings where the victim of a crime sought compensation following an acquittal of the accused person in criminal proceedings were also challenged in the European Court of Human Rights. In *Ringwold v Norway,*[21] the applicant applied to Strasbourg complaining that the Norwegian Supreme Court's judgment awarding the alleged victim compensation entailed a violation of his right to a presumption of innocence under Article 6(2). The Court held that, unlike in *O*, the compensation claim was not a consequence of and concomitant to the criminal proceedings and therefore Article 6(2) was not violated.[22]

Similarly, in *Y v Norway,*[23] a person acquitted in a criminal trial challenged the award of compensation to the victim's parents arguing that it was a violation of his rights under Article 6(2) to the presumption of innocence. The European Court of Human Rights held that because the language employed by the High Court, upheld by the Supreme Court, overstepped the bounds of the civil forum, it had thereby cast doubt on the correctness of that acquittal. Accordingly, there was a sufficient link to the earlier criminal proceedings which was incompatible with the presumption of innocence. Accordingly, Article 6(2) was held to apply to the compensation proceedings and was held to have been violated by the national court's decision to award compensation.

---

[19] *ibid*, n 16, p 530.

[20] *O v Norway* App no 29327/95, 11 February 2003.

[21] *Ringvold v Norway* App no 34964/97, 11 February 2003.

[22] In a dissenting judgment, Judge Costa stated that both the presumption of innocence and the acquittal would be deprived on any useful purpose if judgment were given against that person in civil proceedings. The better option would be to set up a compensation fund for victims of crime.

[23] *Y v Norway* App no 56568/00, 11 May 2003.

"Trying to Have it Both Ways" — On the First Judgments of the Court of First Instance Concerning EC Acts Adopted in the Fight against International Terrorism

Dr Laurent Pech*

Article III-322 of the defunct EU Constitutional Treaty formally empowered the Council to adopt "restrictive measures" against natural or legal persons and groups or non-State entities, when it implements the EU's Common Foreign and Security Policy (CFSP). The drafters of the Lisbon Treaty rightly decided to reproduce this provision[1] and maintain another unprecedented provision which expressly gives the European Court of Justice of the European Communities (ECJ) jurisdiction to rule on proceedings reviewing the legality of European decisions providing for these types of restrictive measures.[2] In so doing, the Lisbon Treaty addresses, although insufficiently, the unacceptable shortcomings of the current Treaty arrangements in relation to the CFSP.[3] Indeed, while the European Union and the European Community are officially said to be based on the rule of law,[4] the jurisdiction of the ECJ is extremely limited outside the EC pillar and even within this pillar, the provisions governing the *locus standi* of private applicants have been narrowly construed by the ECJ itself.[5] Besides, the increasingly important number

* *Jean Monnet* Lecturer in EU Public Law, School of Law, NUI Galway.

[1] See new Article 188K TFEU. It is important to note that the Lisbon Treaty, unlike the abandoned EU Constitutional Treaty which repealed and replaced the current EU and EC Treaties, "merely" amends these two treaties. Furthermore, it was decided that the *Treaty Establishing the European Community* (EC Treaty) should be renamed the *Treaty on the Functioning of the European Union* (TFEU).

[2] See new Article 240a TFEU (formerly Article III-376(2) EU CT).

[3] For a recent and exhaustive study, see MG Garbagnati Ketvel, "The Jurisdiction of the European Court of Justice in Respect of the Common Foreign and Security Policy" (2006) 55 ICLQ 77.

[4] By virtue of Article 6 TEU, the EU is said to be founded on the principle of the rule of law. This provision also provides that the EU respects fundamental rights, as guaranteed by the 1950 European Convention for the Protection of Human Rights and Fundamental Freedoms and as they result from the constitutional provisions common to the Member States, as general principles of Community law.

[5] Article 230 EC requires a private applicant to satisfy a number of criteria before he/she can challenge, in the Community Courts, an act other than one addressed to him. See e.g. *Union de Pequeños Agricoltores* [2002] ECR I-6677 Case C-50/00 P. The restrictive interpretation of these criteria has been criticised as not providing sufficient legal protection for the individual.

of EC "restrictive measures" aimed at identified individuals[6] have been adopted although the EC Treaty does not provide an explicit legal basis for the possibility of adopting economic and financial sanctions (e.g. freezing of funds) against individuals.

In two fascinating and highly detailed judgments delivered on the 21 September 2005, the Court of First Instance of the European Communities (CFI) appears to have addressed some of these concerns almost as if the provisions of the Constitutional Treaty previously mentioned were already in force. Indeed, in the cases of *Yusuf* and *Kadi*,[7] the CFI has demonstrated a "generous" attitude both with regard to the issue of standing of legal and natural persons affected by restrictive measures adopted in connection with the fight against terrorism, and with regard to the interpretation of the Treaty provisions governing the Council's power to adopt those restrictive measures.

To briefly summarise the background to the dispute, in 1999, the United Nations Security Council (UNSC) adopted a resolution aimed at the Taliban and at the individuals and entities associated with them, which required that all the Member States of the UN freeze the funds and other financial resources of the persons concerned. Following the "9/11" atrocities, the UNSC adopted additional resolutions to include Osama bin Laden and the Al-Qaeda network among those whose funds may be frozen. Rather than challenging measures of the UNSC before the UNSC itself — not a surprising decision considering the absence of due process at UN level[8]— the applicants, all residents in Sweden with the exception of Mr Kadi (resident in Saudi Arabia), sought to challenge before the CFI the Council Regulations putting into effect in the Community the UNSC resolutions.[9]

---

[6] They are also called "smart sanctions" as they have progressively replaced general trade embargos aimed at a country.

[7] *Ahmen Ali Yusuf and Al Barakaat International Foundation v. Council of the EU and Commission of the EC* (hereinafter: *Yusuf*) [2005] ECR II-3533 Case T-306/01,; *Yassin Abdullah Kadi v Council of the EU and Commission of the EC* (hereinafter: *Kadi*) [2005] ECR II-3649 Case T-315/01. All the applicants have since appealed the judgments of the CFI before the ECJ. At the time of writing (Spring 2006), the cases (C-415/05 and C-402/05) are still pending.

[8] See generally Council of Europe, Committee on Legal Affairs and Human Rights, *UN Security Council Black Lists*, Report by D Marty, AS/Jur (2007) 14, 19 March 2007. The persons concerned by the contested UNSC resolutions have nonetheless the possibility of presenting their case to the UNSC Sanctions Committee for review through the Government of the State of which they are nationals on in the territory of which they reside. In truth, this procedure can sometimes lead to some positive results as two of the original applicants were removed from the list of persons to whom the freezing of funds applies following a submission to the Sanctions Committee by the Swedish Government on their behalf.

[9] The applicants originally sought annulment of Council Regulation (EC) No 467/2001 of 6 March 2001 prohibiting the export of certain goods and services to Afghanistan, strengthening the flight ban and extending the freeze of funds and other financial resources in respect of the Taliban of Afghanistan. As this Regulation was repealed by Council Regulation (EC) No 881/2002 of 27 May 2002 imposing specific restrictive measures directed against certain persons and entities associated with Osama bin Laden, the Al-Qaeda network and the Taliban (OJ 2002 L 139, p 9), the applicants were allowed by the Court to alter their claims, pleas in law and argument as to seek annulment of this Regulation.

Thanks to the presence of an EC Regulation rather than a pure CFSP act,[10] the applicants were successful in bringing an action against the Council before the CFI on the basis of Article 230 EC.[11] Remarkably, both judgments remain unfortunately silent on the issue of *locus standi* under this Article but there is little doubt that the applicants were directly and individually concerned as their names appeared in Annex I to Regulation No 467/2001 and later on, in Annex I to Regulation No 881/2002.[12] With regard to the Council's power to impose economic sanctions on individuals, the CFI held that Articles 60 EC and 301 EC, together with Article 308 EC, offer a sound "cumulative"[13] legal bases for the adoption by the Council of ("smart") sanctions directed at the persons or entities associated with the rulers of a specific country, or directly or indirectly controlled by those rulers. Considering that Articles 60 EC and 301 EC exclusively refer to measures taken against "third States" and the fact that the CFI is ready to admit that Article 308 does not constitute, of itself, sufficient legal basis for Regulation No 881/2002, this conclusion definitely illustrates an impressive exercise of judicial creativity.[14] It is questionable, however, whether such creativity was warranted. According to the Court, in a rather astonishing *obiter dictum*, we live in a world where "States can no longer be regarded as the only source of threats to international peace and security" and therefore, "the Union and its Community pillar are not to be prevented from adapting to those new threats by imposing economic and financial sanction ... on associated persons, groups, undertakings or entities developing terrorist activity".[15] To follow such a rationale, we might as well write off the principle of conferred competences as far as the fight against terrorism is concerned. The Court's bold statement might nonetheless be explained by Article III-322 of the EU Constitutional Treaty which indicated a prior consensus between the Member States to expand the Union's competence in this particular field.

---

[10] In the absence of EC implementing measures, the CFI ruled that it lacked jurisdiction in the *Segi v Council* [2004] ECR-II 1647 Case T-333/08. The applicants sought compensation for the damage allegedly suffered as a result of the applicants' name having been included in the list of terrorist persons, groups and bodies, pursuant to Common Position 2001/931/CFSP. They alleged breach of their fundamental rights.

[11] On 27 May 2002 the Council adopted Common Position 2002/402/CFSP concerning restrictive measures against Osama bin Laden, members of the Al-Qaeda organisation and the Taliban and other individuals, groups, undertakings and entities associated with them and repealing Common Positions 96/746, 1999/727, 2001/154 and 2001/771/CFSP (OJ 2002 L 139, p 4). Because this CFSP act required implementation by means of Community measures, the Council adopted Regulation No 881/2002, on 27 May 2002, on the basis of Articles 60 EC, 301 EC and 308 EC.

[12] Annex I contains the list of persons, entities and bodies affected by the freezing of funds imposed by the Regulation. The Commission is empowered to amend or supplement Annex I on the basis of determination made by either the UNSC or the "Sanctions Committee", a committee of the Security Council set up by Resolution 1267 (1999).

[13] *Yusuf*, para 166; *Kadi*, para 130.

[14] The United Kingdom, traditionally prompt to criticize any extension of the powers of the EC/EU and prevent "competence creep" through the use of Article 308, intervened in these two cases to defend the Council's broad interpretation of its powers.

[15] *Yusuf*, para 169 ; *Kadi*, para 133.

Although the competence question would certainly deserve a more substantial analysis, this note will focus solely on the alleged breach of the applicants' fundamental rights. Faced with the delicate argument that the contested EC regulation providing for the freezing of assets of persons associated with Osama bin Laden, the AL-Qaeda network and the Taliban, and adopted by the Council in order to implement various decisions of the UNSC, infringes fundamental rights as recognised in the Community legal order, the CFI has offered two landmark rulings. Its reasoning is nonetheless quite Byzantine. Indeed, the Court first appears to renounce jurisdiction by ruling that it lacks jurisdiction to call indirectly into question the lawfulness of UNSC resolutions in the light of EC law or of fundamental rights as recognised in the EC legal order. Subsequently, and quite surprisingly as it appears *prima facie* in contradiction with its previous assertion, the CFI elaborates a sophisticated exception to its lack of jurisdiction: it grants itself the power to indirectly review UNSC resolutions in light of the fundamental rights falling within the scope of *jus cogens*.

The Principle: UNSC Resolutions and EC Acts Implementing those Resolutions Fall Outside the Scope of the CFI's Judicial Review

No less than 28 paragraphs expose the CFI's understanding of the relationship between the international legal order, on the one hand, and the Community and national legal orders, on the other hand.[16] The Court's conclusion is clear if not rather surprising as it implies that all EC Member States are "monist" States, i.e. states in which the obligations of the Member States of the UN under the UN Charter prevail over any other legal obligation. For EU Member States, this means that their UN obligations prevail over their obligations under the EC Treaty as well as their obligations under the ECHR. Regarding the relationship between the UN Charter and the domestic law of the Member States of the UN, a "rule of primacy" is derived by the CFI from the principles of customary international law and in particular Article 27 of the Vienna Convention on the Law of Treaties according to which a State may not invoke the provisions of its internal law as justification for its failure to perform a treaty. The same rule of primacy is said to govern the relationship between the UN Charter and international treaty law by virtue of Article 103 of the Charter, which provides that obligations of UN members under the Charter prevail over any obligations under any other international agreement. Finally, and decisively as the EC regulations were adopted on this basis, the rule of primacy is extended to decisions contained in a resolution of the UNSC in accordance with Article 25 of the UN Charter, under which the Members of the United Nations agree to accept and carry out the decisions of the Security Council. In other words, for the CFI, resolutions adopted by the UNSC under Chapter VII of the UN Charter are binding on all the EC Member States. The Member States must, accordingly, take all measures necessary to ensure that those resolutions are put into effect. This leads to an additional and unusual duty, coming from a Community Court which is normally inclined to guarantee the effectiveness of EC law: the Member States must "leave unapplied any provision of Community law, whether

[16] See *Yusuf*, paras 231-259; *Kadi*, paras 181-208.

a provision of primary law or a general principle of law, that raises any impediment to the proper performance of their obligations under the Charter of the United Nations".[17]

Although the EC is not a member of the UN, the CFI plainly affirms for the first time that the EC must also be considered to be bound by the obligations flowing from the UN Charter in the same way as are its Member States, not by virtue of the UN Charter but by virtue of the Treaty establishing the EC. By analogy with the case of *International Fruit* in which the ECJ ruled that the EC is bound by the GATT,[18] the CFI recalls that the Member States, when they concluded the Treaty of Rome in 1957, were bound by their obligations under the UN Charter[19] and that they have undertaken to ensure that the EC itself, following the conferral of some powers to it, should exercise those powers with a view to not infringing the obligations imposed on its Member States by virtue of the UN Charter or of not impeding the performance of their obligations which stem from that Charter.[20] An additional and more "positive" obligation also falls on the EC: it is required to adopt all the provisions necessary to allow its Member States to fulfil those obligations.

Having regard to the rule of primacy deduced from the rules of customary international law and the consequent obligation on the EC to give effect to UNSC resolutions within the sphere of its powers, the CFI ruled that it had no authority to call into question, "even indirectly", the lawfulness of UNSC resolutions in light of EC law or of fundamental rights as guaranteed in the Community legal order.[21] The Court previously explained why it could not annul the contested regulation. As Regulation No 881/2002 solely implements at EC level the obligation placed on the Member States to give effect to several UNSC resolutions, were it to decide to nullify the regulation on the ground that it violated the applicants' fundamental rights, "such annulment would indirectly mean that the resolutions of the Security Council concerned themselves infringe those fundamental rights. In other words, the applicants ask the Court to declare by implication that the provision of international law at issue infringes the fundamental rights of individuals, as protected by the Community legal order."[22]

A Surprising Exception: UNSC Resolutions May be Indirectly Scrutinized by Reference to Universally Recognised Fundamental Rights as Protected by *Jus Cogens*

Immediately following the statement that it lacked jurisdiction to review, even indirectly, UNSC resolutions through EC acts implementing those resolutions, the

---

[17] *Yusuf*, para 240; *Kadi*, para 190.

[18] *International Fruit Company and Others* [1972] ECR 1219 Joined Cases 21/72 to 24/72.

[19] To be entirely exact, Germany was not yet a member of the UN in 1957. The CFI evacuates this difficulty, in a somewhat cavalier fashion, on the basis of an international agreement signed in 1954. See *Yusuf*, para 237; *Kadi*, para 187.

[20] See in particular Article 297 EC.

[21] *Yusuf*, para 276; *Kadi*, para 225.

[22] *Yusuf*, para 267; *Kadi*, para 216.

CFI, rather surprisingly, held that it was nonetheless "empowered to check, indirectly, the lawfulness of the resolutions of the Security Council in question with regard to *jus cogens*, understood as a body of higher rules of public international law binding on all subjects of international law, including the bodies of the United Nations, and from which no derogation is possible."[23]

This assertion seems at first difficult to reconcile with what the Court previously asserted. A sound judgment, it may be argued, should have concluded either that the Court had jurisdiction or lacked jurisdiction. The Court's argument, however, is both more subtle and perplexing. To follow the Court's logic, it has no jurisdiction to indirectly rule on the lawfulness of UNSC resolutions *in light of EC law* but it has jurisdiction to rule on the legality of EC acts implementing UNSC resolutions *in light of peremptory norms of general international law*. This reasoning is intriguing as it leads to the *de facto* transformation of the CFI into an international Court with the self-granted power to exercise indirect judicial review of UNSC resolutions on the basis of a controversial body of international norms.[24] This is a far cry from the ECJ's finding that the EC must respect international law, on the one hand, and that EC law "must be interpreted, and its scope limited," [25] in the light of the relevant rules of customary international law, on the other hand.[26]

Should one be convinced that the CFI can claim jurisdiction if only in the name of the EU's commitment to the rule of law and the fact that the contested act is after all an EC regulation challengeable under Article 230 EC, for this author, it would then have been preferable to rely on the general principles of EC law as a standard of review. In order to carry out genuine judicial review, Community courts ought to apply clearly identified and demanding EC legal standards. As a matter of fact, in the case of *Bosphorus* (see case note of Professor Rick Lawson), the ECJ agreed to review, without any perceptible hesitation, the lawfulness of a provision of

---

[23] *Yusuf*, para 277; *Kadi*, para 226.

[24] For a classic study criticizing the uncertainties inflicted on the international normative system by the fragmentation of normativity that the theory of *jus cogens* has brought in its wake, see P Weil, "Towards Relative Normativity in International Law?" (1983) 77 AJIL 413. In his reply to Professor Weil, ten years later, U Fastenrath suggests, by contrast, that "the concept of *ius cogens* is another indication of an emerging global society. Through this instrument, worldwide perceptions of justice may be expressed. Whereas such perceptions have to date been crude and inconsistent, this merely points to the fact that we are but at the beginning of a process which has hitherto led us from the law of coexistence to the law of cooperation; the path to a true constitution of the global society remains open and untrodden before us", "Relative Normativity in International Law" (1993) 4 EIJL 305, p 341.

[25] *Poulsen and Diva Navigation* [1992] ECR I-6019 Case C-286/90, para 9.

[26] Furthermore, if the ECJ has accepted that questions of validity of an EC regulation could be determined not only on the basis of EC norms but by the rules of international law, the Court has been cautious enough to hold in the case of *Racke* that "because of the complexity of the rules [of customary international law] in question and the imprecision of some of the concepts to which they refer, judicial review must necessarily ... be limited to the question whether, by adopting the suspending regulation, the Council made manifest errors of assessment concerning the conditions for applying those rules", Case C-162/96 [1998] ECR I-3655, para 52.

Regulation No 990/93, which implemented at EC level the sanctions against the Federal Republic of Yugoslavia adopted by the UNSC, exclusively in the light of fundamental rights and the principle of proportionality as guaranteed by the EC legal order.[27] The CFI's decision to refer instead to the notion of *jus cogens*, as defined by Article 53 of the Vienna Convention on the Law of Treaties,[28] does not seem warranted and is certainly rather perilous in practise.

Apart from the fact that the precise identification of all these norms of international customary law which cannot be set aside by treaty or acquiescence remains a controversial exercise,[29] it is difficult to understand how the CFI could come to the conclusion that "international law thus permits the inference that there exists one limit to the principle that resolutions of the Security Council have binding effect: namely, that they must observe the fundamental peremptory provisions of *jus cogens*".[30] To argue that this conclusion can be deduced from Article 53 and Article 64 of the Vienna Convention on the Law of Treaties is to misapprehend the more limited and specific purpose of those provisions which is to govern the situation when a treaty, and not a UNSC resolution, may become void.[31] Finally, there is considerable uncertainty as to whether what the Court calls "the mandatory provisions concerning the universal protection of human rights" falls within the scope of *jus cogens*. "The least controversial examples of the class",[32] as Ian Brownlie puts it, are the prohibitions of aggression, genocide, racial discrimination, crimes against humanity and one may also add, the prohibition of torture, slavery and the principle of self-determination. Even though a certain number of legal scholars and

---

[27] To dismiss the applicant's claim that the impounding under that regulation of an aircraft it owns, the ECJ solely refers to its case-law to rule that the fundamental rights invoked by *Bosphorus* Airways are not absolute and that their exercise may be subject to restrictions justified by objectives of general interest pursued by the Community. See *Bosphorus* [1996] ECR I-3953 Case C-84/95, para 21. For an exhaustive commentary, see I. Canor, "'Can Two Walk Together, Except They be Agreed?' The Relationship Between International Law and European Law: The Incorporation of United Nations Sanctions Against Yugoslavia Into European Community Law Through the Perspective of the European Court of Justice" (1998) 35 CMLR 137.

[28] "A treaty is void if, at the time of its conclusion, it conflicts with a peremptory norm of general international law. For the purposes of the present Convention, a peremptory norm of general international law is a norm accepted and recognized by the international community of States as a whole as a norm from which no derogation is permitted and which can be modified only by a subsequent norm of general international law having the same character."

[29] It may be worth quoting the classic *Oppenheim's International Law* RY Jennings and A Watts eds, (9th ed, Longmans, 1992) at pp 7-8: "Such a category of rules of *ius cogens* is a comparatively recent development and there is no general agreement as to which rules have this character. … The full content of the category of *ius cogens* remains to be worked out in the practice of states and in the jurisprudence of international tribunals."

[30] *Yusuf*, para 281; *Kadi*, para 230.

[31] See, however, for a recent article arguing that the UNSC's decision-making power is not free of legal constraints and that, in particular, *jus cogens* applies to acts of the UNSC, A Orakhelashvili, "The Impact of Peremptory Norms on the Interpretation and Application of United Nations Security Council Resolutions" (2005) 16 EIJL 59.

[32] I Brownlie, *Principles of Public International Law* (6th ed, OUP, Oxford, 2003) at pp 488-489.

human rights lawyers have sought to add fundamental rights to this list of customary law rights, there is as yet no consensus and it is rather audacious to affirm that all fundamental rights can be regarded as peremptory norms.[33]

Irrespective of the rather unpersuasive character of the Court's analysis regarding the scope given to the notion of *jus cogens*, the two judgements are instructive insofar as the Court grants itself the power to determine "whether the superior rules of international law falling within the ambit of *jus cogens* have been observed, in particular the mandatory provisions concerning the universal protection of human rights".[34] In the present cases, the Court had to answer three arguments put forward by the applicants: that the contested regulation deprived them of their right to property as protected by the Community legal order, that it breached their right to a fair hearing and right to an effective judicial remedy also as protected by the Community legal order.

Logically, in light of what it previously held, the CFI indicates that the applicants' claim in relation to an alleged violation of their right to property will be examined by the "sole criterion of the standard of universal protection of the fundamental rights of the human person falling within the ambit of *jus cogens*",[35] and not by reference to Article 1 of the First Protocol to the ECHR.[36] It is regrettable, however, that the CFI does not find it necessary to specify how the right to property has become a peremptory norm of international law if we except a brief mention to Article 17 of the Universal Declaration of Human Rights, and why should only an "arbitrary" deprivation of that right be regarded as contrary to *jus cogens*.[37] Regardless of those uncertainties, the Court explains at great length why it must reject the applicants' claim: the freezing of their funds constitutes an aspect of the sanctions decided by the UN in the context of the legitimate fight against international terrorism and furthermore; it is a precautionary measure which does not affect the very substance of the applicants' right to property but only the use of their financial assets; and finally, that the UNSC resolutions provide for a means of reviewing the overall system of sanctions and for a procedure enabling the applicants to present their case to the Sanctions Committee for review.

---

33 See A Orakhelashvili, *op. cit*, p 64–66.

34 *Yusuf*, para 282; *Kadi*, para 231.

35 *Yusuf*, para 286; *Kadi*, para 235.

36 The right of every natural or legal person not to be deprived of his possessions has been recognised in numerous occasions in the case law of the ECJ. In *Hauer*, the Court held that "the right to property is guaranteed in the Community legal order in accordance with the ideas common to the constitutions of the Member States, which are also reflected in the first protocol to the European Convention for the protection of human rights", Case 44/79 [1979] ECR 3727, para 4. The exercise of the right may be subject to restrictions justified by objectives of general interest pursued by the Community as long as those restrictions do not constitute, with regard to the objective pursued, a disproportionate and intolerable interference, impairing the very substance of the right.

37 *Yusuf*, para 292; *Kadi*, para 241.

As regards the right to a fair hearing, although well-established in the case law of the ECJ as a fundamental principle of EC law,[38] the CFI itself recognizes that it does not constitute a rule of *jus cogens*. Accordingly, the CFI should have stopped at this stage. This is not, however, what the Court did. On the contrary, the Court describes at great length the mechanism for the re-examination of individual cases set up by the UNSC resolutions and according to which the persons concerned may address a request to the Sanctions Committee, through their national authorities, to be removed from the list of persons affected by the sanction or to obtain exemption from the freezing of funds. While certainly interesting, these developments have no *raison d'être* as the Court previously emphasised that it could only check, indirectly, the lawfulness of the UNSC resolutions in the light of the higher rules of general international law falling within the scope of *jus cogens*.

Finally, concerning the alleged breach of the right to an effective judicial remedy, the Court of First Instance also rejects the arguments raised by the applicants. First, the Court is satisfied that the review of the lawfulness of the contested regulation it has operated, in particular with regard to *jus cogens*, demonstrates that the applicants have benefited from an effective judicial remedy as a matter of EC law.[39] Second, while there is no international court with jurisdiction to rule on actions brought against decisions taken by the Sanctions Committee, the Court is satisfied — without further justification — that "such lacuna in the judicial protection available to the applicants is not in itself contrary to *jus cogens*."[40] The Court also apparently considers that it is enough to state that "in the circumstances of this case, the applicants' interest in having a court hear their case on its merits is not enough to outweigh the essential public interest in the maintenance of international peace and security in the face of a threat clearly identified by the Security Council",[41] to convince the legal community that the rule of law may quietly be set aside as long as the "restrictive measures" adopted by the UNSC and aimed at individuals, are re-examined on a regular basis with the additional possibility of petitioning the Sanctions Committee through the applicant's government of residence and/or citizenship.

The first judgments given by the CFI in relation to EC acts adopted in the context of the fight against international terrorism leaves one somewhat puzzled. In the end, it

---

[38] It is settled case law that "observance of the right to be heard is, in all proceedings initiated against a person which are liable to culminate in a measure adversely affecting that person, a fundamental principle of Community law which must be guaranteed even in the absence of any rules governing the proceedings in question", *Liesrestal* [1996] ECR I-5373 Case C-32/95, para 21. That principle requires that the addressees of decisions which significantly affect their interests should be placed in a position in which they may effectively make known their views.
[39] In *Johnston*, the Court held that the principle of effective judicial control, i.e. the existence of a judicial remedy, "reflects a general principle of law which underlies the constitutional traditions common to the member states" and has been enshrined in Articles 6 and 13 of the ECHR, Case 222/84 [1984] ECR 1651, para 18.
[40] *Yusuf*, para 341 ; *Kadi*, para 286.
[41] *Yusuf*, para 344 ; *Kadi*, para 289.

is questionable whether the Court's revolutionary approach was worth adopting or was not actually revolutionary enough.[42] Its power to annul an EC act implementing UNSC resolutions, and indirectly rule on the lawfulness of these resolutions, with regard to *jus cogens* is likely to remain perpetually theoretical and controversial: theoretical because the CFI is unlikely to ever have the political courage to stand up even against a manifest violation of fundamental rights; controversial because the Court has decided to review EC acts implementing UNSC resolutions with regard to *jus cogens* rather than in light of fundamental rights as guaranteed by the Community legal order. On shaky legal grounds, the Court wants to have it both ways: it does not want to disturb the international legal order by plainly affirming its power to review indirectly UNSC resolutions on the sole basis of EC law and yet, because it has the legitimate concern to protect the fundamental rights of EC residents, it transforms itself as an agent of compliance with *jus cogens*.

An interesting interpretation has likened the cases of *Yusuf* and *Kadi* to the adoption, at Community level, of the "*Solange*" reasoning.[43] In 1974, in the so-called "*Solange I*" judgment, the German Federal Constitutional Court challenged the ECJ by ruling that it reserved the power to set EC law aside in the case of a Community norm violating German fundamental rights.[44] And indeed, while knowing that it should never exercise its self-granted new jurisdictional competence to annul an act implementing a UNSC resolution for fear of a political cataclysm, the CFI may have been tempted to solemnly proclaim its role as a guardian of fundamental rights and formally advance the rule of law in our globalised world by benignly reminding the UNSC that it must pay due attention to peremptory "fundamental human rights" when it interferes with the rights and duties of individuals.[45] If the cases of *Yusuf* and *Kadi*, now pending before the ECJ,[46] could convince the UNSC to take due process seriously and the community of States to grant the International Court of Justice with some power of judicial review,[47] praise would then have to be given

[42] See also P Eeckhout, "Community Terrorism Listings, Fundamental Rights, and UN Security Council Resolutions. In search of the right fit" (2007) 3 *EuConst* 183. He argues that the Court of First Instance's approach has the worst of both worlds as it does not fit the ECJ's case law on the protection of fundamental rights and is not required by international law.

[43] See D Symon, F Mariatte, "Le Tribunal de première instance des Communautés: Professeur de droit international?" (2005) 12 *Europe* 6, p 10.

[44] BVerfGE 37, 271, reported in English at [1974] 14 *CMLR* 540.

[45] For further references and recent developments, see E Flynn, "The Security Council's Counter-Terrorism Committee and Human Rights" (2007) 7 HRLR 371.

[46] In his Opinion on the *Kadi* case (C-402/05), delivered on 16 January 2008, Advocate General Poiares Maduro argues — rightly in my view — that the Court of First Instance erred in finding that it had only limited jurisdiction to review Council Regulation (EC) No 881/2002 and further contends that the Court of Justice must annul this Regulation, in so far as it concerns the appellant, on the ground that it infringes his fundamental rights as recognised by Community law.

[47] The CFI could then replicate the "*Solange II*" ruling and finally admit that it will no longer control, indirectly through EC acts implementing them, the compatibility of UNSC resolutions with fundamental rights as protected by *jus cogens*. In the so-called *Solange II*, the German Constitutional Court agreed it will no longer exercise its (theoretical) jurisdiction thanks to the development of effective EC protection. BVerfGE 73, 339, reported in English at [1987] 3 CMLR 225.

to the CFI regardless of its Byzantine reasoning at times and its contentious choice to review the contested regulation with regard to *jus cogens* rather than on the basis of EC standards.

EDITOR'S NOTE: This case note was written prior to the decision of the European Court of Justice. In a Grand Chamber judgment, issued on the 3rd of September 2008 (Joined Cases C-402/05 P and C-415/05 P), the Court of Justice ruled that the EC judicature has jurisdiction to review measures adopted by the EC giving effect to resolutions of the UNSC and held that EC regulation 881/2002 infringed Mr Kadi and Al Barakaat's fundamental rights under EC law. Accordingly, the Court set aside the judgments of the Court of First Instance analysed in this casenote and annulled EC Regulation 881/2002 in so far as it concerned Mr Kadi and the Al Barakaat International Foundation. The ECJ decision will be analysed in the next issue of the *Irish Human Rights Law Review.*

Investigation of Disappearances: *Gongadze v Ukraine*[*]

Aoife O'Donoghue[**]

The discovery of Heorhiy Gongadze's body, which was found over 100 miles from Kiev where he disappeared on the 16 September 2000, had major political repercussions within the Ukraine. Gongadze's wife brought an application to the European Court of Human Rights after unsuccessful attempts to receive adequate answers to questions regarding his disappearance and death, although several police officers were subsequently charged in relation to the disappearance.

Mr Gongadze was a journalist and editor of a leading Ukrainian newspaper *Ukrainska Pravda*, a paper which was strongly critical of the Kuchma-led Government of the Ukraine. Prior to his disappearance he repeatedly told friends, relatives and colleagues that he was being threatened by government officials under the guise of a purported criminal investigation. For a period, he had also been followed by a car when travelling to and from work. The harassment led him to write an open letter to the Prosecutor General seeking protection. This request was ultimately turned down as it was claimed that there were no grounds for criminal proceedings against the alleged harassers. Mr Gongadze disappeared on 16 September 2000.

The day after Mr Gongadze's disappearance his wife petitioned the District Police Department of Kiev. On 18 September — though this date was disputed by the Government who argued that it was 19 September — a murder investigation began, which included searches and interviews at locations where Mr Gongadze was last seen.

On 2 November a decapitated body was found in Tarashcha. An initial autopsy concluded that this person died about the time of Mr Gongadze's disappearance. Mr Gongadze's relatives found out about the existence of this body from a brief newspaper article and subsequently identified it as his body through jewellery and old scars. A fragment of skin was taken by the relatives for independent analysis.

Subsequent to this, the body was removed by the Government to Kiev and all documentation relating to the initial forensic investigation that occurred upon discovery of the body was confiscated. At various stages throughout the Government investigation, different forensic analyses undertaken by various

*(Application No. 34056/02) European Court of Human Rights (Second Section) 8th November 2005, [2005] ECHR 34056/02

** School of Law, University of Durham.

groups were carried out on the body. The local expert who conducted the initial autopsy was prohibited from talking about his investigation. The Deputy Minister for the Interior had announced (on 16 November) that the body found in Tarashcha was buried in the soil for approximately two years.

The applicant then requested to be identified as a civil party to the investigation at Tarashcha, to identify the jewellery and to organise a forensic examination to establish that the body was that of her husband. This request was refused. Next, the applicant asked that the body not be cremated until it was established that it was that of her husband. On 29 November the applicant was recognised as a civil party in the Gongadze case although the request that both cases be joined was refused. In December 2000 the Prosecutor General announced that DNA analysis could not be done for the time being as Mr Gongadze's mother was ill, a suggestion which the deceased's mother rejected at the time. On the 10 December 2000, the applicant was permitted to participate in an identification exercise but was unable to positively identify her husband. A DNA sample was taken from the deceased's mother but a request for foreign expert analysis was refused and the Prosecutor General announced that the Tarashcha body was not that of the deceased. Several other DNA investigations were made which led to several foreign experts stating that it was highly probably that the Tarashcha body was that of Mr Gongadze.

In January 2001 the Prosecutor General informed the Ukrainian parliament that it was highly probable that the Tarashcha body was that of Mr Gongadze although there had been unconfirmed reports of sightings of Mr Gongadze in November and December of 2000. The applicant's status as a civil party in the Gongadze case was annulled. The Perchersky District Court recognised the applicant's and the deceased mother's right to be civil parties though unusually this was not granted. The Tarashcha body was then released to the applicant for burial. A death certificate was not issued, no burial has taken place and the body is still in Kiev.

Grani Magazine, a Ukrainian journal, then published the name of four officers whom it alleged took part in the surveillance of Mr Gongadze. This raised more questions regarding the government's involvement. On 26 January 2001 the applicants were again recognised as civil parties, apparently due to a Council of Europe resolution passed regarding the death of Mr Gongadze. The State refuted this, stating that it was due to the discovery of additional forensic information which confirmed that the Tarashcha body was indeed that of Mr Gongadze.

In March of 2001 the applicant filed a complaint regarding negligence in the conduct of the investigation. This complaint was apparently mislaid and the applicant was advised to resubmit the complaint. In May of 2001 the Minister of the Interior announced that the two murderers of Mr Gongadze — apparently drug dealers who were without political motive — had died and that the investigation was now closed. This was contradicted and it was then disclosed to the applicant that new information had become available and it would be premature to state that the investigation was now closed. The applicant requested that the FBI be involved: this was refused. There were also continuous refusals to have the case file made available. As the forensic evidence was still ambiguous the applicant requested that access to these files and eventually registered a complaint against the GPO, however the court would not hear this until the case came before it. It was not until August 2005 that the applicant was allowed access to the criminal case file.

In July of 2002 a new Prosecutor General was elected and confirmed that the investigation had had a number of irregularities. In October 2002 another forensic investigation took place in Switzerland: this confirmed that the body discovered at Tarashcha was definitely that of Mr Gongadze. In November of 2002 the prosecutor of the Tarashcha case was convicted of negligence in the investigation of the case although he was absolved from serving his sentence under an amnesty law. In January of 2003, a chairman of a parliamentary committee announced that those responsible for the death worked in the police force. The parliament than requested that the GPO investigate the possibility that Mr Kravchenko, who was the Minister of the Interior at the time of the disappearance, had a role in the death. The Prosecutor General then began investigating the involvement of senior officials in that department. In May 2003 a Mr G was arrested for his possible involvement in collusion with the police. He died in prison in unclear circumstances. After his death, letters, which were later confirmed to be that of Mr G, asserted that senior police and officials were involved in the death of Mr Gongadze. In October 2003, Lieutenant-General Pukach, an official at the Ministry of the Interior, was arrested for alleged involvement in the disappearance; he was later released on his undertaking not to abscond. The Prosecutor General was dismissed by the President in October of 2003.

These were the complicated series of events which the European Court of Human Rights examined when considering the application of Mrs Gongadze against the Ukrainian Government.

The Court first looked at the alleged violation of Article 2 ECHR, recalling that there were both positive and negative obligations on the State, not only to refrain from the intentional and unlawful taking of life but also to take appropriate steps to safeguard the lives of those within its jurisdiction. This included, according to the Court, a positive obligation on the State to put into place such procedures as would deter offences, including enforcement measures, as well as the protection of persons whose lives were at risk. However, the Court did acknowledge that there were limits as to the State's ability where this task was impossible or imposed a disproportionate burden. The Court stated that, for this positive obligation to apply, it must be established that the State knew or ought to have known at the time of the existence of a real and immediate risk to an identified individual or individuals from a third party and that the State failed to take such measures as was in their power that might reasonably be expected to avoid the risk.[1] The question was whether the State failed to comply with its positive obligations.

The Court noted that there was a high probability that police officers were involved in the disappearance and murder of Mr Gongadze. It also noted that Mr Gongadze had written an open letter to the Prosecutor General and went on to note that the State would be aware of the vulnerability of a journalist writing about politically

[1] *Kiliç v Turkey* [2004] ECHR 40498/98.

sensitive topics. The Court also noted that the GPO, under domestic law, was obliged to supervise the activities of the police and investigate allegations against them. It noted that the GPO was clearly negligent in its response to Mr Gongadze's letter finding that these complaints contained therein and the subsequent events that revealed the possibility of State involvement in his death were neglected or simply ignored. The fact that quickly after the change of Government in the Ukraine the alleged offenders were identified and charged raised doubts as to the seriousness of the authorities under the previous government in their efforts to investigate events thoroughly. The Court concluded that there had been a substantive violation of Article 2 ECHR.

The Court then proceeded to look at the investigation into Mr Gongadze's death under the procedural aspects of Article 2 ECHR. The Government maintained that there were objective reasons for the delays in the investigation and that it had been sufficiently effective. The Court asserted that Article 2 must be read in conjunction with a state's general duties under Article 1 ECHR and that these in combination create an obligation to provide an effective official investigation.[2] The investigation is the state's responsibility and must not rely on next-of-kin to lodge complaints once the incident has been brought to a state's attention. A State must also ensure that an investigation, inclusive of the collection of evidence, is to a standard that will allow for the determination of whether the use of force was justified and to allow for the identification and punishment of those responsible.[3] The court also clearly stated that there is a requirement of promptness and that this is essential in maintaining confidence in an authority's ability to maintain the rule of law. Finding that there was a procedural violation of Article 2, the Court noted that for quite a period of time the Ukrainian authorities were almost entirely engaged in disproving any State involvement rather than in finding the truth of what had occurred.

The Court then examined the alleged violation of Article 3 of the Convention. The applicant maintained that the atmosphere of fear and uncertainty as well as the differing information given to the applicant during the investigation led to a violation of Article 3. The Court referred to a number of Turkish cases that raised similar arguments. It asserted that for there to be a violation of Article 3 in this kind of situation certain special factors which lead to suffering of a dimension and character that could be distinguished from the emotional distress which will be regarded as inevitable in situations where close family members disappear must arise. The Court then examined the circumstances of the case, particularly the attitude and behaviour of the official investigating authorities to the applicant and her family, and concluded there had been a violation of Article 3 ECHR.

In relation to Article 13 ECHR which requires the provision of effective domestic remedies the Court found that no effective investigation had been undertaken for four years. The compensatory remedy available under Ukrainian domestic law was only available against identified persons and as there had been no outcome in

[2] *Kaya v Turkey* [2005] ECHR 36150/02.
[3] *Güleç v Turkey* [1998] ECHR 21593.

criminal proceedings due to the ineffectiveness of the investigation the Court found that there was a violation of Article 13.

The death of Heorhiy Gongadze was a major turning point in the post-Soviet development of Ukrainian politics. This journalist's investigation into the corruption that was rife in this post-Soviet State illustrates the difficulties that some of these countries are experiencing in developing their political and social infrastructures to a point where a state's reaction to overt public criticism is lawful, proportionate and reasonable. This criticism, that is now nominally at least permitted, must be allowed to flourish and the reaction of states must be informed by the democratic free speech standards protected by the European Convention on Human Rights. There have been several cases before the European Court of Human Rights dealing with restrictions on political parties in these post-Soviet states as well as cases involving journalists.[4] It will be interesting to see how the Court's jurisprudence will evolve into future cases that come before it from former Soviet states as communism becomes a more distant memory. The transition to the kind of liberal democracy underpinned by the Convention will be effected largely by political and economic factors but judicial intervention from Strasbourg will also continue to be important.

[4] Including the following examples (although this is by no means an exhaustive list): *Rekvenyi v Hungary* (2000) 30 E.H.R.R. 519; *Partidul Comunistilor (Nepecerista) and Ungureanu v Romania* [2005] ECHR 46626/99; *Ždanoka v Latvia* [2006] ECHR 58278/00; *Cumpana and another v Romania* [2004] ECHR 33348/96.

Index

O